Modern Phonology

Theoretical Linguistics 2

Modern Phonology

Alan H. Sommerstein

University of Nottingham

University Park Press

© Alan H. Sommerstein 1977

First Published 1977 by
Edward Arnold (Publishers) Ltd London

First published in the USA in 1977 by
University Park Press
Chamber of Commerce Building
Baltimore, Maryland 21202

Library of Congress Cataloging in Publication Data

Sommerstein, Alan H.
  Modern phonology.
  (Theoretical linguistics)
  Includes bibliographical references and index.
  1. Grammar, Comparative and general—Phonology.
I. Title. II. Series.
P217.S59   414   77-12173
ISBN 0-8391-1172-X

Printed in Great Britain

Acknowledgements

It is my pleasant duty to express my gratitude to those who have assisted me with advice and criticism or with information and copies of published or unpublished papers, and particularly to Sidney Allen, Bernard Comrie, Andrew Crompton, Erik Fudge, Fred Householder, Robert King, Peter Matthews, James McCawley, Gary Miller, Linda Norman, and Geoffrey Sampson; also to all those others from whom I have over the years learned something about phonology, without whom this book would never have been. None of them is responsible in any way for its shortcomings.

The series editor, Pieter Seuren, deserves special mention. He it was who suggested to me the idea of the book, and who ensured that its gestation was not even more protracted than it has proved to be.

Both King's College, Cambridge, and the University of Nottingham have helped me in every possible way, and the Library staff at Nottingham must have a special word of thanks. And lastly, if I have persevered to complete the work, it has been because of the encouragement of my wife and the ineradicable cheerfulness of my daughter Louise.

Nottingham, December 1975   Alan H. Sommerstein

For my mother and father

Contents

1 Aims and Principles

Phonology is a branch of linguistics: phonetics is often considered not to be. Phonetics deals with the capabilities of the human articulatory and auditory systems with respect to the sounds and prosodic features available for use in language, and with the acoustic characteristics of these sounds and features themselves. A knowledge of the elements of articulatory phonetics is assumed throughout the present work.

Phonology, in a sense, begins where phonetics leaves off. It is concerned with the ways in which the sounds and prosodic features defined by phonetics are actually used in natural languages. This general definition would be accepted by all schools of thought. Differences begin to arise when one attempts to make the goals of phonology more specific, to frame, if you like, the question which it is the object of phonological inquiry to answer.

In the present century there have been two main views on how to frame this question. Almost all the phonological theories that have been developed during this time can be ranged in one or other of the two camps defined by these two questions.

One view is that the proper question to ask is 'What phonic features (a) serve in the language under investigation, or (b) are capable of serving in natural language, to distinguish one utterance from another?' This was the dominant orientation of phonology from the mid 1920s to the mid 1960s, and is still not without influence; it has sometimes been called *classical phonology*.

The second view is that the proper question is 'What are the principles determining the pronunciation of the words, phrases and sentences of a language; and to what extent are these principles derivable from more general principles determining the organization in this respect of *all* human languages?' Putting the question this way means looking at phonology less as a means for reducing the literally infinite variety of human articulation to what is, for each language, a relatively small number of essential distinctions, and more as a code whereby the grammatical structures known as sentences are given audible form. The most important, though as we shall see not the only, school to have chosen this second orientation is that which, developing mainly since the appearance in 1959 of Morris Halle's *The Sound Pattern of Russian*, has come to be known as *generative phonology*.[1]

Acceptance of the orientation of classical phonology has usually led to one

---

[1] The term is unfortunate, because in most versions of generative phonology the phonology does not in any recognized sense generate anything; but it is established usage, and the reader should regard the term as an arbitrary label.

variety or another of *phonemics*, so called from the *phoneme*, the name given to the minimal unit of sound serving to keep utterances apart. The motivation for phonemics is this: physically, objectively, no two speech sounds are exactly alike, even those that occur in corresponding positions in utterances which are 'intentional repetitions of one another. Consequently the number of different sounds that can be used in language is infinite, since there is no limit to the amount of speech that human beings can produce. But any given language will only utilize a limited number of differences of sound to carry differences of meaning. Consider, for instance, the articulation of a labial stop consonant followed by a vowel. Vocal cord vibration (voicing) may begin before, simultaneously with, or after the release of the stop closure, and both the 'before' period and the 'after' period are infinitely subdivisible; but English utilizes only one distinction along this axis. An English labial stop belongs to one of two classes: one, roughly speaking, including all those in which voicing lags after release (such as the initial stop of *pat*); the other, those in which voicing begins at or before release (such as the initial stop of *bat*). It is not necessary to learn finer details about voice-onset in order to speak English intelligibly, though the mastery of such details may be highly desirable if one wishes to avoid giving the impression of a 'foreign accent'. A difference of sound which is utilized by a language is termed a *distinction* or *(distinctive) opposition* or *contrast* in that language.

Different languages, moreover, have different sets of contrasts. In present-day Cypriot Greek (Newton 1972), consonants contrast with one another along the axis of length, e.g. [éforos] 'fertile' against [éforos] 'superintendent'; in English there is no such contrast. Even where two languages both have a contrast along the same axis, the points along that axis may be differently divided up; Hindi, like English, has a contrast along the voice-onset axis, but it divides this axis into *three* ranges, roughly one with voicing preceding release, one with it simultaneous, and one with it following. The stops in the three ranges are usually transcribed with *b*, *p*, *ph* for the labials, and analogously in other positions; thus Hindi *p* falls within the range of English *b*. A dramatic illustration of how languages can differ in this way is given by Bühler (1931). Phonetically (thinking now in terms not of what can be distinguished by an ideally perfect recording device, but just of the ear of a trained phonetician), the Caucasian language Adyge has as many vowel sounds as German. But it has only one axis of distinctiveness for vowels, the high-mid-low dimension, which it divides into three ranges; all other differences in vowel quality are wholly determined by the surrounding consonants; so that phonologically speaking the vowel systems of Adyge and German are utterly disparate.

The 'phonemic principle', in its simplest terms, is that the differences of sound that must be discussed in a phonological description of a language are all the contrasts of that language and only those. A *phonemic transcription* then is one such that no two contrasting sounds are represented by the same symbol, and no two sounds occupying the same range as each other on all the axes of distinctiveness are represented by different symbols. (This definition begs a few questions, some of which will be answered in the next chapter, while others have never been satisfactorily answered.)

On this view, then, a phonological description centres on a phonemic transcription, or phonemic representation. 'Below' this level—nearer to the phonetic data—there will be statements about systematic but non-contrastive variation. Here for instance will come, in the phonology of English, the statement that all vowels are somewhat longer before voiced than before voiceless consonants (compare the length of the vowel in *bid* and *bit*); such variation is termed *allophonic variation*, and two or more sounds which differ non-distinctively but are in the same range on all the axes of distinctiveness are called *allophones* of the same phoneme.

'Above' the phonemic level—in the direction leading towards grammar—there will be statements concerning the situations which occur in all languages, where one and the same grammatical form is realized, in different morphological or phonological contexts, as two or more phonological forms: e.g. that the plural suffix in English is pronounced [z] in one set of contexts, [s] in another set, and [ɪz] in a third. (That this is not allophonic variation is proved by observing that in *loose, lose, Suez*, the three phonological forms in question contrast with one another.) Such phenomena, involving alternative phonemic realizations of a single morphological unit, are termed *morphophonemic alternations*.

This brief description of the essentials of classical phonological analysis will be elaborated in Chapter Two. But it is important at present to observe one not quite obvious consequence of the classical orientation. If phonology is the discipline which determines what phonic features function distinctively (in Language or in a language), then it ought to follow that the only evidence of which use may be made in phonological studies is evidence about sound (that is, the raw phonetic data of speech) and evidence about which utterances are distinct (that is, informants' judgements on which utterances are, and which are not, repetitions of one another). All other information, and in particular morphological and grammatical information, will then have to be excluded from phonology, at least until a phonemic system has been set up on purely phonetic evidence. After that has been done, grammar and phonology can be linked by giving an account of morphophonemic alternations.

Not all classical phonologists explicitly restricted their evidence in this way; but all were to some extent affected by this notion of their aims. K. L. Pike, who in a famous series of articles (see especially Pike 1947; 1952) argued that grammatical evidence could be relevant to phonemic analysis, failed to convince (at the time) for precisely this reason.

Of the many important contributions made to phonology by the classical phonemicists, one must be mentioned now: an extremely convenient notational convention, which will be used throughout this book. It has long been customary to enclose phonetic transcriptions in square brackets, thus [pʰæn] for English *pan*: note that the stop is marked as aspirated and the vowel as nasalized, both non-distinctive (allophonic) features in English. When phonemic transcriptions were first used, they were likewise placed within square brackets. But this led to an impression, especially among those unfamiliar with phonemics, that phonemics was an inaccurate kind of phonetics; [pæn] for *pan* seemed to imply, falsely, that the stop was unaspirated and the vowel oral. And in truth the use of square brackets was misleading. They seemed to promise a phonetic transcription, and that gives information about pronunciation. A phonemic transcription gives information primarily about the place of each sound in a system of contrasts. For this reason a different notation is now used for the latter; they are enclosed within oblique strokes, e.g. /pæn/. Individual phonemes are represented in the same way, e.g. English /p/, Russian /tʲ/. Note that whereas phonetic notation is language-independent, phonemic notation is language-dependent: each language has its own system of contrasts, and (in classical phonemics) the / ... / notation should never be used without some indication, express or implied, of the language being referred to.

Some of the theories we shall be discussing have nothing directly corresponding to the phonemic representations of classical phonemics. In these theories the / ... / notation may be used rather differently; its use will be explained in the proper place. Where neither the square-bracket nor the oblique notation is used, what is given is a conventional orthographic form; such forms are given in *italics*.

Suppose now that we take the second view of the business of phonology—that its task is to ascertain the principles that determine the pronunciation of the words, phrases and sentences of a language, and how far these principles are universal. To answer this question fully we must have as our phonological description a set of statements using which we can take any word, phrase or sentence and deduce its pronunciation; and the description must be so explicit that no room is left for doubt or ambiguity, except in cases where the language itself freely permits alternative pronunciations of the same grammatical structure. Morphophonemic alternation, which in classical phonology is rather peripheral, is of crucial interest in a phonology of this type, for morphophonemics deals precisely with the ways in which the grammatical units are realized as complexes of phonological units; it was only a slight exaggeration when an unsympathetic critic (Hockett 1968, 81) remarked that 'by the "phonological component" he [Chomsky] means what most of us call morphophonemics.'

To point out this difference in emphasis is not to say that generative phonology, or other theories with the same basic orientation, does or should ignore the phonetic facts. On the contrary, their goal is to account for these facts; if the result of applying to a sentence, in the proper manner, the statements (or *rules* as they are more often called) which make up the phonological description does not tally with the empirically known pronunciation of that sentence, the description is to at least that extent wrong.

The major theories of this second class regard phonology as an integral part of a full linguistic description. Such a full description of a language states, again with complete explicitness, what the well-formed sentences of the language are, their grammatical structure (syntax), meaning (semantics)—and pronunciation (phonology). The exact relationship between these components varies from theory to theory. In the 'standard theory', so called, of Chomsky (1965b), the grammar first defines the class of well-formed sentences by their syntactic structure, and then derives from the syntactic structure of each sentence its meaning and its pronunciation by separate sets of rules. Other theories define, or take as given in advance, the class of meanings of sentences, deriving the class of grammatical forms from these by one set of rules, and then the class of pronunciations from the grammatical forms by another set. Stratificational theory defines a class of meanings, a class of pronunciations, and several classes of intermediate representations, independently and in parallel, and specifies by sets of 'realization rules' which members of different classes are representations, at different levels (*strata*), of the same sentence.

In all these theories, however, we can isolate a phonological component of the grammar.[2] This consists of explicit rules which establish correspondences between a set of *underlying representations* (called 'morphemic' in stratificational theory, sometimes called 'morphophonemic' or 'systematic phonemic' in generative phonology) and a set of *phonetic representations*.

Underlying representations are not subject to the constraints on phonemic representations mentioned on p. 2. In particular, the attempt is usually made to set them up in such a way that a grammatical unit with alternative phonetic realizations, whether these would be described in classical phonology as allophonic variants or as morphophonemic alternants, has only one underlying representation—which may or may not be identical with one of its phonetic realizations. For in a phonology that concentrates on how grammatical units (small or large) are pronounced, the notion of phonological contrast, basic to phonemics, is relevant only peripherally if at all. What is important is rather to account for the variant pronunciations of one and the same grammatical element; and the best way of doing this, where it is possible, is to show how these pronunciations can be derived, by phonological processes of some generality, from one and the same underlying form.

Equally clearly, theories of our second class cannot be bound by the restrictions, mentioned on p. 3, which classical phonology imposes (or ought logically to impose) on what constitutes valid evidence. But what, in these theories, *does* constitute valid evidence, and what arguments can be used to justify or refute one or another analysis?

It is worth while to begin answering this by going back half a century to the first clear statement, in modern phonology, of the idea that the really significant level in phonological description is one that directly indicates the relationship between phonology and grammar: Edward Sapir's classic article 'Sound Patterns in Language' (1925).

At the beginning of the article it might seem that the author was simply concerned to emphasize the distinction between phonology and phonetics, and in particular that (as all schools agree) phonology studies speech sounds not in isolation but in systems, or, as he says, patterns. But continuing, it becomes clear that his 'patterns' do not meet the conditions of classical phonemics (which, to be sure, had not then been made explicit by anyone).

Sapir imagines a language which has, among other sounds, a pair of fricatives [s] and [z]; of these [z] does not occur at the end of a word. Some grammatical units end in [s] when they happen to be the last element of a word, in [z] otherwise; others have [s] in all positions. A classical phonemic analysis of such a language would have to assign all occurrences of [s] to a phoneme /s/, and all

---

[2] Though recent work strongly suggests that the isolation is not complete, in that some syntactic processes depend on phonological information and some phonological processes depend on information not available in superficial syntactic structure.

occurrences of [z] to a phoneme /z/; for it is assumed that the [s] which alternates with [z] covers precisely the same phonetic range as the [s] which does not alternate. But this is not what Sapir does. He assigns to the phoneme /z/ not only [z] but also those occurrences of [s] where it alternates with [z], and to /s/ only the non-alternating instances of [s]. With what justification? 'How,' as Sapir imagines an objector asking, 'can a sound be assigned a "place" in a phonetic pattern over and above its natural classification on organic and acoustic grounds?'[3]

His answer is: 'Because of a general feeling of its phonetic relationships resulting from all the specific phonetic relationships (such as parallelism, contrast, combination, imperviousness to combination, and so on) to all other sounds.' And he gives a very interesting example of this. Objectively (and classical-phonemically), English [ŋ] (the sound which occurs finally in *sing* and medially in *singer*) is a velar nasal related to [m] and [n] in exactly the same way as the velar stop [g] is related to [b] and [d]. But 'psychologically it cannot be grouped with [the other nasals] because, unlike them, it is not a freely movable consonant (there are no words beginning with [ŋ]). It still *feels* like [ŋg], however little it sounds like it.'

But now, the modern student will ask, what evidence can we have about these 'feelings'? Surely all we can know is what the native speaker tells us; and surely his 'feelings', in so far as they are conscious, may be conditioned by quite irrelevant factors (most obviously, in the case of a literate speaker, orthographic convention), and in so far as they are not conscious, are not directly accessible to the linguist. We cannot base analyses on such an insecure foundation.

In a later paper (1933), Sapir seeks to provide some independent evidence of the reality of his 'sound patterns' and of the phoneme in the sense in which *he* used the term (not the classical sense). He assumes that

> if the phonemic attitude is more basic, psychologically speaking, than the more strictly phonetic one, it should be possible to detect it in the unguarded speech judgments of native speakers who have a complete control of their language in a practical sense but have no rationalized or consciously systematic knowledge of it. 'Errors' of analysis . . . may be expected to occur which have the characteristic of being phonetically unsound or inconsistent but which at the same time register a feeling for what is phonemically accurate.

Sapir goes on to give several examples, not all of which are entirely cogent. One, however, is very strong indeed; in fact when Twaddell (1935) was trying to abolish the evidence for 'the phoneme [in *any* sense] as a mental or psychological reality', he was unable to find a satisfactory counter-argument to this example.

In Sarcee, an Athapaskan language, there are two words, both pronounced [di‿ni⁻] (where the horizontal lines represent pitch levels), meaning respectively 'this one' and 'it makes a sound'; I shall refer to them as D1 and D2. Sapir's informant insisted that the two words sounded different, but was unable to specify

---

[3] Had Sapir been writing a few years later, he would have said 'phonemic' or 'phonological' rather than 'phonetic'; in 1925 the terminological distinction between phonetics and phonology was not yet in general use.

any phonetic difference between them, nor was Sapir able to hear any consistent difference; but whereas Sapir thought he could sometimes detect differences in stress, tone, and aspiration, the informant suggested quite another distinction, namely that D2 'ended in a "t"'. But no [t] was audible. Morphophonemically, however, the informant was quite accurate. For while D1 is underlying /di_ni⁻/, D2 is underlying /di_nith⁻/; note that the suffix which, added to D1, yields the form [di_na:⁻], with D2 gives [di_ni⁻thi⁻]. We therefore have here evidence that a phonetically fairly naive native speaker can believe that words which in point of fact are homophonous are not so, and can believe this on morphophonemic grounds.

This conclusion seemed to many contemporaries of Sapir to involve phonology in two serious problems. One was that if the really significant phonological representation must take account of morphophonemic factors, it followed that it was not possible to make a phonological analysis without first identifying the grammatical units. But, it was argued, such identification itself presupposes a phonemic analysis; so that there is a circle, into which we can never break. The other was due to the refusal of Bloomfield, Twaddell, and most other American linguists of the period to admit the use, in 'scientific' linguistic description, of unobservable 'mental' entities, such as Sapir's phonemes professedly were; for, as Twaddell put it, to them 'the scientific method [was] quite simply the convention that mind does not exist.'

For all this, no one was able to explain away Sapir's evidence, anecdotal though this was. Rather, the problem was quietly ignored, and it remained established doctrine that phonology must avoid the two sins of the last paragraph, 'mixing of levels' and 'mentalism'.

All the phonological theories of the second class that we are going to discuss in this book are like Sapir's in that they crucially involve mixing of levels; although one, stratificational grammar, manages by its mode of construction to keep levels separate in presentation, it does not suggest that they must or can be kept separate in analysis. Probably no recent phonological theory crucially involves mentalism, and that includes Sapir's own; for Sapirian phonological representations can normally be analysed out without reference to native speaker intuitions; but almost all class two theories assert the 'psychological reality' of their theoretical constructs, and are not for that reason considered unscientific.

For those who condemned unobservable explanations as unscientific made two mistakes. The less important relates to the obvious fact that an event may itself be unobservable and yet lead to observable consequences by which a hypothesis involving the event in question may be checked: almost any branch of science dealing with objects which are either very small or very distant can furnish examples. The more important is that mental states and events are not in fact unobservable in principle.[4] The issues are well stated by Chomsky (1965b, 193f):

> The mentalist . . . need make no assumptions about the possible physiological basis for the mental reality that he studies. In particular, he need not deny that there is such a basis. One would guess, rather, that it is the mentalistic studies

[4] It was not only a damaging but also an unnecessary admission when Postal (1966, 156), in asserting that the domain of linguistic structure was a mentalistic one, added that it was 'unobservable as such.'

that will ultimately be of greatest value for the investigation of neurophysiological mechanisms, since they alone are concerned with determining abstractly the properties that such mechanisms must exhibit and the functions they must perform.

...The behaviorist position is not an arguable matter. It is simply an expression of lack of interest in theory and explanation. This is clear, for example, in Twaddell's critique (1935) of Sapir's mentalistic phonology, which used informant responses and comments as evidence bearing on the psychological reality of some abstract system of phonological elements. For Twaddell, the enterprise has no point because all that interests him is the behavior itself, 'which is already available for the student of language, though in less concentrated form.'

Twaddell would have had a ready answer to Chomsky's charge: namely that what Chomsky calls explanation is in fact pseudo-explanation, 'the logical fallacy of "explaining" a fact of unknown cause by giving that unknown cause a name and then citing the name x as the cause of the fact', x in this case being 'mind'. But this is not what the mentalist is doing. The claim is, rather, that the explanation of many linguistic facts[5] lies in what are presumably neurochemical patterns in the brain; that we do not yet have the techniques to detect these patterns, but in the meantime we can say that they must be such as to be capable of accounting for certain relationships, which we then proceed to describe.

As for the objection to mixing of levels, this appears to rest on a confusion whose clearing-up is one of the most important advances of recent linguistic theory. The confusion is that between a theory and a procedure. If the objection to mixing of levels were an empirical claim that phonological patterns in language are wholly independent of grammatical patterns, it would probably never have been made. The evidence is all the other way. It is true that instances of independence can be cited. One that became a classic in the 1950s was the English word *Plato*, which has[6] an allophone of the diphthong /ei/ that is elsewhere typical of word-final position, being considerably longer than in apparently similar words such as *cater* and *potato*, and further, in many varieties of American English, has an aspirated alveolar stop [tʰ]—a typically initial allophone— rather than the flap [D] which is usual in these dialects in the middle of a word after a stressed vowel: in short, it behaves phonologically like two words—yet grammatically it is not merely a single word but an indivisible grammatical unit, a single *morpheme*.[7] The phenomenon of liaison in French provides another example: in certain cases a word-final consonant is phonetically more closely bound to the initial vowel of the next (grammatical) word than to the word of

[5] The same argument of course applies to other aspects of human (and indeed animal) behaviour.
[6] At least for some speakers.
[7] The *morpheme* is generally defined as a 'minimal meaningful unit' or a 'minimal unit relevant to grammatical analysis' (these definitions are not in general equivalent, but they give an idea of what the term is about). A word may comprise several morphemes; thus *meaningful* consists of *mean* (verb) + -*ing* (noun-forming suffix) + -*ful* (adjective-forming suffix); *definitions* might be analysed as consisting of *de*- (prefix) + -*fin*- (root, not found as a separate word but extractable from *final, finite*, etc.) + -*it*- (stem-forming suffix found in many Latin-derived words) + -*ion* (noun-forming suffix) + -*s* (plural ending); *give*, on the other hand, is a one-morpheme word, no part of it being separately meaningful or having separate grammatical significance.

which it itself grammatically forms part. But there is no escaping from the fact that in a wide variety of languages many phonological phenomena are to a high degree predictable from the position of grammatical word boundaries, nor from the fact that phonological distinctions can often be established between grammatical categories. French liaison itself can exemplify this: it is sensitive to such distinctions as that between an adjective-noun sequence and a noun adjective sequence (*anciens ouvriers* [ɑ̃sjɛ̃zuvrie] 'former workers' with liaison, but *ouvriers anciens* [uvrieɑ̃sjɛ̃] 'ancient workers' without it; for the principle cf. Schane 1967). In any such case, to keep the grammar and phonology wholly independent of one another is either to stultify the phonology, or to compel oneself to say the same thing twice in different parts of one's description.

If the requirement of no mixing of levels is not empirically based, there are two other possible explanations of it. One is the rationale of Wells (1947): 'Phonemics takes the point of view of the hearer. Now the hearer, in order to interpret correctly an utterance that he hears, must rely on two separate sources of information: (a) the heard sounds . . . ; (b) the extra-linguistic context (including his knowledge of what the utterance may or must mean). For the purpose of sharply distinguishing between what can be learned from one source and what can be learned from the other, phonemics makes a point of recording nothing but what is conveyed by (a).' This argument presupposes that the investigator is concerned to answer the *first* of the two questions with which we began this chapter; given that presupposition, the argument is irrefutable; but it has nothing to say to those who are interested in the *second* question.

This leaves the possibility that the requirement of no mixing of levels is a methodological one: that assertions about phonology which are not based purely on the phonic data (which are all that is directly observable) are for that reason unscientific. But to accept such a principle is, it has been argued, to misunderstand the nature of scientific method. In science we frame and test hypotheses. It does not in the least matter how these hypotheses are arrived at in the first place; it is the exception rather than the rule for an interesting hypothesis to be reached by a mechanical procedure, such as phonemic analysis essentially is.[8] Rather, what makes a hypothesis scientific or unscientific is whether it can be stated what kind of empirical evidence will tend to confirm it, what kind will tend to disconfirm it, and what kind will definitively refute it. And there is no reason why this general scientific principle should not be valid for phonological analysis.

Leaving aside, then, questions of analytic procedure as not relevant, what kind of evidence is germane to the validity of a phonological analysis?[9] There are two kinds of possible justification: internal and external.

Up till very recently, generative phonologists relied almost exclusively on internal justification. The weakest internal justification—though none the less essential—is *consistency*: an analysis must, in the words of W. W. Sawyer,[10] 'answer either *yes* or *no* to any question you put to it, and . . . never answer both

---

[8] What was said by Hockett (1968, 117) of mathematics applies equally to all sciences: 'The discovery of an algorithm [a rigorous procedure, such as a machine can carry out] for anything automatically renders the matter trivial, and mathematicians lose interest.'

[9] A clear conspectus of methodological principles of generative phonology is given by Zwicky (1975).

[10] *Prelude to Mathematics* (Penguin, Harmondsworth, 1955) 167.

yes and *no* to the same question.' In the case of phonology, this means that any given phonetic representation must be linked by the phonological component to one and only one underlying representation, except where there is independent reason to suppose ambiguity; that any given underlying representation must be linked to one and only one phonetic representation, except where there is free variation; and that phonetic representations that do not in fact occur in the language in question must not be linked to any underlying representation at all.

The most frequently cited kind of internal justification for phonological analysis is *success in capturing generalizations.* Simply, this means that an analysis which describes a single phenomenon by a single statement is better (other things being equal) than one which requires two or more statements to describe the same phenomenon. A second principle, often used in conjunction with the first, is that the phonological processes assumed should if possible be such as are known to be normal and in some sense 'natural' in language generally. There has been a justified tendency in the last few years to place greater emphasis on the second principle where (as not infrequently happens) it comes into conflict with the first; for it is easier to find independent evidence bearing on the question whether this or that process is frequently found in various languages, than it is to find such evidence on the question whether a given set of data constitute a 'single phenomenon'. Note that the two principles do not mean that an analysis requiring many statements of little generality, or a rule that is known from no language other than that for which it is posited, is necessarily wrong; only that it is *prima facie* suspicious, and to be rejected if a preferable analysis is found. Probably all languages have areas of their phonology where large-scale generalization is impossible, and very many seem to have unique rules (though, as we shall see in Chapter Nine, it has lately been argued that in this last respect appearances can be deceptive).

Related to the notion of generalization is an antinomy much referred to by generative grammarians when attempting to justify or refute analyses, that of *independently motivated* v. *ad hoc.* This is based on a principle (valid for all sciences) which is thus expressed by Botha (1971, 229): 'The postulation and use of linguistic and grammatical concepts . . . must be motivated by showing that they are required for diverse reasons, no two of which are interdependent. . . . It is further required that the general linguistic principles, structural descriptions and rules taken as wholes be independently motivated' in the same sense. One might here wish to quarrel with the words 'must' and 'required'. Both in linguistics and elsewhere, the principle distinguishes between better and worse hypotheses, not between right and wrong ones.

An example of the working of the principle of independent motivation may be taken, again, from French. A very large number of French words, which in all normal styles of speech end in a consonant, are in certain special styles (such as poetry and song) treated, in some environments, as ending in a vowel [ə]: e.g. [pɔrt] 'door', [grãd] 'large (fem.)' [ɛm] 'like' (1st/3rd person singular), [ɛl] 'she'. Most generative phonological analyses assign all these words underlying forms with this final vowel. This is not done for any one reason in particular but because a variety of independent considerations point the same way; for example:

1. Another large class of French words has a 'movable' final consonant, present in some environments and absent in others: e.g. [grã(t)] 'large (masc.)', [vjø(z)] 'old (masc. pl.)', [ã(n)] 'in'; the list would be much longer still if we added the words in which the movable consonant appears overtly only when a suffix is added, e.g. [par] 'share', cf. [part-až-e] 'to share out'; [pari] 'Paris', cf. [pariz-jɛ] 'Parisian'. Since the identity of the movable consonant (or even whether there is one at all) is in any particular case quite unpredictable, the natural solution is to include them in the underlying representations; but in that case some distinct underlying representation must be found for the words that end in a consonant that is *always* present on the surface. The representation with final /ə/ suggests itself, especially in view of the other considerations to be mentioned.

2. The assumption of the underlying /ə/ makes possible a uniform phonological shape for certain morphemes, e.g. the feminine ending in adjectives will always have the underlying representation /ə/.

3. In certain positions word-final [ə] is actually heard even in normal speech: e.g. [dã lə mɔd] 'in the world', [gardə-bu] 'mudguard'. It might be argued that this could be accounted for by assuming /ə/ not to be present in underlying representations but to be inserted by rule under appropriate conditions; but apart from the fact that this conflicts with the other evidence favouring the presence of /ə/ in underlying representations, it can be shown[11] that such a solution cannot be made to work.

4. Movable final consonants, when present on the surface, are closely bound phonetically to the initial vowel of the following word; fixed final consonants are not. This dissimilarity finds an explanation if at the underlying level some other element, such as /ə/ would be, intervenes between a fixed final consonant and the initial segment of the next word.

5. The vowel of the feminine definite article /la/ drops when the succeeding word begins with a vowel. If underlying /ə/ is not recognized, a special rule will have to be set up purely for this one case; if underlying /ə/ is assumed, its deletion and the deletion of the vowel of /la/ can be regarded as special cases of a general rule dropping unstressed word-final vowels. For the main stress of a French word falls on the last vowel which is not /ə/[12]; but certain words, and among them the definite article, normally bear no stress at all.[13]

These are merely a selection, and they could be supplemented by a good many other considerations of a more technical nature. If the facts of French had been such that only one of these considerations had held good, the positing of underlying /ə/ might with some reason have been criticized as *ad hoc*. As it is, when we further note that the dropping of unstressed vowels is a phonetically very plausible and very frequent process (particularly when they directly follow stressed syllables, as word-final French /ə/ always does except in monosyllables),

---

[11] The demonstration is due to Andrew Crompton.

[12] On the surface this stress is not appreciable except before a pause.

[13] In the rare circumstances in which the definite article is stressed its vowel is not dropped even before a vowel: cf. *le ou les voyages* 'the journey or journeys', where the singular and plural articles are stressed for contrast with one another.

and that in general, in most languages, if any vowels are dropped in any circumstances /ə/ is normally among them if the language has that vowel at all— when we take all this into account, the arguments for this analysis become well-nigh irresistible.[14]

But it must again be emphasized that independent motivation is not obligatory, merely desirable. An analysis parts of which are *ad hoc* is, to be sure, acceptable only *faute de mieux*; but it is not unacceptable merely because parts of it are *ad hoc*.

A fourth type of internal justification is based on simplicity. In some theories, notably stratificational grammar and early versions of generative phonology, a 'simplicity metric' is set up, based on the notation defined by the theory; each proposed description is given a value, usually inversely proportional to the number of symbols of certain types it uses, and the highest-valued description accounting for a given set of facts is considered the best. Such simplicity metrics have usually run into problems, finding that the clearly inferior of two alternative descriptions turns out to be more highly valued by the metric; for some time the natural reaction was to revise either the metric or the notation to avoid such conflicts. But as soon as you do this you are no longer really using simplicity as a criterion; rather you are taking a blend of the criteria that you do use to judge competing analyses and labelling it simplicity. Thus formal simplicity is now used to any extent as a criterion only in stratificational grammar, which appears to have been remarkably successful in avoiding conflicts of the kind mentioned. In the other senses in which 'simplicity' has been employed in discussions of evaluation in phonology, it is hard to see that it means anything other than generality or naturalness.

The criteria we have discussed are all useful, but they are all *internal*, at least in the sense of being dependent on a particular theoretical perspective. This is so even in the case of criteria like generality and naturalness. Why *should* we assume that the more general solution is necessarily the better one? Dell (1973b, 266) is right to point out that this assumption is actually an empirical hypothesis, 'that during language learning children exploit to the full all the regularities they are capable of uncovering in the utterances they hear around them, and memorize only what cannot be predicted by rule.'[15] Is the hypothesis correct?[16] As far as naturalness is concerned, does it not very largely depend on our preconceptions? For if a certain type of rule occurs very often in various languages, that *may* reflect not the languages themselves but the way they have been analysed. It is worth remembering that the whole concept of assimilation, almost the paradigm case of

[14] On the whole subject of French '*e muet*' see the relevant portions of Schane (1967) and Dell (1973b).

[15] I have throughout tacitly translated quotations from works not in English.

[16] Neuropsychology apparently suggests it isn't: 'the indications . . . are that, instead of storing a small number of primitives and organizing them in terms of a large number of rules, we store a large number of complex items which we manipulate with comparatively simple operations. The central nervous system is like a special kind of computer which has rapid access to the items in a very large memory, but comparatively little ability to process these items when they have been taken out of memory' (Ladefoged 1972a, 282). Of course, statements of this degree of vagueness cannot be treated as criteria for linguistic descriptions, but they show the need for caution in using the much-favoured (and in its place, essential) generality principle. See now Hsieh (1976) for a trenchant critique of the generality principle on psycholinguistic grounds, with references to earlier work.

a natural type of rule, was rejected at one time by a whole school of phonologists (the prosodists: see Chapter Three). We should welcome some *external* criteria of adequacy.

Here again, we can begin with a weak and obvious criterion, which has, in fact, been tacitly assumed throughout the previous discussion: namely that the phonological description, in conjunction with the grammatical description, should correctly state the sound-meaning relationship which is mediated by grammar and phonology. That is, given a phonetic representation P, we want the description to tell us: (a) whether the language being described, L, contains a sentence S of which P is the phonetic representation; (b) if so, what other phonetic representations, if any, S can have; (c) whether S is semantically anomalous, univocal or ambiguous, and if ambiguous how many possible interpretations it is capable of; and (d) some kind of specification of what these interpretations are.

Of these requirements, (c) and (d) belong to grammar and semantics. A phonological description of L that gives correct answers to (a) and (b) for *all* logically possible phonetic representations (answering 'no' to (a) for those which the language does not allow at all, e.g. *[fkerŋumt] in English)[17] may be said to be *observationally adequate* (Chomsky 1965a).

In the same work Chomsky recognizes two higher levels of what purports to be external justification; these, however, are controversial, and in practice are very little appealed to.[18] *Descriptive adequacy* consists in correspondence between the description and 'the linguistic intuition of the native speaker (whether or not he may be immediately aware of this).' This at once recalls the arguments of Sapir (1925) (see pp. 5–6), and is open to the same objection that these 'intuitions', if accessible at all, may be conditioned by irrelevant factors. Moreover, is there any evidence that the 'intuitions' in question are consistent even between different speakers of the same language or dialect? Linguists investigating their native languages have been known to have sharply divergent views on what is an 'intuitively satisfactory' analysis; how much more then will unsophisticated native speakers differ on the point.

The third and even higher standard of adequacy is for Chomsky a property not of grammars,[19] but of *linguistic theories.* A linguistic theory is regarded as a set of universal conditions which all grammars of possible human languages must obey: that is, it defines what is and what is not a possible grammar. Chomsky assumes that the child possesses an innate mechanism for deducing the full structure of the language he has to learn from the data presented to him, and a linguistic theory is *true* to the extent that it approximates this mechanism.[20] The

---

[17] In linguistic description the asterisk is regularly used to indicate that the form in question is inadmissible in the language under discussion. In historical linguistics its function is rather different: there it means that the form so marked is not attested either in contemporary speech or by written records, but is hypothesized to have once existed in order to explain some attested form or forms.

[18] Though some linguists seem to use 'descriptive adequacy' as a synonym for 'observational adequacy'.

[19] Recall (p. 4) that in generative theory the 'grammar' of a language is a full description including semantics, syntax and phonology.

[20] I know this definition only from a letter of Chomsky's quoted by Hockett (1968); but, though Chomsky does not elsewhere make it explicit, it fits well with his other expositions of the questions of adequacy and of 'innateness'.

structure of the innate mechanism is supposed to be determinable via a study of linguistic universals: plainly any such mechanism must be such as to ensure that no child can ever deduce, from any set of data that he might be presented with, that the language he is learning has a structure that neither is nor could be[21] found in any human language. In Chomsky (1965a) this level of adequacy is called 'explanatory adequacy'.

Descriptive adequacy and 'truth' are not very easily relatable to any empirical data likely to be available for some time to come, and the search has recently been intensified for other external criteria for phonological descriptions. This movement began when Kiparsky (1968a) found some isomorphisms between the kinds of statement that are needed in phonological description and the kinds of phonological change that are known to occur; in a later paper (1972b) Kiparsky mentions several other kinds of evidence that can tell for or against phonological analyses: child language; language pathology (aphasias and the like); direct psychological experimentation; treatment of loanwords; orthography (which must, of course, be used with caution, especially where the writing system is long-established); metrics. Some of these have been made use of by phonologists for a long time; it is only necessary to recall how Jakobson (1942) showed that certain universals about the make-up of consonant and vowel systems tallied with the order of acquisition of phonemes by children and their loss by aphasics. At present, however, for generative and similar phonological analyses, only two of these criteria are being effectively used—linguistic change and the treatment of loanwords.[22] The criterion of linguistic change may be of particular help in one kind of situation: where the nature of a phonological change implies that those in whose speech the change took place were intuitively analysing their language in a particular way just before the change. If for example Sarcee (cf. pp. 6–7) were to undergo a change whereby it dropped word-final vowels, and D2 (surface [di_ni⁻], underlying /di_nith⁻/) were to be unaffected by the change, this would strongly support Sapir's analysis of the data.[23]

A last external criterion that must not be overlooked is *phonetic plausibility*. A proposed rule is phonetically plausible if it can be shown that its effect is to make either the production or the perception of speech easier, in at least one respect,[24]

[21] 'Neither is nor could be', because some statements which are true for all existing languages may for all we know be 'accidental universals'—they may be true merely because all the languages that violated them have become extinct. Only one language in the world is known to have apico-labial stops (viz. Umotina: Hockett in Martin 1956, 683), and in today's world it is only too easy to envisage this South American language disappearing, in which case, if records of it also happened to be lost, linguists a thousand years hence might wrongly conclude that a language having apico-stops was not a possible human language.

[22] Very recent work, however, has shown increasing interest in child phonology, and it is possible that the next revolution in the subject will come from this direction: a phonological grammar composed of principles each of which can be shown to be actually acquired by the child learning the language. As of 1975, however, such a project is still scarcely on the horizon. The evidence of speech errors has also been put to use: see Hyman (1975, 21f.) and references there, as well as p. 235 below on 'natural processes'.

[23] Even more so, of course, if some change (e.g. a rule loss, a reordering, a restriction on a rule's generality) were to result in the previously 'abstract' /th/ reappearing on the surface: cf. examples in D. G. Miller (1973b, 374–8).

[24] A change that makes production or perception easier at one point may make it more difficult at

than it would have been had the grammar of the language not contained the rule in question. The phonologies of most languages, however, contain rules that are not phonetically plausible: typically these rules are partly, or even wholly, conditioned by grammatical categories and features, and it is a moot point (to which we shall return in Chapter Nine) whether they belong in the phonological component at all.

Thus our two questions lead to two very different kinds of phonology, producing different kinds of description by different methods and judging them by different sets of criteria. Since they are not trying to do the same thing, they are not necessarily inconsistent with one another; indeed, attempts have been made (most notably by Schane 1971) to use the classical-phonemic notion of contrast in generative phonology. Most theories of the second class profess to be interested in explanation; classical phonemics does not; but there is no reason why the morphophonemic and allophonic statements of a good classical phonemic analysis, and language universals derived from a large number of such analyses, should not have as much explanatory power as the rules of a good generative phonological analysis. There is reason, as we shall see later, to believe that the dichotomy between morphophonemic and allophonic statements, imposed by the principles of classical phonemics, sometimes forces the analyst to miss generalizations; but it is equally a fault of generative phonology that it provides no direct means of determining whether two or more segment types are not in surface contrast, even though some phonological processes probably need access to such information. In short, if one were asked which of the two questions with which we started it was the proper business of phonology to attack, the best answer would be: both.

This book will be mainly concerned, as the present chapter has been, with phonological description of languages as they are at given points in time, *synchronic* phonology; the study of phonological change, historical or *diachronic* phonology, will be dealt with mainly in the last chapter. The two cannot be rigidly separated, for even the ordinary native speaker has some diachronic knowledge: if he is young, he knows that his grandparents speak in ways in which he would not speak himself; if he is old, he knows that some innovations have been taken up by the younger generation. These differences may affect phonology as much as any other part of language. But in general, when dealing with synchronic phonology, we will abstract away from them.

Classical phonemics will be the subject of the next chapter; then two other theories will be dealt with which have played a significant part in the phonological work of the last thirty years. Chapter Five will consider the nature of the ultimate units of phonology. Generative phonology will be the theme of Chapters Six to Nine, first in the form which has been canonized by *The Sound Pattern of English*, followed by discussion of some fields in which subsequent research has suggested that the *SPE* model may be unsatisfactory, and in many of which important issues remain unsettled.

---

another point; or a change that eases production may hamper perception, or *vice versa*. A perfect equilibrium is never attained. This is a substantial part of the reason why phonological change is always going on.

2 Classical Phonemics

2.1 Segmental phonemics

As has been said, the basic notion of phonemic analysis is that of *contrast*, and it is on the basis of contrast that phonemic systems are set up for languages.

Phonemic analysis has a very long history. The notion of phonemic contrast was known to the Indian grammarian Patanjali in the second century B.C. (see Jakobson 1960/1971, 394), and in the West is virtually explicit in an eleventh-century Icelandic treatise (cf. Haugen 1950); it was rediscovered by J. Winteler in the 1870s, and the term 'phoneme' was first used in approximately its present sense by M. Kruszewski in 1880. For many years, however, phonemics was on the one hand not very clearly distinguished from phonetics, and on the other tended to be regarded as a branch of psychology rather than of linguistics: the name 'psychophonetics' given to the field by J. Baudouin de Courtenay, generally regarded as the greatest figure in the prehistory of phonology, is symptomatic.[1]

The theoretical foundations for a purely linguistic phonemic analysis were laid just before and just after the first world war, largely by Russian scholars such as L. Ščerba and N. F. Jakovlev; but the edifice itself was constructed between the 1920s and the 1940s, simultaneously and at first largely independently, in Prague and in America. Phonemic analysis as here to be expounded follows essentially the American tradition; the major emphases of the Prague School version of classical phonemics, where they differ, will be discussed later.

2.1.1. Analytic procedure

Let us begin by making two big assumptions. First, that we know what language we are interested in. The assumption is far from being trivial; no language is wholly homogeneous, and it is only too easy for a phonemic analysis to be vitiated by the fact that the data on which it is based derive from two or more dialects whose differences crucially affect the analysis.[2] The idiolects[3] which form our data

[1] On the early history of the phoneme and related concepts, see Krámský (1974); the reference to Kruszewski is provided by Isačenko (1956, 313).

[2] This is a condemnation of so-called *overall pattern* analyses such as the analysis of American English phonemes by Trager and Smith (1951). Such analyses considered a group of related dialects, and any contrast found to be present in one of the dialects was in principle taken to be part of the 'overall pattern' of the whole group. Such an analysis may have some practical utility in that it establishes a sort of language-specific phonetic grid which can be used by dialect investigators; but it cannot be regarded as a *phonemic* analysis of anything, for the phonemic system of one dialect cannot be made to depend upon contrasts in another dialect of whose very existence most speakers of the first dialect are unaware.

[3] Idiolect: the form of speech employed by a particular person (speaking, we should add, in one and the same stylistic register).

must either all have the same system of contrasts or at least have a substantial common core; in the latter case the differences must be clearly stated, and evidence from one dialect must not be applied to the analysis of another unless the differences can be shown to be immaterial to the point under discussion.

The second assumption is that we have succeeded in carrying out a phonetic *segmentation* of a corpus of utterances in the language in which we are interested: that is, that we have exhaustively divided it into individual 'sounds' or *phones* of the kind that are represented by single symbols in such systems as the International Phonetic Association's alphabet, and have noted the *prosodic features* (pitch, loudness, length) of each segment of each utterance that is capable of carrying prosodic variations. We are here begging the question whether such segmentation has any theoretical validity; it is a tool of analysis, all schools use it as such, and for this purpose experience has proved it satisfactory.

What we now have is a *narrow phonetic transcription*, which, if ideally accurate, would show that every phone-token was different from every other. A great reduction, however, can immediately be effected by the following simple principle:

If A and B are phones found in the data, and native speakers always regard   **1**
the utterance XBY as a repetition of XAY whatever X and Y may be
(provided XAY is a well-formed utterance in the language), then so far as that
language is concerned A and B may be regarded as variants of a single phone.

In all that follows the phonetic transcription will be assumed to have already undergone this reduction, and the term 'phone' should be interpreted accordingly.

It will always be possible to group the phones into sets such that no two members of any set occur in the same *environment*, or if they do, native speakers regard utterances differing only by the substitution of one of them for the other as repetitions of one another. The environment of a phonetic (or phonological) element is defined as the phonetic (respectively, phonological) elements preceding and following it, up to the boundary of the utterance; this includes prosodic features, and the utterance boundary itself is considered as part of the environment.

Let us look at a partial example of such grouping. Among the segment types found in a phonetic transcription of a reasonable-sized corpus in English will be:

		cf.	
[t]		*stop*	**2**[4]
[tʰ]	(aspirated)	*top*	
[t˺]	(unreleased)	*hatpin*	
[t̪˺]	(dental, not alveolar)	*eighth*	
[tʲ]		*not yet*	
[ṭ]	(slightly retroflexed)	*trap*	

Now all these can be grouped into a set meeting the conditions just mentioned. For example, with most speakers, [t̪˺] occurs only when the immediately

---

[4] This is not intended as a complete statement of the allophones of English /t/; it ignores, for instance, the important phenomenon of glottalization (Higginbottom 1965).

following segment is the dental fricative [θ], and none of the other segment types of (2) occurs in this environment. Technically, [t̪⁻] is described as being in *complementary distribution* with each of the other segment types mentioned. On the other hand, when a stop, a nasal, or utterance boundary immediately follows, either [t] or [tʰ] can occur; these two phones are therefore not in complementary distribution. But if, in any of these environments, we replace [t⁻] by [tʰ] or vice versa, we never by so doing change one utterance into another regarded by speakers of the language as a non-repetition of the first; these phones are therefore said to be in *free variation* in these environments (and, as it happens, in complementary distribution in other environments).

I have several times spoken of native speakers regarding utterances as repetitions or non-repetitions of one another. How do we test this? We cannot just present our informant with utterances like [hæt⁻pʰɪn] and [hætʰpʰɪn] and ask him 'Are these the same or different?' For our informant's response may be based not on phonological contrast but on factors such as the acuteness of his ear, or his knowledge that the two utterances are 'the same word', or even a hunch that 'there must be a catch in the question somewhere'. Nor can we ask him 'Do they mean the same thing?'; for we may then be surprised to learn that there is no phonological contrast between [íːðə] and [áiðə],[5] or between [æbətwaː] and [slóːtəhæus], etc. To find out whether two utterances did in fact contrast phonologically, the technique most often used was that known as the 'pair test'. Given two utterance types,

> we ask two informants to say these to each other several times, telling one informant which to say . . . and seeing if the other can guess which he said. If the hearer guesses right about fifty per cent of the time then there is no regular descriptive difference between the utterances [i.e. they are free variants— AHS]; if he guesses right near one hundred per cent, there is. (Z. Harris 1951, 32–3.)

This test will always reveal a contrast if one exists;[6] but it *may* also appear to reveal a contrast where none exists. This would no doubt happen, for instance, if the two utterances in question were the English word *run* pronounced respectively with a retroflex [ɻ] and a trilled [r]. So the validity of putative contrasts revealed by the pair test may be checked by another test, described by Contreras and Saporta (1960).[7] Two putatively contrasting items are recorded, and each is

---

[5] Here and hereafter, the elements of diphthongs are linked by a subscript curve.

[6] Recently Labov (1974) has shown that a speaker may consistently use slightly different phones (clearly distinguishable by instrumental methods) in different sets of words while (i) asserting that the words are homophonous and (ii) unable to distinguish between them in another virtually identical idiolect, or in his own recorded speech. Such a speaker has productive control over the distinction, but not perceptual control; neither the pair test nor the repetition test will reveal the existence of a contrast, and it is questionable whether such distinctions should be regarded as phonemic (any more than would a distinction which a speaker could perceive but not produce). They are none the less real, and it would appear that such 'half-contrasts' may be found over substantial areas and persist for perhaps centuries without the phones in question either merging of moving further apart. Perhaps we need to distinguish a productive and a perceptual phonemic system; the classic tests for contrast relate only to the latter.

[7] And for some mysterious reason totally ignored, by both defenders and opponents of classical phonemics, ever since.

played back to the informant ten times, the two items being intermixed in random order, and the informant being asked to repeat each item as he hears it. A repetition is correct just in case it contains the same choice for the putatively contrastive feature as the item of which it is a repetition. Contreras and Saporta found that informants scored 18 out of 20 or better on all and only those pairs of items which really were in phonological contrast.

The repetition test is rather a laborious affair, and in most cases we will be content to take a short cut and ask: is the putative contrast *ever* paralleled by a difference in meaning? We do not test this out on a single pair of utterances, for we might hit on one of those cases where genuinely contrasting phonological forms are used with the same meaning. But if, looking at all the material we have in the language (and checking back with our informants), we find that the difference in pronunciation *never* converts one utterance into another that is consistently said to differ in meaning, we conclude that there is no real contrast.

Having established, for each pair of phones in the language, whether it is a pair in free variation, complementary distribution or a mixture of the two, or whether its members are in contrast, the next step in phonemic analysis is to group the phones into sets all of whose numbers are in free variation and/or complementary distribution with one another. This step gives rise to two problems.

First, the notion 'complementary distribution' as we have used it up to now, defined in terms of utterance-long environments, is both clumsy and inadequate. Its clumsiness can be overcome by technological brute force (e.g. computerization); its inadequacy cannot. The problem is that two phones which are in phonological contrast may nevertheless, in terms of utterance-long environments, be in complementary distribution even in the (infinite) corpus consisting of all the well-formed utterances in the language. All phonemic analyses of English agree that it has a phoneme /ž/, found medially in such words as *measure* and finally in certain pronunciations of *rouge, beige* and other more or less naturalized French loanwords, and contrasting with the other consonants of English and in particular with its voiceless counterpart /š/ (initial in *shoe*, medial in *washer*, final in *rush*). But at least in many idiolects of English there is no utterance-long environment in which both [ž] and [š] can be found. Rather, the two phones are said to contrast because they both occur in the environment 'followed by pause, preceded by [éi]'—cf. *beige. Paish*—, in the environment 'followed by [ə], preceded by [ɛ́]' cf. *measure:thresher*— , and perhaps in certain other similarly defined 'environments'. That is, not utterance-long environments are considered, but rather 'relevant' environments. What, though, is meant by 'relevant'?

The key notion here is one that we have already met in another connexion: that of *generalization*. The only way in which the distribution of [š] and [ž] can be stated is by listing the morphemes, words, utterances which have the 'allophone' [š] and those which have [ž]; there is nothing *phonological* about the principles that determine their distribution.[8] Contrast the distribution of the genuine allophones of /t/ given in (2), which is determined by purely phonological factors.

---

[8] As a whole, that is. There are in fact certain phonological restrictions on the distribution of both phonemes, but these do not amount to complementary distribution.

If, however, we adopt the notion of relevant environment, based on that of generalization, we must abandon the hope of complete methodological rigour. What *is* a phonological generalization? We have taken extreme cases. But even in these it could *à la rigueur* be argued that a statement in purely phonological terms of the restrictions on [š] and [ž], or a statement in non-phonological terms of the restrictions on the allophones of /t/, is possible; true, it is fiendishly complicated, but there may very well be cases in which the issue is rather finely balanced. It has, however, long been recognized that complete methodological rigour is a chimera,[9] and we may be content with the following principles:

Two or more phones are capable of being phonemically identical only if it is **3a** possible to formulate a set of general phonological statements such that, for every (utterance-long) environment in the language, it is the case that either:
    none of the phones in question can occur in that environment; or,
    all of them can occur in it; or,
    the general phonological statements fully and correctly predict which of them can occur in that environment and which cannot;
    and if, further, the difference between two of the phones in question never carries a difference in meaning.
In all phonemic analysis, phones are to be presumed distinct until the **b** contrary is proved;[10] in other words, any real doubt about (for example) the generality of a phonological statement must be resolved in such a way as to make the affected phones contrastive.

Even these principles are not entirely watertight, but if they failed it could only be because the phonemes in question were exceedingly rare.[11]

Note that although we have given up complete methodological rigour, statements about complementary distribution remain empirical statements; any such statement can be falsified, in the last resort, by producing a minimal pair, i.e. two utterances whose sole point of difference is the difference between the allegedly complementary phones, and which differ in meaning.

The second and perhaps even more important problem is that there is not in general a single grouping of phones that meets the criteria we have stated; frequently there are several, giving rise to what is called 'the non-uniqueness problem'. For example, the phone [t̪⁻] that we considered earlier is in complementary distribution with [tʰ], but it is also in complementary distribution with [pʰ], [kʰ], and a good many other phones. With which of these

---

[9] E.g. by Hockett (1955, 147), who says it is necessary that 'the analyst . . . to some extent learn the language with which he is working', renouncing the hope that many American linguists had earlier cherished of being able to formulate rigorous procedures for arriving at correct analyses of languages which the investigator did not know.

[10] Cf. Pilch (1968, 69–70).

[11] Pilch (1968, 72) gives an example which shows it is possible that there might be phonemes for which general phonological statements of distribution were *accidentally* possible, in which case (3) would wrongly regard them as non-contrastive; but the example involves three phones each of which is assumed to occur once only in the language. Such possibilities might be controlled by testing whether forms violating the statements of distribution are accepted as nonsense words.

should it be grouped? For it cannot be grouped with all the phones with which it is in complementary distribution, since some of these contrast among themselves. Under such circumstances appeal is often made to the criterion of *phonetic similarity*. This criterion has been formulated in various ways by various scholars. The weak form is:

Of the various possible groupings of phones, choose that which maximizes the phonetic similarity between phones belonging to the same group.   **4**

But this still permits us to make groupings which do not reflect the nature of the language. For example, [h] and [ŋ] are in complementary distribution in English: the former occurs only if a stressed vowel follows or a juncture[12] precedes, the latter never occurs when either of these conditions obtains. Neither can be grouped with any phone more phonetically similar to itself than the other is. Yet to group them together would certainly not be a good analysis. A stronger form of the phonetic similarity condition was therefore preferred by many linguists (e.g. Trubetzkoy and Bloch), namely that in order to be grouped, a set of segment types not only had to meet the distributional requirements already mentioned but also had to have phonetic features in common *which no segment outside the set had*; these may be called the defining features of the group. On this criterion, [h] and [ŋ] could not be grouped; for virtually the only phonetic feature they share is that they are not vowels, and this feature is of course shared by many other phones as well.

Many otherwise possible analyses are excluded by the criterion of phonetic similarity, but some non-uniqueness still remains. It frequently happens that we find three phones, two of which are in contrast while the third is in complementary distribution with each and phonetically similar to each in about the same degree. Such cases are sometimes called cases of *neutralization*: the opposition between the first two phone(me)s is, as it were, suspended in a particular environment, in which a phone appears that has the features common to both but cannot unequivocally be identified, at least at first sight, with either. To take once again the example from English, [pʰ] and [b] contrast in various environments, but neither occurs after [s]; instead, in this environment we find voiceless, unaspirated [p]. With which of the other two should this [p] be grouped? Does it, in other words, belong with the /p/ phoneme or the /b/ phoneme?[13]

It is possible that phonetic similarity may be able to give a decision here. Davidsen-Nielsen (1969) found the relevant phonetic features of the three phones to be as follows:

[pʰ]: fortis, voiceless, aspirated.   **5**

---

[12] For juncture see p. 40.

[13] The situation is exactly analogous with the alveolar and velar stops. Actually there are two potential minimal pairs, *distain:disdain* and *disperse:disburse*, yet nobody, so far as I know, has ever tried to determine the simple question whether English speakers can tell these apart—although an answer to that would decide the whole question of the phonemic assignment of the voiceless unaspirates (so long as it turned out that voiceless unaspirates were actually being used in *distain* and *disperse*). The discussion in the text should be taken as referring to a (possibly imaginary) idiolect in which the 'simple question' is answered in the negative.

[p]: fortis, voiceless, unaspirated.
[b]: lenis, voiced or voiceless, unaspirated.

If this is correct, [p] is closer phonetically to [pʰ] than to [b], for it differs from the former by one feature, from the latter by one feature obligatorily and optionally by a second.[14] But the difference in degree of closeness is rather tenuous, and there may well be dialects in which [p] is absolutely equidistant between the other two phones. What do we do then?

It seems preferable, on the whole, to classify [p] with the /p/ phoneme. The reason is one of what is generally and rather vaguely termed *pattern congruity*. If we choose to classify [p] with the /p/ phoneme, then English will (within syllables) have /sp/ clusters but no /sb/ clusters; if we classify it with the /b/ phoneme, *vice versa*. Now there is a clear sense in which the opposition between /s/ and /z/ in the English phonemic system is the same as the opposition between /p/ and /b/; to avoid begging questions, let us call the feature concerned Feature X. In general, clusters of obstruents[15] in English must agree in the value of Feature X. We have clusters /ps bz/, for example, as in *caps* and *cabs* respectively, but no */pz bs/. But if we classify [p] with the /b/ phoneme, this generalization will no longer hold; we will have clusters /sb sd sg/ but no /sp st sk/. As a result, the principles governing the arrangement of phonemes relevant to one another, the *phonotactic* rules, will be unnecessarily complicated. If we assign [p] to the /b/ phoneme, the relevant part of the phonotactics will have to say:

When a stop precedes any obstruent, or a fricative precedes a fricative, the   **6a**
two must agree in the value of Feature X.
When a fricative precedes a stop, the stop must have the 'weaker' value of   **b**
Feature X.

If we assign [p] to the /p/ phoneme, the relevant phonotactic statement will be:

When an obstruent precedes an obstruent, the two must agree in the value of   **7**
Feature X.

The term 'pattern congruity' has been used in the literature to mean two rather different things. One is phonotactic simplification, as above. The other is a preference for more symmetrical over less symmetrical phonological systems. Consider the obstruent system of standard German. Leaving aside affricates, this contains at least the following stops and fricatives:

/p	t	k	**8**
b	d	g	
f	s	š	
v	z		/

There are also, phonetically, palatal and velar fricatives [ç x]—e.g. [báːx] 'stream', [bέːçə] 'streams'—which we shall assume to be in complementary

---

[14] In spite of this Davidsen-Nielsen (1969) assigned the voiceless unaspirates to the /b d g/ phonemes, giving phonetic similarity as the ground for doing so; more recently (1975) he has argued, on the basis of an investigation of speech errors, for treating them as realizations of an archiphoneme (cf. p. 23).
[15] An *obstruent* is a stop or fricative. A consonant which is not an obstruent is a *sonorant* or *resonant*.

distribution.[16] The problem is: assuming that these two fricatives are allophones of one phoneme, where does this phoneme fit into the diagrammed system (8)?

The answer is given at once by the diagram There is only one vacant 'slot' for a voiceless fricative, and that is as the counterpart of the velar stops /k g/. Otherwise, we will be forced to reckon *five* different places of articulation for German obstruents although only four ever contrast. For this reason it is customary to symbolize the fricative under discussion by /x/, the usual fricative counterpart of /k/. It is also largely for this reason that so much effort has gone into proving that the two fricatives *are* allophones of one phoneme in the face of apparent counter-evidence.

The reader should, by the way, be warned against supposing that this is primarily a question of symbols, transcriptions, and system diagrams. The question at issue is whether German obstruents have five distinct positions of articulation (labial, dental, palato-alveolar, palatal-or-velar, and velar) or only four: the choice of symbols is merely a way of showing clearly where we stand on this question. The example may further serve to emphasize that a phonetic transcription is useless as a guide to pronunciation unless the allophonic rules are known.

Another criterion for use in cases of phonemic non-uniqueness is that of phonetic plausibility (see Chapter One, p. 14f.): are the morphophonemic and particularly the allophonic rules implied by a proposed analysis explicable in phonetic terms, and if they are not, is there an alternative analysis, meeting the other criteria laid down, that avoids this drawback?

It must be said that there are many phonologists, even among those who hold in general to the phonemic theory, who would say that for at least some cases of non-uniqueness it is wrong in principle to force a resolution along the lines here indicated, e.g. to try to classify the English voiceless unaspirated stops with either the /b d g/ or the /p t k/ phonemes. They would say that the insistence on setting up a single phonemic system valid for the whole language ('once a phoneme always a phoneme', as it has been epigrammatically put) is a mere prejudice arising from the fact that Western writing systems follow this pattern; after /s/ in English there is no distinction between the two classes of stops, and we should not try to pretend that there is. Some would say that the voiceless unaspirated stops were instances neither of /b d g/ nor of /p t k/, but of 'archiphonemes' which had all the shared features of /b p/ (resp. /d t/, /g k/) but were neutral as to Feature X: this view of neutralization is associated with the Prague School.[17] Others would say that voicelessness, which undoubtedly *is* a characteristic of clusters like English [sp st sk], ought not to be marked independently for each phoneme in the cluster, since that would imply (falsely) that one consonant in the cluster can be voiced or voiceless regardless of what the others are; rather voicing or voicelessness should be assigned to the cluster as a whole. On this view a pair of contrasting words like *staffs* and *starves* might be represented thus:

---

[16] Actually the complementary distribution is not quite perfect, and many attempts have been made to show that what appear to be counter-examples are not really such.
[17] The term 'archiphoneme' appears to be due to Jakobson (1929).

$$\begin{array}{llll}
/s & t & a\!: & f & s/ \\
vl\text{---} & & vl\text{---} \\
/s & t & a\!: & f & s/ \\
vl\text{---} & & vd\text{---}
\end{array}$$

9a

b

Such features, whose domain is longer than one segment, have been termed 'phonemic long components'; a developed form of the same notion is found in prosodic phonology (see Chapter Three).

For the present we will continue to maintain the principle of a single all-embracing phonemic system for each language.

We have now, we hope, by the use of the criteria of complementary distribution, phonetic similarity, pattern congruity and phonetic plausibility, exhaustively classified the very large number of phone types in a language into a much smaller number of classes. These classes are the *phonemes* of the language.

2.1.2 Defining the phoneme

The notion of the phoneme as a class of sounds is perhaps the simplest to understand; it is that of Jones (1950), Chao (1934), and Hockett (1942). Chao's definition may serve to introduce one or two points of uncertainty:

> A phoneme is one of an exhaustive list of classes of sounds in a language, such that every word in the language can be given as an ordered series of one or more of these classes and such that two different words which are not considered as having the same pronunciation differ in the order or in the constituency of the classes which make up the word.

Chao intended that definition as a statement of the *communis opinio* at the time he was writing; he himself saw a weakness in it, and subsequent work soon uncovered another. The second weakness was the emphasis on words. Within a few years some linguists, notably Bloch, Trager and Hockett, became doubtful of the methodological respectability of assuming words as given in advance of a phonemic analysis, and noted further that the Chao definition exluded intonation from phonemics (though it did not, of course, exclude lexical tone in tone languages); they therefore, in effect, replaced 'word' in the definition by 'utterance'.[18]

The weakness seen by Chao himself was, as the title of his paper indicates, the problem of non-uniqueness; and in the next ten to fifteen years criteria were elaborated for choosing among alternative analyses. Hockett (1942) lists six properties of phonemic systems which he calls criteria, though four of them are in fact not so much criteria as necessary conditions for a phonemic analysis to be tenable at all. Three of the four are straightforward enough: phonetic similarity, complementary distribution, and completeness (i.e. the analysis must account for all utterances in the language). The fourth is one we have not met so far: Hockett calls it the requirement of *non-intersection*. Every phoneme is taken to be defined

---

[18] An utterance is 'any stretch of talk, by one person, before and after which there is silence on the part of that person' (Z. Harris 1951, 14). It should be possible during the analysis to determine which silences are genuine pause or utterance-end and which mere hesitation.

by a conjunction of phonetic features; and every phone which has those defining features must be a member of that phoneme. This entails that all occurrences of one and the same phone must be assigned to one and the same phoneme. This seems commonsensical enough; yet it can have embarrassing results.

Consider a language[19] which has, among other phonemes, two velar stops /k g/ and two nasals /m n/, each occurring in a wide range of environments. Before a velar stop, the only non-labial nasal that is found is a velar nasal [ŋ]; if this were the only environment in which this phone occurred, we would naturally regard it as an allophone of /n/. We find, however, that the same phone occurs in contrast with /n/: there are clusters of the form [mn], [nn] and [ŋn], and the last-named type are often found at morpheme junctions where the first morpheme in other environments ends in /g/. This kind of anticipation of nasality would be a very plausible kind of allophonic variation; and if [ŋ] were only found in [ŋn] clusters we would have little hesitation in assigning it to the /g/ phoneme.

Hockett's principle exludes such an analysis. The velar nasal is the same wherever it occurs; it must belong to the same phoneme wherever it occurs. This cannot be the /n/ phoneme, because we have seen that [ŋ] contrasts with [n]. It might be the /g/ phoneme, but this could only work if the language had no [gg] sequences,[20] and even then such a solution would complicate the phonotactics and violate phonetic plausibility. The only remaining possibility is to regard /ŋ/ as a distinct phoneme, although at least one of its defining features is always predictable wherever it occurs. Many phonemicists have regarded this principle (sometimes called the 'invariance condition') as too strong. It becomes unnecessary if we take the units of analysis to be, not phones as such, but phones in given environments; we can then treat [ŋ] before velars and before /n/ as two different analytic units and assign them to different phonemes, if that is preferable from the point of view of the analysis as a whole. Such a situation is called *partial overlapping* of phonemes; *complete overlapping*, in which one and the same phone is one and the same environment is assigned to different phonemes, was hardly ever allowed by classical phonemicists, because it could never be shown to be necessary on purely phonetic grounds.

As a criterion for choosing between alternative analyses which meet the first four requirements, Hockett uses pattern congruity; in his later *Manual of Phonology* (1955) he glosses this as 'symmetry both of phonemes and of allophonic variation'. Phonetic plausibility is not mentioned in the 1942 version, though in 1955 it makes an appearance as 'phonetic realism' and is made an absolute requirement, any grouping of phones which necessitates phonetically unrealistic allophonic statements being thereby shown to be invalid. Hockett's last criterion is economy, by which he means minimization of the total number of phonemes; this is scarcely mentioned in the later treatment, where it is clearly regarded as much less important than pattern congruity and phonetic realism. In other senses, however, economy has been used as a criterion by various classical phonemicists, most notably by Bloch (1950), who takes it as a requirement that the *descriptive statements* should be as few and general as possible; he implies

[19] The situation described is essentially that which appears to have held in classical Latin.
[20] Classical Latin did have such sequences, e.g. in [ággeris] 'of a rampart', so that in its case even this solution would not be available at all.

(*ib.* 112) that this criterion has priority over that of pattern congruity (which, indeed, it in part subsumes). It will be seen that no final agreement on criteria was ever reached.

The differences of view in this period about the nature of the phoneme are more notable for ontological ingenuity than for any empirical distinguishability between the various definitions. Points of view before 1935 are summarized and discussed by Twaddell (1935); after that time the only account of the phoneme that had much influence, other than the 'class of sounds' view, was that of the Prague School, to which we shall come in due course. Nor did such differences much affect phonemic analyses. On the whole, it is correct in retrospect to view 'classical phonemics' as a single theoretical position in phonology.

2.1.3 An illustrative analysis

What follows is a specimen of a phonemic analysis in the classical tradition. In order not to have to begin with a full presentation of the phonetic data (which would take up a disproportionate amount of space) I shall take English as the language of analysis, and, in particular, my own dialect, which is a variety of standard (southern) British English. The phonological system of English can conveniently be divided into four subsystems: the consonant, vowel, pitch and stress systems.

The notions 'consonant' and 'vowel' are clear enough intuitively, but their phonological definition presents some difficulties. Both are closely linked with the syllable, which we shall have occasion to discuss at some length in Chapter Eight. For the present we may say, combining suggestions of Jones (1960, 23) and Hockett (1955, 91), that a vowel is any phoneme such that

all of its allophones are so produced that 'the air issues in a continuous   **10a**
stream through the pharynx and mouth, there being no obstruction and no
narrowing such as would cause audible friction' (Jones); and in addition
it is *capable* of occurring as the nucleus of a syllabic peak, though it may (or   **b**
may not) also occur in other positions (Hockett).

(To define the term 'nucleus of a syllabic peak' would lead us on to the thorny ground of the nature of the syllable: at present an example may suffice. In the five-syllable phrase /nju̱:ka̱:sl̩kæ̱unsl̩/ *Newcastle Council* the five underlined phonemes are peak nuclei; two of them are syllabic consonants.)

Any phoneme which is not a vowel is a consonant, even if it can occur as a syllabic peak nucleus.

The definition (10) seems to come closer than any other I know of to the way the terms are actually used by phonologists relatively unconcerned with demarcation disputes.

The consonant system is not particularly problematic in English. Let us first take the consonants that occur in one important environment: in initial position[21] before a vowel. Here there seem to be twenty-two contrasting units; the five I have starred are the only ones that present problems:

---

[21] Strictly, of course, this means *utterance*-initial position; although most of the utterances we shall be dealing with (except as regards pitch and stress) will in fact consist of just one word, it should be remembered that at the present stage of the analysis the word has no status.

/p cf. *pat*   **11**
 t   *tack*
*č   *chat*
 k   *cat*
 b   *bat*
 ḍ   *dad*
*ǰ   *jack*
 g   *gap*
 f   *fat*
 s   *sat*
 š   *shack*
 v   *vat*
 z   *Zack* (personal name)
 m   *mat*
 n   *nap*
*θ   *thatch*
*ð   *that*
 l   *lap*
 r   *rat*
*w   *wag*
 j   *yap*
 h/   *hat*

In my dialect and many others there is a contrast between *witch* and *which*, which could be accounted for in one of two ways: by adding an extra phoneme /ʍ/, the voiceless counterpart of /w/; or by analysing the initial of *which* as a cluster /hw/. The latter view seems preferable on various grounds (it has in fact been generally preferred by phonologists). The initial of *which* is not usually voiceless throughout its duration;[22] so an analysis as /hw/ would not greatly complicate the allophonics of /w/ (which in any case is sometimes devoiced after a voiceless consonant) or of /h/ (which is normally realized as a voiceless anticipation of whatever segment follows). The analysis /hw/ is better for pattern congruity; the cluster is phonotactically parallel to /hj/ in *huge, human*, etc., whereas /ʍ/ as a voiceless resonant would be isolated, and from a general linguistic point of view unusual.

There is no doubt that /θ/ and /ð/ contrast phonemically; but one might nevertheless feel that such a statement conceals an important fact. For /ð/ occurs in initial position only in *grammatical* morphemes: the archaic second person pronoun *thou* (*thee, thy, thine*), the definite article, the root of a demonstrative (*that, there, then*, etc.): /θ/, on the other hand, occurs initially only in *lexical* morphemes. This is complementary distribution, but not of a kind that a classical phonemic analysis can recognize; nor could the regularity be stated in the morphophonemic rules, since no alternation is involved. If the regularity is to be stated at all, it must be as part of a set of principles governing the phonemic make-up of morphemes.

[22] Scottish usage differs here; I mention this only because this particular contrast is often exemplified from Scottish English, which is where it survives most vigorously.

The affricates /č ǰ/ raise one of the traditional problems of classical phonemics, the problem of 'un ou deux phonèmes'. There are certain parts of the stream of speech which we find particular difficulty in deciding whether to treat as single segments or as segment sequences: affricates are typical, but we shall meet the same problem in relation to diphthongs, and in other languages there are many segment/sequence types with which it arises: examples are rounded, palatalized and prenasalized consonants, nasalized and retroflexed vowels. The uncertainty is most acute where the doubtful piece is clearly divisible into two or more phases each of sufficient duration to make it reasonable to think of describing it as a separate segment, and yet the bond between the phases is closer than is normal between separate segments: indeed Bloch (1950) by implication restricted the possibility of diphonematic interpretation to pieces of this kind, but this is probably too strong. From time to time we find an unanalysable segment (unanalysable in phonetic terms, that is) in complementary distribution or free variation with a phonetically similar segment sequence: for example[23] there probably exist dialects of English in which a nasalized alveolar flap [D̃] is in free variation with the sequence [nt] in words like *painting*, and from many points of view it would be advantageous to analyse the flap as /nt/. The best criteria to follow seem to be these:

A piece consisting of phonetically distinguishable subpieces may, provided   **12a** the whole piece is contained within the same syllable and comprises a single articulatory movement and does not markedly exceed in duration other single phonemes of the language,[24] be analysed either as a single phoneme or as a sequence of phonemes, whichever better satisfies the ordinary criteria of phonemic analysis.

A piece not so divisible may be analysed as a phoneme sequence only if it is   **b** in complementary distribution or free variation with a phone sequence actually occurring in the language, and contains no distinctive features not present in at least one member of that sequence.[25]

The two English affricates satisfy the preconditions of (12a); a monophonemic interpretation is therefore possible. We accordingly turn to the ordinary criteria of analysis.

It has more than once been suggested that the question is decided at the outset by the existence of contrasts between [č] and [tš]; A. Hill (1958, 37) cites *courtship:ketchup* as a near-minimal pair. It is, however, unclear to what extent such contrasts are a matter of 'juncture' (see p. 40); and syllable boundary (which is, after all, a phonological and/or phonetic fact) is probably also relevant—all occurrences of [tš] where it is said to contrast with [č] seem to straddle syllable boundary, which [č] never does. It is therefore best to proceed on the assumption that the existence of such contrasts cannot be demonstrated.

[23] The example is based on Z. Harris (1951, 92).
[24] These are the first three 'rules' laid down by Trubetzkoy (1939, 57ff), except that the qualification 'markedly' is not his.
[25] So Pilch (1968, 110); it is possible that the last-mentioned condition is too weak. Pilch adds the further condition, which classical phonemics strictly would not admit, that there must be a 'particularly close morphophonemic relationship' between the phone and the phone sequence in question.

The main evidence must come from pattern congruity. There seem to be four important arguments here, not all of which point the same way.

(i) The combinatorial possiblities of the affricates are much more restricted than those of simple stops. In particular, initially they cannot cluster with any other consonant whatever, whereas any simple stop can be followed at least by /r/. This argues for a cluster interpretation of the affricates.

(ii) If the affricates are regarded as unit phonemes, they fit neatly into a 'hole' in the stop system as the counterparts of the fricatives /š ž/. The force of this argument is diminished by the consideration that in English stop types and fricative types do not on the whole pair off very well; there are two fricative positions (as against one stop position) in the denti-alveolar region, and none in the velar region.

(iii) If the affricates are regarded as clusters, the phoneme /ž/ will have a rather odd distribution: instead of occurring only after vowels, it will occur after vowels and after /d/. This tells, rather more strongly than the previous argument, in favour of a unit-phoneme interpretation.

(iv) In general stop-fricative clusters are rare in English. They occur medially, though only at morpheme junctions; they occur finally, though (apart from the affricates under consideration) almost exclusively where one of the various suffixes of the form /s/ or /z/ is involved; but in initial position, apart from a minute number of recent loans, /tš/ and /dž/, if we adopted that analysis, would be the only stop-fricative clusters to occur.

The weight of argument from pattern congruity is therefore in favour of a unit-phoneme interpretation; but the matter cannot be said to have conclusively decided, and many analysts have favoured a cluster interpretation. Explicitly or implicitly, these have used other criteria than those used here. Harris (1951, 21), for instance, seems to imply that if a piece *can* be segmented into subpieces which can be referred to phonemes needed anyway in the language, it *must* be so segmented; Cohen (1952) adopts a cluster interpretation simply on the ground that, in some positions at least, /tš/ is in contrast with both /t/ and /š/, /dž/ with both /d/ and /ž/; Pilch (1968, 89f) requires the splitting up of any sequence [XY] for which there can be found a 'partly like, partly unlike' sequence [XZ] or [WY], so that we would have to analyse diphonemically, /tš dž/, because of /tr dr/ etc.

If from utterance-initial position we turn to utterance-final position (after a vowel), we find occurring there easily recognizable counterparts of all the phonemes of (11) except the last four, /r w j h/.[26] We also find two other sounds that do not at first sight seem to be classable with any of the phonemes of (11): [ž] as in *beige*, and [ŋ] as in *bang*. Are these separate phonemes?

One might for a moment think of classifying [ž] as an allophone of /r/. It is pronounced in the same region of the mouth (though it is laminal rather than apical), and, like /r/, is very frequently accompanied by non-distinctive lip rounding; it differs chiefly in being an obstruent. But as soon as we proceed beyond one-word utterances it becomes clear that the two contrast:

---

[26] For the possibility that allophones of some of these are to be recognized in the second elements of certain diphthongs, see below, p. 32f.

The beige is a nice colour.   13a
The bear is a nice colour.   b

We must therefore take /ž/ to be a separate phoneme.

There remains [ŋ]. This too must be treated as a separate phoneme. We have already seen (above, p. 21) that it cannot be grouped with /h/, and similar objections exist to a grouping with /r/ or /j/; while though, on certain analyses of the vowel system, it would be in complementary distribution with [w]—with which [ŋ] does exclusively share certain phonetic properties (they are the only velar, non-lateral resonants)—still such an analysis is never adopted, on grounds of pattern congruity and phonetic plausibility. It is asymmetrical to find one phoneme with both nasal and semivowel allophones beside two nasal phonemes and one semivowel phoneme displaying no such variation; and though nasal/semivowel allophony is by no means unknown, it is implausible for it to depend purely on position in the syllable, with nasality in the environment having no effect whatever.

Investigation of consonants occurring in other positions reveals no new contrasts, and we may set up the consonant system of this variety of English as follows:

$$
\begin{array}{lllll}
/\text{p} & \text{t} & \text{č} & \text{k} & \qquad\textbf{14}\\
\text{b} & \text{d} & \text{ǰ} & \text{g} \\
\text{f} & \theta & \text{s} & \text{š} \\
\text{v} & \text{ð} & \text{z} & \text{ž} \\
\text{m} & \text{n} \\
& \text{l} & \text{r} \\
& & \text{j} & \text{w} \\
& & & \text{h}/
\end{array}
$$

Let us now consider the vowel system. In (15) are listed all the different syllabic peaks in my speech. The transcription on the left is that which will be used in the present discussion; that on the right is a more precise one based on the Jones cardinal vowels, which will enable the interested reader to relate my vowel system to, for example, the description of Gimson (1970). The peaks are numbered for reference, the numbering being that of Daniel Jones.[27]

1	[iː]	[ïi]	as in:	*peat*
2	[ɪ]	[ë]		*pit*
3	[e]	[ɛ]		*pet*
4	[æ]	[ɛ̞]		*pat*
5	[aː]	[ɑː]		*part*
6	[ɔ]	[ɒ]		*pot*
7	[oː]	[ǫː]		*port, bought*
8	[ʊ]	[ö]		*put*

(right column, numbered **15**)

[27] In the transcription on the right, a superscript double dot indicates centralization; a subscript dot a vowel closer than cardinal, a subscript hook one more open than cardinal; a single dot to the right of the letter indicates a half-long vowel.

9	[uː]	[üu]	as in	*boot*
10	[a]	[ä]		*putt*
11	[əː]	[əː]		*pert*
12	[ə]	[ə]		*parade* (first syllable)
13	[ei]	[ei̭]		*pate*
14	[əu]	[əö̭]		*boat*
15	[ai]	[äë]		*bite*
16	[æu]	[aö]		*pout*
17	[ɔi]	[ɔḙ̈]		*Boyd*
18	[ɪə]	[ëə]		*peered*
19	[eə]	[ɛə]		*pared*
21	[uɔ]	[öə]		*moored*[28]

All these contrast with one another, except for 12 which occurs only unstressed and might possibly be grouped with its nearest neighbour phonetically, 11; but whether we can do this depends on exactly how we decide to phonemicize stress, so for the present we shall assume that all twenty peak types are phonemically distinct. This is, however, far from determining how their distinctness should be represented in a phonemic analysis.

The main problems that arise are these:

(i) A good many pairs of vowels are distinguished by one or more of the features of length, diphthongization and vowel quality. Which of these features is distinctive and which concomitant in each case?

(ii) For those peak types which we decide to analyse as diphthongs, should the first elements be identified phonemically with vowels occurring as monophthongs . . .

(iii) . . . and should the second elements be regarded as allophones of vowel or of consonant phonemes, or perhaps as phonemes *sui generis*?

(iv) Where we decide length is distinctive, how should the long vowels be analysed—as geminates, as vowels plus a length phoneme, or what?

The first question is the most important, and there has perhaps been too much of a tendency towards monolithic answers. It is better to ask, as Pierce (1965) tried to do, which features native speakers actually treat as diagnostic for each pair of contrasting vowels. The answer seems to be that the 'long' or 'complex' peaks[29] fall into several groups. Types 5 and 11, central or nearly central vowels without significant diphthongization, are distinguished from 10 and 12 almost entirely by length; the same applies in a scarcely less degree to the distinction between 18, 19, 21 and 2, 3, 8 respectively, for the so-called 'centring diphthongs' are often

[28] The jump in numbering is due to the fact that I do not distinguish Jones's peak types 7 and 20. The distinction between these and 21 is also somewhat precarious, many (perhaps all) words with 21 having alternative forms with 7; but since this free variation is not reciprocal— it is inadmissible, for instance, to pronounce *pour* like *poor*—7 and 21 must still be regarded as distinct peak types in my speech.

[29] These terms refer to the class consisting of peaks 1, 5, 7, 9, 11, 13–19, 21. Neither term is very happy; not all these peaks are phonetically diphthongal, and not all of them are consistently longer than the 'short' or 'simple' peaks. Nevertheless they are a natural class, as their distribution shows: they are the only peak types capable of occuring under stress in utterance-final position.

scarcely diphthongal at all and not seldom quite monophthongal. Types 1, 7 and 9, peripheral vowels with slight or no diphthongization, are distinguished from 2, 6 and 8 by vowel quality; variations of length and diphthongization scarcely affect identification if quality is held constant. And for types 13–17 diphthongization must be regarded as distinctive; most of them, indeed, cannot plausibly be put into one-to-one correspondence with any 'simple' peak at all.

If for the time being we ignore the five distinctively diphthongal peaks, we are left with a basic system of ten vowels distinguished by quality: /i ɪ e æ a ɔ o U u ə/. Of these, /ɪ e a U ə/ have contrasting long and short forms, differing only slightly or not at all in quality; /i o u/ occur only long, /æ ɔ/ are traditionally described as occurring only short, though in fact they can be quite long in some environments. The question of how to analyse the long vowels can most conveniently be left until we have considered the diphthongs.

The first question concerning the diphthongs is whether to treat them as single phonemes (which happen to be 'gliding' rather than 'steady-state'[30]) or as phoneme sequences. The criteria of (12) do not help us; they merely allow us to adopt a single-phoneme analysis if pattern congruity, phonetic plausibility, etc., point that way. Pattern congruity is the only criterion that has anything much to say on the subject. From the phonotactic point of view, if we analyse the diphthongs as phoneme sequences we shall need some very restrictive phonotactic rules to account for the fact that so few of the logically possible vowel-vowel (or vowel-semivowel) sequences actually occur;[31] we may add that almost all morphophonemic alternations treat peaks, simple or complex, as indivisible units, and there is no particularly close morphophonemic relationship between a 'complex' peak and the 'simple' peak that phonetically resembles its first element. On the other hand, the vowel system is already unusually crowded; ten vowels distinguished by quality is a lot by world standards, particularly as none of them is back unrounded or front rounded; another five independent phonemes would accentuate this abnormality still further. In addition Pierce (1966) points out that some at least of the diphthongs—14, 15, 17—have a mean duration nearly twice as long as the average for other peaks, which raises questions as to whether criterion (12a) is satisfied after all.

The arguments are fairly evenly balanced. We shall here opt for a two-phoneme analysis, not least because it is this type of analysis that raises further questions of interest.

There is now no reason not to identify the first elements of the diphthongs with the basic vowels phonetically closest to them; we therefore provisionally phonemicize them (begging for the moment the question of the second element) as /ei̯ ə̯u ai̯ æu̯ oi̯/.[32]

The second elements of the diphthongs might plausibly be identified phonemically (i) with the half-close vowels /ɪ U/; (ii) with the close vowels /i u/; (iii) with the semi-vowels /j w/. Provided syllable division is taken into account, they are in complementary distribution with all three.

---

[30] These terms should not be taken too seriously; no speech sound is really steady-state.

[31] It was because Trager and Smith's analysis of English was an overall-pattern one that they were able to avoid this argument.

[32] The retention of the subscript link is also rather question-begging.

The problem with treating the second elements of diphthongs as allophones of any kind of vowel phoneme lies mainly in the criterion of non-intersection. As may be seen from (15), the end points of diphthongs range from fully close to mid, extending over the allophonic range both of /i u/ and of /i ʊ/, and unless we are to treat them as *four* different phonemes (which would offend against the spirit, if not perhaps the letter, of the principle of complementary distribution, and even so might well not do complete justice to the facts) we cannot identify them with vowel phonemes at all.[33]

There is, on the other hand, no impediment to phonemicizing the second elements of diphthongs as /j w/: indeed there are several points in favour of such an analysis. The necessary phonetic invariants are palatality (resp. velarity), absence of closure or friction, and *non-syllabicity* (that is the property of not being a peak nucleus; cf. p. 26). There is marked symmetry of allophonic variation; for just as the second element of a diphthong has a closer or opener pronunciation according to the vowel preceding, so prevocalic /j w/ have a closer or opener pronunciation according to the vowel following. And there is phonotactic simplification in that /j w/, like the majority of consonant phonemes, can now end as well as begin a syllable. It is true that they can only appear after a limited range of vowels; but they are not alone in this, e.g. /ŋ/ cannot appear after any of /i o ʊ u ə/.

We therefore definitively phonemicize the five diphthongs as /ej əw aj æw oj/.

This decision more or less rules out any possibility of analysing the long vowels as geminates; for that would wreck the phonotactic generalization that a syllable contains at most one vowel. There still, however, remain three possibilities.

(i)   Treat the long vowels as single phonemes with length as one of their features.
(ii) Treat them as sequences of a vowel and a 'prolongation' phoneme.
(iii) Treat them, like the diphthongs, as sequences of a vowel phoneme and a consonant phoneme.

The third solution is not as unreasonable as it might seem. It does not contradict our finding that these vowels are distinguished from their short counterparts solely or mainly by length; for it is perfectly possible that a consonant phoneme might be realized in certain environments as prolongation of a vowel. More importantly, while only three of the five distinctively long vowels are in free variation with phone sequences, all five are in complementary distribution with such sequences: to wit, each distinctively long vowel [V:] is in complementary distribution with the sequence [V:r], the latter occurring where a vowel follows without break (e.g. *peering, pairing, sparring, mooring, purring*), the former everywhere else.[34] Hence these long vowels satisfy the condition (12b) for two-phoneme analysis of single phones, since naturally their distinctive features are precisely the same as those of the first members of the sequences in question!

[33] But in generative phonology, where the criterion of non-intersection does not apply, it may well be possible, and even preferable, to analyse the second elements of diphthongs as vowels; diphthongs will then be sequences of unlike vowels, while 'long vowels' will be sequences of like vowels. See Lass (1976, 21ff.)

[34] In the case of /a:/ this may not be quite true; it would hold, though, for those idiolects (mine is not one of them) in which the insertion of so-called 'intrusive /r/' between /a:/ and a following vowel is invariable.

However, this gets us no further unless we can analyse the [V:r] sequences themselves in such a way that the long vowels turn out to be allophones of vowel phonemes already set up, conditioned by the environment 'preceding /r/'. And in fact this cannot be done; for all the basic vowels except /ʊ/ occur before /r/ and are there represented by their normal allophones; cf. *key-ring, mirror, herring, marry, hurry, porridge, two wrists* (contrasting with *tourists*), *labourer*. Thus the long vowels cannot be analysed as sequences of a basic vowel plus /r/; an analysis with /r/ could be maintained only by positing at least four new vowel phonemes of extremely restricted distribution, and this would more than obviate any advantage the analysis could claim by way of giving a freer distribution to the /r/ phoneme.

We are thus left with the first and second alternatives for the analysis of the long vowels. Of these. it might well be argued that the second is not in the spirit of the principles of phonemic analysis that have here been put forward; a phoneme which is not realized by any phone at all, but only by the prolongation of another phone, is not provided for by those principles. If we take this course we are really treating length as a prosodic (suprasegmental) feature, in the same manner in which (as we shall presently see) stress and pitch are normally treated; stress and pitch phonemes also are not realized as phones. And there are languages in which it is definitely advantageous to analyse length in this way. Is English one of these languages?

The advantages of recognizing a length phoneme are very considerable. Except in point of length, the distinctively long vowels bear a very close phonetic resemblance to the corresponding basic vowels, much closer than any other peak types bear to each other. The analysis with a length phoneme not only keeps the complexity of the vowel system within reasonable bounds, but preserves an attractive feature of the rejected /Vr/ analysis: the long vowels, being composed of two phonemes, are made similar in form to the diphthongs, just as they are similar in distribution. As an added bonus, it is now possible to account automatically for the fact that certain of the basic vowels are always long: the phonotactics will specify that they can occur only with the length phoneme. There appear to be no disadvantages.

Our final picture of the English vowel system, then, is this:[35]

> *Basic vowels*
>
> | | Front | Central | Back |
> |---|---|---|---|
> | Close | /i/ | | /u/ |
> | Half-close | /ɪ/ | /ə/ | /ʊ/ |
> | Half-open | /e/ | | /o/ |
> | Open | /æ/ | /a/ | /ɔ/ |
>
> *Semivowels:*   /j w/
> *Length phoneme:*   /:/

16

[35] There are many discussions of the English vowel system from the standpoint of various forms of classical phonemics. Some of the possibilities for standard British are discussed by Gimson (1970, 96ff); Swadesh (1947) analyses all the 'complex' peaks as vowel sequences, A. Cohen (1952) as single phonemes. In the United States the dominant tradition has been that initiated by Bloch and Trager (1941), who treated the 'complex' peaks as vowel-semivowel sequences; Pierce (1965; 1966) prefers to treat as many as possible as single phonemes, and insists on the importance of vowel quality. Cf. also Haugen and Twaddell (1942); Kurath (1957).

The phonotactics allow a syllabic peak to consist of a basic vowel alone or followed by a semivowel or the length phoneme, subject to restrictions which (17) details.[36]

First element	Second element				
	zero	/:/	/j/	/w/	17
/i/	no	yes	no	no	
/ɪ/	yes	yes	no	no	
/e/	yes	yes	yes	no	
/æ/	yes	no	no	yes	
/ə/	yes	yes	no	yes	
/a/	yes	yes	yes	no	
/u/	no	yes	no	no	
/U/	yes	yes	no	no	
/o/	no	yes	yes	no	
/ɔ/	yes	no	no	no	

It will be observed that although there are four basic vowel phonemes on the front axis and four on the back axis, there are never more than three contrasting positions on either axis if we distinguish between short and long vowels; also that in diphthongs the dimension of openness/closeness is not used distinctively at all.

2.2 Prosodic features

We now pass to *prosodic* or *suprasegmental* features, of which the most typical are stress and pitch. These can be distinguished from the *inherent* or *segmental* features in two main ways. Firstly, prosodic features are essentially *relative* in a way that inherent features are not. As Lehiste (1970) points out, such a characteristic as 'the rounding of a vowel . . . can be established for each vowel without necessary reference to adjacent sounds. The stressedness of a vowel, on the other hand, cannot be established without comparing the vowel with another segment in the sequence'; and similarly it is impossible to tell whether a given syllable is linguistically high-pitched or low-pitched until the pitch of other syllables in the utterance is known.

Secondly, prosodic features do not respect the segmentation established on the basis of inherent features. On the one hand the domain of a prosodic feature is very frequently a syllable, and may be a word or even longer: e.g. in the Japanese phrase *uma no asi no iro* 'the colour of the horse's leg', the domain of the prosodic feature 'high pitch' is the whole piece *-ma no asi*, in accordance with the general principle that a Japanese phrase, except for its first syllable,[37] is high-pitched as far as its main accent (inclusive) and low-pitched thereafter. On the other hand, the value of a prosodic feature may change in the middle of a segment.[38]

Nevertheless it would be in principle possible to treat prosodic features for phonological purposes in the same way as inherent features—to regard high-pitched vowels and low-pitched vowels, stressed and unstressed vowels, etc., as

[36] A full description would, of course, also have to include details of allophonic variation.
[37] Or rather the first *mora*. See McCawley (1968, ch. 3), from whom the example is taken.
[38] There is often no other motivation for reanalysing such segments as segment sequences.

different phones and hence, inevitably, as distinct phonemes. (Stress and pitch variations on consonants would normally be allophonic.) This is never in fact done: the reason appears to be that languages typically have some morphemes whose phonological realizations are composed solely of prosodic features, and which occur simultaneously with morphemes whose realizations are composed of segmental features; phonemic analysis can handle these situations adequately only if prosodic features are abstracted as independent phonemes. For example, the English utterance *yes?* consists of a segmental morpheme and an intonation contour, each of which is found independently elsewhere.[39]

A considerable number of prosodic features can be identified for English,[40] but we shall look only. at the two which have been the subject of phonological investigation for longest: pitch and stress.

2.2.1 Stress

The phonetic nature of stress remains a matter of controversy. The best evidence at present is that perceived loudness (which is by no means the same as objectively observed intensity) correlates with certain forms of muscular effort in the lung region. See Ladefoged (1967); Lehiste (1970); and Lieberman (1970), who emphasizes the increase of subglottal air pressure. Loudness itself is not the sole auditory component of what practical phoneticians call stress. Pitch and duration are relevant cues as well; indeed they are often found to be more important determining factors for perceptual stress discrimination than loudness is. What is evidently happening is that the hearer is using all available information to determine the degree of muscular effort with which each syllable was uttered, and what we call stress corresponds not to the data he uses or any part of it, but to the conclusions he reaches.

Uncertainty about the phonetic nature of stress, however, does not necessarily preclude phonological investigation of it; for phoneticians familiar with a language generally have little difficulty in agreeing on which syllables of the language are more stressed, which less stressed, and which not stressed at all. In English there are two clear contrasts.

(i)   *Strong v. weak syllables.* In most pronunciations, the noun *ímport* and the verb *impórt* are identical in their consonant and vowel phonemes. Since they certainly contrast, this contrast must reside in their stress patterns. We therefore set up, to begin with, two contrasting stress phonemes: *strong stress*, which we symbolize by /'/ over the vowel of the stressed syllable, and *weak stress*, which needs no symbol, being understood to occur with every vowel on which /'/ is absent. Non-compound words (other than some which perform purely grammatical functions) have exactly one strong stress.

(ii) *Nuclear v. non-nuclear strong stress.* An utterance consists of one or more pieces each of which, in general, corresponds to a complete intonation

---

[39] On the whole phonologists have not been very good at explaining why inherent and prosodic features should be differently treated. The argument in the text is due to Z. Harris (1944, 182), who, however, goes on to argue (on other grounds) for what is in effect a prosodic treatment of many features that have usually been regarded as inherent.

[40] For a full treatment see Crystal (1969).

contour; and in each intonation contour one syllable, the *nucleus* or *centre*, is stressed much more heavily than the remaining strong syllables. Thus (18a) and (18b) contrast:

(What's John going to do?—) Jóhn's góing to síng.   **18a**
(Who's going to sing?   ) Jóhn's góing to sing.   **b**

This requires us to set up a third stress phoneme, *nuclear stress*, symbolized by /"/; it is often called *sentence stress* because it is never contrastive at the word level, but a sentence may contain more than one nuclear stress; indeed it may contain more nuclear stresses than intonation contours, e.g. (19) contains (on the most likely rendering) two intonation contours but three nuclear stresses:

I sáid that cáts éat báts, nót the óther wáy róund.   **19**

Now phonetically there are many more differences in stress levels within the word than the simple strong-weak contrast we have provided for. The syllables of such a word as *aristocracy* are often all pronounced with perceptibly different degrees of stress. It is not clear whether these differences are in all cases predictable from the segmental and syllabic make-up of the word and the position of strong stress; but no two utterances ever seem to be distinguished solely by different degrees of non-strong stress. It is striking, too, that as Sledd (1962) pointed out, analysts who regard some of these further differences as phonemic often cannot agree on how to phonemicize one and the same utterance token, even though they are native speakers of the language. Unless better evidence appears, it seems safest not to set up more than the three contrasting stress phonemes—weak, strong and nuclear—here proposed.[41]

Before leaving stress, a word on the term *accent* is in place. Accent may be defined as prominence given by means of a prosodic feature or combination of prosodic features to a particular syllable or mora of a word in contrast with others. The definition is no more than indicative: it is not hard-and-fast, and does not imply that a word can have only one accented syllable or mora. The traditional distinction between accent languages on the one hand, and tone languages on the other (in which *each* syllable was said to bear one of a number of phonemically distinctive pitches), cannot be rigidly maintained: intermediate types exist, some of which it would be hard without arbitrariness to assign to either limb of such a dichotomy.[42] For example, the Kyoto dialect of Japanese (McCawley 1968) has phonemic distinctions of pitch at two points in the word. The first mora may be either high or low pitched; in the latter case it is always immediately followed by a rise to high. Then, regardless of whether the word started high or started low and rose to high, there may be a fall to low later in the

---

[41] The Trager-Smith analysis sets up four stress phonemes, of which the first two correspond to our 'nuclear' and 'strong'. This *may* be necessary for American English, for which A. Hill (1958, 17) finds a near-minimal pair in *Phárisee:fállacy*, where the final syllables have the same vowel but differ in stress, though neither has strong stress: in British English there is a vowel difference. Our three distinctive degrees of stress correspond (under different names) to those used by Stockwell (1972), who gives a useful conspectus of comparative stress terminology, and to those recognized by Hirst (1976) in his simple yet comprehensive analysis of the discrete aspects of English prosodics (except that Hirst adds a feature to account for a distinctive, extra heavy stress on certain nuclear syllables).
[42] Cf. Williamson (1970).

word; the position of this fall, if it occurs, is what is distinctive. The pitch contrast in the first mora is of a type characteristic of tone languages; the distinctive fall in pitch later in the word, whose position can vary, is typical of accent languages. For what above all distinguishes accentual uses of prosodic features from other uses is that whereas for prosodic features in general (just as for inherent features) the basic question is 'what?' (which of the various possible features or feature values is selected at each point?), for accent the basic question is 'where (does the accent fall)?'. Sometimes the position of accent is entirely predictable in relation to word boundaries; that does not make the question 'where?' trivial, for the position of accent remains distinctive on the utterance level, and indeed is an important cue for determining the position of word boundaries themselves. Where the position of accent is not thus predictable, it can serve to distinguish words (cf. English *ábstract* 'not concrete': *abstráct* 'remove') or phrases (cf. Russian *rádostʲ ljubʲítʲ* 'joy in loving': *rădostʲ ljubítʲ* 'to love joy'[43]; but this function is rarely of more than marginal importance. The primary function of accent has been described thus by Allen (1973, 87) as 'grouping together, with itself as the focus of attention, a sequence of syllables having a single semantic function—in other words, to "individualize" the word unit.' It must be emphasized that 'accent' and 'stress' are different categories: stress is a phonetic feature, accent is not.

2.2.2 Pitch

Pitch is not distinctive in English at the word level, except in so far as it is one of the clues the hearer uses for determining the position of strong and nuclear stresses. At the utterance level, on the other hand, pitch is very definitely distinctive; indeed there are an infinite number of pairs of utterances distinguished solely by their pitch contours. But pitch contours in English (and many other languages) differ from the normal run of phonological elements in more than one important respect. The function of phonemes is to distinguish meaningful forms; save by accident, they are not themselves meaningful forms. If you were to take an utterance and remove all the vowels, or all the nasals, or even all the stresses, you would be converting a sequence of complete morphemes into a sequence of incomplete morphemes. But if you similarly removed the pitch contour, what you would have left would still be a sequence of complete morphemes and would still have the same grammatical structure.[44] Thus the sequence of morphemes *He's béen to the dŏctor* can be combined with with these three pitch contours (among others):

He's been to the doctōr	**20a**
He's been to the dóctor	**b**
He's been to the doctór	**c**

[43] See Jakobson (1937/1962, 255).

[44] This is a slight oversimplification. Thus Halliday (1964) points out that in the sentence *I dídn't cóme because he tŏld me*, a pitch contour ending with a fall implies that the negative is attached to *come* ('It was because he told me that I didn't come'), while one ending with a rise attaches the negative to the causal clause ('It wasn't because he told me that I came'). Facts of this kind, however, are usually

The first is a straightforward factual statement, the second a yes-no question; the third affirms that there has been a visit to the doctor but implies that this may not be the whole story (does the speaker think (s)he is suspected of not taking sufficient steps to help the patient? did the doctor make an unwelcome diagnosis? something of that kind). Prosodic phenomena which have these characteristics (their semantic relevance is essentially to clauses or sentences as wholes rather than words or phrases; and they do not form part of, and do not affect the grammatical relations between, wholly or partly non-prosodic morphemes) are termed phenomena of *intonation*. (Note that the term is here defined so as to leave open the possibility that other features than pitch might be used in the same way; indeed there is a case (Crystal 1969) for arguing that in English tempo, pause, rhythmicality, and some other features are in fact so used.)

The second major peculiarity of intonational phenomena is that they often lack that essential characteristic of phonemic units, *discreteness*. Phonemes do not shade into each other. If someone used a word which he pronounced [pe̱in] with a voiceless unaspirated bilabial stop, this would not be interpreted as having a meaning intermediate between those of *pain* and *bane*; it would be regarded as a mispronunciation of one or other of these words. With intonation, to a great extent, it is otherwise: many of the variables whose values define pitch contours behave *continuously* rather than discretely. It is possible to identify contrasting utterances, but tokens intermediate between them are interpreted as having intermediate meanings. Features which behave in this way are not amenable to phonemic analysis, because there is no basis for disregarding any perceptible difference however small. The nondiscreteness of intonational variables, strongly argued for over many years by Dwight Bolinger, emerges clearly from the careful analysis of Crystal (1969), who recognizes for English only one discrete variable, 'the direction of pitch movement within [and after][45] the most prominent syllable of a tone-unit': level, falling (20a), rising (20b), falling-rising (20c), rising-falling.

To the extent that intonational features are continuously variable in the sense just indicated, phonology, and for that matter morphology and syntax, have nothing to say about them. Phonology imposes discrete categorization on continuous sound; grammar and lexicon impose discrete categorization on continuous reality. Intonation, with the exception mentioned, maps certain continuously variable aspects of reality (largely relating to the speaker's attitudes) into continuously variable aspects of sound, bypassing, as it were, all discrete linguistic structure. It will therefore not be further treated here.[46]

---

assigned to 'deep' syntax, or to semantics, rather than to 'surface' syntax; on the surface, whatever the intonation, the grammatical attachment of the negative is to *come*.

[45] The postnuclear 'tail' always continues the final pitch direction of the nuclear syllable, though eventually, particularly if the tail is long, its pitch may level out (Crystal 1969, 223); and very often this final direction is much more clearly detectable from the tail than from the nuclear syllable itself, especially where there is a change of direction as in the falling-rising nucleus.

[46] Discrete phonological treatments of intonation in English show a fair degree of convergence, though they use very different notations. In the stretch covered by a single contour (an 'intonation group') the key points are the first syllable, the first strong syllable or *head*, and the nucleus, and the main variables are: the pitch of the first syllable, which determines the pitch for the stretch up to, but not including, the head; the pitch on which the nucleus begins; and the direction of pitch change thereafter. British analysts tend to treat these elements themselves as primes, and use a diagrammatic

It should be noted that the recognition of the intonational feature 'direction of pitch movement' makes the phoneme 'nuclear stress' redundant; for nuclear stress falls always and only on syllables having one or another value for this intonational feature. We shall, however, continue to use /"/ as a cover-symbol where the choice between the various directions of pitch movement is unimportant.

2.2.3 'Juncture'

In addition to segmental and prosodic phonemes, classical phonemic analyses of English and of other languages have often recognized one further type of phoneme, *junctures* (a confusing term: 'disjuncture' would have been better, and was occasionally used). The object of positing junctures was to avoid having to make allophonic statements in terms of non-phonological elements such as words and their boundaries. Junctures were defined in terms of phonetic phenomena that occurred typically (but by no means invariably or exclusively) in the neighbourhood of such boundaries: 'phonetic manners of transition from one phoneme to another such that differences in the timing, stretching, releases, pitch contours, intensity, scope, and the like of a sequence of segmental and suprasegmental phonemes contrast with other occurrences of phonetically similar ... phonemes' (Trager 1962). Such effects are indeed demonstrably present, particularly in the matter of timing;[47] but it is another matter to show that it is these effects that the hearer makes use of to identify word boundaries. The experiments of O'Connor and Tooley (1964) point decidedly the other way: they found that people's ability to locate word boundaries in minimal-pair phrases taken out of sentence context (like *may name: main aim*), though better than chance, was far below their ability to make ordinary phonemic discriminations.[48] It appears that in identifying word boundaries listeners rely not so much on the phonetic clues collectively labelled 'juncture', or on the fact that many phonemes in many languages have special word-initial or word-final allophones, as on the context, linguistic and non-linguistic, and their knowledge of the language; and thus that Chao and other early investigators, and subsequently Pike, were right to permit reference to word boundaries in phonemic analysis. Somewhere in our description the phonetic effects of word boundary must, of course, be stated, and it must also be stated in what circumstances these effects are not manifested and in

---

notation; American phonemicists, starting with Wells (1945), have used a limited number (usually four) of 'phonemic pitch levels', analysing the contours as successions of such levels. The American system thus makes finer distinctions among levels than the British system (which recognizes only a simple high-low contrast), but except in tails (for which special 'terminal contour' phonemes are brought in) can refer to pitch directions only indirectly via the levels. The British approach may be exemplified by Kingdon (1958); the American approach found its classical expression in Trager and Smith (1951).

[47] See A. Hill (1958) and Joos (1962— delivered in 1957). Earlier attempts to determine the phonetic correlates of juncture phonemes had foundered on the fact that no invariant set of defining features could be set up for them as was possible for all other phonemes.

[48] We have noted that phonemic identification is normally over 90% correct. O'Connor and Tooley report an average of 67% correct word boundary identification, and the highest percentage they give for any one pair of phrases is 89.

what circumstances word-boundary-like effects are found where there is no word boundary. But for this a special phoneme is not needed.

2.3 Alternations

We have thus arrived at a phonemic analysis for English which, to briefly recapitulate, is as follows:

Consonants: /p t č k b d ǰ g f θ s š v ð z ž m n ŋ l r j w h/   **21**
Vowels: /i ɪ e æ a ɔ o U u ə/
Length: /:/
Strong stress: /'/
Pitch direction: level, rise, fall, fall-rise, rise-fall.

A full phonological description would also contain a set of allophonic statements and a set of *phonotactic* statements detailing the arrangements of phonemes within morphemes or within words; and besides these, a set of statements accounting for the alternations of those morphemes whose phonemic shapes are not constant.

2.3.1 The allomorph approach

One manner of describing alternations which had, for some mysterious reason, a considerable vogue at one period of classical phonemics, was to simply list, for each morpheme, the phonemic shapes it could assume, and the environments in which it could assume each shape. To do this is to pretend that there is no generality about morphophonemic alternations, which is patently untrue. In German, for instance, *every* morpheme which can take a phonemic shape with /b/ or /d/ or /g/ as final segment and which can occur directly before word boundary has in that position a phonemic shape identical to the other except that the final segment is /p/ or /t/ or /k/ respectively. This is evidently a single fact, and it is utterly pointless to state it separately for each morpheme.

2.3.2 Classical morphophonemics

A more satisfactory, and also much used, method of morphophonemic description was that which I shall now outline.

It was first necessary to establish which strings of phonemes were the phonemic realizations of morphemes, or, in the terminology of Harris (1951), which strings of phonemes were *morphemic segments*, also known as *morphs*; next to group these morphs into morphemes, using much the same principles of contrast, similarity, pattern congruity, etc., as were used in the grouping of phones into phonemes. This was considered the essential first step in grammatical description, rather than part of phonological description; and although the search for distributional methods of analysis which would make possible 'the construction of a grammar with no appeal to meaning' is an interesting study, it cannot be discussed here. We shall assume that we have arrived at a list of the morphemes of the language, with the shapes they can assume in the various environments in which they can occur: just such a list, in fact, as constitutes, on the view previously mentioned, a full morphophonemic description. Since *alternation* is definable as the relationship which exists between any two or more phonemic shapes of one and the same morpheme which are not in free variation, this may also be regarded as a list of all the alternations in the language. These may be classified into the following types.

2.3.2.1 *Suppletions*

These are the cases, found in most languages, in which a morpheme has alternant phonemic shapes (*allomorphs*) which differ so radically from one another, and in a manner so different from any other alternation in the language, that no statement can usefully be made about the alternation other than the mere listing of it as one that occurs. Thus the English plural suffix for nouns has, in certain environments, the allomorphs /ən/ or /rən/ (the latter combined with a vowel change) instead of the normal, phonologically conditioned alternants /z/, /s/ and /ɪz/ (cf. *oxen, children*); in other environments the same function is performed by one or another vowel change (cf. *mice, geese, women*) or by the replacement of such suffixes as /əs/ and /ɪs/ by /aj/ and /iːz/ respectively.[49] The French verb root whose most frequent allomorph is /al/ 'go' also appears in the phonologically unrelated forms /v/ (cf. /va/ 'goes') and /i/ (cf. /ira/ 'will go (3rd sg.)'). Such forms are treated as allomorphs of one morpheme because their grammatical behaviour is parallel to that of other allomorphs of the same morpheme, or to that of other morphemes which do not alternate or which alternate in regular ways.

2.3.2.2 *Morphologically conditioned alternations*

A morpheme may have different allomorphs depending on the identity or grammatical status, rather than the phonological shape, of the morphemes constituting its environment. For example, several English noun-stem morphemes (e.g. *hoof, knife, wife, house*) have allomorphs with voiced final consonants before the plural suffix—but not before the phonemically identical possessive suffix. This is not suppletion, for the phonological relationship between the alternants is obvious; but it depends on grammatical, not phonological conditions. Again, many morphemes have allomorphs with stressed final syllable (and vowel changes) before the suffixes *-ic, -ical*, but not before *-ize, -ism, -ist: phonológical, catastróphic, anagrammátic, económic*, but *phonólogist, catástrophism, anagrámmatize, ecónomist*.

2.3.2.3 *Phonologically conditioned but non-automatic alternations*

A morpheme may have varying allomorphs depending on the phonemic environment (including pitch and stress conditions and the position of

[49] This very common situation in which a grammatical category is realized, not by the addition of phonemic material, but by the substitution of one bit of such material for another bit, was often a headache for classical morphophonemics. If *goose:geese* was the regular pattern of English plural formation we would probably treat the discontinuous /g . . . s/ as the stem and extract a singular infix /uː/ and a plural infix /iː/. Since, however, plurality is with overwhelming frequency represented by an additive suffix, and if a singular infix were recognized all its forms would be irregular, we must treat the singular /guːs/ as a single morpheme. In that case, how do we analyse the plural? For discussion of some possibilities see Hockett (1954).

boundaries or junctures). If such an alternation occurs in *every* morpheme of a given general phonological form in a given phonemic environment, it is *automatic*;[50] otherwise, it is *non-automatic*. An example of a non-automatic phonologically conditioned alternation is that of /k/ and /s/ in several English morphemes such as *-ic*: such morphemes have /s/ whenever /i/ or /ɪ/ or /aj/ immediately follows, and /k/ otherwise. Cf. *septicaemia, scepticism, criticize*, but *septic, sceptical, authenticate*. It is non-automatic because many morphemes end in non-alternating /k/, and many others in non-alternating /s/, and there is no phonological way to tell which morphemes alternate and which do not. Thus alternations of this kind are still in a sense morphologically conditioned—only not by the identity of other morphemes, but by that of the alternating morpheme itself.

2.3.2.4 *Automatic alternations*
As has already been alluded to, many morphemes in certain English dialects alternate between forms ending in a long vowel and forms in which this vowel is followed by /r/. Where a consonant or pause follows, this alternation is automatic; for in these dialects /r/ cannot be directly followed by a consonant or pause. But before a vowel (whether in the same word or not) the alternation is sometimes automatic and sometimes not. Where the long vowel is /o:/ the alternation is non-automatic: for some morphemes (*lore, sore*) the presence of /r/ is obligatory if the next morpheme begins with a vowel (unless a pause intervenes), for others (often homonymous: *law, saw*) it is no more than optional at word boundaries, and word-internally the /r/ never shows up at all. For /a:/, in certain dialects, it is automatic: whenever a word ends with /a:/, and the next word (not separated by pause) begins with a vowel, the /r/ appears. Yet the sequence /a:V/ is permitted by the phonotactics of the language, cf. *baaing*. For /e:/, finally, the presence of /r/ is not merely automatic, but phonotactically necessary, or in Wells's terms 'narrowly automatic'; /e:/ can never be followed without pause by a vowel.

2.3.2.5 *Alternation statements, morphophonemes, and base forms*
Leaving aside cases of suppletion, we now seek to state the other alternations in as general a manner as possible. The canonical form for alternation statements devised by Z. Harris (1951) is given below, with an illustration.

In the following group of morphemes (which may be a mere list or a phonologically or grammatically defined class or, in the limiting case, all the morphemes in the language)	In *hoof, knife, wife, mouth, house* . . .	**22a**
the following phoneme or phonemic sequence (which the morphemes contain when not in environment **d**)	the phonemes /f θ s/ if morpheme-final	**b**
is replaced by the following phoneme or phonemic sequence	are replaced by /v ð z/ respectively	**c**

[50] This is an informal statement of the definition given by Wells (1949).

when the morpheme occurs in the following environments (which may be phonological or consist of a morpheme or class of morphemes)	when the morpheme occurs directly preceding the plural suffix	d

An optional further step is to set up what are termed *morphophonemes*. All 'the phonemes which replace each other in corresponding parts of the various members of a morpheme' (Harris 1951) are, *in that morpheme*, members of one morphophoneme; if different morphemes show alternations between the same phonemes in the same environments, all the phoneme occurrences which take part in such identical alternations belong to the same morphophoneme. Thus in the case of the English /k ~ s/ alternation, the relevant occurrences of /k/ and /s/ (but not other occurrences of these phonemes) may be taken to be members of one morphophoneme that might appropriately be labelled //c//.[51]

Note that some morphophonemes may have zero as a member: the English morphophoneme whose other member is morpheme-final /r/ does, for example. To avoid this and further complications (such as the problem of the kind of alternation which involves two phonemes changing places, known as metathesis), Harris sometimes used morphophonemes some or all of whose members were not phonemes but phoneme sequences; this, however, is rather an artificial expedient, and difficulties of this kind may have been among the factors leading to the general abandonment of the morphophoneme concept in the early 1950s.

An alternative was available to the notion of the morphophoneme as a class of phonemes. This was to treat the various phonemic shapes of a morpheme as environmentally conditioned modifications of a constant *base form*. The base form could, if one liked, be spoken of as composed of morphophonemes, but these morphophonemes were in no sense classes of phonemes-in-environments: they were separate theoretical constructs set up, not in accordance with any mechanical procedure, but in such a way as to make the alternation statements as few and as simple as possible. This method of description was frequently used by Sapir amd Bloomfield;[52] it is directly ancestral to the underlying forms and rules of generative phonology. The status of morphophonemic representations and base forms, however, was never really decided: did they play a real role in the functioning of language, as it was generally accepted that phonemic representations did, or were they no more than 'artefacts of analysis or conveniences for description' (Hockett 1961)? Predominantly the latter answer was returned; and as a result, in contrast with the voluminous literature by classical phonemicists on criteria for phonemic analysis, there is very little about criteria for morphophonemic analysis. After all, morphophonemic or base-form representation was not indispensable; a language could be described without it (viz. by the listing of alternants as described above, p. 41).

---

[51] Double oblique strokes are one of a number of notational devices that have been used to indicate that a representation is morphophonemic.

[52] See the analyses of Southern Paiute by Sapir (1933) and of Menomini by Bloomfield (1939).

2.3.3 Classical phonemics: conclusion

A phonemic, an allophonic, a phonotactic and a morphophonemic analysis complete the phonological description of a language on the classical phonemic model. And the literature of classical phonemics is very largely about problems of analysis: how to phonemicize, how to represent unusual allophonic or morphophonemic situations, whether word boundaries should be taken into account, how stress and pitch contrasts should be represented, etc.—together with the presentation of actual analyses of the phonology of particular languages. With the striking exception of Hockett (1955), the general properties of phonological systems were little discussed; the question of the general properties of morphophonemic systems was hardly even raised.

2.4 Prague school phonology[53]

At the same time, mainly in Europe, another approach to phonology was being developed, in which these general properties were placed, as it were, in the centre of the stage. This is usually known as *Prague School* phonology, after the Prague Linguistic Circle, whose members, above all Trubetzkoy and Jakobson, were its principal practitioners in the 1920s and 1930s. In many respects it runs parallel to classical phonemics: its definitions of the phoneme, for example, lead to phonemic representations which do not differ in any important way from those resulting from definitions like that of Hockett. But Prague School phonology has a separate importance of its own because of the attention it devoted to areas largely neglected by American phonologists—areas of great importance.

A feature of Prague School phonology that might seem peripheral, but in fact explains many of the particular interests of the school, is its attitude to phonetics. Classical phonemics (in America at any rate), being much under the influence of an ultra-empiricist philosophy of science which, in one version, insisted not merely (as all empirical science does) that all scientific statements be testable by observation but also (a quite different thing) that all such statements be paraphrasable in observational terms, tended to be embarrassed by the fact that the phonetic representations on which phonemic analyses were based seemed to be no more than arbitrary segmentations of what was without doubt objectively a continuous stream of speech. The solution usually resorted to, in theoretical discussion, was to deny the linguistic validity of these phonetic representations; thus Bloomfield (1933, 84; the remarks in square brackets are mine):

> Having learned to discriminate many kinds of sounds, the phonetician may turn to some language, new or familiar, and insist upon recording all the distinctions he has learned to discriminate, even when in this language they are non-distinctive and have no bearing whatsoever. [This, of course, is exactly what the linguist making a preliminary phonetic transcription must normally do.] ... The chief objection to this procedure is its inconsistency. The phonetician's equipment is personal and accidental; he hears those acoustic

[53] It is not possible in the space available here to give the phonological ideas of the Prague School the attention they deserve. For a fuller account see Vachek (1966) and Fischer-Jørgensen (1975, ch. 3).

features which are discriminated in the languages he has observed. Even his most 'exact' record is bound to ignore innumerable non-distinctive features of sound. . . . Only two kinds of linguistic records are scientifically relevant. One is a mechanical record of the gross acoustic features, such as is produced in the phonetics laboratory [such a record being continuous and unsegmentable]. The other is a record in terms of phonemes, ignoring all features that are not distinctive in the language.

It should be said that a great deal of analytical work was carried out, not least by Bloomfield, in disregard of this doctrine; most of it could not otherwise have been carried out at all. Efforts were increasingly made to provide an observational basis for phonetic segmentation.[54] But not all linguists could keep up with, or even fully understand, these fine-spun theoretical discussions; whereas they had all read Bloomfield's book. So in practice, throughout the period of classical phonemics, the Bloomfield doctrine continued to be widely followed. It was not considered reprehensible, in giving a phonological description of a language, to list the phonemes without making any statement about their allophones or about their phonetic characteristics; and even the more systematic kind of morphophonemic descriptions usually referred to lists of phonemes rather than to classes of phonemes defined by shared phonetic features (cf. the canonical form of statement suggested by Harris, given in (22) above).

In Prague School phonology, on the other hand, a place was carefully worked out in the theory for phonetic representations and for the notion 'speech sound'. Trubetzkoy (1939) points out that since the details of allophonic variation have to be stated specially for each language, allophony cannot be a purely physiological matter but must have psychological correlates. Many a phonemicist might have said that 'each phoneme has its own "psychological equivalent"—namely the acoustic and motor representations which correspond to it': when Trubetzkoy said it, he replaced 'phoneme' by 'speech sound'.

It is this insistence on the psychological reality of the speech sound that makes its definition necessary. For the purpose of this definition, Trubetzkoy supposes that we have already made a phonemic analysis of the language in which we are interested. Next, taking, presumably, something like Bloomfield's 'mechanical record of the gross acoustic features', he concentrates on those points in the speech continuum at which the features distinctively characteristic of a particular phoneme occur. The conjunction of *all* the peculiarities (whether phonologically relevant or not) which occur at just that point in the stream of speech then constitutes a speech sound.

For this definition to work it is, of course, necessary to have a definition of the phoneme which is logically independent of the notion 'speech sound'. Trubetzkoy's definition of the phoneme meets this requirement; it may be

---

[54] Thus Bloch (1948), partly using notions suggested by Hockett (1942), postulates that 'phonetic segmentation of speech *as perceived* is possible', and defines a *phase* as an interval during which an organ is perceived to remain in one place or move in one direction or be set in vibration; a *change-point* as the moment when, with respect to any organ, a phase begins or ends; and a *segment* as a maximal utterance fragment containing no change-points whatever. This is an excellent codification of normal practice; but it hardly answers Bloomfield's point about the subjectivity of perception.

regarded as beginning with the comparison of minimally differing, but unsegmented, *utterances*:

> By ... phonological opposition we thus understand any phonic opposition capable of differentiating cognitive meaning[55] in a given language. Each pole of such an opposition we term a *phonological* (or *distinctive*) *unit*. ... Phonological units that, from the standpoint of the language in question, do not admit analysis into shorter phonological units in sequence we term *phonemes*.

Even so there remains a serious objection to Trubetzkoy's approach to the problem of the speech sound. This is that there is no reason to suppose that it will always be possible, either by acoustic or even by articulatory analysis, to identify for each phoneme a point in the stream of speech at which all its distinctive features occur simultaneously. It might well seem more promising, whatever we do on the phonemic level, to regard as the basic units of phonetic representation not speech sounds but the features themselves. We have noted, when considering the question of one-phoneme or two-phoneme interpretation of affricates, diphthongs and the like, that the criteria applied are predominantly phonological rather than phonetic; and in general it is perfectly possible to regard phonetic segmentation as merely a preliminary, tentative step in the process of phonological analysis, rather than as itself having linguistic validity. This need not affect Trubetzkoy's sound conclusions on the psychological reality of allophonic phenomena; for these can be stated in terms of features just as well as in terms of segments. A discrete phonetic representation is essential to phonological description; a uniformly segmented phonetic representation need not be.

However, what is crucial about this aspect of Prague School phonology is its emphasis on the phonic matter, as well as the phonemic form, and it is this that made it possible for the Prague School to make so much progress in the field of general phonology. For if the phonic matter of languages is important, and since it is the same for all the languages of the world, it is to be expected that numerous non-trivial statements about the nature of phonological systems can be made which will hold true for all languages. If the phonic matter is disregarded, there is nothing to distinguish a system of phonological oppositions from any other system of oppositions; so if the phonic matter is irrelevant to phonology, it is not to be expected that phonological systems will share significant peculiarities not shared by other systems of oppositions (such as, to use Trubetzkoy's examples, systems of gestures or of flag signals).

It is the former of these two alternative expectations that is borne out: and the work of Prague School phonologists contains a wide variety of statements intended to hold good for all the languages of the world. In the case of vowel systems, for example, Trubetzkoy makes such statements as:

> In triangular two-class vowel systems, [where] back rounded or 'dark' vowels are opposed to front unrounded or 'clear' vowels ..., the maximally

---

[55] In the original 'intellektuelle Bedeutung'; a recent English translation has 'lexical meaning', but this is too restrictive, seeming as it does to exclude phonic differences signalling grammatical rather than lexical distinctions, as well as discrete intonational differences such as those of (20).

open vowel phoneme *a*, standing outside the opposition, is a back unrounded vowel.

In any vowel system, the 'darkest' and the 'clearest' classes of vowels always contain the same number of degrees of saturation [an auditory term corresponding to the articulatory dimension of openness: i.e. there are always exactly as many degrees of openness among back rounded vowels as among front unrounded vowels—a universal of dubious validity].

In three-class vowel systems the intermediate class [consisting of front rounded or back unrounded vowels] cannot contain more vowel phonemes than either of the extreme classes.

It is thus to the Prague School that we owe much of the development of general phonology, the phonology, as it might be termed, of Language rather than of languages.[56]

As we have seen in considering the Praguian notion of the phoneme, the starting point in phonological analysis for the Prague School was not, as in contemporary American and British work, the 'sound' but the 'opposition': the relationship between two words, phrases or sentences which were differentiated in cognitive meaning by the presence at some point within them of different phonic peculiarities, or by the presence of a peculiarity in one of the two and its absence in the other. A typology of oppositions was developed, whose detail need not concern us here;[57] and the questions that we typically find arising in Prague School work are: what are the possible oppositions in natural languages? what oppositions, and of what types, *must* occur in *any* natural language? when does the existence in a language of one opposition imply the existence of another? when does the existence of one opposition exclude the existence of another? etc. These are not, or not primarily, questions of analysis; they are questions of what phonological systems are like.

That last statement raises an important issue which is perhaps worth a digression. It is implicit in the work of Trubetzkoy and Jakobson, and eventually (notably in generative and stratificational phonology) we shall see it being made explicit, that a language in some sense 'has' a phonological system, and that the task of the phonologist is to 'discover' this system. But (it may be, and has been, objected) this is an assumption without warrant. The data used by the linguist, be he phonologist or grammarian, consist of utterances, and a phonological description is an attempt to state certain regularities that hold good over these utterances, not to describe some 'system' that 'lies behind' them. One linguist may attach more importance to some regularities than to others, another's preferences may be the reverse; both are equally valid, though there may be criteria of simplicity and elegance which would make one form of statement preferable to another. Universal phonology of any kind is, on this view, a misleading chimera; for what are presented as statements about phonological *systems* are in reality statements about phonological *descriptions*, and reflect, not facts about language, but facts about the descriptive habits of linguists.

---

[56] The first systematic investigations of language acquisition from the phonological point of view were, not surprisingly, made in this tradition: see Jakobson (1942).

[57] Cf. Trubetzkoy (1939), section on 'Logical classification of distinctive oppositions'.

This view, which I have presented in an extreme form in which it would not perhaps be maintained by anybody,[58] received in the early 1950s the designation 'hocus-pocus linguistics'. The contrary view (sometimes called the 'God's-truth' position) can also be held with various degrees of emphasis; its main thesis is perhaps best formulated by Starosta (1971):

> If each speaker has a single internalized grammar, then any theory which purports to represent that grammar is subject to empirical disconfirmation. . . . If there is no single right answer, no theory is disprovable; and then linguistics is not science, at least not in the common modern sense of the word.

This is rather an oversimplification. For linguistic hypotheses to be empirically disprovable, it is not necessary that they be claims about the organization of a 'single internalized grammar'; but it *is* necessary—and here to the present author the God's-truth position seems decisively superior—that they make *some* kind of claim to physiological and/or psychological reality: otherwise linguistics is indeed not a science, but a game, and one moreover in which you can make your own rules.[59]

I have briefly mentioned above (p. 23) the Prague School attitude to neutralization and their concept of the archiphoneme. This must now be considered further.

Before, I illustrated neutralization with the case of English plosives, which in most positions show a contrast between /p t k/, voiceless, aspirated (if released), and fortis, and /b d g/, lenis, never aspirated, and often voiced. After /s/, however, there is no contrast, or, as Trubetzkoy would put it, the opposition of voice is here *neutralized*, the archiphoneme being represented by a voiceless, unaspirated, fortis stop. We must first define the terms used here, and then look at the consequences of this view of neutralization for phonological theory generally.[60]

Neutralization is generally taken to be applicable only to *minimal* oppositions, i.e. to pairs or sets of phonemes which are alike in every feature but one: thus an opposition /t/: /d/ can be neutralized, but not an opposition /t/:/b/—for the latter pair of phonemes differ both in voice and in place of articulation. Any apparent neutralization of /t/ and /b/ would also have to involve some third phoneme such as /p/ or /d/ which differed minimally from each of them, and would thus really be the product of *two* neutralizations.

A minimal opposition, then, is neutralized in a given (set of) phonic

---

[58] Though Matthews (1972, 20 n. 2) seems at least very close to this position, rejecting as he does the Chomskyan term 'descriptive adequacy' on the grounds that it 'suggests that one is actually "describing" something'.

[59] A respectable case might be made for a linguistics which was not empirically refutable but which did make truth claims: most kinds of historical scholarship find themselves from time to time in the same position. But what would we say of a historian who professed himself unconcerned with whether events (not directly attested) which he hypothesized had actually happened, and interested only in whether they accounted simply and elegantly for the data; one who was prepared to say that two incompatible hypotheses were alike valid?

[60] The following account of neutralization incorporates an extension of classical Prague School doctrine proposed by Haas (1957), though not his terminological innovations. The original doctrine applied only to *privative* oppositions (those consisting in presence *v.* absence of a feature), and consequently the problem of phonemes not participating in a neutralization but sharing all the common features of the phonemes that did participate could not arise.

environment(s) when in those environments the opposition is never used to distinguish cognitive meanings. In such environments (*positions of neutralization*), the two phonemes which are the terms of the opposition are considered not to occur; what does occur is (the representative of) an *archiphoneme*, defined as 'the set of distinctive peculiarities common to the two phonemes'; if any phoneme not participating in the neutralization shares the same common peculiarities, the archiphoneme is also taken to include the *disjunction* of the peculiarities which differentiate the participating phonemes from each other. (The definition is capable of extension where more than two phonemes are neutralized.) Thus the archiphoneme of English /t d/ where these are neutralized is simply 'alveolar plosive'; where English /t k/ are neutralized (viz. at the start of a syllable where /l/ follows), 'voiceless plosive' would not adequately specify the archiphoneme (for /p/, also a voiceless plosive, does not participate in the neutralization), and we must define it as 'voiceless plosive, alveolar or velar'.

Note that phonetically an archiphoneme may well be realized identically to one of the phonemes of which it is a neutralization: this does not affect its archiphonemic status, which is due not to its pronunciation but to the lack of contrast. Thus in English, after /æw/, there is no contrast between syllable-final /d/ and /g/. What occurs is to all intents and purposes identical with what is elsewhere a realization of /d/; nevertheless, in *this* position, it realizes the archiphoneme of /d/ and /g/.

This treatment of neutralization has as a consequence that one can no longer speak of *the* phonemic system of a language as if there were only one. For the total inventory of phonemes and archiphonemes used in a language will not meet the conditions we have agreed to impose on phonemic systems. The archiphoneme of /p b/, for example—let us call it /P/—is phonetically similar to /p/ and in complementary distribution with it, and likewise is phonetically similar to /b/ and in complementary distribution with it. But if we ignore the archiphonemes when setting up the phonemic system of the language, then the system will fail Hockett's test of 'completeness', since it will not be possible to describe every utterance exhaustively as a sequence of phonemes.

Thus, in the Praguian view, a language must be regarded as having 'beside the general system of phonemes or of prosodic features . . . *partial systems* which hold only in given phonic contexts and in which only some of the phonological devices of the general system are used' (Trubetzkoy 1939). A full analysis must thus specify not only the general system but the partial systems and the contexts in which each of them is applicable.

A possible example of a partial system in English would be the range of consonant[61] contrasts in the position between a preceding vowel and a following obstruent where (a) the latter is word-final and (b) no morpheme boundary intervenes between the two consonants. (Note that in classical American phonemics we could not impose a restriction like (b); Prague School phonology does not regard grammatical and morphological information as necessarily taboo.)

---

[61] For this purpose we will take the term 'consonant' to exclude semivowels. Proper names are ignored throughout.

A classical phonemicist would claim that in this position the following phonemes occurred:

Phoneme	Can occur before	Examples	23
/p/	/t s/	apt apse	
/t/	/s/	blitz	
/k/	/t s/	act axe	
/d/	/z/	adze	
/f/	/t/	lift	
/s/	/p t k/	lisp list ask	
/m/	/p f/	lamp nymph	
/n/	/t dǰ θ s š z/	tent tend change	
		month bounce	
		bench bronze	
/ŋ/	/k/	bank	
/l/	/p t č k b dǰ	help belt belch	
	f θ s š v/	milk elbow weld	
		bulge elf wealth	
		pulse welsh	
		twelve	

The phonemes /č b ǰ g θ š v ð z ž r/, it would be said, do not occur in this position.

What would a theory taking full account of neutralization make of this set of data? First, we would note that the evidence for the occurrence of /d/ in the stated environment is very thin: *adze* is in fact the only word ending with a cluster /dz/ not divided by a morpheme boundary; and we might well decide to treat it as a mere exception, a violation of English phonotactics. If so, our putative phonemic system is reduced to /p t k f s m n ŋ l/: nine phonemes, compared with the twenty-one consonant phonemes (excluding semivowels and /h/) of the full system.

But now we observe several things about this system. One is that the opposition of voice/aspiration, so important in other positions, is in this position totally irrelevant: all obstruents are voiceless. Another is that there are no contrasts among liquids and no contrasts among nasals: the three nasal 'phonemes' are all in complementary distribution and should be represented by a single archiphoneme. The contrasts between alveolar and palato-alveolar articulation, and between the two types of apical fricative represented by /θ/ and /s/, are likewise neutralized.

The more revealing way of describing this system, therefore, would be something like (24), where all symbols represent archiphonemes:

$$\begin{array}{ccc} /\text{P} & \text{T} & \text{K} \\ \text{F} & \text{S} & \\ \hline & \text{N} & \\ \text{L} & & / \end{array}$$

24

with only seven contrasting elements. Here /P T K/ are neither distinctively voiced nor distinctively voiceless; /T S/ have no place-of-articulation features other than 'coronality' (for which see Chapter Five, p. 100); and /N L/ have no distinctive features whatever other than 'nasal' and 'liquid' respectively.

In more restricted environments, even smaller phonological systems may be found. Thus before plosives other than /t/, there are no contrasts whatever among obstruents, the archiphoneme 'obstruent' being represented by a voiceless sibilant; in this position therefore there are only three contrasting elements in the system, 'obstruent', 'nasal', 'liquid'.

There is, be it noted, nothing arbitrary about these 'partial systems'; though distinct from the 'general system', they are closely related to it. An archiphoneme is always a set of properties common to two or more phonemes of the general system; it cannot be defined by any other set of properties.

Linked, in the Prague School view, with the notion of neutralization is that of *markedness*. A privative opposition (cf. note 60) by definition sets the presence of some phonic peculiarity over against its absence, so that one of the terms of such an opposition is, as it were, positive and the other negative. The positive pole of a privative opposition is termed the *marked* pole (member, term) and the other the *unmarked*.

It might be the thought that it could be determined on purely phonetic grounds which oppositions were privative and which were their marked terms; but this procedure was not followed, for such objective phonetic determination is not always possible. Consider the opposition between oral and nasal consonants (or vowels for that matter). Almost intuitively we say that this is a privative opposition, with the nasals having the positive peculiarity—presumably the acoustic peculiarity of nasal resonance. But one could argue plausibly from the articulatory point of view that it was the oral sounds that had a positive peculiarity, viz. the raising of the velum (which requires muscular effort); and there might even be a case for saying that, since it was impossible to decide between the two positions mentioned, the opposition should not be regarded as privative at all.

For objective evidence on such questions recourse was had to the phenomena of neutralization, in particular to the question what type of sound appeared as 'representative of the archiphoneme' in positions of neutralization. Now not all such cases are relevant. Sometimes, as in the case discussed on pp. 21–22, the sound found in these environments is merely intermediate between the terms of the opposition. Sometimes the appearance, in positions of neutralization, of one term of an opposition rather than another is clearly explicable from the context; consider the realizations of the archiphoneme /N/ of (24). The cases that are of interest are those where one term of an opposition appears to the exclusion of the other in a position of neutralization *without* there being anything in the phonic context to account for the choice. In such circumstances, claims Trubetzkoy, the opposition is (with certain well-defined exceptions[62]) always privative, and the term which appears in positions of neutralization is always the *unmarked* term.

Thus we have seen that in English, where an obstruent follows in the

---

[62] Viz. where the opposition in question was one 'of which the terms are characterized by different degrees of the *same* feature' (*gradual* opposition), rather than by the presence or absence of a feature (private opposition) or by the presence of different features in the opposed phonemes (equipollent opposition). Openness in vowels, and pitch, are typically gradual oppositions, though if along either of these axes there is no more than a two-way contrast the opposition in question can be considered privative.

circumstances specified on p. 50, all oppositions among coronal occlusives are neutralized in favour of the alveolar plosive [t], representing an archiphoneme /T/, and all oppositions among coronal fricatives are neutralized in favour of the voiceless alveolar fricative [s], representing an archiphoneme /S/. Nothing in the particular environments explains why the representative of the archiphoneme should be alveolar, nor why it should be voiceless.[63] Since, further, the evidence from other positions of neutralization (to the extent that the choice of representation is not contextually determined) is entirely consistent with this, the theory tells us that we must regard all the oppositions in question as privative, and /t/ and /s/ as the unmarked terms of all of them. That is, /t/ is unmarked for voice as against /d/, for 'stridency' as against /č/; /s/ is unmarked for the same two features as against /z/ and /θ/ respectively, and also for 'compactness' as against /š/.[64] This is in English, note; in other languages the marked-unmarked relation may be reversed, and some of the oppositions may even not be privative.

In this way, some of the most valuable information about the nature of a phonological opposition can paradoxically be gleaned from those cases where the opposition does not function.

The combination of the insights of American classical phonemics with those of the Prague School would have yielded a strong and interesting theory of universal phonology, though, as will be seen in following chapters, such a theory would still be regarded by many today as defective in important aspects. As it happened, such a synthesis never really occurred. But it is important to note that the later work of Jakobson (subsequently joined by Halle), which eventually led to the development of generative phonology, was carried out essentially within the Prague School tradition, that is, with a view to a universal theory in which phonetics was to play an important role. It is unlikely that any amount of work in classical phonemics, with its emphasis on the individual language and on procedures of analysis and its Bloomfieldian distrust of impressionistic phonetics, would have produced similar results.

[63] This is a slight oversimplification, omitting a step in the argument. Coronal obstruents in this position are always voiceless because the obstruents that follow them are also always voiceless; it is the latter fact (and analogous facts in other positions of neutralization) that is hard to explain in contextual terms.

[64] The labels for the oppositions are taken from the later work of Jakobson, which will be discussed in Chapter Five. Trubetzkoy regards the oppositions here termed 'stridency' and 'compactness' as equipollent (cf. note 62), not privative, but he does not explain how this can be so in view of the facts of neutralization.

③ Prosodic Phonology

3.1 Feature smear

We have already observed certain difficulties into which the simple and plausible theory of classical phonemics ran from a very early stage of its development. We pass now to consider another class of difficulty which provides a logical motivation for a phonological theory markedly different from, and in one sense directly opposed to, all forms of phonemic analysis.

The class of phenomena in question, some of which have already been discussed from a different point of view under the heading of neutralization, may be conveniently labelled *feature smear*. Feature smear occurs whenever the same phonetic peculiarity, or a set of closely related phonic peculiarities, are found in several successive segments over a domain clearly delimitable in phonological terms.

Suppose there is a language such that ordinary phonemic analysis establishes three vowel phonemes /i a u/ and a number of consonant phonemes including /h/. Suppose further that all the consonants other than /h/ are audibly palatalized before /i/ and audibly labialized before /u/, and that /h/, as is very often actually the case, is realized phonetically as a voiceless onset of the succeeding vowel. Then what reason have we, it might be asked, for treating the vowel quality as distinctive (phonemic) and the consonant modifications as redundant (non-phonemic), rather than the other way round? It is true that Hockett's criterion of economy (cf. p. 25) will answer this question, since the saving of the two vowel phonemes if we treat vowel quality as non-distinctive will be more than outweighed by the trebling of the consonant inventory; but economy is not a very strong criterion, and in any case its use begs the question whether we should have to choose between the two analyses at all. Why should we not in this language treat palatalization and labialization as features of the syllable as a whole? After all, this is how we treat stress and pitch; why should the same treatment not be extended to other features, if they behave comparably?

An inadequacy of both classical and Praguian phonemics, deeper than a mere problem of choice between analyses, appears when we consider the vowel system of Turkish.

Turkish has eight vowels. These are distinguished by the features front-back, unrounded-rounded, high-low, and every possible combination of these features occurs, as shown in (25) opposite.

In word-initial syllables all these vowels contrast with one another. In non-initial syllables, however, there are far fewer contrasts. Rounding is not distinctive

	Front *unrounded*	*Front* *rounded*	*Back* *unrounded*	*Back* *rounded*	**25**
High (close)	i	y	ɯ	u	
Low (open)	e	ø	a	o	

for low vowels, those that occur being phonetically unrounded. Subject to this, vowels in non-initial syllables normally[1] agree in frontness or backness, and in rounding or non-rounding, with the vowel of the preceding syllable. The effect of this is that all the vowels of a word have the same value for backness (all back or all front); while as far as rounding is concerned, all the vowels have the same value for the feature until one comes to the first non-initial syllable that has a low vowel, after which all the remaining vowels in the word are unrounded. Thus the addition to the stem /jol/ of two high-vowel suffixes results in a form which is phonemically /jolumuz/; but if the low-vowel suffix /lar/ is added directly after the stem, the vowels of the succeeding suffixes are given an unrounded pronunciation, so that phonemically the word is /jollarɯmɯz/.[2]

Classical phonemic theory, however, commits us to specifying *every* vowel that occurs as a term in the eight-vowel system (25)—even though, in a great many contexts, the phonology of the language actually offers no more than a two-way choice, high *v.* low. The Praguian theory of the archiphoneme obviates this redundancy; but in one respect it gives a false impression. It claims in effect that the backness and rounding, or lack of it, of (most) vowels in non-initial syllables in Turkish is linguistically irrelevant. It is not; and neither is any 'determined' or 'redundant' feature. For redundant features are only redundant *if the distinctive features are successfully transmitted to the listener;* and since articulation and hearing are both always imperfect, and there is also imperfection in, and interference on, the channel of transmission to be reckoned with, the distinctive features very often are not successfully transmitted. In such circumstances the 'redundant' features in effect assume distinctive function; and, since the message is successfully transmitted without the help of the 'distinctive' features, *they* are presumably redundant!

The argument to which this might lead is clear. A smeared feature is distinctive, at least potentially, at *every* point at which it is found; Praguian phonemics compels us to specify it as distinctive at one point only, and redundant everywhere else. American phonemics is inconsistent; in some cases it likewise confines distinctiveness to one point, in others it asserts, just as falsely, by representations such as /jollarɯmɯz/, that points of potential distinctiveness are also points of choice. Both theories to some extent confuse the abstract with the concrete, on the one hand the choice between two linguistic forms which differ as minimally as the phonological principles of the language will allow, on the other hand the points in the stream of speech at which that choice is manifested. We need a theory that is able to say simultaneously that smeared features are single entities *and* that they are manifested at more than one point.

[1] There are some exceptions, and the principles apply differently and less fully to Arabic and other loans. This would be treated in prosodic theory by the setting up of a separate phonological system for loanwords, as in Henderson (1951). In general prosodic theory does not require or expect that phonological statements should be exceptionless.
[2] Examples from Waterson (1956).

C

An attempt at such a theory within the general tradition of American phonemics was made by Zellig Harris[3] in what was called the theory of *long components*.

3.1.1 Long component analysis

The object of positing long components is said to be 'to have a simpler statement of the phonetic facts about the language . . . [either by] reducing the number of phonemes, or the complexity of allophonic variation within each phoneme, . . . [or] eliminating the limitations of distribution upon each phoneme' (Harris 1945, 241); the goal is to ensure that 'each phoneme contrasts with each other in every position'[4] (*ibid*. 243).

Some features have the property that they are either present or absent over the whole of a syllable, word, or other stretch of speech (the *domain* of the feature), but cannot be present in one part of a domain and absent in another part. Any such feature may be abstracted as a long component. Within the domain of the component, all segments to which the component is relevant are represented by 'archiphonemic' symbols, and the long component is interpreted as an instruction to add certain features to these archiphonemes. For instance, the two Turkish forms mentioned on p. 55 might be represented thus in a long-component analysis:

$$\text{Rd}———\quad \text{Rd}– \qquad\qquad\qquad \textbf{26}$$
$$\text{Bk}———\quad \text{Bk}————$$
$$\text{/jAllmIz/}\quad\text{/jAllArImIz/}$$

where the horizontal lines indicate the extent of the domains of the components, and somewhere in the description it is stated that the component /Rd/ makes all vowels round, and /Bk/ makes all vowels back, within their respective domains, while in the absence of these components vowels are unrounded or front as the case may be.

Long-component analysis in its standard Harrisian form can capture several types of phonological generalization, but it is subject to a severe restriction. This is that the features which are abstracted as long components must themselves be phonemic. The data for a long-component analysis, in fact, are not phonetic data but the output of a completed phonemic analysis. The result is that this type of long-component theory probably could not deal with the palatalization-labialization example we first considered, any more than Praguian phonology could. For palatalization and labialization of consonants would already have been eliminated from consideration at the stage of phonemic analysis and would be no part of the data for a long-component analysis.

This objection is met in the form of componential analysis proposed by Hockett (1947b), where the components, whether 'long' or confined to a single segment, were established directly from the phonetic record, all and only those components being noted which were 'independent or only partially dependent';

---

[3] See Welmers and Harris (1942) and Harris (1944; 1945; 1951).
[4] Presumably we should understand 'within a given subsystem'; it is not easy to see in what interesting sense all consonants could contrast with all vowels, all vowels with all pitch phonemes, etc.

the analysis in terms of components was then regarded as the primary phonological analysis, that in terms of phonemes being an optional extra. Hockett's components, like classical phonemes (and unlike Harris's long components), had to have invariant phonetic correlates.

3.2 The prosodic approach

Neither of these forms of componential analysis ever came into wide use. Meanwhile and quite independently, in Britain, a form of phonological analysis was being developed which bears close superficial resemblances to componential analysis (though there are far-reaching theoretical differences), and which combines Harris's abandonment of the invariance condition with Hockett's virtual substitution of the component for the phoneme. This is generally known as *prosodic phonology*.

According to prosodic phonologists, phonemics in all its forms gives undue weight to the contrastive or 'paradigmatic' aspect of phonology, and to neglect the 'syntagmatic' aspect, the relationships between smaller units of structure within larger units (how consonants and vowels cohere in syllables, syllables in words, etc.) This charge is not perhaps fully justified, since syntagmatic statements are normally made in the phonotactic section of a classical phonemic description; but the aim of prosodic phonology is, among other things, to integrate syntagmatic and paradigmatic statement in a single unified description.

To this end, a basic role is given to smeared features and to other peculiarities that can be regarded as characteristic of a unit of structure (phrase, word, syllable, syllable initial, etc.) rather than of a segment as such. It is these peculiarities (and certain others mentioned below) that are termed *prosodies*.[5] When all possible prosodies have been extracted, the remaining facts are described in terms of segments or *phonematic* (n.b. not phonemic) *units*. This phonological statement is linked to phonetics by a set of statements detailing the phonetic realizations or *exponents* of each prosody, phonematic unit, or combination of such elements, in general or in particular environments.

No full account has ever appeared of the theory and practice of prosodic analysis. The originator of the theory, J. R. Firth, wrote little on the subject, and his pupils have testified that it is not always easy to deduce his detailed views from his written or oral statements. What follows is therefore an attempt to extract the principles of the school from (for the most part) its published work.[6] Fortunately, at the period of the main development of prosodic analysis (which may be said to cover the years 1948–60), its chief practitioners were working close together and under the immediate influence of Firth, and in fact the differences of view that emerge from their work are far less important than the identities.

[5] This is a technical term of the theory and has nothing to do with the more usual sense of the adjective 'prosodic' as it was employed in Chapter Two.

[6] In addition, I wish at this point in particular to express my gratitude for the help given and the information supplied to me by Professor W. S. Allen, and to emphasize that I am wholly responsible for any misinterpretations or errors.

3.2.1 Types of prosodies

Some critics (e.g. Postal 1968) have spoken of 'a certain arbitrariness in whether phenomena are to be treated as prosodies or [in terms of] segments'; and certainly the audience to whom Firth delivered his trail-blazing lecture (Firth 1948) must have been baffled by this question. In practice, however, most of the phenomena that were recognized as prosodies could be classified under four main heads, and we shall presently see that these can in turn be brought under a single rubric.

1   First, there are features such as length, stress and pitch, those in fact which are termed 'prosodic' by phonologists working in other traditions. In prosodic phonology, however, they are no more and no less 'prosodic' than the other classes of features discussed below. Their domain is most often, perhaps, a mora or a syllable; but the domain of an intonation is usually a whole sentence. One might even recognize suprasentential prosodies (e.g. of style and voice quality) whose domain could be an entire discourse or even the entire linguistic output of a particular speaker.
2   A second class of prosodies is formed by features which, though not prosodic in the traditional sense, resemble the features of the first class in having an extended domain. Most typical of these are the smeared features. Since prosodic theory does not regard the phonemic notion of contrast as of any particular importance, no notice is taken of whether smeared features are phonemic (distinctive) or not; rather any phonic peculiarity, or set of related phonic peculiarities, which 'extend[s] over more than one place in the phonological structure [i.e. more than one segment] or ha[s] implications for more than one place' (Bendor-Samuel 1966) is treated as a prosody. Under this heading, therefore, come the whole range of phenomena usually dealt with as 'assimilation' (whether 'morphophonemic' or 'allophonic'). Dissimilation is also included, though this requires rather more complex exponence statements; Allen (1951), for instance, considering Sanskrit, in which no syllable may both begin and end with a phonetically aspirated consonant, treats aspiration as a syllable prosody which may not have a phonetic exponent in more than one segment.[7]
3   Also treated as prosodies ('junction prosodies') are those features and combinations of features whose occurrence marks the presence of a boundary between structural units. A wide range of phenomena are covered by this. In a language, for instance, in which word stress is fixed (as in Czech, where it always falls on the initial syllable) or restricted in position (as in Modern Greek, where not more than two syllables may intervene between the stressed syllable and the end of the word), stress is taken to be a phonetic exponent of a junction prosody focused[8] on the word boundary. Note that this is still the case even where the

[7] This shows the meaning of the phrase 'have implications for more than one place'. The syllable prosody of aspiration is only realized at one place within the syllable; but the *non*-aspiration of a consonant at the other end of the syllable is equally an exponent or 'implication' of the prosody, since it is determined by the phonological principle of the language which the prosody embodies.
[8] Although prosodies normally have an extended domain, it is often obvious that they 'originate' from a single point in structure, e.g. a syllable prosody of nasalization from a nasal consonant, Turkish vowel harmony from the vowel of the initial syllable. This 'point of origin' is termed the *focus* of the prosody. All junction prosodies are focused on the boundaries whose presence they mark.

accent serves in addition a distinctive function: where it does, it will be said to serve as the exponent of two different prosodies. Thus in Modern Greek /píno/ means 'I drink', while /pinó/ means 'I am hungry'; a prosodic analyst would here set up at least two prosodies: one of junction (whose exponents would include, *inter alia*, stress and length on one of the last three syllables preceding the boundary), the other a syllable prosody of accent (its exponents being stress on the syllable forming the domain of the prosody and length on its vowel).[9]

Another instance of a junction prosody would be a sequence of segments which can only occur across a boundary. For instance, in English (more precisely: in the Germanic and Romance strata of the English vocabulary[10]), an occlusive with oral closure and nasal release is found only at a major morphological boundary, e.g. in *catnap, topmost, wet-nurse*[11]: the occurrence of such an occlusive would therefore be treated as an exponent of a junction prosody. The 'terminal contours' of some American analyses of English intonation (see Chapter Two, note 46) would probably be regarded as exponents of phrase-boundary prosodies.

Features of this type were discussed by the Prague School, which termed them 'boundary signals' (Grenzsignale); but their status within the school's general phonological theory was never made very clear. Prosodic theory, treating them simply as one class of prosody, is here more successful.[12]

4   The last class of prosody comprises what may be termed diagnostic features: features which are characteristic of a particular structural position, a particular section of the vocabulary, a particular grammatical category, or a particular style of speech.

(a)   In many languages, occlusive consonants are released only in syllable-initial position, and remain unreleased in syllable-final. In such a case release (often called 'plosion') is a *marker* of syllable-initial position, and it is generally (as by Henderson 1949) treated as a prosody. This is a prosody of a markedly different type from the others we have considered so far, since its exponents are confined to a single segment; it is considered a prosody because it characterizes the segment not *qua* segment but *qua* syllable-initial—metaphorically, it is not so much a part of the railway carriage as a label indicating its position in the train.[13] Similarly, there may be prosodic markers of syllable-final position, phrase-final position, etc., or even of word- or phrase-medial position (cf. note 12).

(b)   In almost all languages which include substantial numbers of loan-words, their phonological structure differs somewhat from that of 'native' forms. There will thus be phonic peculiarities occurring only in loans, and phonic peculiarities

[9] To avoid duplication one might think of making the accent prosody itself an exponent of the junction prosody; but this would be to confuse their distinct functions—the junction prosody is demarcative, whereas the accent prosody has the function of individualizing the word-unit (cf. p. 38) and also a distinctive function.

[10] Cf. below, on prosodies of class 4b. It should be pointed out that words are assigned to one or another stratum according to their phonological and morphological peculiarities, not according to their etymology.

[11] There are a few exceptions such as *partner* (unless this is regarded as a derivative of *part*); and as usual the principle does not apply to proper names, e.g. *Rednal, Dropmore, Witney*.

[12] Trubetzkoy's 'negative' Grenzsignale, which are elements and combinations of elements whose presence indicates that there is *not* a boundary (of a particular type) in the neighbourhood, would no doubt count as markers of medial position in a prosodic analysis: cf. below, on prosodies of class 4a.

[13] This analogy is due to T. Hill (1966).

occurring only in native forms. Often the situation is more complex than this, as in English, where it is probably necessary to recognize four main vocabulary divisions (Germanic, Romance, Greek, and what we may call 'exotic'). In discussing vocabulary divisions of this kind, Henderson (1949; 1951) seems to imply that their special features should be regarded as prosodic. Thus, e.g., nasally released occlusion in English, when not an exponent of a junction prosody, will be an exponent of a diagnostic prosody of 'Greekness' (e.g. in *atmosphere*, when pronounced /ǽpm-/ as it not infrequently is) or 'exoticness' (e.g. in *sputnik, nudnik*[14]). On the other hand, voicelessness, when combined with the other features characteristic of the phonematic unit *w*, is an exponent (in those English dialects in which it is found) of a diagnostic prosody of 'nativeness'.[15]

(c)   An example of a diagnostic prosody of grammatical function is the case (p. 27) of English [θ] and [ð], where voicing of this fricative in initial position may be regarded as an exponent of a word prosody marking non-lexicality. Similarly Sprigg (1954, 153) seems to treat aspiration in Tibetan as an exponent of a prosody because it marks intransitivity.

(d)   Finally, there are style prosodies; these are not much discussed in the literature, but Henderson (1949) pays particular attention to variation in pronunciation as between slow and fast speech. The phonetic characteristics of fast speech can be exceedingly diverse; but as they are all referable to the same causal factor, they are all classified together as 'linking prosodies'.

This listing of types of prosodies may well have seemed very unsystematic to the reader, but on examination he will find that they all have this in common: in every case there is some link between an affected segment and something outside itself, either other segments (1 and 2), boundaries (3 and 4a), grammatical or lexical factors (4b and 4c), or style (4d). And the general nature of the concept 'prosody' within this theory can perhaps best be captured by the following definition:

A phonic peculiarity is regarded as prosodic just in case it is related to some   27
aspect of the context.[16]

'Context' must here be understood in the widest possible sense. It includes the linguistic context, phonological, grammatical and lexical; but it also includes the *context of situation*, that is both 'the context of concurrent human activity' and 'the entire cultural setting of speech and the personal history of the participants', as Langendoen (1968) explains it. Context of situation enters chiefly into the discussion of style prosodies: phonology can vary almost as much as vocabulary according to the situation in which speech takes place (public importance of the

---

[14] But not e.g. *beatnik*, which is (perhaps we had better now say was) a derivative formed within English with the help of an exotic suffix; here nasal release is a junction prosody. The difference is that *beat-* is the ordinary English morpheme *beat*, whereas neither *sput-* nor *nud-* is an English morpheme at all.

[15] The question of vocabulary divisions and the setting up of special phonological systems for them has also received a good deal of attention from classical phonemicists of various schools. See, e.g., Mathesius (1929; 1934); Fries and Pike (1949); and Pilch (1965) with the comments of Daneš and Sivertsen.

[16] The definition is my own. Sometimes prosodic analysts treat features as phonematic when they might have been treated as prosodic: e.g. Henderson (1966) on some features in Vietnamese which are diagnostic of initial or final position.

occasion, social relationship of speaker and addressee, sex of speaker (in some languages), etc.)

Prosodic phonology may thus be seen as an attempt to extract from the phonetic record all peculiarities which have an explanation, complete or partial, outside themselves. It is in this sense that the prosodies are *anima vocis*, 'the soul of speech', as Firth (1948) called them. Prosodies, on this theory, comprehend everything that is interesting about the phonology of a language, leaving to the phonematics only those phenomena which have no repercussions outside the segment in which they occur, 'which predict nothing and which are correlated with nothing'.[17]

3.2.2 Polysystemicism and related matters

Certain theoretical assumptions, which are not logically implied by prosodic theory, were nevertheless held by almost all prosodic phonologists, at least in the early days of the school. One of these was the assumption that it was wrong to seek for language universals; this followed naturally from the 'hocus-pocus' orientation of the school (cf. pp. 48f).[18] Thus in principle, for prosodic theory, an analysis of the phonology of one language can neither be justified nor objected to on grounds relating to another language.

But prosodic theory went further than this. From the very beginning[19] it was insisted that phonological analysis should be *polysystemic*. This term covered not only the recognition of separate phonological systems for different structural positions and different strata of vocabulary, corresponding to the 'partial systems' of the Prague School or the 'coexistent systems' of Fries and Pike (1949), but also the possibility of establishing separate phonological systems for different grammatical categories or lexical classes. But prosodic theory went much further than the Prague School or, indeed, any other theory of phonology, in asserting that the terms in different phonological systems, even within one and the same language, were totally unrelated to one another. They might be represented by the same symbol, but this was only due to the practical impossibility of finding enough different symbols. It followed that an analysis of *part* of the phonology of a language, e.g. the phonology of monosyllabic roots or of the nominal complex, could not be disconfirmed to any degree at all by showing that it was inapplicable to other parts of the language. This principle may well seem astonishing; but it was held:

> It should be emphasized that there is no presupposition that the exemplifications of one grammatical category will be describable within the

---

[17] The phrase is that of Postal (1968, 133), who uses it in an entirely different connection, with reference to rule-exception features in generative phonology; phonematics in prosodic phonology is as peripheral as that.

[18] Cf. the statement of Robins (1957): '. . . Linguistic structures and systems must likewise be thought of not as pre-existing or discoverable in any literal sense, but rather as the product of the linguist in working over his material.' Clearly, if linguistic structures and systems do not exist, it makes no sense to claim that similar structures and systems occur in widely different languages (though this did not stop Firth, at any rate, making such claims).

[19] The polysystemic hypothesis is already explicit in Firth (1935) and Butlin (1936), long before prosodic theory as a whole was elaborated.

same framework of phonological statement as those of another category. It may, however, and not infrequently does happen, that at least certain sections of two or more such frameworks are 'isomorphic', in the sense that they involve systems of equal magnitude, the exponents of whose terms are susceptible of identical statement. From the point of view of economical presentation it is clearly an advantage to exploit such isomorphisms. But at the same time it is essential to realize that any exploitation of this kind is a *generalization* and not an *identification*. There can be no identification of function between terms of various systems established within the description of any one corpus. (Allen, 1956).[20]

Note here that even the 'isomorphisms' admitted to exist—which are given only presentational, not theoretical significance—can be found only between 'systems of equal magnitude': if one phonological 'system' has more or fewer terms than another within the same language, no 'isomorphism' can be set up between them and no 'generalization' stated. Thus in this framework the English initial and final consonant systems have nothing in common. A revealing juxtaposition may be found at the end of Palmer (1956a):

> All these complications are avoided if the approach is polysystemic. It is not required that the exponents of gemination shall be the same for all types of plural, . . . and, still less, that the phonological analysis shall be integrated with the analysis of other, unrelated data.
>
> APPENDIX I. A very similar, though more simple, statement could be made for the verbal forms. . . .

In polysystemic theory, this similarity is of no interest.

The reason for this attitude appears to lie in a phenomenon not unknown in the history of linguistics (as of other sciences), the extension of an important new insight beyond its proper domain. The insight was that it was often unrevealing to try to describe a whole language in terms of a single phonemic system: the illegitimate extension was that therefore systems should be multiplied whenever possible, and further that they should be considered unrelated to one another. The extension seems to have resulted from the interaction of the original insight with Firth's view of language in general as intimately related to contexts of situation. If 'unity is the last concept that should be applied to language' (Firth 1935), it may well be thought incumbent on the linguist to seek the maximum of diversity. But the hypothesis founders on the simple fact that on any reasonable analysis, different subsystems of the phonology of one language show far more similarity, on the average and in comparison with subsystems of the phonology of different languages, than can possibly be attributed to chance.

Another important feature of most (though not all) work in prosodic phonology is the rejection of what is known as 'the biuniqueness requirement' of

---

[20] It should be said that this extreme position was not held for long: Robins (1967, 167f) treats non-identification of terms in systems set up for different structural positions as an option available to the analyst, not as a theoretical requirement. It seems beyond doubt, however, that in the 1950s, the most vigorous period of the history of prosodic phonology, non-identification *was* a theoretical requirement.

classical phonemics. This requirement—which is natural in a theory whose main interest is in identifying phonological contrasts—may be thus expressed:

No two utterances which contrast at the phonetic level may be analysed as **28** phonologically identical, and no two utterances which are phonetically identical, or are in free variation, may be analysed as phonologically distinct.

It is the second half of (28) that prosodic analysis rejects. Admitting as it does the unrestricted use of grammatical criteria in phonology, prosodic analysis considers itself free to give distinct phonological analyses to phonetically identical 'pieces'. There are two German words pronounced [rá:t], one meaning, among other things, 'councillor' (plural [ré:tə]), the other meaning 'wheel' (plural [ré:də(r)]). A prosodic analyst might very well treat the final [t] of the first word as an exponent of the phonematic unit *t*, but that of the second as an exponent of the phonematic unit *d* plus a diagnostic prosody marking final position (one of whose exponents is devoicing of obstruents). Prosodic representations are thus similar in some ways to the morphophonemic or base-form representations discussed in the last chapter; there are, however, considerable differences, even apart from the non-linear, non-segmental nature of prosodic description. In particular, the prosodic (phonological) representations are mapped on to the phonetic data by a single set of statements giving the 'phonetic exponents' of each unit or combination; there is no intermediate level like that of classical phonemics. Prosodic writers frequently note that this eliminates the need for any statements of morphophonemic alternation. What they do not note is that it simultaneously complicates the statements of phonetic exponence: there is simplification only in the sense that it ceases to be necessary to posit two unrelated types of mapping statements, 'morphophonemic' and 'allophonic'.

3.3 An example

We are now ready to look at an example of prosodic analysis. The analysis is my own, and probably does not take into account all the possibilities of prosodic statement.

I propose to consider monosyllabic utterances in English, and for convenience I will arbitrarily restrict myself to monosyllables of the form CVC.[21] What properties of such monosyllables (apart from stress and pitch) might be regarded as prosodic?

One very likely candidate is voicing. The contrast between *bat* and *bad* does not reside solely in the voicing of the final consonant of the latter; *bad* also has a perceptibly longer vowel, and if, experimentally, you cut the vowel of *bad* short, you will find that the word sounds most unnatural. This association of syllable-final voicing with vowel length occurs throughout English (even when the syllable ends with a consonant cluster: contrast *sent* with *send*). Syllable-initial voicing, on the other hand, has no effect on the vowel.

[21] It is possible that most if not all grammatically simple monosyllables in English might be treated in prosodic analysis as (C)V(C) syllables. Most consonant clusters show smeared features of some kind, and there are very few pairs of clusters which differ only in the *order* of their components. So T. Hill (1966) in effect treats English [spr] as a single consonant, a 'sigmatized and rhotacized' labial stop.

This is one of a number of reasons[22] for treating the English syllable as consisting of two components, an *initial* and a *final*, the former corresponding to everything that precedes the vowel, the latter to the vowel and everything that follows it. This division has, interestingly, some empirical confirmation from the study of speech errors: a wrong pairing of initial with final (e.g. 'key and take' for *tea and cake*) is far more common than such errors as the interchange of final consonantisms (which would give, for *tea and cake*, 'teak and kay').

Making this division of the syllable, we can now set up, for the final, a *v-prosody*, whose main exponents are voicing throughout the final and prolongation of the vowel articulation, and in opposition to this a *v̌-prosody*, whose main exponents are shortening of the vowel articulation and voicing terminating with the first obstruent articulation.

It does not necessarily follow that voicing should also be treated prosodically in the initial. However, in utterances of the structure with which we are concerned, voicelessness in initial position is always accompanied by aspiration, and further (if, stretching the facts a little for the sake of illustration, we assume that utterance-final stops are unreleased) aspiration is diagnostic of the initial, as is the plosive release itself; therefore we can reasonably extract two initial prosodies, *plosion with aspiration* and *plosion with voice*. Thus voicing is a prosodic feature in all positions.

Another candidate for prosodic status is nasality. Phonemically there are no nasalized vowels in English; but phonetically there are. All finals of CVC syllables are one or two types: oral vowel + oral consonant, or nasalized vowel + nasal consonant. In prosodic phonology there is no need to regard one of the two parts of the final as having inherent nasality and the other as having conditioned nasality: rather, we set up an *n-prosody* for the final whose exponent is, simply, lowering of the velum.[23]

It does not seem possible to regard nasality as prosodic in the initial, where it is neither smeared nor diagnostic.

There may be a similar argument for treating as prosodic the distinction between [č ǰ] on the one hand and [k g] on the other. At least in the author's dialect, there is a marked difference between the vowel articulations in *rich*, *ridge* and those in *rick*, *rig*: in the latter the vowel is rather higher and more front. Before labial and alveolar consonants the vowel articulation is virtually identical with that of *rich*, not that of *rick*; so perhaps we should speak of a *k-prosody* whose exponents are dorsal articulation of the final consonant, and raising and fronting of the vowel articulation if it would in any case be high and front. There are also peculiarities of vowel articulation associated with final [l], so that this consonant articulation too should be regarded as an exponent of a prosody.

Thus we find that the system of consonantal phonematic units for the last place in the syllable is very restricted, consisting at most of the seven elements $p, t, č/k, f, θ, s, š$.[24]

---

[22] In general, there are far more interdependencies between the occurence of vowels and final consonants than between vowels and initial consonants: cf., again, Hill (1966).

[23] Were we including in our description syllables with more than one postvocalic consonant, we would have to give the exponent as 'lowering of the velum continued until perceptibly after oral closure has been effected' to allow for clusters like [nt] of which the second element is non-nasal.

[24] Final nasals will be treated as exponents of the stop phonematic units and the nasality prosody.

In the initial, as already mentioned, voicing is (probably) prosodic, and nasality is not. There are no other smeared features. There are, however, three features which are diagnostic of the initial: presence of [h], of [r], and of the 'clear' variety of [l]. These would be treated as prosodies of the initial, leaving the following system of consonantal phonematic units for this position: $p, t, č, k, f, \theta, s, š, m, n, j, w$.

As far as the vowel units are concerned, prosodic analysis very often, in a diversity of languages, finds it to be the case that the distinction between front and back vowel qualities is not to be treated phonematically. This is because there are generally perceptible differences in the articulation not only of the vowels but also of certain surrounding consonants. In pronouncing, say, [kɪk kek kæk kak kɔk kʊk], it is not only the vowel that changes; the point of articulation of the velar also moves back, and in the latter two syllables the consonants as well as the vowels are uttered with slight and strong lip rounding respectively. It is for this reason that we would probably wish to abstract what prosodic analysts have traditionally called *yotization* and *labiovelarization* as syllable prosodies. Denoting these by superscript ^{j} and ^{w}, we may account for the six 'short' peaks that occur in monosyllabic utterances by positing the following phonematic and prosodic systems:

Phonematic units: *I, E, A*   29
Syllable prosodies: ^{j}, ^{w}
Occurring complexes of phonematic units and prosodies:

^jI — exponent	[ɪ]
^wI	[ʊ]
^jE	[e]
A	[a]
^jA	[æ]
^wA	[ɔ]

We have also, however, to consider the 'long' or 'complex' peaks. We have previously seen that in a phonemic analysis there is good reason to consider some of them bisegmental, and the rest as composed of a vowel phoneme and a length phoneme; in a prosodic analysis the semivowel offglides, just as much as the length, must be regarded as exponents of prosodies. In most cases there is a clear difference of quality between a vowel occurring as a simple peak and the most closely comparable vowel occurring as the first element of a complex peak: see the second column of (15), pp. 30f, remembering that the notation there used can capture only a very few of the perceptually distinguishable points in vowel space.

In the absence of the rigid conditions on phonemic analysis, there are some advantages in a rather Trager-Smithian interpretation of the complex peaks; in particular it obviates any need to increase the number of vowel phonematic units. Trager and Smith (1951), following Bloch and Trager (1941), analysed all 'complex' peaks as sequences of a vowel and one of three semivowel offglides, palatal /j/, velar /w/, and a lowering/centralizing glide which they identified with the phoneme /h/; the peaks which in our classical-phonemic analysis (pp. 30–35) we treated as containing the length phoneme /:/ were distributed among these three classes, /i:/ being treated as /ij/, /a:/ as /ah/, etc.

In a prosodic framework, as just mentioned, the semivowel offglides must be replaced by prosodies, whose domain is the 'final': *postpalatalization*, which may be represented by ^{i}: *postlabialization*, represented by ^{u}; and *postcentralization*, represented best by ^{r} in view of such alternations as [béə]: [béərɪŋ].

This gives us what appears to be a very simple analysis of the English stressed vowel system. Phonetically there are at least twenty contrasting peaks. Our classical phonemic analysis had nine vowel phonemes, two semivowel offglides, and a length phoneme. The prosodic analysis requires just three phonematic units, two syllable prosodies, and three final prosodies.

However, we cannot stop there. A full description must also state (i) which prosodies can cooccur with one another and with given phonematic units, and (ii) what the phonetic exponents are of each prosody and each phonematic unit. (i) is simply a phonotactic statement, which is sometimes said to be rendered unnecessary by prosodic analysis;[25] (ii) is universally agreed to be necessary in order to make the analysis empirically testable.[26] The phonetic exponence statement is here presented—or, more strictly, a fragment of it; for ideally the phonetic exponents of phonological units should be stated in terms directly and immediately relatable to instrumental observation.

Exponents of phonematic vowel units:
Phonematic unit A: Relatively open vowel articulation; the exponents of any syllable prosodies manifested only to a slight extent.

Phonematic unit E: Basically mid to half open vowel articulation tending to greater closeness in the presence of final prosodies ^{i} and ^{u} and greater openness in the presence of syllable prosody ^{w}.

Phonematic unit I: Relatively close vowel articulation; the exponents of both syllable and final prosodies manifested to a high degree.

For all phonematic units, in the absence of any syllable prosody, the articulation is central to back and lip rounding is absent: i.e. *A* is then realized as [a], *E* as [ə], *I* would be realized as something like [ʉ] except that it never occurs unaccompanied by a syllable prosody.

Exponents of syllable prosodies:
Prosody ^{j}: Raising of the front of the tongue throughout the syllable, resulting in prevelar articulation when consonant unit č/k and k-prosody (cf. p. 64) are present. Spreading of lips, again throughout the syllable.

Prosody ^{w}: Raising of the back of the tongue, resulting in postvelar articulation when consonant unit č/k and k-prosody are present; rounding of lips.

Exponents of final prosodies:
Prosody ^{i}: Raising of the front of the tongue in approximately the last third of

---

[25] Because, if units A and B (be they prosodic or phonematic) are linked by any kind of distributional regularity, it is always possible to posit a prosody whose domain is the union of the domains of A and B, and whose exponence statements embody the distributional regularity. The problem with this approach is that the newly posited second-order prosodies may well themselves be subject to distributional regularities, and there is risk of an infinite regress.

[26] This appears to be the meaning of the favourite Firthian phrase 'to secure renewal of connection'.

the vowel articulation and in what follows up to the end of the syllable; more peripheral articulation over the first two-thirds of the vowel.

Prosody [u]: Raising of the back of the tongue and rounding of the lips in the last third of the vowel and in what follows to the end of the syllable; more central and slightly more open articulation over the first two-thirds of the vowel.

Prosody [r]: Generally, more open and more central articulation of the whole vowel, with a movement to a mid central position at its conclusion if this represents either a lowering or a centralization. When, however, this prosody occurs in combination with phonematic unit *E* and prosody [w], it has no exponents except that mentioned immediately hereafter.

All final prosodies have as an exponent a prolongation of the vowel articulation.

I append a table of correspondences between the peaks recognized in our phonemic analysis (see (16) and (17)) and the possible combinations of phonematic units and prosodies in the present analysis. It is a table of correspondences, not of identities; apart from other anisomorphisms between the two types of analysis, the exponents of the prosodies are not confined to the vowel but extend over other parts of the syllable. Syllable prosodies are represented by left-hand superscripts, final prosodies by right-hand superscripts.

$/\mathrm{I}/$	...	$^{j}\mathrm{I}$	$/\mathrm{i{:}}/$	...	$^{j}\mathrm{I}^{i}$	**30**
$/e/$	...	$^{j}\mathrm{E}$	$/\mathrm{I{:}}/$	...	$^{j}\mathrm{I}^{r}$	
$/æ/$	...	$^{j}\mathrm{A}$	$/e{:}/$	...	$^{j}\mathrm{E}^{r}$	
$/a/$	...	A	$/a{:}/$	...	A^{r}	
$/ɔ/$	...	$^{w}\mathrm{A}$	$/ə{:}/$	...	E^{r}	
$/\mathrm{U}/$	...	$^{w}\mathrm{I}$	$/o{:}/$	...	$^{w}\mathrm{E}^{r}$	
$/ej/$	...	$^{j}\mathrm{E}^{i}$	$/\mathrm{U{:}}/$	...	$^{w}\mathrm{I}^{r}$	
$/aj/$	...	A^{i}	$/u{:}/$	...	$^{w}\mathrm{I}^{u}$	
$/oj/$	...	$^{w}\mathrm{E}^{i}$	$/æw/$	...	$^{j}\mathrm{A}^{u}$	
			$/əw/$	...	E^{u}	

The above is a slight and partial sketch of a prosodic analysis of one fragment of English phonology. It perhaps illustrates the statement made earlier, that while phonemic analysis was primarily concerned with paradigmatic relations such as contrast, prosodic analysis was as concerned or more concerned with syntagmatic relations. As in the sketch just given, syllable structure was usually stated prior to giving details of prosodic and phonematic phenomena within the syllable, the reverse of the usual classical phonemic procedure whereby the phonemes were listed first and syllable structure was mentioned, if at all, only in the logically posterior phonotactic statement: here the prosodic treatment, with its explicit recognition of the fact that segments are not isolated but participate in higher-order structures, may well be preferable.

3.4 Conclusion

Prosodic phonology, historically speaking, drew much-needed attention to aspects of phonological structure which classical phonemic theory had tended to neglect (the practice of the best classical phonemicists is another matter). Of particular interest is the abandonment of the biuniqueness requirement, anticipating what generative phonology has often regarded as one of its own most important innovations. The same is true of some aspects of the polysystemic approach, notably the recognition of the distinctive phonological behaviour of words of foreign origin and in some cases of particular grammatically defined classes. And clarity in the presentation of analyses was much improved by prosodic analysts' usual practice of working 'downwards' from the abstract phonematic and prosodic elements to their exponents, rather than 'upwards' from the phonetic data to the phonemics and then the morphophonemics.

The reasons for the failure of prosodic phonology to gain wide acceptance are in part mere historical accidents; but the theory does have certain drawbacks in itself, above all the great complexity of the descriptive statements it requires.

This complexity has two main sources. One is the polysystemic approach in its extreme form, with its insistence that terms in different systems should not be identified with one another. This leads to a great deal of repetition within different parts of the analysis. The other source of complexity is the phonetic exponence statements. Prosodic phonological analyses were based wherever possible, especially in later work, on the principle of 'a single formula, a lexical-item phonological formula, for each lexical item' (Sprigg 1966, 431);[27] otherwise put, they were essentially morphophonemic. It was thus necessary to embody all of what a classical phonemicist would call morphophonemic alternation and allophonic variation in a single set of exponence statements; and what is more important, these statements were of a very restricted kind, being all of the following form:

> The prosody/phonematic unit X has the exponent(s)   **31**
> Y_1 in the environment(s) Z_1
> Y_2 in the environment(s) Z_2
>
>   . . .
>
> Y_n in the environment(s) Z_n

where each environment Z_i had to be defined in terms of phonological and/or grammatical elements. In very many cases this will result in unnecessary complications, as Palmer (1956b, 161) in effect admits:

> In the completed statement [of certain harmonic phenomena in Tigre] two kinds of prosodic system are required. The terms of the one system, involving 'vowel harmony', will be referred to as α and α, and the terms of the other, involving 'vowel-consonant harmony', will be referred to as ϕ and ϕ. Since openness is a feature (though not the only feature) of both α and ϕ, *the analysis will be greatly complicated if the data considered for the statement of one prosody differ in terms of the other* [emphasis mine: AHS]

—because it will then be necessary to include in the description of the exponents of each of the prosodies reference to the exponents of the other. The

---

[27] This aim does not seem easy to reconcile with polysystemicism. Consider the situation where two allomorphs of one morpheme have corresponding segments in different positions in the syllable, e.g. *n* in English *(do)n't* and *not*. In such cases the corresponding segments are, on the standard assumptions of prosodic phonology, unrelated, being terms in different systems.

complications could in great measure have been avoided by stating the exponents of one of the prosodies by reference to the structure existing *after* the exponence statement for the other prosody had been put into effect: what is also known as sequential rule application. The reason why this was not done was, in part at least, that prosodic phonology positively welcomed complication, as reflecting 'the highly complex patterns of language' (Firth 1948). But most complexities in the world are due to a great multiplicity of simple factors; and the business of a phonological theory, as of any scientific theory, is to point these factors out. We do not need theoretical assistance to appreciate that the patterns of language are highly complex.

4 Stratificational Phonology

As we saw in Chapter One, the notion 'mixing of levels' is ambiguous. On the one hand there is mixing of levels in *analysis*, where the linguist uses higher-level (e.g. grammatical) information to justify a particular lower-level (e.g. phonological) description; it is now generally agreed that this is not objectionable. On the other hand there is mixing of levels in *presentation*, which is, to a greater or lesser extent, a characteristic of many theories. Generative phonology is particularly liberal with this kind of level-mixing; it allows both grammatical conditions on phonological rules[1] and phonological conditions on syntactic transformations.

Stratificational grammar developed in the 1960s, and one of its main claims is that mixing of levels in presentation is an offence against the way language is organized.[2] To understand stratificational phonology it is necessary first to have a view of the complete organization of a stratificational grammar (SG).

4.1 Organization of a stratificational grammar

Language can be viewed in various ways—a set of habits, a set of sentences, a set of rules or organizing principles, are among the possibilities. To Sydney Lamb, the founder of SG, language is essentially a *code*. Like any other code, it links a set of *messages* with a set of *signals*. In the case of language, the messages are what can be labelled conceptual structures, and the signals consist of phonic material, either as articulated by the speaker or as received by the hearer. The speaker *encodes* the message into a signal; the hearer *decodes* the signal into what, errors and ambiguities apart, should be the speaker's original message. It is an axiom of SG that the encoding and decoding mechanisms are describable by one and the same set of statements, merely read in opposite directions.

SG holds that both the encoding and the decoding processes take place in a small number of discrete stages, and that each stopping-place, as it were, corresponds to a distinct level of linguistic organization, or *stratum*. It follows that a linguistic description must consist essentially of two interrelated parts.

The encoding-decoding device consists of a set of statements defining the relationship of the units of each stratum to the strata 'above' (nearer the

[1] See Chapter Six, pp. 151–5.

[2] At least, this was so before Lamb (1971) proposed to revise the theory to incorporate 'bypassing lines' which in fact make it possible, *inter alia,* to express syntactic conditions on phonological alternations, though not vice versa. As Lamb recognizes, this makes language much less stratified than he previously thought it to be; the strata have undergone a 'partial coalescence'. In the rest of this chapter I do not discuss this innovation further; little has been published on it beyond Lamb's rather programmatic statement.

conceptual level) and 'below' (nearer the phonic level). These statements between them describe the *realization* of a message as a signal, or vice versa, and collectively they are termed the *realizational portion* of the grammar. In the domain of phonology they correspond roughly to morphophonemic and allophonic rules.

At right angles, so to speak, to this 'vertical' organization, each stratum has its own 'horizontal' organization independent of the other strata. This defines the elements of the stratum and their possible combinations, up to the largest unit relevant at that stratum; it is termed the *tactics* of that stratum (cf. 'phonotactics').

In the version of stratificational theory presented by Lockwood (1972b), there are six strata: those of gnostemics, sememics, lexemics, morphemics, phonemics and phonetics. Of these the first two are chiefly relevant to semantics. The lexemic tactics (lexotactics) defines the syntactic possibilities of the language, while the morphotactics defines the possibilities of word structure and to some extent also the structure of phrases. Morphophonemic phenomena are handled by realizational statements between the morphemic and phonemic strata, with the help (as will be seen) of the phonotactics. The phonetic stratum is said by Lockwood to 'provide for non-distinctive phonetic facts'; its details have apparently not yet been worked out,[3] but presumably the tactics of this stratum will define a set of possible phonetic representations for the language in question.

4.2 The phonemic stratum

All the strata have a common general structure. The diagram which follows of the organization of the phonemic stratum could, with a change of prefix (e.g. replace *phon-* and *morph-* by *lex-* and *sem-* respectively), do equally well for most of the others. Note that the 'emes' of a stratum are its minimal tactical units; they are, however, themselves composite, being composed of smaller units, the primes of the stratum, marked by the suffix *-on* (like elementary particles in physics). In the diagram boxes with curved ends stand for types of linguistic unit; boxes with flat ends stand for sets of statements, whether tactic or realizational.

The central point of the stratum is that marked 'phonemes'.[4] This is not quite the classical phonemic level: that corresponds rather to the SG level of 'phonemic signs'. The level of phonemes is slightly more abstract, since it has base forms for those alternations which are dealt with in the phonemic alternation pattern. These alternations are a subset of the alternations traditionally termed morphophonemic; most other such alternations are dealt with in the morphonic alternation pattern which describes the phonemic realization of morphons (traditional morphophonemes, and the primes of the morphemic stratum). The only alternations not handled in one or other of these patterns are suppletions, which being totally irrelevant to phonology are described in higher alternation patterns still.

How is it decided whether a given alternation is morphonic or phonemic? Lockwood's criterion is as follows (Lockwood 1972b, 232):

---

[3] At any rate, it had not been when Lockwood was writing, and it has not come to my notice that it has been done since.

[4] The shape of the box at that point will be explained in due course.

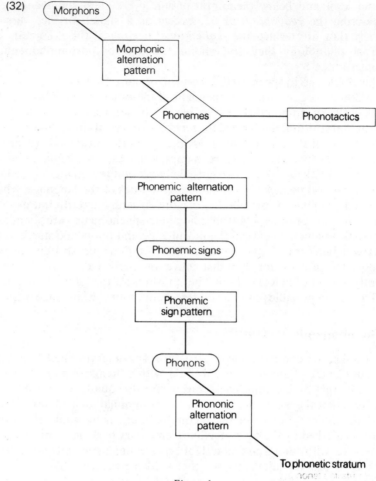

Figure 1

The morphonic alternation pattern will handle the kinds of alternation which are better treated in terms of whole segments than in terms of components.[5] ... The phonemic alternation pattern will deal with the alternations better treated in terms of components.

However, it is another axiom of SG that for all alternations,[6] the conditioning environment can be stated in terms of the tactics of the stratum to which the alternation belongs. For both the alternation patterns with which we are concerned, this stratum is the phonemic: so all conditioning environments for morphonic and phonemic alternations alike must be statable in terms of the phonotactics. Now—speaking in general terms, not purely of SG—there are basically two ways of stating the conditioning environment of a realization rule.

[5] 'Component' in SG = 'feature' in many other theories.
[6] There is a small class of exceptions, but these are nowhere characterized and it is not clear how they fit into the picture, so I have ignored them.

One is in terms of the level of representation on which the *input* to the rule stands, e.g. an environment for a morphophonemic rule stated in morphophonemic terms: this type of environment statement is regular for allophonic rules in classical phonemics and for all rules in standard generative phonology. The other is in terms of the level of representation on which the *output* of the rule stands, e.g. conditions on a morphophonemic rule stated in phonemic terms; outside SG this type of statement has until recently been little used, but various proposals for making use of 'surface phonetic constraints' in generative phonology are essentially proposals to introduce conditions of this kind into the theory.[7] Let us call these two types of conditioning *input conditioning* and *output conditioning* respectively. Then SG recognizes rules of both kinds. Some rules are most easily stated as input-conditioned, and these will go in the phonemic alternation pattern; others are most easily stated as output-conditioned, and these will go in the morphonic alternation pattern. But it is clear that it is not logically necessary that the assignment of alternations by this test coincide with their assignment by Lockwood's criterion previously stated. But since every alternation has to be assigned to one alternation pattern or the other, we can only conclude that SG asserts that, as a matter of contingent fact,

All morphophonemic alternations are best stated either as output- **33** conditioned alternations in terms of segments, or as input-conditioned alternations in terms of components.

Now this is an empirical claim, and an interesting one. It is an empirical claim because in SG 'best stated' is a notion defined rigorously in terms of a precise simplicity measure, details of which will be given later: the best account of a given set of phenomena is the simplest in terms of that measure. It is unfortunate that stratificational writers seem unaware that (33) *is* an empirical claim, and do not attempt to support it, since if it were found to be valid it would be very strong evidence in favour of the SG approach to phonology.

The phonotactics traces almost the whole sound system of the language, except for allophonic variation. It gives a certain amount of information about the arrangements of components in segments, viz. such as can be made in statements of the form 'All phonemes belonging to such-and-such an independently motivated phonotactic class contain such-and-such a component'; and it gives full information on the arrangement of phonemes, on the one hand in clusters, on the other hand in syllables, phonological words, and higher-rank phonological units. But the phonotactics does not venture outside the realm of phonology; in particular it does not deal with the 'phonemic composition of morphemes', for the very good reason that in SG[8] morphemes are not composed of phonemes. 'The elements of a stratum,' says Lamb, 'are obviously unique to that stratum'; and in SG a unit on one stratum cannot be *composed of* units on another stratum. Rather a morpheme (more accurately, a morphemic sign) is composed of morphons which are *realized by* phonemes. The phonotactics therefore can take no

---

[7] Made to some degree under the influence of SG ideas on the subject—if I can speak as one (though not the first) who has made such a proposal. More on this in Chapter Eight.
[8] And not only in SG. Already in 1931 Trubetzkoy had pointed out (*TCLP* 4, 295) that 'the morphophoneme is a part of the morpheme, while the phoneme is a part of the syllable.'

account of morpheme boundaries; word boundaries are another matter, since SG assumes, like many varieties of classical phonemics, that a unit which it is reasonable to call a word can be defined phonologically.

The phonemic signs, which are closely comparable to classical phonemes (most importantly, they satisfy the biuniqueness requirement), consist of phonons; the manner in which phonons combine to form phonemic signs is the concern of the phonemic *sign pattern*. In general, a given phonemic sign does not contain all the phonons present in the segment which it represents; many of the latter are phonotactically determined. For example, most if not all languages must be analysed as having (*a*) a phonon 'vocalic' and (*b*) a phonotactic class 'vowels'; and (*a*) is a component of just those segments that realize phonemes belonging to the class (*b*). Clearly it is wasteful to say in the phonotactics that such and such phonemes are vowels and *also* to say in the phonemic sign pattern that the corresponding phonemic signs contain the phonon 'vocalic'. Consequently an SG will represent this phonon as arising directly from the phonotactics, and the phonemic signs representing vowels will not contain it.[9]

The phonons stand for individual features of articulation such as 'vocalic', 'labial', 'unvoiced'. They are positive terms only; there is, for instance, no phonon 'not labial' or 'not unvoiced'.[10] They are therefore sometimes known as *singulary* (or *unary*) features, in contradistinction to the *binary* (in some cases *multinary*) features that we shall meet in the next chapter, which consist of an axis plus a specification of position on that axis, e.g. [+labial], [−nasal], [2 stress].

4.3 Types of linguistic relationships

A favourite stratificational description of language is 'a network of relationships'; and in all strictness SG does not recognize 'linguistic objects' (except at the phonetic and conceptual extremities of the network) but only relationships—though it is nevertheless convenient to speak, as I have done, in terms of 'units' and 'elements'. This orientation (like the notion of strata itself) comes to SG from the work of Louis Hjelmslev (e.g. Hjelmslev 1948; 1954; 1961; see also Fischer-Jørgensen 1975, 114–143), which is noteworthy among other things for its emphasis on the 'form' of the relationships that constitute linguistic structure rather than the 'substance'—articulation and sound—in which that structure is manifested: an approach that is open to the objection (cf. p. 47) that it fails to do justice to differences between language and other symbol-systems, or to the fact that to no small extent the 'substance' determines the 'form'.

SG is far from ignoring substance: the phonons are intended to correspond to specifiable phonic properties. But substance is encountered only at the periphery of language, in sound and (it is held) in conceptual structure; in between there is pure form, pure relationship.

[9] To represent this kind of possibility one might add to diagram (32) a broken line running from 'phonotactics' to 'phonons'.

[10] Lockwood (1969; 1972a; 1972b) has developed a theory of markedness, differing in some respects from Prague School theory, which allows the 'unmarked' member of a set of related phonic properties to be represented by the *absence* of a phonon. The question which member of such a set is unmarked is taken to be a matter to be decided for each language separately, and the basic criterion is simplicity of the total description.

The most distinctive claim of SG is that all the linguistic relationships that exist, whether tactic or realizational, within or between strata, belong to a very small number of types (the present figure is about eleven), the most important of which are definable in terms of three simple dichotomies:

Does the relationship involve a single higher-level or higher-stratum **34a** element realized by or consisting of two or more lower-level or lower-stratum elements (together or as alternatives), or conversely? (DOWNWARD *v.* UPWARD)

Between the two or more elements referred to in (a), does there exist any **b** relationship of sequencing or priority? (ORDERED *v.* UNORDERED)

Are these two or more elements found together, or are they alternatives? **c** (AND *v.* OR)

In the realizational portion of the grammar, relationships hold between one or more higher-level or higher-stratum elements (the *realizates*) and one or more lower-level or lower-stratum elements (the *realizations*); but they are always either one-many or many-one relationships, never many-many. In the tactic portion, the relationship is one of constituency (composition) rather than realization. In either case it may be conveniently represented by the symbol /, which stands for 'is realized as' or 'consists of' as the case may be.

The basic notation system of SG is a graphic one.[11] The grammar of a language is modelled as a vast diagram, with conceptual substance at the top and phonic substance at the bottom; every linguistic element, on whatever stratum, corresponds to some line segment in the diagram; by tracing the connections of this line it is possible to determine the elements on other strata, and ultimately the conceptual and phonic elements, to which in various environments it corresponds, and also its role in the tactics of its own stratum. Where a line divides, and at certain other points, there are *nodes*: each type of node symbolizes a particular type of relationship between the element(s) represented by the line(s) entering the node from above and the element(s) represented by the line(s) entering it from below. In the realizational portion of the grammar, the former are the realizates, the latter the realizations.

The choices offered by the three basic dichotomies of (34) give rise, in theory, to eight major types of relationship; one of these, however (the upward ordered or), appears not to occur. The remainder function as follows:

Figure 2

---

[11] There is an interesting anticipation of this system (though without distinction between different types of relationship) in Henderson's (1948) analysis of consonant cluster types in Lushai; the interested reader might like to try redrawing Henderson's diagram on the normal stratificational pattern.

(i)   The DOWNWARD UNORDERED AND, symbolized, when algebraic instead of graphic notation is used, by such formulae as $a/b \cdot c$: '*a* is realized as (consists of) *b* and *c* occurring simultaneously.' This type of relationship appears, for instance, in a phonemic sign consisting of several phonons; similarly a phonological phrase might be analysed as consisting of two simultaneous parts, an intonation contour and a residue.

(ii)   The DOWNWARD ORDERED AND, symbolized a/bc: '*a* is realized as (consists of) *b* and *c* in that order.' All hierarchical structure in phonology can be expressed by relationships of this kind, e.g. the composition of clusters or of syllables; so can epenthesis, which may be treated as the realization of one morphon by two (successive) phonemes.

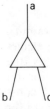

Figure 3

(iii, iv)   The UPWARD UNORDERED AND, symbolized $x \cdot y \mathbin{/} z$: '*x* and *y* occurring simultaneously are realized as *z*,' and the UPWARD ORDERED AND, symbolized $x\,y/z$: '*x* and *y* occurring successively are realized as *z*.' These are used for what is termed portmanteau realization,[12] of which a well-known morphophonemic example is the realization of the French morpheme sequence *à le* as the single phoneme /o/. Examples of the upward unordered and are more difficult to find in phonology; a case in point might be that stress and the syllabic peak, which at some level in the phonotactics are presuably separate elements, are manifested as a single phoneme (a stressed vowel).

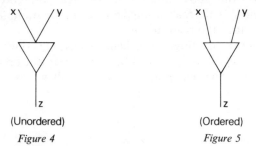

(Unordered)	(Ordered)
Figure 4	*Figure 5*

(v)   The DOWNWARD UNORDERED OR, symbolized $a \mathbin{/} b\,,c$: '*a* is realized as *b* or *c*.' In the realizational portion of the grammar, this relationship denotes free variation or optionality (conditioned variation is handled by another mechanism—see below). In the tactics the downward unordered or is used for most paradigmatic relationships, e.g. that between the phonotactic unit 'vowel' and the various vowel phonemes.

[12] The term is originally due to H. Dumpty (see *Alice through the looking glass,* ch. 6).

Figure 6

(vi)   The DOWNWARD ORDERED OR, symbolized $a / b + c$: 'a is realized as b if the appropriate conditioning factor is present, as c otherwise.' This is SG's mechanism for handling conditioned alternations. Each of the branches below the node is tested in turn, from left to right, to see if the conditioning factors for any of the preferred realizations are present; the actual realization in a given environment is the first one reached where these factors do prove to be present. If the conditions are not met for any of the preferred realizations, then the rightmost (lowest preference) realization is chosen. The node thus corresponds to a morphophonemic rule, for instance, of the type: 'Morphophoneme $//M//$ is realized by phoneme $/P_1/$ in environment E_1, by $/P_2/$ in environment E_2, . . . (etc.) . . . and by $/P_n/$ elsewhere.'

Figure 7

All branches of a downward ordered or, except the rightmost, must lead to an ENABLER node (graphic symbol: a black circle), which gives effect to the conditioning factors mentioned in the last paragraph. The enabler stands at the bottom end of a 'conditioning line' which branches off higher up from a line or lines representing the element(s) that constitute the conditioning environment. The conditioning environment may precede, follow or be simultaneous with the conditioned element; in the example given here, it follows. The diagram represents the realization of the English morphon $/F/$,[13] which occurs in such morphemes as *knife* and *shelf*, as the phoneme $/v/$ in the presence of the plural suffix morphon $/Z/$ and as the phoneme $/f/$ elsewhere; it is accompanied by an algebraic statement of the alternation.[14]

---

[13] In SG writings it is normal for the symbols for all types of elements (phonemes, morphons, lexons, etc.) to be enclosed in single obliques; where necessary an abbreviation for the type of element (P for phoneme, MN for morphon, etc.) may be added as a superscript before the left-hand oblique.
[14] One problem with the device here described is that certain alternations may be conditioned by both preceding and following context: I have not found these discussed in the SG literature, but it would seem natural in such circumstances to allow two enabler nodes and two conditioning lines (possibly three, if there was also a simultaneous environment) to be associated with one downward ordered or.

(Note that in SG diagrams, line crossings have no significance unless they are marked by a node; it is just that, with only two dimensions to play with, we cannot avoid them. In algebraic statements, ‖ introduces an environment;——X means 'before X'; X—— means 'after X'; + means 'or if the above condition is not satisfied';—— means 'any environment at all'. Thus the statement given may be read: 'MN/F/ is realized as P/v/ when it is followed by MN/Z/; if that condition is not satisfied it is realized as P/f/ in all environments.')

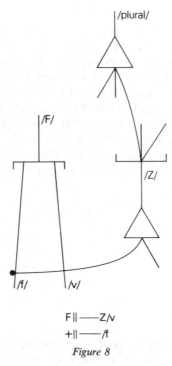

$$F \parallel \text{———} Z/\text{v}$$
$$+ \parallel \text{———} /f$$

Figure 8

(vii) The UPWARD UNORDERED OR, symbolized *x*, *y* / *z*: 'either *x* or *y* is realized as *z*.' In the realizational portion of the grammar this node denotes *neutralization*—a term used by stratificationalists in a more general sense than usual, to refer to any situation where a higher-level distinction between two or more elements is not reflected by a lower-vowel distinction. In this sense, for instance, the phoneme /f/ which is one of the realizations of the morphon /F/ is also, by neutralization, the realization of the non-alternating morpheme /f/. This situation is diagrammed in Figure 10.

Figure 9

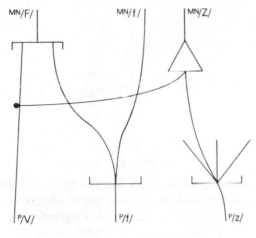

Figure 10

In addition to the basic seven node types and the enabler, two other types of node perform special functions:

(viii)   The COORDINATION NODE (graphic symbol: a semicircle), symbolized algebraically by $p \mid (q)^*$: 'p is realized by (consists of) an arbitrary number of elements of type q.' In tactic patterns on all strata, it is sometimes necessary to describe a situation where a single higher-rank element can contain an unlimited number of lower-rank elements all of the same kind. The ordinary nodes are incapable in principle of describing such a situation,[15] and the coordination node has been added for this reason. It is chiefly used in syntax, but can have uses in phonotactics, as when one wishes, for instance, to state the syllabic structure of words; thus in English, though in fact any given dialect contains a longest word, in principle there is no limit to the length of words, and a coordination node is necessary if this fact is to be stated in the grammar.

Figure 11

(ix)   The REDUPLICATION NODE. In many languages we find that certain morphemes are realized by phoneme sequences whose only constant property is that they are identical to some phoneme sequence in their environment; or, even more commonly, the phononic composition of a phonemic sign is variable but one phonon is always identical to one that appears in a neighbouring segment

---

[15] An exactly similar problem was faced by transformational-generative syntax when dealing with coordination, and likewise had to be solved by positing a type of relationship not used elsewhere.

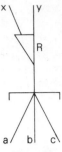

Figure 12

(what is usually termed assimilation). Such a relationship is difficult to express using the notations so far mentioned, and so a special node is used for the purpose (represented by a vertical wedge in the above diagram). The diagram is thus interpretable: *y* is realized as either *a*, *b* or *c*; *x*, where it precedes *y*, is also realized as either *a*, *b* or *c*, but the realization of *x* must be the same as the realization of *y*, so that the only possible realizations are *aa*, *bb*, *cc*. A situation where consonants were palatalized before a front vowel and labialized before a rounded vowel might be represented as in the acompanying diagram. The line ending in a small circle stands for zero, i.e., in this case, the absence of both the feature 'front' and the feature 'rounded'.

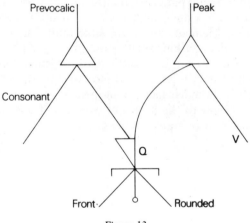

Figure 13

It is also possible for the reduplicative element to follow the reduplicated element ('progressive assimilation').

An algebraic representation of the situation just diagrammed might be:

$$\begin{aligned}&\text{Prevocalic/Consonant} \ \cdot = Q \qquad\qquad\qquad \textbf{35}\\&\text{Peak} \qquad\quad /Q \cdot V\\&Q \qquad\qquad\quad /\text{Frontal, Rounded, } \theta\end{aligned}$$

If we were dealing with a progressive assimilation, the equals sign would follow the label of the reduplication node instead of preceding it.

We have not so far considered one very important type of relationship in SG: the relationship between elements in tactic patterns and elements in the realizational component. Generally speaking, it is the *emes* of the stratum in question (phonemes, morphemes, etc.) that embody this relationship, since they are at once realizational units (realizing the *ons* of the next higher stratum) and the minimal units of the tactics of their own stratum. They are represented in the graphic notation[16] by a special type of node known as a *diamond*.

A typical diamond representing, say, a phoneme has the form shown in the accompanying diagram. The upper right-hand line connects to the phonotactics, and represents the phoneme in its tactic aspect; following this line we shall come to nodes that tell us the combinations in which this phoneme can figure, the phoneme classes to which it belongs, etc. The upper left-hand line connects the phoneme to the morphon or morphons of which it is a realization, and the lower right-hand line connects it to the phonemic sign or signs which are *its* realizations.

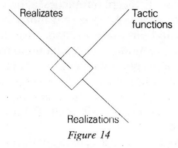

Realizates   Tactic
                    functions

Realizations

Figure 14

Not all diamonds, however, have this full form. Sometimes, for one reason or another (e.g. to provide a conditioning environment for an alternation), a phoneme must be posited of whose presence there is no overt marker—whose realization is zero. Such units are called *zero phonemes* or *upward-determined phonemes*, and may be represented by diamonds with connections to the phonotactics and to the level of morphons but no connections downwards, indicating that the phonemes in question have tactic functions and realize morphons but are not realized by any phonemic signs, phonons, etc.

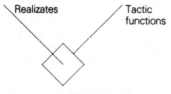

Realizates   Tactic
                    functions

Figure 15

The converse of the zero phoneme is the *empty phoneme* which does not realize any morphon. The epenthetic vowel that appears in certain occurrences of the English plural, possessive, third person singular, and past tense formative (e.g. *waited, houses*) is a likely example. An empty phoneme is naturally indicated by a diamond with a connection to the tactics and a realizational connection downwards but not upwards, as in Figure 16 overleaf.

---

[16] There is no established algebraic notation for diamonds.

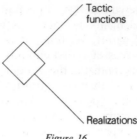

Tactic
functions

Realizations

Figure 16

It is also sometimes the case that a morphon, in addition to or instead of being overtly realized as a combination of phonons, has an effect on the tactical choices that are possible at the phonetic stratum. Consider, for instance, the effect of the accent morphon on the vowel system of Belorussian (Lockwood 1972b, 223). If this morphon is not present, the phonotactics allows for only a three-vowel system /i a u/; but the presence of the accent morphon results in a change in phonotactic possibilities, and a five-vowel system must then be provided for. Such situations are described in SG by locating the diamond representing the phoneme in question in the middle of the phonotactics instead of at its base, and allowing it to control choices in the phonotactics; in diagrams such controlling lines originate from the lower left side of the diamond. I reproduce (opposite) Lockwood's diagrammatic representation of the Belorussian situation, in which, for clarity, I have lettered the lines.[17]

A vowel in Belorussian (line *a*) consists of the phonon 'vocalic' (line *b*) plus one of the three choices leading from line *c*. In accordance with the principle of the ordered or, we first try line *e* to see if the realization of the morphon 'accent' occurs at the position in which we are interested (i.e. if line *d* is activated). If the answer is yes, the phoneme 'accent' (represented by the diamond) occurs, to be realized by the corresponding phonon (line *g*); and its occurrence presents us with the tactical choice arising out of line *h*. This line leads to the following possible combinations of phonons: front (via lines *l-q-s*); labial (via lines *l-q-t*); high and front (via *l-q-s* and *k-m-r*); high and labial (via *l-q-t* and *k-m-r*); or nothing at all (the zero element being chosen instead of line *j*). These five possibilities, in conjunction with 'vocalic', correspond to the vowels /e o i u a/ respectively. Suppose, however, line *d* is *not* activated. Then one of the two inputs 'from above' to the diamond is missing, and consequently we cannot get past it (thus the diamond, it will be seen, plays roughly the same role as an enabler node). We retreat along line *e* to the ordered or, and take either line *f* (which leads to 'high, front' via *n-r* + *p-q-s*, or to 'high, labial' via *n-r, p-q-t*) or the zero element; the former choice corresponds to the vowels /i u/, the latter presumably to /a/ (which, under this feature system, will be the 'unmarked' vowel).

4.4 The evaluation of alternative descriptions

It is generally the case, despite the paucity and simplicity of the descriptive devices that SG makes available, that it allows a given set of data to be analysed in more

17 I have also replaced some downward ordered *or* nodes by unordered ones.

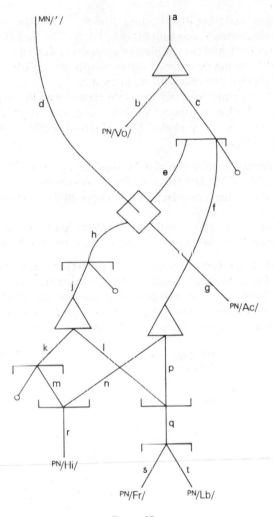

Figure 17

than one way; hence it becomes very important to establish criteria to choose between them. External justification (see Chapter One) has not been employed to any significant extent; instead SG has concentrated on a simplicity criterion, and much work has been done on the problem of so defining 'simplicity' that the description selected by the theory as simplest is also the one that seems to the linguist to capture significant generalizations best. At various times, various different simplicity measures have been put forward. The most recent is based directly on the number and complexity of the nodes required in a graphic representation of a description. It is as follows.

Considering separately each node in a diagram, count the number of lines leading from it (in all directions). Two lines per node are allowed free, since any node must have at least three lines leading from it;[18] each line beyond two leading from a given node counts as one unit of complexity. The 'scores' from all nodes of a diagram are totalled, and the simplest of competing descriptions is then defined to be the one with the lowest score. If two descriptions score the same on this test, the simpler of them is the one with fewer nodes.[19]

Take a simple example. Suppose a certain type of unit in the phonotactics of a language (call it 'initial obstruent cluster') can consist of the phonemes or phoneme sequences /p t k sp st sk/. This situation might be described in three plausible ways, among others:

An initial obstruent cluster is one of the following: /p t k sp st sk/, the first **36a** three being segments, the last three segment sequences.

An initial obstruent cluster consists of a stop optionally preceded by /s/; a **b** stop is either /p/ or /t/ or /k/.

An initial obstruent cluster is one of the following: /p t k s͡p s͡t s͡k/; all these **c** are single segments, the last three having the feature 'presibilated'.

From these verbal statements it is not at all easy to see which of these alternatives is the simplest. Let us therefore diagram the three descriptions, each in two parts: for the choice between them has consequences for two different parts of the grammar, the phonotactics and the phonemic sign pattern.

First, the three alternative phonotactic descriptions.

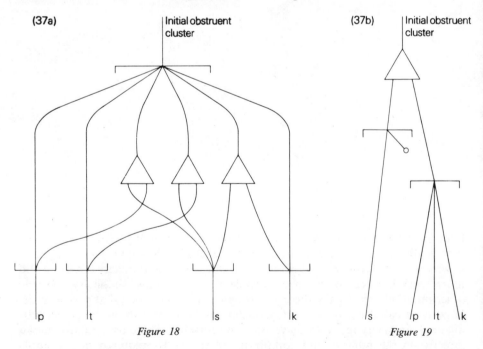

Figure 18   *Figure 19*

[18] Exceptions to this statement are diamond nodes for empty and zero elements, and the coordination node; these are treated as degenerate nodes and ignored completely.
[19] As in the line count, degenerate nodes (see previous footnote) are ignored.

(37c)

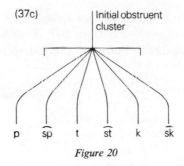

Figure 20

Diagram (37a) has eight nodes; one of these has seven lines running out of it, one four, and the remainder three, a total of 29; allowing two free lines per node the 'cost' of description (36a), from the phonotactic point of view, comes to 13. In (37b) there are three nodes and a total of ten lines; cost 4. And (37c) has one node which is the focus of seven lines, so that its cost is 5. Thus from the SG point of view, (36b) appears to provide marginally the best phonotactic description.

This is confirmed if we now look at the phonemic sign patterns which the various descriptions require. Descriptions (36a) and (36b) lead to the same set of phonemes and phonons:

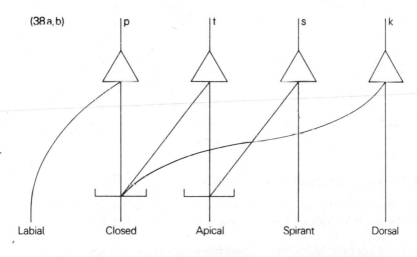

Figure 21

This has six nodes, so that 12 free lines are allowed; the actual number of lines is 19, so the cost of this part of the description is 7 (giving a total cost of 20 for description (36a) and 11 for (36b)).

Description (36c), with its single-segment 'presibilates', requires a different phonemic sign pattern: see (38c) overleaf.

Here we have eleven nodes, with 40 lines against a free allowance of 22; so that the cost is 18 in the phonemic sign pattern and 23 overall. Thus (36b) is, for SG, the simplest of the three descriptions and (36c), despite its considerable initial appeal, the most complicated.[20]

(38c)

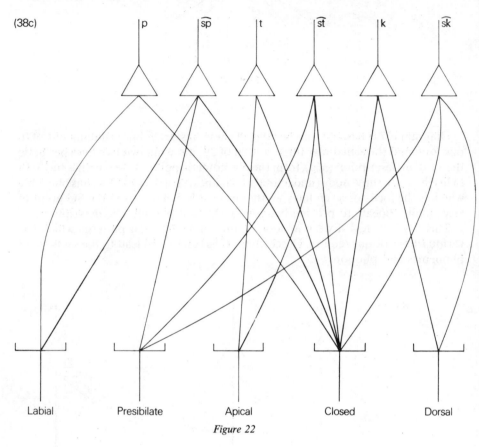

Labial   Presibilate   Apical   Closed   Dorsal

Figure 22

4.5   Two illustrative descriptions

I shall now present, as a partial example of stratificational description, a fragment of the phonotactics of English and a fragment of the morphonic alternation pattern.

The phonotactic fragment concerns word-initial clusters beginning with an obstruent. The possibilities are:

> Single obstruent: /p t č k b d ǰ g f θ s š v ð z/   **39**
> Plosive + liquid: /pl kl bl gl pr tr kr br dr gr/
> Fricative + liquid: /fl sl fr θr šr/

[20] It should, however, be borne in mind that the extra complexity introduced by description (36c) *might* be wiped out by greater simplification in the grammar as a whole, e.g. by unification of the description of initial and final 'presibilates'.

Fricative + nasal: /sm sn/
Fricative + plosive: /sp st sk/
Fricative + fricative: /sf/
Fricative + plosive + liquid: /spl skl spr str skr/

In (40) I diagram the phonotactics of this class of clusters.[21]

(40)

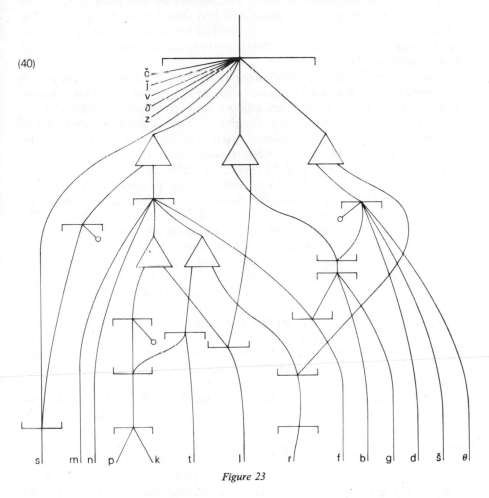

Figure 23

(40) actually accounts not only for initial obstruents and clusters beginning with obstruents but also for initial /l r m n/; it is in fact simpler for it to account for these initial resonants than not to.

In the morphonic alternation pattern, I will consider a relationship which in generative phonology has been called Velar Softening. As is well known, certain

---

[21] It is easy to determine which of two or more given stratificational descriptions is the simpler, but very hard indeed to determine whether one given description is the simplest possible. I do not make this claim for (40); it is meant merely to give an idea of the form that part of a tactic pattern in a stratificational phonology of English might take.

D

morphemes in English end with phonemic /k g/ in some environments, but with /s ǰ/ respectively in others; cf. *critic:criticize, reduction:reduce, ideologue:ideology, regal:regicide.* At one time the conditioning environment for this alternation will have been easily specifiable, the fronted consonant being found always and only before front vowels. In present-day English things seem much more complex. Quite apart from the fact that many morphemes do not participate in the alternation at all, those which do participate may show a 'hard' consonant before a front vowel (cf. *regalia, allegation* contrasted with *alleging*) or a 'soft' consonant before a back vowel (cf. *criticize*) or before a consonant (*reduced*) or in word-final position (*reduce, allege*).

As usual, it is difficult to justify a particular stratificational solution because to do so would involve proving a negative—that no simpler solution could account for all the facts. The analysis which follows, however, might be a candidate.

As in all cases where a phoneme participates in a particular alternation only in some of its occurrences, the natural first step is to set up special morphons for the alternating segments, let us say MN/K G/, contrasting with MN/k g/ which are realized as non-alternating Pk g/. The special morphons will be realized as P/s ǰ/ under certain conditions, and as P/k g/ elsewhere, and to state the conditions we will want an ordered or-node with its left-hand branch leading to an enabler.

But now, what is the conditioning environment for the fronted realization? On the surface we can distinguish three cases: where the alternating consonant is followed by a full vowel; where, as in *regal* and *regent*, it is followed by a reduced vowel; and where, as in *induce, induced, induceable, induction*, it is followed by a consonant or a word boundary or a fully productive affix.

Before a full vowel things are easy, broadly speaking. The alternating consonants have a fronted realization before P/ɪ e ə: i: ɪ: aj/ and not before any other peak types. This seems almost a paradigm case of an alternation 'better treated in terms of whole segments' (cf. p. 72); for neither these six peak types nor indeed /s ǰ/ form a simply definable class in terms of components. It is thus confirmed that the morphonic alternation pattern is the proper place for this relationship to be described.

Before the reduced vowel PS/ə/ either the fronted or the non-fronted realization may occur; which of them actually occurs is determined by whether the reduced vowel alternates with one of the six peak types mentioned in the previous paragraph. Thus we have a fronted realization of MN/G/ in *regent*, because in this suffix the reduced vowel realizes a morphon which is elsewhere realized as PS/e/: compare *resident*, formed with the same suffix, with its derivational cognate *residential*. In *regal*, on the other hand, the reduced vowel realizes a morphon elsewhere realized as PS/ej/, as in *regalia*, and /ej/ is a peak type that conditions a non-fronted realization. We therefore do not need to extend the above statement about full vowels to account for what happens to MN/K G/ before reduced vowels; we need only assume that vowel reduction is handled by the phonemic alternation pattern, and that a unit /ə/ makes its first appearance at the level of phonemic signs. This first appearance can come no lower than this, because the relationship between phonemic signs and the phonetic stratum is a biunique one; and it can come no higher, because if there were a phoneme /ə/ it would not be possible to specify in the phonotactics the

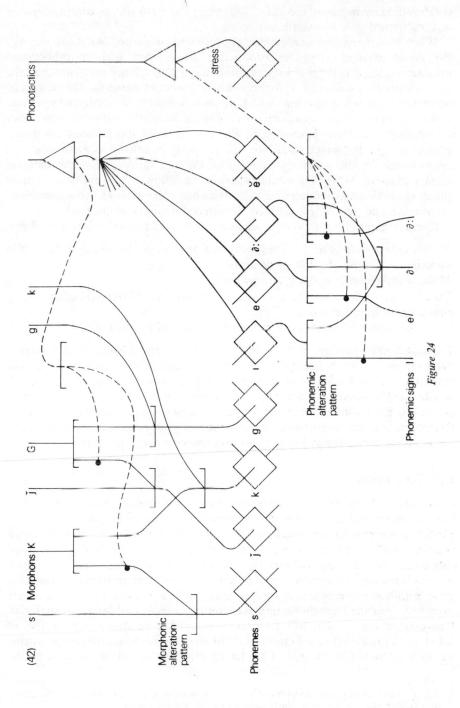

Figure 24

conditioning environment for Velar Softening, and a morphonic alternation can be conditioned *only* by the phonotactics.

When the alternating consonant is not followed by a vowel, what can we say? We could arrange to ignore productive affixes; but such morphological information sits ill in the phonotactics, and in any case will not account for all the cases of fronted realization not preceding a vowel (let alone for the difference between, say, *reduce* and *allege*, which do show softening in word-final position, and *critic* and *analogue*, which do not). Suppose instead[22] that we assume, both as a morphon and as a phoneme, an element /ĕ/ which has no realization as a phonemic sign, but which does have the property of serving as a conditioning environment for the softening alternation. We can suppose that this element occurs whenever ^{MN}/K G/ would otherwise be followed by a morphon whose phonemic realization is something other than one of the six peak types previously mentioned, and yet ^{MN}/K G/ have a 'softened' realization themselves.

The statements, then, needed to account for this alternation will be as follows:

^{MN} /K G/ are realized as ^{P}/s ǰ/ respectively if any one of ^{P}/ɪ e ĕ i: ɪ: ə: aj/   **41a**
immediately follows; as ^{P}/k g/ otherwise.

^{MN}/k g/ are realized as ^{P}/k g/ everywhere.   **b**

^{P}/ɪ e ə: / are realized as ^{PS}/ɪ e ə: / when the phoneme /'/ (stress) occurs   **c**
simultaneously; otherwise as ^{PS}/ə/.[23]

^{P}/ĕ/ is an *upward-determined element* (cf. p. 81) and is realized as zero.   **d**

Thus a complete account of this alternation will require a description of part of three patterns: the morphonic and phonemic alternation patterns, and the phonotactics. In (42), where these are diagrammed, 'conditioning lines' (cf. p. 77) are, in accordance with a useful convention, shown broken; also, to avoid clutter, only those morphons and phonemic signs are shown that are directly relevant to the alternation, the others being merely indicated by upward and downward links on diamond nodes (these links are always shown where they exist).

4.6 Conclusion

As has already been observed, the theory of stratificational grammar represents a very strong and interesting hypothesis about the nature of language. Up to the present, however, it has been more developed as a theoretical model than used as a practical tool. There are two reasons for this. One is the purely practical difficulties in its use, particularly the difficulty of determining whether a given analysis is the simplest possible, and perhaps also the graphic notation, which for most people is not easy either to take in as a whole or to analyse once it gets anywhere near the degree of complexity found in most real language material. The other reason is that SG as so far developed is incapable in principle of handling many of the facts of language.[24] Most of these intractable facts, it is true, are in the domain of syntax; but SG being a theory that sets great store by the

---

[22] This is an adaptation to the purposes of SG of a proposal by Chomsky and Halle (1968, 220).
[23] An oversimplification, no doubt, but it will do for our present purposes.
[24] See the criticisms of Sampson (1974).

homogeneity of organization of the various strata, an inadequacy on any one stratum reflects on the whole theory.

More strictly within phonology, there are also doubts. The theory has implications which are empirically testable and are far from being self-evidently true, and no attempt has been made to substantiate them; we have noted one such (p. 73). And while it is well adapted to making generalizations in cases where the same complex conditioning factors turn up in the statement of different alternations (for then the conditioning factors can be stated once and for all in the relevant tactic pattern, and a downward or-node can connect them to the various alternations which they govern), it has in this field two drawbacks. One is that it is by no means so easy to express generalizations about conditioning factors which, though obviously related, are not identical. The other is that, since formal simplicity is the sole criterion, the theory cannot distinguish between complex conditioning factors of types reasonably likely to occur in natural language and those which could never occur: this is the fruit of its Hjelmslevian emphasis on form as against substance.

Nevertheless SG remains a theory well worth knowing about, in particular for its analysis of the types of relationship that can obtain between underlying elements and their realizations and for its insistence on the central role of phonotactics in phonology.

5 Phonological Primes

5.1 Beyond the phoneme

One of the most important questions in phonology is: what are the basic, minimal units of phonological description? In much classical phonemic work the basic unit was the segment, in the shape of the phoneme; one notes in particular the definition of the phoneme by Bloomfield (1926) as a '*minimum* same of vocal feature' (emphasis mine). Such an approach, however, has certain inherent difficulties.

If Bloomfield's definition is taken literally, it asserts that phonemes are incapable of division into smaller units which are also 'sames of vocal feature', i.e., in effect, that each phoneme is to be treated as if it were completely unlike every other phoneme. On this basis a phonological description might (and many did) consist of simply:

> a list of symbols denoting the phonemes of a language;
> for each phoneme separately, a statement of the morphophonemic alternations in which it participates;
> for each phoneme separately, a statement of its allophones with the environments in which they occur.

But a description on these lines is inevitably going to involve a great deal of redundant statement and to miss generalizations. In English, for instance, it would have to be stated separately for each of /p t k/ that they are aspirated before a vowel provided /s/ does not precede; separately for /k/ and for /g/ that they are more front or more back according to the following vowel; separately for each of /p t k b d g/ that they are optionally unreleased in final position, etc. There are two ways of capturing the desired generalizations, ways which are in some respects equivalent to one another, and both of which have a respectably long history: by grouping phonemes into *classes*, and by dissecting them into *features*.

We have seen both approaches at work in stratificational phonology. The phonotactics organizes phonemes into classes according to their behaviour in combination and their distribution; the phonemic sign pattern analyses them into phonons according to their phonic features; and very frequently the two groupings coincide, and a phonotactic class turns out to consist of just those phonemes that share a particular phonon or set of phonons. Or, to put it in a more theoretically neutral way, *the morphophonemic behaviour of a phoneme depends very largely on its phonic correlates.*

Stratificational phonology, as we have seen (p. 74), provides a mechanism for expressing relationships of this kind; but the links between classes and features are so numerous and extensive that rather than regarding them, as SG does, merely as short cuts superimposed on what is basically an indirect relationship between classes and features by way of phonemes (which alone figure in both the tactic and the realizational portions of the phonology), there is much to be said for one of three alternative forms of organization:

allowing the classes to determine the features directly;   **43a**
treating the features, rather than the phonemes, as the basic units of   **b**
phonological description, and allowing them to determine the classes;
deriving both features and classes from some third set of entities distinct   **c**
from both.

Now Occam's razor (the maxim 'Entities are not to be multiplied beyond necessity') warns us against postulating an otherwise unmotivated *tertium quid* from which both phonemic classes and phonic features are to be derived. Of the other alternatives, (43a) retains the phoneme as basic, since in a classification the objects classified are logically prior to the classes. It is easy to see how the morphophonemics and allophonics of a language might be described on such a system. In addition to the list of phonemes, the description would include a set of statements defining classes of phonemes; morphophonemic and allophonic statements would then refer, not to phonemes as such, but to these classes and to set-theoretical functions of them such as their unions and intersections.[1] There has been a considerable literature on problems of phoneme classification.[2]

But today the preponderance of opinion is in favour of alternative (43b), treating the feature as the true basic unit. For there is an asymmetry between classes and features. Every feature in a feature system defines two classes of phonemes, those which have the feature and those which do not; and since the features are based on phonic parameters, it is to be expected that these classes (as well as many of the secondary classes based on combinations of features rather than single features) will be relevant to phonotactics and to morphophonemic alternations. Further, since phonic features rest ultimately on the human vocal apparatus, which is the same for all languages, there is reasonable hope of setting up an adequate *universal* feature system. With phonotactic classes, on the other hand, it is purely providential if every class happens to define a phonic feature, and, since phonemic systems are by definition language-particular, there can be no such thing as a universal system of phonotactic classes.

5.2 Feature theory

5.2.1 Development

The genesis of modern work on phonological feature theory is indissolubly linked with the name of Roman Jakobson.[3] At first, as Jakobson has since pointed out

[1] The *union* of two or more sets is the set of all items belonging to at least one of them; the *intersection* of two or more sets is the set of all items belonging to every one of them. Thus of two sets 'A, C, E' and 'B, C, D', the union is the set 'A, B, C, D, E', while their intersection is the one-member set 'C'.
[2] See for example Swadesh (1934); Fischer-Jørgensen (1952); Vogt (1954).
[3] In the late 1940s some American linguists such as Hockett (1947a; 1947b) and Bloch (1950) made extensive use of feature analysis, Hockett at least asserting explicitly that for him phonemes were not

(1962, 641), this was done within a framework of assumptions essentially the same as that of classical phonemics. Jakobson (1949), for instance, takes a single language at a time (say French), and considers first minimal phonemic oppositions ('minimal' in the Prague School sense, cf. p. 49): thus in French the phoneme /b/ is minimally opposed to each of the phonemes /m v p d g/. He then groups minimal oppositions into sets using the usual criteria of phonemic analysis, notably phonetic similarity and, above all, complementary distribution: thus not only is the opposition /b :m/ to be identified with /d :n/, but /b :g/ is to be identified with /m :ɲ/ and with /v :ž/ even though /g/ is velar,/ɲ/ palatal, and /ž/ palato-alveolar. For differences of point of articulation within the range covered by these phonemes are never contrastive in French. Continuing to group features in this way, Jakobson concludes that for consonants French has only five distinctive oppositions: nasality, tenseness (called voicing by others), continuance, and gravity and compactness (acoustically defined equivalents of place-of-articulation features). It is the classical method of phonemic analysis, applied to oppositions (or to the features they define) instead of to phones.

   The emphasis, however, gradually changed; and feature theory in its best known forms takes a rather different starting point. It seeks to categorize, not the phonemes or phones or oppositions of a given language, but the sounds of human language in general in terms of position on a large number of phonic axes; and then it uses this categorization, in a simpler form, to define automatically a set of classes, either of sounds in language in general or of sounds or phonemes in a particular language. It thus implicitly makes the claim that the great majority of phoneme classes that need to be set up in describing particular languages can be shown to be natural (in a sense which will be defined below) in terms of a universal phonetic system.

   As already indicated, the feature, not the phoneme, is the ultimate unit in phonological theories of this kind; more precisely, the ultimate unit is an ordered pair consisting of a symbol representing a position on an axis followed by the name of the axis, e.g. [3 stress], [1 round]:[4] such an ordered pair may be called a *specified feature*. A *segment* is a simultaneous bundle of such specified features.[5]

---

genuine linguistic units but a matter of transcriptional convenience. The inspiration, however, appears to have come originally from Jakobson, whose lectures Hockett at any rate is known to have attended; the elaboration of the method thereafter seems to have proceeded on parallel but independent lines. Jakobson's work in turn was a development of his and his Prague School colleagues' study of distinctive oppositions.

[4] It is conventional always to enclose specified features within square brackets. Following the principle implicit in terms like 'primary' and 'secondary' applied to stress, it would seem natural to assign low integers to those cases where the property named is present to a high degree; thus a segment specified as [1 round] would be very strongly rounded. For all features except stress, however, the reverse practice is at least as common, [2 round], for instance, being more rounded than [1 round]; context will normally disambiguate.

[5] Halle (1962), in an unfortunate moment, said that segments 'lack all systematic import' in generative phonology (which is feature-based). This statement, which has led to a great deal of misunderstanding, must have been due to a desire to distinguish the theory clearly from the popular segment-based version of classical phonemics. In fact, there are, and always were, certain types of operation in generative phonology, notably deletion, insertion and permutation, which can only be performed on segments, not on specified features; and as Matthews (1973) remarks, the problem of generative phonology (and other theories too) has not been too little, but too much, attention to the segment.

By the 1950s (e.g. Jakobson, Fant and Halle 1952; Jakobson and Halle 1956), Jakobson and his associates were putting forward the very strong hypothesis that just twelve features were sufficient to describe all contrasts (other than prosodic contrasts) in all human languages. The features were defined both in acoustic and in articulatory terms, but the former type of definition was considered more important, and as a result some superficially quite disparate classes of sounds fell together in this treatment. The feature of 'compactness', for example, was held to be characteristic of open vowels as against close ones, and of velar and palatal consonants as against labial and dental ones.

With investigation and analysis of a variety of languages it later came to be found, on the one hand that contrasts existed in various natural languages which the twelve Jakobsonian features could not handle (e.g. sometimes two different kinds of opposition, which Jakobson had assumed to be in universal complementary distribution and subsumed under a single feature, were found in one or another language to be separately distinctive), on the other hand that the classifications implied by those features were not always those required by the morphophonemic and allophonic phenomena actually found in natural language.

For example, as already mentioned, the Jakobsonian system distinguished velar from palatal consonants by the feature 'compactness' (or its mirror image 'diffuseness'), so that if a velar consonant became palatal, its specification for this feature would be taken to have changed. But when palatalization was found as a secondary articulation in, say, a dental or labial consonant, it was represented by a distinct feature of 'sharpness'. Thus no unified statement could be made of the type of phonological change or morphophonemic rule, quite common in natural languages, whereby in the same environment (usually before front vowels and front glides) velar consonants become palatals while other consonants acquire a secondary palatal articulation.

For this and other reasons Halle, McCawley and others proposed during the 1960s various changes in and especially additions to the Jakobsonian feature framework. The tendency was to replace acoustically by articulatorily defined features. This phase culminated in the codification of the revised theory by Chomsky and Halle (1968, chapter 7). Since 1968 there have been two divergent trends in work on feature theory. One, represented by Halle and his associates, has concentrated on perfecting, defending, revising, improving and applying the 1968 proposals. The other has sought to replace them completely on the ground that the features in many cases fail to correspond to identifiable and measurable phonetic parameters: here the dominant figure has been Ladefoged. In addition a great many individual proposals have been made for the recognition of new features or groups of features.

5.2.2 Criteria

The basic difference between the two major schools is not rooted in any fundamental disagreement about the criteria to which regard is to be had in setting up feature systems; rather it turns on the data—the findings of experimental phonetics—and the question how these data are to be interpreted in terms of neural and muscular activity. The criteria for feature systems formulated by Schane (1973a), who essentially maintains the Chomsky–Halle system, on the one hand, and by Ladefoged (1965; 1972a; 1971; 1975),[6] on the other, are remarkably similar. They may be treated under three heads: phonetic specifiability, completeness/universality, and morphophonemic relevance.

5.2.2.1   Phonetic specifiability

Every feature must have determinable phonetic correlates; these may relate to the manner of production of the relevant sounds, or to their acoustic nature, or both. In addition, Schane allows 'perceptual' correlates, which Ladefoged rejects on the ground that claims about perceptual invariants are not capable of empirical falsification (Ladefoged 1973). Here, in a sense, both parties are right: we may grant that at present to talk of the perceptual correlates of a feature is little more than to say that certain sounds stike our ears (and brains) as similar to one another, although it is always possible that new methods of investigation may be devised to obviate this objection; but we must also grant that nobody would think of setting up a feature with only perceptual correlates unless there were facts that it was needed to account for—morphophonemic rules, perhaps, or historical changes, probably a good many of them, which treated a certain group of sounds alike although they had nothing articulatorily or acoustically in common. It is perhaps best to accept 'perceptual' features while remembering that we really have no idea what their correlates are, and that they are not explanations, but explananda.

In his earlier work Ladefoged laid down a rigid requirement that 'sounds differing in terms of a feature should differ only in degree, and that the differences should be quantifiable in terms of a single measurable parameter'; this, he held, ruled out a great many of the features proposed by Jakobson, and later by Chomsky and Halle. The requirement, however, is not basic to the difference between the two schools of thought, for in his *Preliminaries* (1971) Ladefoged relaxed it. The difficulty seems to have been that the requirement had proved impossible to apply to some major features such as syllabicity, which nevertheless the system could not do without. It does not seem an insuperable difficulty; two much more important major class features, 'consonant' and 'vowel', do not appear in Ladefoged's basic feature system at all, being regarded as 'cover-features', 'labels for groups of phonological units' (Ladefoged 1965, 66), not terms in a phonetic theory, and a feature like syllabicity could be treated in the same way.[7] The feature system of the *Preliminaries* would then meet Ladefoged's earlier requirement. The requirement itself may be too absolute; like that discussed in the previous paragraph, it seems to overestimate our knowledge in many branches of phonetics. It should be regarded as a guide, placing the burden of proof on any proposal that deviated from it.

---

[6] The order is that of writing; the dates are those of publication.

[7] Though one sympathizes strongly with what Ladefoged (1971, 81) says about syllabicity: 'We will . . . assume that a neurophysiological definition is possible, even if we cannot at the moment state it in any way.'

5.2.2.2 *Completeness/universality*

Obviously a universal feature system, such as it is now generally accepted it should be our aim to construct, must be capable of distinguishing between any two phones which contrast in any actual language. But both Schane and Ladefoged go further than this, and therefore further than Jakobson, requiring an adequate feature system to be capable of accounting also for some allophonic differences, at least all those that have to be specially mentioned in the phonological description of particular languages (as opposed to those which are more or less automatic, universal coarticulation effects). It may also happen that pairs of phones exist which never differ either phonemically or allophonically for the simple reason that they never occur in the same language, but which are phonetically different enough so that a bilingual could not substitute phone [X] of his first language for phone [X′] of his second when speaking the latter without being guilty of a 'mispronunciation' or a 'foreign accent' or the like; these differences too must be accounted for by a universal feature system.

5.2.2.3 *Morphophonemic relevance*

An adequate feature system—and here Schane is again in full agreement with Ladefoged (1971, 4)—must, so far as possible, be such as to bear out the implicit claim of all modern feature theory that 'the great majority of phoneme classes that need to be set up in describing particular languages can be shown to be natural . . . in terms of' the system (p. 94); or, as a generative phonologist would say, that the great majority of input descriptions and conditioning environments for phonological rules can be formulated in terms of such natural classes. The customary definition of 'natural class' is a class of segment types which, in the feature system that is being used, can be defined with fewer features than any of its members. Thus in English, on the Jakobsonian feature system, /p k f/ form a natural class; the features [+grave, −voice] pick out these segment types and no others, while each individual segment type in the class requires at least one additional feature for its identification. The class /p k s/, on the other hand, is not natural (under the Jakobsonian or any other feature system I know of); its simplest definition is as the class of segments which are [−voice] and either [+grave, − continuant]   or   [− grave, − compact, + continuant, + strident]—a total of seven features, far more than are needed to define /p/ or /k/ or /s/ individually.

In the nature of things this criterion is more difficult to apply than the other two. The morphophonemic rules of a language generally owe their origin to a complex of historical causes and are often not expressible in terms of natural classes. The historical changes themselves may be expected to be phonetically motivated where they are not morphologically motivated; but even if it proved to be the case that all phonological changes were expressible in terms of the natural classes furnished by some otherwise satisfactory feature system, it is almost certainly impossible to devise a feature system such that all the natural classes it defines can be shown to play a role in phonological change. The criterion of morphophonemic relevance is thus of more value in confirming the systematic status of a feature than in disconfirming it.

5.3 The features

The discussion of individual features and groups of features which follows is based on the presentation in the seventh chapter of Chomsky and Halle's *Sound Pattern of English* (1968; henceforth, throughout the book, this work will be referred to as *SPE*). An explanation of the *SPE* proposals is followed in each case by a review of criticisms and alternative suggestions.

5.3.1 Major-class features

The first categorization of segments imposed by the feature system is an elaboration of the consonant-vowel dichotomy into three dichotomies. A segment, first of all, is either *syllabic* or non-syllabic;[8] syllabicity is defined in *SPE* only in terms of the apparently intuitive notion 'syllabic peak', and advance on this position will be possible only when we understand much better than we do now what gives to the syllable the individuality and identifiability it so clearly possesses.[9] Vowels are syllabic, and so are those consonants which constitute syllabic peaks, such as the final nasal in those pronunciations of English *button* in which the oral closure made for the [t] is not released, so that the nasal stop follows the oral stop without a break and the second syllable is vowelless: [bát⁻n̩]. It has often been assumed that only resonant consonants can be syllabic, but this is certainly wrong. Quite frequently fricatives are syllabic, the best-known examples in the literature being from some Chinese dialects (Chao 1934) and Bella Coola, a Salishan language of British Columbia (discussed by Hockett 1955, 57 and by Greenberg 1962); the latter, on some analyses, also has syllabic stops. But it is not necessary to go so far afield; English too has both syllabic fricatives and syllabic stops. There is a minimal contrast between *stall* (noun), with a short sibilant and unaspirated [t], and *'s tall* 'it is tall' with a rather longer sibilant and the aspirated [tʰ] characteristic of syllable-initial position; and likewise between *cue, queue, Q* on the one hand, and on the other *'kyou* 'thank you', which is often pronounced with a stop closure as long as the normal duration of a syllable, a silent syllable which is moreover accompanied by the muscular effort which is a correlate of stress.[10] Semivowels or *glides* are the non-syllabic counterparts of vowels.

Cross-cutting the classification by syllabicity is one by the feature of *consonantality*: consonantal sounds are those produced with a close constriction

[8] In its main discussion of the feature system *SPE* retains the Jakobsonian feature of 'vocalicity'; in a later excursus, however (*SPE* 354), Chomsky and Halle come to the conclusion that this feature should be abandoned in favour of syllabicity, and this change has been generally accepted. Vocalicity distinguished vowels and liquids (vocalic) from obstruents, nasals and glides (non-vocalic), not a very well motivated categorization either from a phonological or (as Ivić 1965 remarked) from a phonetic point of view. But cf. now Grace (1975).

[9] Fant (1971), however, offers a tentative acoustic definition based on 'a weighted sum of second and first formant intensity relative to that of an adjacent phonetic segment.'

[10] An elegant lesson if one is tempted to equate stress with loudness! On the question of syllabic obstruents see further Bell (1970), Hoard (1971b). In many languages syllabicity could be regarded as a redundant feature, its value being predictable from that of other features (sometimes grammatical information is required in addition), and Lass and Anderson (1975) claim that this is true of all languages; but its morphophonemic relevance makes it nevertheless essential to an adequate feature system.

(at least close enough so that, other things being equal,[11] friction would result) in the upper part of the vocal tract (excluding the glottal area). Thus all vowels and glides are non-consonantal; so are those 'consonants' in whose production the only constriction is in the glottal region, such as [h] and [ʔ]— these latter indeed, being non-consonantal and non-syllabic, are frequently (and not very appropriately) also termed glides.

Within the class of consonantal, non-syllabic segments—'consonants' in a narrower sense[12]—the most important distinction is that between obstruents and resonants. The distinction is defined in *SPE* in terms of the possibility of what is there called 'spontaneous voicing', a phonetically questionable notion; but the distinction itself is exactly the familiar obstruent-resonant dichotomy. Chomsky and Halle seem to have thought that only 'consonants' could be obstruent; Fromkin (1970) pointed out that if the *SPE* definition was taken rigorously, so-called 'laryngeal glides' like [h] and [ʔ] were also obstruent, as were voiceless vowels. The obstruence of 'laryngeal glides' tends to be confirmed by the fact that [h] often proves to be morphophonemically related to fricatives and [ʔ] to stops.[13] Ladefoged (1975) defines sonorance in terms of acoustic energy.

The major-class features meet to a high degree the condition of morphophonemic relevance; they have been subjected to some criticism on the score of phonetic specifiability, but Ladefoged (1971) accepts sonorance and syllabicity as primary features. In the last few years, however, an attack has been launched on the major-class features on what might be thought its home ground, morphophonemic relevance. This is associated with the revival (Zwicky 1972; Hooper 1974a; Hankamer and Aissen 1974) of de Saussure's notion of a hierarchy of segments ranging from the most open or sonorous, the low vowels, to the most closed (stops). Hankamer and Aissen propose a main hierarchy which is universal (stops— fricatives— nasals—lquids and glides—vowels) and subhierarchies within at least some of these classes which are apparently language-specific.[14] The weakest point in the proposal is that no phonetic characterization is offered for the new multi-valued feature of 'sonority'. The strong point is that the hierarchy captures morphophonemic generalizations which the *SPE* major-class features are unable to capture. It has been pointed out[15] that in various natural languages there are morphophonemic rules which apply or refer to the following classes of segments: stops and fricatives, fricatives and nasals, nasals and liquids, liquids and glides; and there is no possible system of binary cross-classifying features that can make all these into natural classes.

[11] In liquids and nasals, other things are not equal, for either (as in trills) the constriction is only intermittent or (as e.g. in nasals and laterals) there is an alternative unobstructed air passage. But since, in the absence of these factors, friction *would* result, the sounds are consonantal.

[12] The term 'consonant', as used in this sense, is to be distinguished from the term 'true consonant', still used in *SPE*, which denoted a segment which was consonantal and non-vocalic; this old term, like the vocalicity feature, is no longer in use.

[13] Cf. now Lass (1976, ch. 6), who argues that glottal stop and [h] are a voiceless stop and a voiceless fricative, both lacking all features related to supralaryngeal articulation.

[14] The distinction between the 'main hierarchy' and the 'subhierarchies' is drawn by me; Hankamer and Aissen do not make it, and consequently do not claim that the hierarchy is universal.

[15] By R. Underhill in a paper (not published so far as I know) to which Hankamer and Aissen refer.

With the hierarchy, on the other hand, in each case we simply need to define two points and say that anywhere between these points the structural description of the rule is met.

It is likely that the sonority hierarchy and the major-class features are both valid. The hierarchy is essentially perceptual, the major-class features essentially productive; and both productive and perceptual factors are capable of being used by speakers to make intuitive generalizations, and of determining or conditioning linguistic change. We shall meet this kind of situation again.

5.3.2 Anteriority and coronality

Apparently because of the basically binary nature of the feature system (discussed further below), the traditional place-of-articulation classes (labial, dental, etc.) have generally been treated by distinctive-feature phonologists, not as so many separate features, but rather in terms of two major binary features. Two features each capable of two specifications will give us four classes, roughly labial, dental, palatal and velar. Further classification is by means of subsidiary features such as 'strident' and 'distributed' or, in the case of palatals, velars and uvulars, by the features of highness, lowness and backness.

In Jakobson's feature framework the four classes were distinguished by the feature of compactness (above, p. 95) and by a feature of 'gravity' so defined that back vowels and labial and velar consonants were grave, while front vowels and dental and palatal consonants were non-grave. Chomsky and Halle replace these features, so far as they relate to consonants, with two new features defined in articulatory terms (*SPE* 304).

A consonant is *anterior* if and only if it is 'produced with an obstruction that is located in front of the palato-alveolar region of the mouth',[16] i.e. if it is labial, dental or alveolar.

A consonant is *coronal* if and only if it is 'produced with the blade of the tongue raised from its neutral position.' Since a raising of the apex of the tongue automatically involves raising of the blade, the only consonants which are non-coronal are on the one hand the labials, which do not involve the tongue at all, and on the other those consonants which are articulated with the body of the tongue only—pharyngeals, uvulars, velars and palatals (but so-called palato-alveolars, being laminally articulated, are coronal). Note that while vowels, since they are not produced with an obstruction, cannot by definition be anterior, a vowel may be coronal if the blade of the tongue is raised; this happens to various degrees in so-called retroflex vowels.

Except by those (such as Ladefoged) who, rejecting all binary classifications in this field as arbitrary, have preferred to work with the traditional multivalued parameter of articulatory place,[17] the feature 'coronal' has been generally

[16] The term 'palato-alveolar' tends to denote a class of sounds (those resembling [č š] in the manner in which friction is produced) rather than a region of the mouth, in spite of the fact that the term heads an (almost empty) column on the International Phonetic Association's chart; the anterior-nonanterior division actually lies between alveolar consonants such as English [s] and post-alveolar consonants such as English [š] (a palatalized and rounded lamino-postalveolar fricative).

[17] Ladefoged has, however, revived the feature of 'gravity'; this feature, or one like it, is needed to account for morphophonemic relationships between velars and labials, and their acoustic

accepted; but there have been grave doubts about the feature 'anterior'.[18] In particular, the definition of the feature seems hard to reconcile with the statement (*SPE* 298) that 'the features . . . relate to independently controllable aspects of the speech event'; this suggests (though it does not actually assert) that the features are meant to have some kind of psychological or physiological reality, and it is hard to claim such reality for the disjunction 'labial or dental/alveolar constriction'—indeed that disjunction bridges one of the few genuine discontinuities to be found in phonetics, the distinction between the lower lip and the tongue as active articulators.

Anderson (1971), for other reasons, proposed to introduce a new feature 'labial', which would be specified plus only for consonants whose primary articulation was labial; Reighard (1972) extended it to rounded vowels and glides, which are often closely related to labial consonants, phonetically and morphophonemically. There are some difficulties with this proposal (for example, there are distinct muscular mechanisms for lip approximation, and they sometimes contrast linguistically),[19] but the direct characterization of labial consonants as just that is vastly preferable to the claim that they are most appropriately defined as consonants which are produced with an obstruction located in front of the palato-alveolar region of the mouth and with the blade of the tongue not raised from its neutral position. The latter is reminiscent of the definition of man as a featherless biped; it works, but as if by accident.

No proposal for making the distinctions among coronal consonants that *SPE* makes by means of the anteriority feature has found wide acceptance; which may perhaps have contributed to the continuance in use of that decidely unsatisfactory feature. Ladefoged (1975) has four specifications for his articulatory-place feature in this region, dental, alveolar, retroflex and palato-alveolar.

5.3.3 Tongue body features

In *SPE* these features are 'high', 'low' and 'back', and in relation to vowels have the meanings that might reasonably be expected; note however that they are defined with reference to the 'neutral position', which is taken, as far as tongue configuration is concerned, to be that of a mid front vowel (*SPE* 300), and consequently that while mid vowels are neither high nor low, central vowels (neither fully front nor fully back) are normally classified as back.[20]

All these features are also used in reference to consonants. Very frequently

similarity, to which the gravity feature refers, meets the condition of phonetic specifiability better than does the coronality feature, which is based on another *SPE* notion that has excited some scepticism—that of a 'neutral position' of the speech apparatus.

[18] See for example Lass (1976, 188–92).

[19] Hence Anderson (1974b) has distinct features 'round' and 'labial' relating to the two main mechanisms, and this may be right; the morphophonemic relationships between rounded vowels (primarily *back* rounded vowels) and labial consonants are probably more appropriately captured by the feature of gravity (cf. note 17)—though this feature is not used by Anderson.

[20] Campbell (1974, 57) points out that there are languages in which central and back vowels contrast minimally with one another. He does not suggest what can be done about this, but the inevitable conclusion is that frontness and backness must be treated as separate features. Palatal consonants will then be [+high, +front] and velars [+high, +back]. So already (for other reasons) Wang (1968), and subsequently (for other reasons again) Hyman (1975, 55).

consonants are palatalized in the neighbourhood of front vowels and velarized in the neighbourhood of back vowels; and dorsal consonants normally vary in their place of articulation according to the frontness or backness of neighbouring vowels. In point of fact, the place of articulation of palatal and velar consonants is the *same* as that of high front and high back vowels respectively—it is only that for the consonants the tongue rises high enough to constrict or block the air flow.

Chomsky and Halle therefore assign to both palatal and velar consonants the specification [+high] and to velars, in addition, the feature [+back]. These features are likewise assigned to palatalized and velarized anterior consonants; these are distinguished from true palatals and velars by anteriority, or whatever features replace anteriority.

In addition, Chomsky and Halle claimed that just as there is an association between palatals and velars on the one hand and high vowels on the other, so there is an association between *pharyngeal* articulation and low vowels such as [a]. In this case the influence often works in the reverse direction, vowels being lowered in the neighbourhood of pharyngeal or pharyngealized consonants (e.g. in some Semitic languages). Thus in *SPE* pharyngeal(ized) consonants are categorized as low and back. The tendency in later work has been to reject this analysis of pharyngealization: the front-back distinction is concerned with the configuration of the *upper surface* of the tongue, and this can have nothing to do with pharyngealization, which involves an approximation of the rear or *root* of the tongue to the pharyngeal wall. Consequently several investigators[21] have made proposals, differing only in detail, for pharyngealization to be treated as a separate feature of 'tongue root retraction'; its counterpart, 'tongue root advancement', is distinctive in, for example, the West African language Akan, where it plays a role in vowel harmony (Stewart 1967).

One of the major criticisms of the high-low-back group of features has been that it allows for only three degrees of openness to be distinctive, since a vowel cannot be [+high, +low]. It is by no means exceptional for four degrees of openness to be contrastive on the surface, and there are languages where it is extremely difficult, if not impossible, to avoid positing a similar four-way distinction in underlying representations. Wang (1968) proposed for this reason to replace the features 'high' and 'low' by 'high' and 'mid', fully close vowels being [+high, −mid], half-close vowels [+high, +mid], and so on. This has various undesirable consequences; for example, it entails that in a language with front vowels /i e ɛ æ/, /i æ/ form a natural class and /i e ɛ/ do not; and Wang's proposal seems only an artifice to enable four-height systems to be described without giving up the claim that at the level of underlying representation all features are binary. As Contreras (1969) and McCawley (1973) have seen, in the domain of vowel openness this claim cannot be maintained. Both have advocated, as has Ladefoged, a single 'height' feature which can take (probably) four distinct specifications.

[21] For example, Hoard (1971b); Halle (discussion on Ali and Daniloff 1972); McCawley (1974); and Ladefoged, who at various times has called this feature 'tension' and 'width'. To the extent that it is valid at all, Chomsky and Halle's feature 'covered' (*SPE* 314) appears to be identical with this feature. Lindau (1975) subsumes tongue root advancement under a feature of *pharyngeal expansion* which also involves a relatively low (*vs.* raised) position of the larynx.

5.3.4 Rounding

Rounding (of the lips) is a straightforwardly definable feature presenting few problems; its relationship to true labiality has been considered above (p. 101 and note 19). In consonants rounding is always a secondary articulation.

5.3.5 Distributedness

This is a feature that made its first appearance in *SPE* (312), where distributed sounds are defined as those 'produced with a constriction that extends for a considerable distance along the direction of the air flow.' The main object of the feature is to capture distinctions among consonants all of which are dental or alveolar (in *SPE* terms, anterior and coronal). In general, in this area laminal consonants are [+distributed] and apicals [−distributed]. The feature has been little used in subsequent work; the length of a constriction is more naturally seen as a consequence than as an aspect of the nature of an articulation, and it is preferable to distinguish apicals and laminals directly.

5.3.6 Nasality and laterality

These features do not seem to require any comment.

5.3.7 Closure and release features

The most important of these is *continuance*, which primarily reflects the major division of obstruent consonants into stops and fricatives. If we define a stop articulation as one in which 'the air flow through the mouth is effectively blocked' (*SPE* 317), we obtain a feature definition which is applicable to resonants as well as obstruents. Nasals will then count as stops, while liquids will be continuants. There is a good deal of variation in the use of this feature. Some analysts regard nasals as continuant, i.e. their definition of a stop omits the words 'through the mouth'; others regard nasals as non-continuant.[22] Contrariwise, if the class of stops is defined more broadly as those consonants in which there is a complete closure *somewhere* along the main path of the air flow, then laterals (and perhaps even trills) will count as stops. The morphophonemic and phonotactic evidence on this question is complicated and partly contradictory (cf. *SPE* 318). It may prove necessary to posit two distinct features, 'occlusive' (for the narrow definition of 'stop') and 'central closure' (for the broad definition); lateral fricatives and lateral resonants would then be [−occlusive, +central closure].[23]

[22] The morphophonemic evidence strongly favours treating nasals as non-continuant; see Anderson (1976).
[23] It might be thought that we would thus be enabled to dispense with the feature "lateral"; but it should be remembered that there are also such things as lateral occlusives (affricates with lateral release) which, but for the existence of the feature 'lateral', would not form a natural class with other laterals.

Not dissimilar to the proposal in the text is the 'mid-closure' feature suggested by Fant (1971). Not only stops, affricates, laterals and trills but also nasals would be marked + for this feature, and, according to Fant, it would render the feature 'consonantal' redundant.

In *SPE*, affricates are distinguished from plosives by the feature 'delayed release' (better 'gradual release', as Anderson 1974b). With this feature there is a minor and a major difficulty. The minor difficulty is that the contrast 'instantaneous versus gradual release' does not allow for those stops (usually syllable-final) which are not released at all; hence Anderson (1974b) treats instantaneous release and gradual release as separate features, unreleased stops being specified minus for both. The major difficulty is that this approach does not adequately capture the relationship between affricates and stop-fricative sequences, which differ only in that the former are single segments and the latter sequences of two segments. For this and a number of other situations where the classic problem 'un ou deux phonèmes' arises, Hoard (1971b) has proposed the extremely useful device of the *complex segment*. A complex segment is a segment which, for at least one feature, has two or more specifications; the phonetic correlates of these specifications are taken to appear in temporal succession. Thus an affricate would be treated as an obstruent which was $[- + \text{continuant}]$; that is, non-continuant to begin with, becoming continuant.[24] The features of instantaneous and gradual release can then be dispensed with, leaving only a contrast released-unreleased (cf. McCawley 1967), which is probably never distinctive at the underlying level.

Several further closure and release features are needed for the description of clicks, ejectives and implosives, all of which have secondary velar and/or glottal closures; for these see *SPE* 319–24.

5.3.8 Tenseness

This feature is one of Jakobson's original set, but in its actual use it has sometimes seemed to be something of a *deus ex machina*. Chomsky and Halle's definition is that

> tense sounds are produced with a deliberate, accurate, maximally distinct gesture that involves considerable muscular effort; nontense sounds are produced rapidly and somewhat indistinctly. In tense sounds, both vowels and consonants, the period during which the articulatory organs maintain the appropriate configuration is relatively long, while in nontense sounds the entire gesture is executed in a somewhat superficial manner.

The tenseness feature can thus subsume a great many of the contrasts, both in vowels and in consonants, that have traditionally been handled under the rubric 'length'; but some such contrasts may be more naturally handled as being between single and double consonants or vowels, and there is undoubtedly also a third class of cases where there is no particular reason for a geminate analysis and none of the differences of quality associated with tenseness, and where the natural analysis is in terms of a separate feature of length. The known cases of the last type all involve vowels.

The most important of the 'differences of quality associated with tenseness' is that tense vowels 'are executed with a greater deviation from the neutral or rest

[24] At the phonetic level it will be necessary to specify the relative duration of the phases of a complex segment.

position of the vocal tract than are [lax vowels]': the meaning of this may be appreciated by comparing the lax English vowels /ɪ a ɔ U/(in the phonemic system of (16) in Chapter Two) with their tense counterparts /iː aː oː uː/. The tense vowels are more fully front, more fully back, more fully close, as the case may be, than the corresponding lax vowels. From the acoustic point of view, Fliflet (1962) found that the following properties were characteristic of non-tense vowels in German, noting that analysis of available spectrographic materials on English yielded similar results:

> Modifications of the formant levels in a 'neutral' direction; a more even intensity distribution over the whole frequency range ... ; more vaguely defined formant outlines; less regular structure of the formants and also of the non-formant areas ...; a different relationship ... in the movement of formants to the frequencies of any following consonants; a generally higher level of disturbance in all spectral utterance-forms of the vowel,

in short 'a blurring of the features that serve to emphasize the individuality of particular vowels.'

Many phonological studies have used the feature 'tenseness' to distinguish between consonants, especially plosives; but it has not usually been made clear on what articulatory characteristics of these consonants such an analysis is based, and the convenience and vagueness of the feature has sometimes tempted excellent phonologists into highly arbitrary analyses.[25] In recent years the tendency has been to turn instead to more detailed investigation of glottal and subglottal activity in sets of consonants whose oral articulations are essentially identical; it is striking that Anderson (1974b), in his detailed discussion of features, does not mention tenseness.[26]

5.3.9 Voicing, aspiration, and related features

In this field *SPE* uses three features, 'voice', 'heightened subglottal pressure', and 'glottal constriction'. A consonant is 'voiced' if in its production the glottis is narrowed sufficiently to make vocal cord vibration possible; it does not follow that vocal cord vibration will actually occur, since other factors may interfere with it, and consequently many consonants traditionally termed voiceless are voiced in *SPE* terms—for example the 'voiceless unaspirated' stops of such language as Spanish and Hindi. (Cf. *SPE* 328.) Heightened subglottal pressure is normally associated with aspirated stops, but an unaspirated stop may have heightened subglottal pressure if it also has a glottal constriction (*sc.* so close as to preclude normal voicing).

These *SPE* features and definitions have now been generally abandoned. It has been shown that the phonetic evidence does not support them: see especially Kim (1970), Lisker and Abramson (1971), and Ladefoged (1973) with the references there cited. In most analytic work, as opposed to discussions of the feature system

---

[25] Some examples are discussed by Anderson (1970).

[26] See now Lass (1976, 15, 39ff.) for a critique of the whole notion of a tenseness feature. Lass points out (44) that 'no one has yet ... demonstrated a pair of vowels that in fact differ only in tenseness: the primary (measurable) differences involved are always in quality and/or length'.

itself, *ad hoc* features based on traditional categorizations have been used—'voicing', 'aspiration' and the like. Meanwhile a number of proposals for new, phonetically specifiable features have been made, of which I will mention two.

Halle (1972) proposes two new pairs of features. The first pair, 'stiff vocal cords' and 'slack vocal cords' (now often abbreviated to 'stiff' and 'slack'), were originally intended to account for high and low pitch respectively. But in obstruents, on physiological grounds, one would expect these vocal cord features to give rise, respectively, to voicelessness and voicing, with an intermediate state of the vocal cords—[− stiff, − slack]—resulting in an intermediate voicing state.[27] It is not, as Halle points out, entirely surprising if voicing and pitch are controlled by the same pair of features. As was noted by Greenberg (1970), it has often been reported in various tone languages that 'voiced consonants . . . lower the pitch of the entire vowel segment or that portion which is immediately adjacent so that, for example, a following high tone becomes a rising tone. On the other hand, a voiceless . . . segment has no such lowering effect. . . . Non-lowering sound types may even on occasion raise pitch.' On Halle's proposal, all effects of this kind can be understood as assimilations.

The second of Halle's feature pairs consists of the features 'spread glottis' and 'constricted glottis'. The latter is similar to the *SPE* feature 'glottal constriction'; the main sound types which are [+ constricted] are glottal stops, ejectives, implosives, glottalized continuants, and vowels pronounced with creaky voice (which requires a narrower glottal opening than normal voice). Spread glottis produces the acoustic effect of breathiness: aspirated consonants, voiceless vowels, and [h] are [+ spread].

The system is a neat one, but as Ladefoged (1973) in particular has pointed out, it has drawbacks. Halle's exposition implies that the state of the glottis for high-pitched vowels is identical with that for voiceless unaspirated consonants, viz. [+ stiff, − slack, − spread, − constricted]—which Ladefoged finds 'clearly contrafactual'. There may also be difficulties in the sphere of morphophonemic relevance. In Japanese, vowels become voiceless between voiceless consonants: a straightforward assimilation. But on Halle's new feature system the voiceless consonants are distinguished as [+ stiff]; and the vowels certainly do not in this environment become [+ stiff], i.e. high-pitched—voiceless vowels are [+ spread]. Nor can we take the rule to be an assimilation of the feature [+ spread]; for not all the relevant voiceless consonants are in fact [+ spread], i.e. aspirated.

Ladefoged's own proposals (Ladefoged 1971; 1972b; 1973; 1975) involve four features, only one of which is binary:

1 *Glottal stricture* can perhaps take as many as ten values: glottal stop, creak, creaky voice, stiff voice, voice, slack voice, murmur, breathy voice, voiceless, spread. Its value for any given phonetic segment must naturally be determined by detailed investigation. But it appears that in no language do more than five values of the feature contrast with one another (Ladefoged 1975, 261).

2 *Voice onset* is a feature of relative timing: it applies mainly to stops, and relates to the elapsed time (positive or negative) between the stop release and the

---

[27] This has not so far as I know been experimentally verified.

onset of vocal cord vibration. There are no 'natural' phonetic divisions, the
domain of the feature being a continuum from voiced, through voiceless
unaspirated, to aspirated; but again no language has more than a three-way
contrast in Voice Onset.[28]

3 *Glottalicity* is a ternary feature distinguishing ejectives on the one hand, and
implosives on the other, from ordinary plosives; *SPE* (322f) uses for this
purpose two separate binary features.

4 *Fortis* consonants are pronounced with increased subglottal pressure. These
consonants may or may not be aspirated; in contrast with the *SPE* system,
aspiration does not presuppose heightened subglottal pressure. Contrasts in
this feature appear to be rather rare; Ladefoged (1971) reports them from only
three or four languages, and Ladefoged (1975) omits this feature altogether.

5.3.10 Stridency

This feature, which was one of the original Jakobsonian set, was retained in *SPE*
mainly for contrasts between certain pairs of fricatives and affricates with the
same or similar places of articulation; strident consonants were said to be
'marked acoustically by greater noisiness than their non-strident counterparts',
e.g. [s] as against [θ], [š] as against [ç]. No precise articulatory definition was
given, and the feature seems to be redundant from the phonetic point of view,
given the other features either of the *SPE* system or of subsequent work; Anderson
(1974b) retains it only as a cover-feature, but it is doubtful whether it is needed
even in this role. See though Ladefoged (1975, 264–5) on 'sibilance'.

5.3.11 Vibration

This is the most important of several new features introduced by Ladefoged. *SPE*
makes no provision for trills and taps, which are [+vibration]; all other sounds
are [−vibration]. Trills and taps may be distinguished from one another by
length ('rate' is Ladefoged's term).

5.3.12 Prosodic features

As these have always been clearly distinguished from the segments on which they
occur, the analysis of these segments into features has not led to any great change
in the treatment of pitch, stress and length. Various attempts have been made to
analyse pitch (e.g. Wang 1967) and stress (e.g. Vanderslice 1972; Vanderslice and
Ladefoged 1972) in terms purely of binary features, and we have noted the
suggestion of Halle (1972) that high pitch and voicelessness are, at one phonetic
level, one and the same thing; but none of these proposals has won wide
acceptance.[29]

Some time ago (p. 94) we were speaking of the features as 'axes' and of their
specifications as referring to 'positions' along these axes, and we were also saying

[28] How a feature of voice onset can be applied to consonants not directly followed by a voiced
segment is problematical; on this see Bhatia (1976).
[29] Cf. now Crystal (1975, ch. 1),

that the feature system imposed a 'categorization' on segments. This implies a very important point in most current feature theory. The 'stream of speech' is continuous; but we have noted that in *SPE* the features are said to relate to 'independently *controllable* aspects of the speech event' (emphasis mine), and the control referred to is presumably exercised by motor commands, which, by the nature of neural organization, must be discrete entities and must be finite in number. Consequently it is assumed, at least by Chomsky and Halle and those who have accepted the general lines of their system, that for each feature there is a finite (and low) limit to the number of possible distinct specifications.[30] These specifications are language-independent (though a given language will not use all possible specifications for all features), and they constitute a true universal phonetic alphabet. Although this hypothesis is difficult to refute (for any apparent counterexample can be neutralized by increasing the limit on the number of possible specifications for the feature in question), it is nonetheless an empirical one.[31]

5.4   Some problems

5.4.1   The naturalness condition

The categorization we have so far been speaking of has been a phonetic one. It is also, however, possible to regard a feature system as imposing a *phonological* categorization of, say, underlying segments. In this case the interpretation of the features cannot be direct, as it is when they are used phonetically. To say that an underlying segment is characterized by a negative specification for the feature 'nasal' is not to say that it is articulated without nasality; for an underlying segment is not articulated at all. Nor is it to say that the phonetic realization of the segment in question is articulated without nasality; for this may not be the case— consider the vowel of English *pan* (cf. p. 3), which is not nasal underlyingly, but is nasal phonetically. Rather, an underlying categorization of a segment with respect to a feature implies that the phonetic realization of that segment is similarly characterized *unless some rule or rules of the phonology require otherwise*—as happens to be the case with *pan*.

The principle that, phonological rules permitting, underlying categorizations imply corresponding phonetic characterizations is called by Postal (1968) 'the Naturalness Condition'. It is not, however, strictly a condition on grammars; for there is no limit to the complexity of the phonological rules a grammar may contain if the facts call for them;[32] rather it is a convention for the interpretation

---

[30] Those who would not agree with this would base their disagreement mainly on rejection of the thesis that all valid features are related to motor commands (or even to higher-order neural events controlling such commands), on the ground, for example, that some features which they consider valid are acoustically defined. Thus we have seen Ladefoged describe his axis of Voice Onset as a continuum, and any categorization along it as arbitrary. I will presently return to the question whether features should be defined articulatorily or acoustically.

[31] For example, it could be experimentally determined whether a language using an excessive number of specifications on some axis was capable of being learnt without explicit phonetic training.

[32] Attempts to limit the 'abstractness' of underlying representations are thus not justifiable on the basis merely of the Naturalness Condition; they must be justified, if at all, on other grounds.

of grammars: all phonetic characterizations not assigned by any phonological rule are understood to be the same as the underlying categorizations.

5.4.2 The binarity hypothesis

Underlying categorizations do, however, in the *SPE* system differ from phonetic ones in one major respect: they are always *binary*. No matter how many possible specifications a feature may have at the phonetic level, the theory requires that at the underlying level it should have two possible specifications only, + and −.[33]

Various justifications have been put forward for the binarity hypothesis. It needs defending, logically, in two directions. On the one hand, it might be—and has been—argued that some features in underlying representations must be allowed to have three or more specifications. In *SPE* itself, stress, though in underlying representations not distinctive at all, is specified in considerable detail (at least five distinct values) by quite early phonological rules, at a stage of derivation when all other features are still strictly binary. We have seen that the high-low dimension in vowels cannot be satisfactorily described except by a multi-valued feature.[34] The same holds for pitch (McCawley 1973); for example, a rule which, in some environment, lowered all pitches one step can be expressed only in a highly convoluted form if pitch is described with binary features. In a number of languages there appears, *prima facie* at any rate, to be a three-way contrast of length, sometimes in vowels (e.g. Wichita: Rood 1975),[35] sometimes in consonants (e.g. some dialects of Lappish: Collinder 1951). In addition, as we have seen, Ladefoged (1971) allows for several underlying three-way distinctions in glottal features, and assigns articulatory place through a single feature which may exhibit as much as a six-way distinction.

I have not seen any convincing justification for the doctrine that all features must be underlyingly binary rather than ternary, quaternary, etc. The proponents of the doctrine often realize it needs defending, but the calibre of the defence is not unfairly represented by the single subordinate clause devoted to the subject in *SPE* (297): 'for the natural way of indicating whether or not an item belongs to a particular category is by means of binary features.'[36] The restriction to two underlying specifications creates problems and solves none.

[33] Originally there was also a third possible underlying specification, 0, signifying that no information at all was provided about that feature in that segment in underlying representation, the specification as + or − being eventually filled in either by a 'morpheme structure rule' or by a phonological rule. It was shown by Stanley (1967) that this device could make possible specious simplifications that reflected no real generalization. See pp. 166–7.

[34] At one time Jakobson and Halle had described the high-low dimension in terms of a single feature with three values, 'compact', 'diffuse', and 'intermediate'; and Jakobson and Halle (1957/1968) actually cite experimental evidence in favour of this treatment.

[35] J. D. McCawley points out to me that there is a similar three-way contrast in some north German dialects, where *Lamm* 'lamb', *Rahm* 'cream', *haben* 'to have' are pronounced respectively [lam ra:m ha::m].

[36] Nobody would take this statement seriously if we were talking about non-linguistic categorizations—if, for instance, we replaced 'item' and 'category' by 'army officer' and 'rank', or 'mammal' and 'order', or 'card' and 'suit'. Binarity is only the 'natural' mode of categorization in a given field if all oppositions in that field are privative (cf. note 60, Chapter Two); which in the linguistic, and even the narrowly phonological, field is neither logically true nor patently true as a matter of contingent fact.

Quite distinct is the question why, if at all, binary features should be preferred to what have been called 'singulary' features—why the unit of phonological description should be a complex entity consisting of a specification and an axis, rather than a simple entity naming a phonological property such as 'voiceless' or 'closed' or 'high'. Of the latter the phonons of stratificational grammar are examples; but the use of the singulary feature goes back a long way.

The main difficulty faced by systems using singulary features is this. If features are non-complex, it is only possible to mark their presence in a segment, not their absence; for if we allow a segment to be marked for the absence of a feature, we are in effect treating that feature as binary. But in that case it is necessary so to arrange the feature system of a given language that no segment type has a feature set that is a subset[37] of the feature set of any other segment type. There cannot, for instance, be a segment (say *p*) with the features 'closed, labial' and another segment (say *b*) with the features 'closed, labial, voiced'. For consider how these segments would be affected by morphophonemic rules. Suppose there to be a rule changing some or all labial stops to fricatives in certain environments. If this rule were stated as

$$\begin{bmatrix} \text{Closed} \\ \text{Labial} \\ \text{Voiced} \end{bmatrix} \rightarrow [\text{Fricative}] \qquad\qquad 44$$

it would of course apply only to *b*. If it were stated as

$$\begin{bmatrix} \text{Closed} \\ \text{Labial} \end{bmatrix} \rightarrow [\text{Fricative}] \qquad\qquad 45$$

it would apply to both *b* and *p*. What, though, if the rule in actual fact applied only to *p*? How could it be stated? Only be referring, in one way or another, to the absence of a feature—which is, again, to introduce binarity by the back door. Whenever we try to formalize a theory of singulary features, we seem to find that it emerges as a notational variant of a theory of binary (or multinary) features.

5.4.3 Articulatory or acoustic features?

One of the most important questions in connection with feature theories is whether features should be defined in articulatory or acoustic terms. As we have seen, Jakobson favoured the latter, Chomsky and Halle the former. There are considerations pointing in both directions.

A feature theory, to the extent that it seeks to account for 'independently controllable aspects of the speech event', must be articulatorily based; for the control is control over muscular movements, not over their acoustic effects. The evidence suggests, too (cf. e.g. Stevens 1972), that we *perceive* speech not directly in terms of sound waves, but in terms of the articulations that we would have to make to generate those sound waves. Thus from the point of view of the requirement of phonetic specifiability, an articulatorily based feature system is all but inevitable.

[37] By saying 'subset' and not 'proper subset' we imply, in addition to the prohibition of situations like that discussed in the text, that (i) no two distinct segment types may have the same feature set (as all systems must require), and more importantly (ii) there cannot be a segment with no features at all (and it is very easy to devise an apparently plausible feature system which proves to violate this).

But there is also a requirement of morphophonemic relevance; and in this connection it matters that morphophonemic rules are in large measure the debris of past phonological changes. Now phonological changes may have various motivations, as we shall see in Chapter Nine; and not the least significant among these are perceptual motivations. Two sounds that are hard for the hearer to distinguish, for instance, may merge; or such a merger may be averted by one of the two acquiring a new feature which makes the distinction easier to perceive. This perceptibility of distinctions is not perceptibility in terms of the 'analysis by synthesis' discussed in the last paragraph; rather, the various distinct segment types must be perceptible as distinct before analysis by synthesis can go to work— in other words we must here be dealing with a purely acoustic level of processing. And it is for this reason that features such as 'grave' or 'sonorant', whose status is dubious at best on the criterion of phonetic specifiability if this is understood, as we have argued it should be, as articulatory-phonetic specfiability, become indispensable as soon as we take the criterion of morphophonemic relevance into consideration.[38]

All through the various forms of distinctive-feature phonology there has been a (usually tacit) assumption that the appropriate features for a universal phonetic alphabet are also the appropriate features for the statement of phonological rules. This now appears not to be the case; and the features to which Ladefoged and others have given the apologetic name of 'cover-features' provide the proof of it.[39] Thus at some stage in a phonological description it will be necessary to 'translate' from one feature system to the other—though many features will certainly be common to both systems.

This is not a problem which will concern us much in the remainder of this book, which is concerned with phonological rules rather than with universal phonetics; and the feature system we shall be using is that of *SPE* with some alterations which seem definitely called for.[40]

5.5 Feature representation of segments and segment classes

Once we have established a feature system, each segment can be represented as a bundle of simultaneous 'specified features', where a specified feature is an ordered pair of a specification[41] and the name of the feature. Thus English /p/ would be defined as the bundle

[38] For further discussion of the need and justification for acoustic as well as articulatory features, see Lass (1976, 197–207).
[39] Not all cover-features that have been proposed are acoustically defined: thus the feature 'lingual' proposed by Lass (1976, ch. 7) covers 'any segment made with the blade or body of the tongue as primary active articulator.'
[40] The most important have been mentioned in the text, and appear in (47). Note that the feature 'continuant' is here assumed to be defined in such a way that /l/ is non-continuant; that 'voice' and 'aspiration' are *ad hoc* features in the absence of a generally accepted system for the description of glottal states; that a segment is specified [+ apical] only if in its articulation the tip of the tongue is used to the *exclusion* of the blade; and that the values of the multinary feature 'height' range from 1 (low) to 4 (high).
[41] A 'specification' is + or − (where the feature is binary) or an integer (where it is multinary); a complex segment will have, for at least one feature, a complex specification, consisting of a sequence of two or more simple specifications.

$$\begin{bmatrix} - \text{syllabic} \\ + \text{consonantal} \\ - \text{sonorant} \\ - \text{continuant} \\ - \text{voice} \\ + \text{labial} \\ \ldots \end{bmatrix} \qquad 46$$

The seven features mentioned are sufficient to define /p/ against all other segment types of *English*; but from the point of view of language in general it is necessary to specify the segment for all other features as well, to distinguish it from many other possible segments which do not occur in English: to say, for example, that it is not rounded, is not implosive, is not velarized, etc.

If we now consider the whole phonological system of a language, it is clearly possible to make a table showing the specification, for all features relevant in the language, of all the segment types in the system. Such a table is called a *classificatory matrix*. It is not part of the grammar of the language, since reference is never made to the table as such in determining the pronunciation of sentences; it merely provides both the student of the language and the linguist with an extremely useful overview of the role of the various features in the phonology of the language. An example of such a matrix follows. It will be seen that the major-class features are listed first, and that features belonging to the same group are listed together.

English Consonants   47a

	p	t	č	k	b	d	ǰ	g	f	θ	s	š	v	ð	z	ž	m	n	ŋ	l	r	j	w	h
syllabic	−	−	−	−	−	−	−	−	−	−	−	−	−	−	−	−	−	−	−	−	−	−	−	−
consonantal	+	+	+	+	+	+	+	+	+	+	+	+	+	+	+	+	+	+	+	+	+	−	−	−
sonorant	−	−	−	−	−	−	−	−	−	−	−	−	−	−	−	−	+	+	+	+	+	+	+	−
continuant	−	−	+	−	−	−	+	−	+	+	+	+	+	+	+	+	−	−	−	−	+	+	+	+
voice	−	−	−	−	+	+	+	+	−	−	−	−	+	+	+	+	+	+	+	+	+	+	+	−
labial	+	−	−	−	+	−	−	−	+	−	−	−	+	−	−	−	+	−	−	−	−	−	+	−
apical	−	+	−	−	−	+	−	−	−	−	+	−	−	−	+	−	−	+	−	+	−	−	−	−
coronal	−	+	+	−	−	+	+	−	−	+	+	+	−	+	+	+	−	+	−	+	+	−	−	−
height	2	2	4	4	2	2	4	4	2	2	2	4	2	2	2	4	2	2	4	3	2	4	4	2
back[42]	−	−	−	+	−	−	−	+	−	−	−	−	−	−	−	−	−	−	+	−	−	−	+	−

English Syllabic Peaks   b

	ɪ	e	æ	a	ɔ	ʊ	ə	iː	ɪː	eː	aː	oː	ʊː	uː	əː	ej	aj	oj	æw	əw
syllabic	+	+	+	+	+	+	+	+	+	+	+	+	+	+	+	+	+	+	+	+
consonantal	−	−	−	−	−	−	−	−	−	−	−	−	−	−	−	−	−	−	−	−
height	3	2	1	1	1	3	2	4	3	2	1	2	3	4	2	24	14	24	14	24
back	−	−	−	+	+	+	+	−	−	−	+	+	+	+	+	−	+−	+−	−+	+
round	−	−	−	−	+	+	−	−	−	−	−	+	+	+	−	−	+−	+−	−+	+
long	−	−	−	−	−	−	−	+	+	+	+	+	+	+	+	+	+	+	+	+

A particular segment type, as we have seen, is represented by a bundle—that is, a conjunction—of specified features. A class of segment types is also normally represented by such a bundle, usually containing fewer features; such a bundle denotes all and only the segment types having all the specified features mentioned (whatever their other specifications may be). Thus the bundle

[42] The liquid /l/ is somewhat arbitrarily given as non-back; phonetically it is back at the end of a syllable, non-back at the beginning, but underlyingly it is relevant that no other coronal consonant is back in English.

$$\begin{bmatrix} -\text{son} \\ +\text{cor} \\ 4\text{height} \end{bmatrix} \qquad \textbf{48}$$

denotes (in English) the class of segment types /č ǰ š ž/.

It is also possible for a class of segment types to be referred to by means of an array of features involving disjunction as well as conjunction. The symbol of disjunction is braces { } surrounding the specified features, or conjunctions of specified features, of which at least one must be present. Thus the partly conjunctive, partly disjunctive class

$$\begin{bmatrix} -\text{son} \\ \begin{Bmatrix} +\text{cor} \\ 4\text{height} \end{Bmatrix} \end{bmatrix} \qquad \textbf{49}$$

denotes all non-sonorants that are *either* coronal *or* high, that is (in English) /t č k d ǰ g θ s š ð z ž/, a class that can also be defined conjunctively as [−son, −lab]. An example of a disjunctive class that cannot be conjunctively defined is

$$\begin{bmatrix} -\text{lab} \\ \begin{Bmatrix} -\text{son} \\ 4\text{height} \end{Bmatrix} \end{bmatrix} \qquad \textbf{50}$$

which comprises all the above segments together with /ŋ j w/ and the vowels /i: u:/.

By suitable combinations of conjunction and disjunction any set of segment types whatever can be defined as a class in this way. Not all such sets are 'genuine' or 'natural' classes, either in the technical sense of p. 97 or in the sense that their members frequently show analogous phonological or morphophonemic phenomena. Nor can we expect them to be; as there pointed out, it is probably impossible to devise a feature system under which the 'formally natural' classes will be all and only the 'intuitively natural' classes. The criterion that *is* used in analysis is that conjunctive classes are preferred to disjunctive classes; for the former assert, and the latter deny, that a generalization exists.

⑥ Generative Phonology I: The SPE Model

Most of the remainder of this book will be about various lines of development in phonological theory that have radiated from the theory elaborated mainly by Morris Halle and Noam Chomsky between about 1955 and 1968, when *The Sound Pattern of English*, which at once became the classic in this part of the field, was published. Subsequent work has tended to take the *SPE* model as a point of departure, begin by pointing out weaknesses that seemed to call for refinement or revision, and only then, if at all, come to the conclusion that this or that weakness was fundamental and required a completely different model of description. And none of these new models has superseded *SPE* in practical use.

In the present chapter, therefore, I shall describe the theory as it is presented in *SPE*, and in the three that follow examine several areas in which there has since been rethinking and controversy.

6.1 The phonological component and the form of phonological rules

Like stratificational phonology, generative phonology (GP) is intended to stand as part of a wider theory of language as a whole, and a phonological description as part of a *grammar*. The grammar enumerates the well-formed sentences of the language; to be more precise, its syntactic and semantic 'components' between them generate a set of formal objects, each of which represents one such well-formed sentence and consists of:

A string of morphemes (also called 'formatives').   **51a**

A specification (usually represented by a tree diagram, or a labelled   **b** bracketing of the string) of the hierarchical organization of this string into grammatical units ('constituents').

A specification of the syntactic, semantic and phonological peculiarities of   **c** each morpheme: information on these is derived from a *lexicon* in which each morpheme[1] is listed with such of its peculiarities as are not predictable by general rule.

A specification of the meaning of the sentence and of those principles of the   **d** language[2] by which its meaning and its form are related.

[1] For arguments for the view that the lexicon should list not morphemes but word-forms (one is tempted to say 'principal parts'), more after the manner of a conventional dictionary, and for some of the consequences of this view for the phonological component, see Linell (1976).

[2] It is these principles (some of them) that are known as 'transformations'; the other principles that define the form-meaning correspondence are the 'semantic interpretation rules', at least on the theory of syntax and semantics presupposed in *SPE*.

The lexicon mentioned in (51c) also contains a specification of the underlying phonological form of each morpheme (this being naturally classable as a 'peculiarity not predictable by general rule'), and the string of morphemes (51a) when converted into this phonological form, supplemented by the syntactic and morphological information of (51b–c), and modified in various minor ways,[3] constitutes the underlying representation which is the input to the *phonological component* of the grammar. As output of the syntactic component, (51a–c) is often called the *surface structure* or, more fully, *surface syntactic structure* of the sentence; the modified structure which is input to the phonological component is sometimes (though not in *SPE*) called a *systematic phonemic representation*.

Phonological rules then apply, changing the values of features and possibly inserting or deleting segments, to convert this representation into a *systematic phonetic representation* of a degree of 'narrowness' such that, at the very least, any two sounds that are distinguished in any human language are differently represented; Bierwisch (1967) requires systematic phonetic representation to 'account for all characteristics beyond the limits of free, individual variation.' On the *SPE* view of the nature of phonetic features, described in the last chapter, it can be regarded as representing a set of instructions issued by the central nervous system to the articulatory apparatus.

Since, as we shall see, phonological rules apply sequentially, one at a time, a sentence may have many phonological representations intermediate between the systematic phonemic and the systematic phonetic. None of these is individually of any theoretical import; in particular, no significance is attached to classical phonemic representation, and a given sentence may well not have any representation that meets the conditions of classical phonemics. It has been argued that from the standpoint of generative phonology such a representation is, for one thing, not necessary and, for another, often not possible, at least not if significant generalizations are to be captured.

It is a main function of a classical phonemic representation to sort out differences between speech sounds into two classes: differences which carry contrasts (marked in the phonemic representation) and differences due to free or environmentally controlled variation (not marked). There are some disputable cases, as we have seen in Chapter Two, on the borderline between these classes (neutralizations, for example), but the general point is clear. And it might naturally be thought that a phonological theory which does not provide for a classical phonemic representation cannot perform this function.

Against this view it might be possible to argue that the contrastive–noncontrastive distinction is no concern of phonological theory; certainly it is not a distinction to which GP has paid much attention. But few if

---

[3] These modifications are the province of the *readjustment component*, whose functions, in *SPE*, are not well defined; it seems mainly to contain those rules of the phonology which must apply before the start of the phonological cycle (cf. p. 163), but it is generally impossible to tell from the form of a rule whether it is a readjustment rule or a phonological rule proper. In contrast Bierwisch (1967) assigns definite functions to readjustment rules (which he calls morphological rules): alteration of syntactic structure in certain cases; assignment of phonological boundaries; phonological realization of some grammatical formatives. His morphological rules, unlike *SPE* readjustment rules, never modify the segments of a phonological representation (except to introduce the realization of a grammatical morpheme).

any have been willing to deny the linguistic significance of the notion; rather they have sought to show, as Postal (1968) does, that GP can indeed capture it, though not in so simple or direct a way as classical phonemics does. Once a classical phonemic analysis of a language has been made, we can say that two utterances in that language are in contrast if and only if their phonemic representations are distinct. To get the same information GP requires that two levels instead of one be consulted: in GP, two utterances are in contrast if and only if their systematic phonemic representations are distinct *and* their systematic phonetic representations are distinct. Identical phonetic representations obviously cannot contrast; while if the same underlying representation can be mapped into distinct phonetic representations, we have free variation (or perhaps variation conditioned by extrasentential context).

The claim that has attracted more attention and controversly is that a representation of the classical phonemic type is not in general *possible*. Two main types of argument have been used in this connection: the first has acquired more notoriety, but is actually somewhat dubious; the second, to which attention has been drawn more recently, is apparently much stronger.

The first type of argument may be exemplified by the classic case presented by Halle (1959) and since discussed *ad nauseam*;[4] it will also give us an opportunity to introduce the notation in which rules in GP are formulated.

In Russian, the majority of obstruents come in contrasting voiced-voiceless pairs, /k g/, /t^j d^j/, /s z/, and so on; but three obstruents, /c č x/,[5] have no distinctively voiced conterparts. Further, Russian like many other languages requires all obstruents forming a cluster to agree in voicing,[6] and for this purpose it is the last obstruent in the cluster that controls the voicing of the whole cluster. Informally, we might state the required phonological rule as follows:

An obstruent which is followed by a sequence of one or more obstruents   **52**
takes the same value for the feature 'voiced' as the last obstruent in this
sequence.

The formal expression of this is:

$$[-\text{son}] \rightarrow [\alpha\text{voice}] / \underline{\qquad} [-\text{son}]_0 \begin{bmatrix} -\text{son} \\ \alpha\text{voice} \end{bmatrix} \left\{ \begin{matrix} [+\text{son}]^7 \\ \# \end{matrix} \right\} \qquad \textbf{53}$$

An alternative and equivalent form of expression, which is regularly used by some phonologists and has the advantage that it can be employed equally well for rules which affect two or more segments simultaneously, is this:

---

[4] The facts of this case are by no means exceptional or isolated; they are typical of what happens when a particular contrast exists over only part of some natural class of phonemes, and even there is neutralized in certain environments.
[5] /c/ is an alveolar affricate; /x/ is a palatal or velar fricative according to environment.
[6] For this purpose /v/, when it ends a cluster, does not count as an obstruent; for this and other reasons it has often been concluded that in Russian phonetic [v] realizes systematic phonemic /w/.
[7] This is what the rule would be like in *SPE* phonology. In more recent work it might well have appeared as a simpler (and intuitively more natural) rule merely assimilating an obstruent to an immediately following obstruent, the rule 'propagating' itself from right to left so that each obstruent, once assimilated, could cause the assimilation of an obstruent directly preceding it. See below, pp. 171–4.

$$[-\text{son}] \quad [-\text{son}]_0 \begin{bmatrix} -\text{son} \\ \alpha\text{voice} \end{bmatrix} \left\{ \begin{matrix} [+\text{son}] \\ \# \end{matrix} \right\} \qquad 54$$
$$\downarrow$$
$$[\alpha\text{voice}]$$

In a rule of the form (53), the symbol or symbols to the left of the arrow constitute the *input*. The symbols, if any, to the right of the oblique stroke form the *environment*; if there is no oblique stroke the rule is understood to apply in all environments. Input and environment between them form the *structural description* of the rule; in a rule formulated in the manner of (54) the parts of the structural description are not distinguished. And the symbols that are not part of the structural description (SD)—in (53) and (54), the one specified feature [αvoice]—constitute the *output* or *structural change* (SC). The generalized forms of (53) and (54) are (55) and (56) respectively, which are, again, exactly equivalent; in each case A and B represent single columns of features, and X and Y sequences of such columns, and X or Y or both may be null:

$$A \rightarrow B \; / \; X \text{——} Y \qquad\qquad 55$$

$$X \quad A \quad Y \qquad\qquad 56$$
$$\downarrow$$
$$B$$

The interpretation of such a rule is as follows: we define a notion of *matching* such that—

A segment of S of a phonological representation matches a column of   57
features C in the statement of a phonological rule if and only if every specified feature of C is present in S.

(57) assumes that all rules are stated in their fullest form, without the use of abbreviatory conventions: each such convention involves some redefinition of the notion of matching. We can now state the interpretation of (55) or (56).

If a phonological representation contains a sequence of segments matching   58
one-for-one, and in the same order as, the columns of X, followed by a segment matching A, followed by a sequence of segments matching one-for-one, and in the same order as, the columns of Y, then the minimum alterations are to be made to the feature specifications of the segment matching A, such that it matches B.

What the input representation contains, other than the sequence matching XAY, is immaterial.

Now consider, with respect to this interpretation, rule (53) or (54) and the underlying representation /dat^{j}bi/, in particular its third segment /t^j/. This segment is non-sonorant, and thus matches (or *meets* or *fits*) the input description (A) of (53). Rule (53) contains nothing corresponding to X (i.e. X is null in this particular rule), so it does not matter what precedes the segment under consideration.[8] What of Y? In this rule Y consists of three columns: for the rule to apply the input segment must be followed by:

(i) $[-\text{son}]_0$—that is, zero or more obstruents. Where a rule contains an expression of the form Z_0, whatever Z may be (a single column, a sequence of columns, or some more complex array), this expression is matched by any of the following: zero; a segment or sequence, as the case may be, matching Z; any continuous sequence of such matching segments or sequences. Thus V_0 is matched by zero, or by one or more successive syllabics;[9] $[V[+\text{nas}]]_0$ by zero, by a sequence of syllabic plus nasal, or by any number of such sequences in succession; $[C_0 V_0]$ by zero, or by one or more sequences of a vowel optionally preceded by a consonant or consonants—in effect, zero or more syllables. The subscript denotes the *least* number of successive occurrences required to constitute a match: thus C_1 means one or more nonsyllables, C_2 two or more, etc. (Note the contrast with C, CC, etc., which denotes sequences of *exactly* one, two, etc., nonsyllabics.) In the case of /dat^{j}bi/ it might be thought that the /b/ provided a match for $[-\text{son}]_0$; but we shall be needing it to provide a match for the next column, and we can quite happily leave the column $[-\text{son}]_0$ to be matched by zero—that is, in effect, treat it as though it were not there at all. The Z_0 notation is one of the devices GP makes available for the situation where a rule applies in a particular environment whether that environment is directly adjacent to the input segment or at a distance, so long, in the latter case, as the intervening segments meet certain conditions.

Halle (1975) proposes to abandon the Z_0 notation in favour of one which specifies, not the conditions the intervening segments must meet, but those they must not meet. Thus a Huasteco rule stressing the last long vowel in a word, or the first syllable if the word contains no long vowel, should, Halle suggests, be thus expressed:

$$V \rightarrow [+\text{stress}] \, / \!\!-\!\! Q \; \# \; \# \quad \text{where } Q \neq X \begin{bmatrix} V \\ +\text{long} \end{bmatrix} Y \qquad 59$$

Where (as will normally happen) a variable like Q matches more than one substring of the string to which the rule applies, it must be interpreted as matching the longest possible substring; Q thus here means 'a maximal stretch containing no long vowel', and the new notation thus unifies what would otherwise seem to be two unconnected subrules.

(ii) $\begin{bmatrix} -\text{son} \\ \alpha\text{voice} \end{bmatrix}$—that is, an obstruent that is either positively or negatively specified for voice, it does not matter which. It might be thought that the mention of voice is redundant and that $[-\text{son}]$ would have been sufficient; as will be seen in a moment, this is not the case. The symbol α is a variable ranging

---

[8] Note that a null left-hand (or, as the case may be, right-hand) environment does *not* mean that the input segment is required to be preceded (resp. followed) by nothing. In a rule which applies only to utterance-initial (utterance-final) segments, the left-hand (right-hand) environment will be expressed as 'pause' or 'utterance boundary', not as null.

[9] The symbols C (consonant) and V (vowel) are handy abbreviatory devices, but not all generative phonologists are agreed on what they are to be taken as meaning. In this book they will be taken to be equivalent to $[-\text{syllabic}]$ and $[+\text{syllabic}]$ respectively.

over the values + and − ;[10] where, as here, the same Greek-letter variable appears in both the SD and the SC, the rule is normally an instruction to *assimilate* the specification of the feature in question to its specification in some segment of the environment, or to the specification of some other feature. For the latter possibility cf.

$$
\begin{bmatrix} V \\ \alpha back \end{bmatrix} \rightarrow [\alpha round] \qquad\qquad 60
$$

(59) makes back vowels round and front vowels non-round. If a *dissimilation* rule is in question, one of the variables will have a minus sign prefixed, it being understood that a minus sign applied to any specification converts it into the opposite specification: e.g.

$$
\begin{bmatrix} +cons \\ +son \end{bmatrix} \rightarrow [-\alpha nas] \, / \, \underline{\hspace{1em}} \, V \begin{bmatrix} +cons \\ +son \\ \alpha nas \end{bmatrix} \qquad 61
$$

This rule (similar to rules which have operated in the history of some Romance languages) dissimilates sequences of like resonants, converting e.g. /nVn/ to [lVn]. Two or more different Greek letters are used only to indicate two or more independent variables, e.g.

$$
[-cont] \rightarrow \begin{bmatrix} \alpha voice \\ \beta nasal \end{bmatrix} / \, \underline{\hspace{1em}} \, \begin{bmatrix} -cont \\ \alpha voice \\ \beta nasal \end{bmatrix} \qquad 62
$$

(61) assimilates a stop in respect of the mutually independent features of voice and nasality (but not in respect of e.g. articulatory place) to a following stop (oral or nasal): e.g. /pn/ is converted to [mn], /ŋb/ to [gb], /bk/ to [pk].

To return to (53), the column $\begin{bmatrix} -son \\ \alpha voice \end{bmatrix}$ is matched by the /b/ of /datʲbi/; we note that it is voiced, and therefore that on this particular occasion α is equal to +.

From time to time proposals have been made to use 'alpha variables' as coefficients of other elements than features. Thus Zwicky (1970b) suggested that the French truncation rule (cf. *SPE* 353ff) might be expressed without using the syllabicity feature whose necessity Chomsky and Halle thought was proved by the rule:

$$
\begin{bmatrix} \alpha vocalic \\ -\alpha cons \\ +foreign \end{bmatrix} \rightarrow \theta \, / \, \underline{\hspace{1em}} \, \# \, \alpha \begin{bmatrix} -cons \\ +vocalic \end{bmatrix} \qquad 63
$$

It is assumed that $-\begin{bmatrix} -cons \\ +vocalic \end{bmatrix}$ means 'not both non-consonantal and vocalic', i.e. 'either consonantal or non-vocalic'; so that the rule means: 'at the end of a foreign word, delete a vowel where the next word begins with a vowel' (α being +) 'and delete a true consonant (not a liquid or glide) where the next word begins with

[10] Or over all the possible specifications of a multinary feature.

E

anything but a vowel'. This device has not won general acceptance; its main effect is to make it easier to write rules referring to disjunctive classes, surely a retrograde step.

(iii)   In the last column of (53/54), $\{^{[+son]}_{\#}\}$, the braces tell us that we have a choice. The expression $\{^{P}_{Q}\}$ in a rule is matched if either P is matched or Q is matched (or both). Thus here a match can be made either by a non-obstruent (resonant or vowel), or by $\#$, that is word boundary (which is assumed to have been inserted by readjustment rules in certain syntactically defined positions).

Thus the SD of (53/54) is completely matched. In full the match can be represented as follows:

$$[-\text{son}] \ [-\text{son}]_0 \ \begin{bmatrix} -\text{son} \\ \alpha\text{voice} \end{bmatrix} \left\{ \begin{matrix} [+\text{son}] \\ \# \end{matrix} \right\} \qquad \textbf{64}$$

/da   t^j (zero)   b   i/

The SC of the rule tells us that we must alter the input segment /t^j/, if necessary, in such a way that it matches [αvoice], that is in this case (cf. above, p. 119) [+voice]. The segment /t^j/ is at present specified [−voice]; we therefore change this to [+voice]. In so doing we have *applied* rule (53/54), whose *output* (differing by one feature from the input) is [dad^{j}bi].

To return now to Halle's argument against classical phonemics, consider now the four underlying representations (65a), the application to which of rule (53/54) yields the representations (65b), which may for our purposes be taken to be the phonetic representations.

dat^{j}l^{j}i	dat^{j}bi	žečl^{j}i	žečbi	**65a**
dat^{j}l^{j}i	dad^{j}bi	žečl^{j}i	žeǰbi	**b**

Now there is no doubt that (53/54) is the most general way of expressing the relationship between (65a) and (65b); and to postulate any kind of intermediate level of representation between these two would result in having to duplicate the rule. But now observe (so runs the argument) that a level meeting the requirements of classical phonemics would in fact be intermediate between (65a) and (65b). Representation (65a) is too abstract: it ignores the difference between [t^j] and [d^j], which in other environments is contrastive. (65b), on the other hand, overdifferentiates: it marks the difference between [č] and [ǰ], which is never contrastive. Yet a classical phonemic representation must mark all and only the differences that are capable of being contrastive; neither (65a) nor (65b) could be a classical phonemic representation, but only something like (66):

$$\text{dat}^j\text{l}^j\text{i} \quad \text{dad}^j\text{bi} \quad \text{žečl}^j\text{i} \quad \text{žečbi} \qquad \textbf{66}$$

And we can only get (66) if we are prepared to split (53/54) into two separate rules, one a 'morphophonemic' rule applying to all segment types except /c č x/, the other an 'allophonic' rule applying just to these three phonemes, thus forgoing the significant generalization that voicing assimilation applies uniformly to all obstruents.

Various objections have been brought against this line of argument:[11] some of

[11] And even against the accuracy of the data adduced: see Christie (1976, 39).

these have been refuted (see e.g. Postal 1968), but two at least have considerable weight.

The first objection is that the argument we are considering is really valid only against the American version of classical phonemics, which requires all differences to be marked that are *capable* of being contrastive. For this and several similar arguments arc based on neutralization, and deal with situations in which a Prague School phonologist, holding that the only differences which should be marked are those which are *actually* contrastive, would make use of the notion 'archiphoneme'. Such a phonologist would say that the true phonological representations of the forms in (65) were:

$$\text{dat}^j\text{l}^j\text{i} \quad \text{daT}^j\text{bi} \quad \text{žečl}^j\text{i} \quad \text{žečbi} \qquad\qquad 67$$

where $/\text{T}^j/$ is the archiphoneme of the pair $/\text{t}^j\,\text{d}^j/$ which before obstruents do not contrast: working with features as our ultimate units, we would no doubt say that the archiphoneme was unspecified for voice. The rule (53/54) applied to these representations gives the correct set of outputs (65b); on this view the rule would always be allophonic, never morphophonemic.

The second and perhaps even more important objection is that, even restricting 'classical phonemics' to its American sense, the conclusion does not follow from the premises. All that has been proved is that in the process of determining ('deriving') the pronunciation of a sentence from its underlying phonological representation, none of the intermediate levels (at which certain rules have applied and others have not) necessarily meets the conditions of classical phonemics. That tells us nothing about the role that such a level might play in speech production or, more importantly, in speech perception. It is significant that Hockett (1965) defines a major assumption of classical phonemics in terms of speech perception:

> The difference between any two distinct sentences of a language is audible to a native speaker in the absence of noise, even if there is no defining context.

By 'distinct' Hockett must here mean 'phonologically distinct'; for he cannot have had any intention of committing himself to the position that homophonous sentences such as those he elsewhere[12] cites, *The sun's rays meet* and *The sons raise meat*, are linguistically identical in all respects, even if spoken with the same intonation. Hockett's assumption is rejected by GP, which in Sapirian fashion (cf. pp. 5–7) holds that *Brown leaves today*, referring to the colour of leaves (where the [v] of *leaves* alternates with [f]), is *phonologically* distinct from *Brown leaves today*, referring to the departure of Brown (where the corresponding [v] does not alternate)—again, even under identical intonation.

Postal (1968, 25) notes this objection but claims that there is no evidence 'that perceptual facts support [classical] phonemics *vis-à-vis* systematic'. But he has restricted his definition of 'perceptual facts' in such a way that the inability of any speaker of English to distinguish between the two sentences *Brown leaves today* (without help from the context) is not a perceptual fact. Postal does make the

---

[12] Hockett (1958, 15)—where he compares the two sentences to identical twins, thus implying that they are *not* one and the same sentence. (Identical twins are not identical; if Bill and Ben were identical, Bill would be Ben and Ben would be Bill.)

solid point that the system of four contrasting stress phonemes usually posited by American phonemicists in the 1950s did not correspond to a four-way perceptual distinction, many of these same phonemicists being unable to hear the contrasts which they set up with any consistency or assurance (cf. p. 37); but as we saw in Chapter Two, that probably was not a correct phonemic analysis.

We must therefore remember that proof that a classical phonemic level plays no role in the GP phonological component does not constitute proof that such a level has no linguistic significance whatsoever.[13] This reservation applies not only to the line of argument followed by Halle but also to the alternative line which we are now going to consider, which is not vulnerable to the other objection raised (p. 121).

This line of argument was first, so far as I know, pointed out by Matthews (1972),[14] who brings the following example.

In Classical Latin it is known (primarily from explicit statements by native speakers) that the phoneme /l/ had two markedly different allophones, one 'clear' (the native term was 'thin', *exilis*) and rather similar to the prevocalic allophone of English /l/, the other 'dark' (*pinguis*, lit. 'fat'), that is, velarized, like English final or preconsonantal allophones of /l/. The evidence of sound-change indicates that at one stage in the history of the language, the 'clear' allophone was used when the lateral was geminate, or when it directly preceded a front vowel, and the 'dark' allophone in all other environments.

Consider now the following data:

/wolo:/	'I wish'	**68**
/wolumus/	'we wish'	
/wolunt/	'they wish'	
/wolui:/	'I wished'	
/wult/	'he wishes'	
/wultis/	'you pl. wish'	
/welim/	'I would like' (present subjunctive)[15]	
/welle/	'to wish'	
/wellem/	'I would wish' (imperfect subjunctive)[15]	

This vowel alternation occurs in full nowhere else, though it is significant that it is found in part in certain verbs whose roots end in /l/:

/impell+ere/ 'drive on': past participle /impul+sus/	**67**
/resil+i:re/ 'rebound': frequentative /resul+t+a:re/	
/sepel+i:re/ 'bury': past participle /sepul+tus/	

[13] And phonemic contrast probably plays some role as one of the factors determining the direction of phonological change, as Schane (1971) has recognized.

[14] Matthews, be it emphasized, is not a generative phonologist, and the conclusions he draws from the example are somewhat different. It is not an isolated example: Newton (1975) notes another (which is, however, factually less certain), and there are probably many more whose bearing on the question has not been recognized.

[15] The Latin subjunctive has many different uses, and the glosses here given merely indicate common meanings of these forms in independent clauses— /welim/ often introducing a mild wish or request or hope for the future, /wellem/ a wish that the present situation were otherwise than it is. The forms are also used in constructions that make it quite clear that /wolo:/ and /welim/ are indicative and subjunctive of the same verb, e.g. /roga:s kʷid welim/ 'you ask what I want?' cf. /kʷid wolo:/ 'what do I want?', and analogously for the imperfect subjunctive.

The generalization is clear. Where /l/ is velarized—in terms of the features we are using, back—the vowel preceding it is back, and *vice versa*.[16] The underlying representations will in all relevant cases have front vowels in the roots, e.g. /wel/, /sepel/; then the rules of (70) will account for the facts with maximal generality, provided—and this is crucial—that rule (70b) applies to the output of rule (70a), which alone creates forms that can satisfy its SD.

$$[+\text{lateral}] \rightarrow \left\{ \begin{array}{l} [-\text{back}] \qquad / \quad \left\{ \begin{array}{c} \underline{\quad} 1 \\ 1 \underline{\quad} \\ \underline{\quad} \begin{bmatrix} +\text{syll} \\ -\text{back} \end{bmatrix} \end{array} \right\} \\ [+\text{back}]\, \text{elsewhere} \end{array} \right\} \qquad \textbf{70a}$$

$$[+\text{syll}] \rightarrow [+\text{back}] / \underline{\quad} \begin{bmatrix} +\text{lateral} \\ +\text{back} \end{bmatrix} \qquad \textbf{b}$$

The application of these rules may be exemplified by the following derivations:

	wel+im	wel+o:	wel+t	wel+le[17]	71
by (70a)	———	weł+o:	weł+t	———	
by (70b)	———	woł+o:	woł ɪ t	———	
by other rules	welim	woło:	wułt	welle	

What though would classical phonemic representations be? Phonetically the initial syllables of [welim] and of [woło:] differed in two ways. The vowel was front in one of them, back in the other; the lateral was velarized in one of them and not in the other. And for classical phonemics the question is which of these two differences constitutes a contrast and which is merely an automatic concomitant of some other difference.

Of the answer to this question there can be no doubt. The difference between [e] and [o] was very frequently contrastive in Latin; one of many minimal pairs is [regat] 'let him rule': [rogat] 'he asks'. The difference between [l] and [ł], on the other hand, is entirely predictable in all cases from phonetic environments and hence cannot be regarded as contrastive. Thus /e o/ are separate phonemes while /l/ is one phoneme; and therefore the appropriate classical phonemic representations for the two forms in which we are interested are /welim wolo:/, with /l/, in each case, unspecified for backness.

Now of these two forms, /welim/ gives no trouble; but /wolo:/ is a form that does not figure in the motivated derivation at all, neither as the underlying form nor as the phonetic form nor as an intermediate form: for at no stage in that derivation is backness positively specified in the vowel and unspecified in the consonant. Thus we see that at least one derivation exists which includes no representation that satisfies the conditions of classical phonemics: in other words, these conditions cannot in any way be made general requirements on the phonological components of generative grammars. As already noted, this does not amount to denying any linguistic significance at all to classical phonemic representations.

[16] The alternation between /o/ and /u/ is a separate matter, having nothing directly to do with the allophones of /l/.

[17] The underlying representation is perhaps /wel+re/, /re/ being the almost invariable infinitive termination; if so, an earlier rule must have assimilated /lr/ to [ll]—earlier, because if the form were *wel+re* when (70) became applicable, the /l/ would be velarized.

6.2 An illustrative analysis

I will now exemplify an analysis on GP lines of a set of phenomena in English of which a stratificational analysis was given in Chapter Four, and then consider in detail other aspects of the theory.

We begin, as before (p. 88), with the fact that the final segment of certain morphemes alternates phonetically between [k] and [s], and of others between [g] and [j]. We note, as before, that the fronted alternants are found before the syllabic peaks [I e ə: i: ɪ: aj] and before [ə] where this alternates with one of these six vowels. This raises the following questions, bearing in mind (cf. p. 5) that GP tries where possible to derive diverse pronunciations of one and the same grammatical element from a common underlying form:

How do we account for the consonant alternation?   **72a**

How do we account for the fact that the fronted alternants are found before   **b**
a set of syllabic peaks which do not constitute a natural class?

How do we account for the fact that the fronted alternants are found before   **c**
some occurrences of [ə] but not before others?

How do we account for the fact (p. 90) that in word-final or preconsonantal   **d**
position either alternant may be found?

How do we account for the fact that some instances of [k g], no matter what   **e**
vowel follows, do not participate in the alternation at all?

In our previous stratificational analysis, we set up special morphons for the alternating segments: we called them /K G/, but these names were purely mnemonic and of no theoretical significance. Our present analysis, by contrast, is made under the 'Naturalness Condition' (p. 108): if we say that the underlying final segment of *ideologue* is /g/, we are saying that other things (that is the phonological rules of the language) being equal to the final segment of the stem *ideologue* will be phonetically [g].

For the alternating consonants we have three choices. We can analyse them as underlying velars, or as underlying /s j/, or as consonants of some intermediate class (say palatals) which become velars in some environments and (palato-) alveolars in others.

Consider first the possibility of regarding the final segments of e.g. *reduce* and *ideologue* as underlying /s j/. At first sight it does not seem to be a serious objection to this that there are numerous cases of phonetic [s j] which do not alternate with velars; after all, there are also numerous phonetic velars which do not alternate with [s j]. There is, however, an important difference. The dividing line between alternating and non-alternating velars is not an arbitrary one, but a line that would have had to be drawn in any case regardless of this alternation; for it corresponds pretty closely with the division, of great importance in English phonology and morphology, between 'Germanic' and 'Latin' morphemes.

I have put these objectives within quotation marks because I am using them in a special and synchronic, not an etymological, sense. For not everything in the English vocabulary which is ultimately derived from Latin is 'Latin' in the relevant sense. For instance, English *count* 'enumerate, enumeration' and *count* '(foreign) earl' are both ultimately derived from Latin, but there is no reason to assign either to the synchronically 'Latin' portion of the vocabulary. Note, for instance, that they do not take any of the typically Latin suffixes -(*at*)*ion*, -*ive*, -*ic*(*al*), -*ity*, etc., and contrast their etymological 'long-lost brothers' *compute* and -*comit*- (as in *concomitant*).[18]

Generally speaking, velars in 'Germanic' forms do not alternate, in 'Latin' forms they do. More than that, velars are simply not found in 'Latin' forms before the six peak types which condition the alternation. There is no such neat dividing line when we look at alternating and non-alternating [s] or [ǰ]; in particular, there are many unquestionably 'Latin' forms (e.g. *sanctity*, *solve*; *judicial*, *junction*) in which [s ǰ] appear before vowels which in alternating forms require the presence of [k g].

In short, if we take /s ǰ/ to be the underlying representations of the alternating consonants, we will need an *ad hoc* feature to determine in what forms they can be realized as [k g] and in what forms not; whereas with /k g/ as the underlying representations the features required are the independently motivated ones indicating the vocabulary divisions.

Some phonologists, especially in the early days of GP, would have preferred to put the argument in a different form. They would have said: if we take /s ǰ/ to be the underlying representations, it will be necessary, for each morpheme in the 'Latin' vocabulary, to specify in the lexicon, by a diacritic feature, whether it is or is not an exception to the rule converting /s ǰ/ to [k g] in certain environments. If the underlying representations are /k g/, this function will be performed by the vocabulary-division feature [±Latin], which is needed in any case, and consequently the grammar will be 'simplified' because all those diacritic features can be omitted from it.

This seems here to be merely a variant of the argument from independent motivation; but it has a much wider bearing. It is ultimately based on the notion of a simplicity metric, on which we touched in Chapter One when considering the internal justification of linguistic hypotheses and again in Chapter Four when we considered the simplicity metric of stratificational grammar. The simplicity metric of GP, in its crudest form, is just this: every specified feature has a 'cost' of one unit, and the simplest (and best) grammar is that whose 'cost' is lowest. But as has been pointed out in Chapter One, the simplicity metric has never been a prime tool for deciding among analyses; and it was early recognized that the metric begged a number of questions, e.g. what was the cost of features like [±Latin] which were not of a phonological nature? what was the cost of a rule that referred not to a complex of features but to an individual morpheme (say past tense)? is it legitimate to 'trade off' simplification of lexical representations against complication of morphophonemic rules or vice versa, and if so what is the 'rate of exchange'? These questions have never been satisfactorily answered, and formal simplicity has long ceased to be used as a criterion in GP.[19]

---

[18] For simplicity I have for the present left aside here the third major subdivision of the English vocabulary, the 'Greek' stratum, which shares many important characteristics of the 'Latin'; velars in 'Greek' forms sometimes alternate, sometimes do not.— On the feature representation of vocabulary divisions see pp. 158–9.

[19] There is a marked decline in confidence in the metric between, say, Harms (1966) and Zimmer (1970). The new evaluation measure tentatively sketched by Kiparsky (1974b), which takes into

Another argument that might be employed has to do with the underlying consonant system of the 'Latin' vocabulary. A corollary, though not a logically inevitable corollary, of the 'Naturalness Condition' is that we are suspicious of proposed underlying consonant or vowel systems which would be highly abnormal as phonetic or classical phonemic systems. The elements of underlying systems are, as it were, conditional ('other-things-being-equal') phonetic segment types; so we expect the systems as wholes to be such that, other things being equal, they would be plausible phonetic systems. And any analysis of the alternating segments which does not make them underlying velars will leave the 'Latin' portion of the vocabulary with a stop system in which velars are entirely lacking, and this although scarcely any language in the world is known to be without velars at the phonetic level.[20] If the alternating segments are regarded as underlying /k g/ we get much more credible underlying stop system /p t k b d j g/.

The second possibility we have to consider is that phonetic [k g] and [s j], where they alternate, are both derived from underlying consonants of some intermediate type. This analysis too would leave the underlying stop system of the 'Latin' vocabulary without velars. It is also vulnerable to a somewhat different version of the argument from the principle of independent motivation, in that the setting up of these underlying consonants is an *ad hoc* addition to the consonant system to account for one alternation; further, there is no non-arbitrary way of deciding what features to assign them. The 'intermediate' analysis seems to have no significant advantages to set against these drawbacks, and few generative phonologists using the *SPE* model[21] would hesitate before deciding in favour of analysing the alternating segments as underlying /k g/.

Having decided on our underlying representations, we might now think it a simple matter to formulate a rule that will convert them to the appropriate surface representations; here is such a rule, the environment description being for the moment left out:

$$
\begin{bmatrix}
-\text{sonorant} \\
-\text{continuant} \\
+\text{back} \\
\alpha\text{voice} \\
+\text{Latin}
\end{bmatrix}
\longrightarrow
\begin{bmatrix}
-\text{back} \\
+\text{coronal} \\
\beta\text{continuant} \\
\gamma\text{height}
\end{bmatrix}
\quad / \ldots \qquad 73
$$

Conditions: if $\alpha = +$, then $\beta = -+$ and $\gamma = 4$.
if $\alpha = -$, then $\beta = +$ and $\gamma = 2$.

(73) illustrates another possible use of variable feature coefficients: to state complex dependencies between input and output features. But the very fact that the dependencies *are* so complex may give us pause about accepting (73). The complexity is due to the fact that the process described in (73) consists of a part common to /k/ and /g/ and parts peculiar to each of them. Would it perhaps make for simpler, more plausible, more 'natural' rules if we separated out the *pars*

---

account other factors besides formal simplicity, is meant to help explain linguistic change rather than to decide among analyses.

[20] Trubetzkoy (1939) finds velars absent only in 'some Slovene dialects of Carinthia'.

[21] The reservation is made because some more recent schools might not accept that a feature-changing rule was involved at all (cf. Chapter Nine).

communis and each of the two *partes propriae* and made them into three separate rules? One way of doing this would be the following:

$$
\begin{bmatrix} -\text{sonorant} \\ -\text{continuant} \\ +\text{back} \\ +\text{Latin} \end{bmatrix} \longrightarrow \begin{bmatrix} -\text{back} \\ +\text{coronal} \\ -+\text{continuant} \\ 2\text{height} \end{bmatrix} \quad /\ldots \qquad 74
$$

$$
\begin{bmatrix} +\text{coronal} \\ -+\text{continuant} \\ 2\text{height} \\ -\text{voice} \end{bmatrix} \longrightarrow [+\text{continuant}] \qquad 75
$$

$$
\begin{bmatrix} +\text{coronal} \\ -+\text{continuant} \end{bmatrix} \longrightarrow [4\text{height}] \qquad 76
$$

Each of these rules would apply to the output of the previous one. The first of them, (74), converts /k g/ in 'fronting' environments to /t͡s d͡z/; this is the *pars communis* of Velar Softening. The other two rules are context-free, and may be said to reflect the fact that English phonotactics does not admit alveolar affricates.[22] The first converts /t͡s/ to [s]; the second is expressed to apply to all alveolar affricates, but in fact, owing to its being ordered after (75), can only apply to /d͡z/ (the only one remaining) which it converts to [j]. Note that (75) and (76) can be *collapsed* into a single *schema*:

$$
\begin{bmatrix} +\text{coronal} \\ -+\text{continuant} \\ 2\text{height} \end{bmatrix} \rightarrow \begin{Bmatrix} [+\text{continuant}] \ /\ [\overline{-\text{voice}}] \\ [4\text{height}] \end{Bmatrix} \qquad 77
$$

This rule (which is exactly equivalent in its effect to the sequence of rules (75, 76)) introduces two important notational conventions. Any rule containing a pair of braces abbreviates two rules (or more): (78a), where X or Z may be null, is an abbreviation for (78b):

$$
X \begin{Bmatrix} Y \\ W \end{Bmatrix} Z \qquad \text{78a}
$$

$$
XYZ, XWZ \qquad \text{b}
$$

The other convention is that of the *simultaneous environment*. We are by now familiar with the identity (79):

$$
A \rightarrow B\ /\ X \text{\textemdash\textemdash} Y \equiv XAY \rightarrow XBY \qquad 79
$$

We now, by extending this to (80), enable ourselves to carry over features of the input segment and state them in the environment description if this is more convenient:

[22] Except (i) across a morpheme boundary, where they should no doubt be treated as sequences of segments rather than complex segments (e.g. in plurals and possessives), (ii) in unassimilated loans, e.g. *tsar*, *blitz*—though even in the latter (75) sometimes seems to be operative in initial position, leading to pronunciations such as [sa:]. The notion of a rule reflecting a phonotactic restriction is foreign to the *SPE* model, which held, rather, that rules *created* phonotactic restrictions, but it does seem to have substantial validity; see further Chapter Eight.

$$A \rightarrow B \ / \ X\left[\ \overline{\text{C}} \ \right] Y \equiv X\begin{bmatrix} A \\ C \end{bmatrix} Y \ X\begin{bmatrix} B \\ C \end{bmatrix} Y \qquad \textbf{80}$$

How can we choose between the alternative rules (73) and (74, 77)? The answer is not automatic unless we hold unquestioningly to the feature-counting simplicity metric. Indeed, it is not automatic even if we do: (73) has nine specified features against fourteen in (74) and (77) combined, but what is the cost of the 'conditions' attached to (73)?

The choice depends to some extent on the weight to be attached to different criteria: at this point a glance back to pp. 10–15 in Chapter One would not be out of place. Many would prefer (74 + 77) because the rules are more plausible and natural than (73): by splitting (73) into its component parts we have in fact made it much clearer why Velar Softening has the effect it has and not some other effect. This is plausibility in the sense of p. 10, where it was said that 'the phonological processes assumed should if possible be such as are known to be normal and in some sense 'natural' in language generally.' There is also the 'phonetic plausibility' of p. 15, which is concerned with the easing of speech production and perception; and here it is fairly clear that (77) eases both by eliminating the need to make and to recognize two contrasts, [$\widehat{\text{ts}} \sim \text{s}$] and [$\widehat{\text{dz}} \sim \text{ʝ}$], which are relatively rare in language generally and otherwise unknown in English, at little if any cost in homonymy. On the other hand, those who are mindful that GP makes claims about psychological reality may wonder if any such reality can be ascribed to these alveolar affricates, introduced more or less *ad hoc* for the purpose of making a rule more plausible. I shall leave the issue unresolved—which is how GP has left it, thus far.

We have still to determine the environment in which (74) is to apply. The first step is clearly to deal with the alternation between the full vowels [ɪ e ə: i: ɪ: a:] and the reduced vowel [ə].

The reduced vowel cannot here be taken as basic, since it is unpredictable which of the six full vowels (not to mention other full vowels with which we are not at present concerned) it will alternate with, and peculiarities not predictable by rule belong in the lexicon (p. 114), hence in the underlying representation. Therefore we must take the full vowels as basic and try to determine under what circumstances they are reduced.

We note that [ə] is always unstressed;[23] and we also note that syllables with full vowels are phonetically more prominent than those with reduced vowels, so that out of context we might judge them to have stronger stress. In our classical phonemic analysis in Chapter Two, we in effect treated these prominence differences as non-distinctive concomitants of vowel contrasts; but this was because, given the assumptions of classical phonemics, the vowel contrasts were needed anyway. In the present analysis there will not at the underlying level be any contrast between full vowels and schwa; at the phonetic level, on the other hand, we will want to state not only this distinction but also all stress distinctions that are linguistically determined (see the definition of systematic phonetic

---

[23] In my dialect a vowel phonetically very close to schwa occurs in the stressed syllable of *worry*, but this is no doubt a conditioned variant of the stressed vowel of *hurry*, so that it can be separately accounted for without invalidating the argument in the text.

representations on p. 115); and no intermediate level has structural significance.

Now in *SPE* it is claimed, with much ingenious argument and a wealth of evidence, that stress in English is almost entirely predictable by rule from phonological structure, morphological make-up and grammatical categorization. This claim has met with considerable criticism, and a number of alternative proposals have been made; we shall here, for the sake of the discussion, accept the *SPE* claim as correct, and note that it extends even to the minor distinctions in prominence with which we are now concerned. We can therefore, as indeed *SPE* does, apply to the output of all these stress rules a rule[24] of

VOWEL REDUCTION   **81**

$$\begin{bmatrix} V \\ -\text{long} \\ -\text{stress} \end{bmatrix} \longrightarrow \begin{bmatrix} 2\text{height} \\ +\text{back} \\ -\text{round} \end{bmatrix}$$

This rule must be *ordered* after Velar Softening; that is, for one thing it cannot apply until Velar Softening has had a chance to apply (though Velar Softening need not actually have applied, for its SD may not have been matched), and for another, once Vowel Reduction has applied, Velar Softening cannot apply. Observe why this must be so. If Vowel Reduction applies first and Velar Softening then applies to its output, it will be impossible to tell which instances of [ə] are derived from vowels permitting Velar Softening before them and which are not. Therefore Velar Softening must apply at a stage when all vowels are still full vowels, i.e. it must be ordered before Vowel Reduction.[25]

So we do not need to make special provision for Velar Softening before [ə], and we seem to be left with the following environment description for that rule:

$$/ \underline{\hspace{2cm}} \left\{ \begin{matrix} I \\ e \\ \text{i:} \\ \text{ɪ:} \\ \text{ə:} \\ \text{aj} \end{matrix} \right\} \qquad \textbf{82}$$

—or in feature terms:

$$/ \underline{\hspace{2cm}} \begin{bmatrix} V \\ -\text{round} \\ (1) \geq 2\text{height} \\ \left\{ \begin{matrix} \begin{bmatrix} -\text{long} \\ -\text{back} \end{bmatrix} \\ \begin{bmatrix} +\text{long} \\ +(-)\text{back} \\ \geq 3\text{height} \end{bmatrix} \end{matrix} \right\} \end{bmatrix} \qquad \textbf{83}^{26}$$

[24] The last rule in the phonology of English as *SPE* presents it, aside from phonetic detail rules which *SPE* omits.

[25] There is a fallacy in this argument. Could not the two rules apply simultaneously? *SPE* phonology does not consider this possibility; but see Chapter Seven.

[26] Some special notational conventions, not in general use, are here needed because of the use made of

No wonder, the reader may well be thinking, that we described this alternation on p. 88 as 'almost a paradigm case of an alternation "better treated in terms of whole segments".' The description in feature terms indeed seems fantastically complicated. But it may be worth while, before accepting our previous verdict, to consider some facts about the English vowel system that may perhaps throw doubt on it.

We can first of all dismiss [ɪ:] and [ə:] from consideration. These very frequently alternate with sequences of vowel plus [r], and GP, being allowed to take morpheme boundaries into account, will have, unlike classical phonemics,[27] no difficulty in analysing them as derived from such sequences, viz. /iːr/ and /er/. The same general principle will apply to all the syllabic peaks which display similar alternations, viz. (to use Jones's numbering as we did in (15), pp. 30f) peak types, 5, 11, 18, 19, 21, and 7 in some of its occurrences. Since we have already seen that [ə] is derived by a very late rule, our twenty peak types are reduced to fourteen:

	ɪ	e	æ	a	ɔ	U	iː	oː	uː	ej	aj	oj	æw	əw	84
height	3	2	1	1	1	3	4	2	4	24	14	24	14	24	
back	−	−	−	+	+	+	−	+	+	−	+−	+−−+	+		
round	−	−	−	−	+	+	−	+	+	−	−	+−−+	−+		
long	−	−	−	−	−	−	+	+	+	+	+	+	+	+	

And the six peak types that condition Velar Softening are reduced to four, /ɪ e iː aj/.

This simplifies the formidable specification (83), but not by much; it is now:

$$/ \underline{\qquad} \quad \begin{bmatrix} \text{V} \\ -\text{round} \\ \left\{\begin{bmatrix} -\text{long} \\ \geq 2\text{height} \end{bmatrix}\right\} \\ \begin{bmatrix} +\text{long} \\ (1)4\text{height} \end{bmatrix} \end{bmatrix} \qquad \textbf{85}$$

Velar Softening, however, is not the only morphophonemic process that cannot be satisfactorily formulated in terms of the syllabic peak system (84). In particular there is a whole series of alternations between short and long peaks that may be said to conflict with the system, in the sense that they pair peak types that have few or no features in common. These are found predominantly, though not solely, in the 'Latin' part of the vocabulary, and are as follows:

---

multinary features and complex segments. A symbol in parentheses denotes a specification that may be present or absent: thus [+(−)back] means 'either [+back] or [+−back]'. Combining this convention with the use of the symbol for 'equal to or greater than', it will be seen that Velar Softening is said in (83) to apply before vowels or dipthongs which, in addition to meeting certain other requirements, are specified for height in one of the following ways: 2, 3, 4, 12, 13, 14. These notations are not used in *SPE*, though variables and conditions are used which have the same effect as the 'equal to or greater than' notation, e.g. in the statement of the Main Stress rule, *SPE* 240.

[27] Cf. pp. 33–4.

ɪ ~ aj	e.g.	divinity:divine	**86**
e ~ i:		kept:keep	
æ ~ ej		sanity:sane	
a ~æw		pronunciation:pronounce	
(or sometimes: a ~ (j)u:		reduction:reduce)	
ɔ ~ ɔw		globular:globe	

There is no straightforward phonological generalization that can be made about these alternations, except that a short and a long peak type is involved in each case; and we might be content to leave it at that, and let the grammar treat each alternation of the series separately, thus implying that the pairings are synchronically arbitrary. But it will be noticed that the first two pairs of (86) are precisely the four peak types that permit Velar Softening: they may be defined as 'the short vowels which are front and [2 height] or higher, and the long peaks which typically alternate with them'; and it will further be noted that a forward shift of velars before front vowels is attested in numerous languages as a historical change, and the higher the front vowel the more likely the shift is to occur. This strongly suggests that we might try to organize the grammar in such a way that at the stage when Velar Softening applies, just these four peak types and no others are front and non-low; which will probably mean deriving [aj i:] from underlying /ɪ: e:/ or the like, and maybe deriving all the pairs of (86) from underlying pairs whose members differ only in length.

We will consider in a moment how to do this. For the present let us observe that this will change the environment description of Velar Softening from (85) to

$$/ \underline{\hspace{1.5cm}} \quad \begin{bmatrix} V \\ -\text{back} \\ \geq 2\text{height} \end{bmatrix} \qquad 87$$

which is not only simpler than (85), but also eminently natural for a velar-fronting rule.

What then are the underlying forms of the vowels of (86)? We have already implied that the underlying representations of [ɪ e] are essentially the same as their phonetic representations, and since the one constant feature distinguishing the right-hand from the left-hand column of (86) is length, it is natural to suppose that surface [aj i:] are underlying /ɪ: e:/. Since, however, most of the peak types in the right-hand column are diphthongal, and since those which are not, [i: u:], can easily be accounted for as monophthongizations of very narrow diphthongs, it may be preferable to treat them as underlying /ɪj ej/.[28] In similar fashion we can treat the pair [æ ej] as underlying /æ æj/.

Over against these three pairs which appear to be underlyingly front stand three pairs whose long members are, in whole or in part, back and round, which it is natural to suppose are all underlying back vowels. The pair [ɔ ɔw] is, leaving

---

[28] In *SPE* all the peak-types of the right-hand column of (86) are treated as underlying long ('tense') vowels, there being no underlying diphthongs; the reason appears to be that diphthongization can be treated as an automatic consequence of length. But it is also possible to treat length as an automatic consequence of diphthongization provided that one has some machinery for indicating that diphthongs are single complex phonological units in a way that, say, VC sequences are not. *SPE* does not have such machinery, each segment being treated as separate from its neighbours; the notion of the complex segment has made this defect good.

aside the difference in rounding between its members, the exact counterpart of [æ ej], and, in parallel fashion, we take it to realize underlying /ɔ ɔw/. The other two long peaks, [(j)u: æw], correspond neatly enough to [i: aj], and would naturally be analysed as underlying /ʊw ow/, but for the fact that the corresponding short vowels are both realized as [a]. Let us, in the interests of generalization, assume that surface [a] does indeed represent underlying /o/ or /ʊ/ according to its alternations.

The underlying vowel system we have now arrived at, with the phonetic realizations of each vowel, is:

/ɪj	[aj	/ʊw	[æw	**88**
ɪ	ɪ	ʊ	a	
ej	i:	ow	u:	
e	e	o	a	
æj	ej	ɔw	ɔw	
æ/	æ]	ɔ/	ɔ]	

What rules (applying, of course, after Velar Softening) will be required to convert the underlying to the phonetic forms?

The most important will clearly be a rule affecting diphthongs only. This rule will have to raise an underlying height specification 1 to 2, raise 2 to 3 (giving /ɪj ʊw, whence [i:u:] by monophthongization: cf. below), and lower 3 to 1; it will in fact, as Chomsky and Halle say, be a 'synchronic residue of the Great Vowel Shift', which in the history of English had approximately this effect on long syllabics (though not in one fell swoop). It will be necessary to ensure that the rule can apply only once to a given input, since if it can reapply to its own output the grammar will go into an endless loop. Consequently the mere abbreviation by means of the brace notation of the three changes just mentioned will not be satisfactory, for rules abbreviated by this notation apply in sequence. Rather it will be necessary to abbreviate the subrules by the use of variable feature coefficients, so that they apply simultaneously:

$$\begin{bmatrix} V \\ +\text{long} \\ \alpha 4\text{height} \end{bmatrix} \rightarrow [\beta 4\text{height}] \qquad \textbf{89}$$

$$\text{conditions: if } \alpha \leq 2, \ \beta = \alpha + 1$$
$$\text{if } \alpha = 3, \ \beta = 1$$

Rule (89) depends crucially for its statability on the use of a multivalued height feature. *SPE*, using the binary features 'low' and 'high', is unable to formulate a convincing single rule employing variables. The rule is therefore split into two, each part being an 'exchange rule': that is, each part converts underlying A to B and underlying B to A. Thus the first part is

$$\begin{bmatrix} V \\ +\text{tense} \\ \alpha \text{high} \\ -\text{low} \end{bmatrix} \rightarrow [-\alpha \text{high}] \qquad \textbf{90}$$

making all tense mid vowels high, and all tense high vowels mid. The use of exchange rules in GP has been much criticized, and it is likely (cf. Anderson and Browne 1973) that they are valid only where they have a morphological function, as in Diegueño where certain verbal plurals are formed by a reversal of the value of the length feature (Schane 1973a, 107, citing D. Walker). The best that can be done with *SPE* features by way of a single Vowel Shift rule would be

$$\begin{bmatrix} V \\ +\text{tense} \\ \alpha\text{high} \\ \beta\text{low} \end{bmatrix} \rightarrow \begin{bmatrix} \gamma\text{high} \\ \alpha\text{low} \end{bmatrix} \qquad \text{91}$$

$$\text{condition: } \gamma = + \text{ if } \alpha = - \text{ and } \beta = -$$
$$\gamma = - \text{ otherwise}$$

which entirely obscures what is going on.

The effect of (89) is to convert the underlying diphthongs / ɪj ej æj ʊw ow ɔw/ to /æj ɪj ej ɔw ʊw ow/. This gets the height specifications more or less right, but a number of adjustments remain to be made. The two diphthongs which are [34 height] must be monophthongized; this can be regarded as an assimilation of the first element of the diphthong to the second, and the nature of the process can be brought out by an alternative form of presentation (which does not change the effect of the rule): instead of

$$\begin{bmatrix} V \\ 34 \text{ height} \end{bmatrix} \rightarrow [4 \text{ height}] \qquad \text{92}$$

we can present the rule as

$$\begin{bmatrix} V \\ 3 \text{ height} \quad 4\text{height} \end{bmatrix} \qquad \text{93}$$
$$[4\text{height}]$$

Note that (92/93) must be ordered after (89); for it applies only to narrow diphthongs derived by (89), not to underlying narrow diphthongs.

It remains to convert /æj ɔw ow/ to phonetic [aj æw ɘw]. In each case this involves reversing the value of the feature 'back', and in the latter two changing [+round] to [− +round]. If these changes were stated as a single rule, this would need to be rather complex to ensure that /ej/ was not affected. It is preferable to separate the rule into two parts, both dissimilatory:[29]

$$\begin{bmatrix} V \\ <2\text{height} \quad 4\text{height} \\ +\text{round} \end{bmatrix} \qquad \text{94}$$
$$[-\text{round}]$$

[29] Once again *SPE's* rules are different, for various reasons, among which are the unavailability of the complex segment notation and the fact that *SPE* is describing a dialect in which some of the relevant diphthongs are differently pronounced.

$$
\begin{bmatrix}
& V & \\
\alpha\text{back} & & \alpha\text{back} \\
1\text{height} & & 4\text{height}
\end{bmatrix}
\qquad \textbf{95}
$$

$$\downarrow$$

$$[-\alpha\text{back}]$$

These rules, applying successively, have the following effect:

Underlying	ej	æj	ow	ɔw	**96**
After (94)	ej	æj	əw	aw	
After (95)	ej	aj	əw	æw	

Finally, a rule is necessary to convert /ʊ o/to [a], and to introduce the palatal onglide (in certain environments only) before [uː].[30]

We have now answered the first three, and in part the fifth, of the questions of (72) with which we began. We have ignored up to now the problem of the 'Greek' vocabulary in English, which includes both alternating and non-alternating underlying velars. Apart from their participation in the Velar Softening alternation there is no difference between these two segment types, and they are best distinguished by a *rule feature* [−Velar Softening].

The notion of rule feature is an expression of the fact that most phonological processes have exceptions. In standard GP, to every rule R there corresponds, at least potentially, a rule feature [±R]. If nothing is said in a lexical entry about such a feature it is presumed to be positively specified;[31] but a segment may be marked minus for one or more rule features either in a lexical entry, or in a *redundancy rule* stating a general property of a class of lexical entries. In our statements of the Velar Softening rule—e.g. (74)—we specified that it could only apply to [+Latin] segments, that is, segments of [+Latin] morphemes. This was not strictly correct, since it can apply to some, but not all, [+Greek] segments as well. Rather there should have been a redundancy rule in the lexicon

$$[+\text{Germanic}] \rightarrow [-\text{Velar Softening}] \qquad \textbf{97}$$

The only specifications for the rule feature that would need to be made in the lexicon would be for certain [+Greek] segments that would be marked [−Velar Softening]; the rest, being unmarked, would be presumed to undergo the rule.

We have still to deal with the fact that in word-final or preconsonantal position, where given the environment description (87) we would expect to find only the unsoftened alternant, the softened alternant sometimes occurs. We can in fact reduce these two positions to one. The softened alternant occurs preconsonantally only before a very few suffixes, most notably those of the plural and of the past tense; and quite generally in English these suffixes have no morphophonemic effects on the form to which they are attached. In *SPE* they are

---

[30] Not to be confused with this is the other [uː], mostly confined to 'Germanic' morphemes, which never takes the onglide; the two frequently contrast with one another, e.g. *coot:cute*. The underlying representation of this vowel is an interesting question which cannot here be gone into.

[31] Unless the feature governs a so-called *minor rule*, in which case the presumption is reversed. Minor rules are used for alternations which, while not found in the bulk of morphemes of any phonologically, morphologically, syntactically and/or semantically definable class, yet occur too often (i.e. in too many forms) to be relegated to the lexicon as individual peculiarities. Cf. pp. 157f.

called 'neutral affixes', and their special status and lack of integration in the word unit is marked by the placing before them of a word boundary, which has the effect of blocking the application of a considerable number of morphophonemic rules.[32] Thus position before neutral affixes can be regarded as a special case of word-final position.

Word-final softening occurs only in a few forms, all, so far as I know, 'Latin'. Typical are *allege* (cf. *allegation*) and *reduce* (cf. *reduction*). Clearly Velar Softening is operating here; but how can these forms be made to meet its SD? Only if the velar in question is underlyingly followed by a non-low front vowel, one of the four which condition Velar Softening.

Now, as it happens, [e] never occurs in word-final position in English. We can therefore assume that it is present in the underlying forms of *allege, reduce*, etc., after the /k/ or /g/, and that there is a rule deleting it. Such a rule is of course quite 'natural', loss of unstressed final vowels being very frequent as a historical change; and there is other evidence unconnected with Velar Softening to support the view that certain stems have an underlying final /e/ which does not show up on the surface.[33]

This completes our GP account of Velar Softening in English. The reader may wish to go over the analysis and see, at each point, how the criteria of analysis explained in Chapter One have been applied.

6.3 Special types of phonological rules

The most frequent type of phonological rule is that of which we have already seen many examples, where for a specified class of segments the values of one or more features are required to be changed, either in a given environment or in all environments. Perhaps the most common of the other varieties is the *deletion* rule, which may be exemplified by the rule deleting word-final /e/ in English mentioned a moment ago:

$$\begin{bmatrix} V \\ 2\text{height} \\ -\text{back} \end{bmatrix} \longrightarrow \theta \;/ \; \underline{\qquad} \; \# \qquad\qquad \textbf{98}$$

When a deletion rule is applied, the deleted segment is entirely eliminated from the form whose derivation is in progress, and the segments (or boundaries) which precede and follow it come to adjoin one another. (Note that θ is the normal symbol for zero; it is not enclosed within obliques, brackets, etc., and is to be distinguished from the phonetic symbols [ø] and [ɸ], which in some founts of type very closely resemble it.)

---

[32] For the effect of boundaries on phonological rules cf. below, pp. 149–151.

[33] On the evidence for /e/–deletion see *SPE*, Index, under '*e*-Elision Rule'. The rule certainly makes some generalizations easier to capture; it may, however, be questioned whether these generalizations have any synchronic reality in speakers' 'linguistic intuitions' (p. 13). By itself the Velar Softening evidence could be otherwise accounted for, e.g. by a minor subrule of Velar Softening applying before word boundary to those forms which were marked plus for it to apply. The whole question of 'abstract analyses'—a not very well-defined term, but one whose denotation most would agree covers /e/-deletion—will be further considered in Chapter Nine.

The converse of deletion is insertion or *epenthesis*. This usually has to be posited when an element whose presence in underlying forms there is no reason to assume appears in a predictable position in the phonetic output. Since an epenthesis rule introduces a completely new column of features into a form, the inserted segment has to be specified for all features; yet such specification is bound to be redundant, since epenthetic segments are normally of types found elsewhere in the language, or at most differ by a single feature from such types. The problem is customarily evaded by designating the output of epenthesis rules with alphabetic symbols instead of in feature terms; it has not been satisfactorily solved.[34]

Epenthesis may be exemplified by an English rule inserting a vowel before the plural, past tense, etc., suffixes in certain environments:

$$\theta \to \text{I} \ / \ \begin{bmatrix} -\text{son} \\ +\text{cor} \\ \left\{\begin{matrix} -\text{cont} \\ -\text{apic} \end{matrix}\right\}_1 \end{bmatrix}_1 \quad \# \ \underline{\quad} \ \begin{bmatrix} -\text{son} \\ +\text{cor} \\ \left\{\begin{matrix} -\text{cont} \\ -\text{apic} \end{matrix}\right\}_1 \end{bmatrix}_1 \quad \# \qquad \textbf{99}$$

The numbered brace notation requires us, whichever choice we make at one pair of braces, to make the same choice at the other pair; i.e. the environment description of (99) is an abbreviation for:

$$/ \left\{ \begin{matrix} \begin{bmatrix} -\text{son} \\ +\text{cor} \\ -\text{cont} \end{bmatrix} \quad \# \ \underline{\quad} \ \begin{bmatrix} -\text{son} \\ +\text{cor} \\ -\text{cont} \end{bmatrix} \quad \# \\[4ex] \begin{bmatrix} -\text{son} \\ +\text{cor} \\ -\text{apic} \end{bmatrix} \quad \# \ \underline{\quad} \ \begin{bmatrix} -\text{son} \\ +\text{cor} \\ -\text{apic} \end{bmatrix} \quad \# \end{matrix} \right\} \qquad \textbf{100}$$

All the types of rules we have considered affect only one segment in a string directly. Some rules, however, must be regarded as affecting two or more segments simultaneously.

The most obvious of these cases is *metathesis*, in which the underlying order of two segments is reversed on the surface. Consider the following data from modern Hebrew. Hebrew has a prefix /hit/, used with both verbs and nouns, denoting roughly 'reciprocity/collectivity': cf. /hit + ʔaḥd + ut/ 'union' ~ /ʔeḥad/ 'one', /hit + nagd + ut/ 'opposition' ~ /neged/ 'opposite'. But where the root begins with a sibilant /c s z š/,[35] these derivative nouns take a different form: the reciprocal/collective derivative of /seder/ 'order' is not */hit + sadr + ut/ but /histadrut/ 'organization, Israeli labour federation'; similarly, for */hit + c- hit + z- hit + š-/ we find /hict- hizd- hišt-/. Clearly this can only reasonably be accounted for by a metathesis rule, which may be stated as follows:

---

[34] Possibly a solution may be available by defining the segment inventory of a language as comprising all segment types, whether underlying or derived, which appear in its phonology (apart from those which are only introduced by phonetic detail rules) and requiring that features unspecified in the output description of an epenthesis rule be so specified as to make the epenthetic segment match a segment in the inventory; but this notion has not been worked out in detail.

[35] These are the only sibilants found in native forms.

$$V \begin{bmatrix} -son \\ -cont \\ +cor \end{bmatrix} + \begin{bmatrix} -son \\ (-)+cont \\ +cor \\ \alpha voice \end{bmatrix} \qquad \mathbf{101}^{36}$$

$$\begin{array}{cccc} 1 & 2 & 3 & 4 \\ & \downarrow & & \downarrow \\ & 4 & & \begin{bmatrix} 2 \\ \alpha voice \end{bmatrix} \end{array}$$

The modification which has here been made to the pattern of statement used for such rules as (54) should be self-explanatory.

Rules modifying two or more segments simultaneously are also needed for other types of phonological processes. For example, a geminate simplification rule could be treated as an ordinary deletion; but do you delete the first or the second of the two consecutive like segments? The choice is arbitrary, and it is preferable to treat the process as a *contraction* or *fusion*.[37] The formulation (102) would be suitable for a deletion; that of (103) is appropriate to a fusion.

$$p \to \emptyset \ / \ \text{———} \ p \qquad\qquad\qquad \mathbf{102}$$

$$pp \to p \qquad\qquad\qquad\qquad \mathbf{103}$$

The converse of fusion may also occur, and it may for analogous reasons be inappropriate to treat it as an epenthetic process. There is no generic name for the converse of fusion, though particular types of it have designations such as gemination, breaking, etc.

6.4 Notational conventions

We have already met a number of conventions which make it possible to combine distinct but related phonological rules in a single statement. The qualification 'but related' is important; as Schane (1973a) has put it, rules may be 'collapsed' in this way only if they involve the same process. What 'same process' means is presumably a question for a theory of natural phonological processes, about which we will say something in Chapter Nine.[38] In the present section we will illustrate some further conventions not previously mentioned.

Perhaps the most important of these is the parenthesis convention. Parentheses are used to enclose elements which may be present or absent in an environment without affecting the applicability of the rule. For instance, a rule of the form

$$V \to [+round] \ / \ \text{———} \ (\#) \ w \qquad\qquad \mathbf{104}$$

[36] As given, this rule leaves the morpheme boundary in place while interchanging the segments flanking it. It is not clear whether this is the correct form of statement; the determination of this question would require an investigation of how phonological rules conditioned by boundaries are found to apply when metathesis rules have applied before them.

[37] Nevertheless *SPE* treats geminate simplification in English as a deletion (of the first of two like consonants), making no comment on the arbitrariness involved.

[38] But empirical confirmation of the validity of a notational convention can come if it is found that the subrules which the convention abbreviates into a schema behave as a unit in linguistic change (Kiparsky 1968a, 179–83), or that they can profitably be treated as a unit in the study of linguistic variation (Labov 1972b, 231–3).

says that a vowel rounds before /w/ whether or not a word boundary intervenes. As an actual example we may take the stress rule of classical Latin. This placed stress on the antepenultimate syllable of a word, if the penultimate syllable had a short vowel and this vowel was followed by no more than one consonant or by an obstruent and a liquid; otherwise on the penultimate; the penultimate was also stressed if the word, while otherwise meeting the conditions for antepenultimate stress, had only two syllables; and monosyllables received stress on their only syllable. The rule can be expressed thus:

$$V \rightarrow [+\text{stress}] \, / \, \underline{\quad} (C_0 (\begin{bmatrix} V \\ -\text{tense} \end{bmatrix} \begin{Bmatrix} C_0^1 \\ [-\text{son}] \begin{bmatrix} +\text{cons} \\ +\text{son} \\ -\text{nas} \end{bmatrix} \end{Bmatrix})V)C_0 \# \qquad \mathbf{105}$$

The environment statement of (105) is an abbreviation for three environment statements, and so (105) itself is an abbreviation for three rules; and not only here, but apparently in all cases where rules are related in such a way that they can be abbreviated by the parenthesis convention, correct results will be given if the rules are applied in the order of (106), that is, the longest expansion first:

$$V \rightarrow [+\text{stress}] \, / \, \underline{\quad} C_0 \begin{bmatrix} V \\ -\text{tense} \end{bmatrix} \begin{Bmatrix} C_0^1 \\ [-\text{son}] \begin{bmatrix} +\text{cons} \\ +\text{son} \\ -\text{nas} \end{bmatrix} \end{Bmatrix} VC_0 \# \quad \mathbf{106a}$$

$$V \rightarrow [+\text{stress}] \, / \, \underline{\quad} C_0 VC_0 \# \qquad\qquad \mathbf{b}$$

$$V \rightarrow [+\text{stress}] \, / \, \underline{\quad} C_0 \# \qquad\qquad \mathbf{c}$$

Each subrule differs from the preceding one by the omission from its environment of one of the parenthesized expressions of (105), the innermost being omitted first.[39]

But one further proviso must be made. Consider a word like /terruit/ '(he) frightened'. Subrule (106a) will correctly stress this word on the antepenultimate syllable. But what now is to prevent (106b) and (106c) from incorrectly stressing the word on the other two syllables as well? Similar problems arise with other sets of parenthesis-abbreviated rules. It is typical of such rules that *only one* of their subrules can apply in any one derivation. Technically, the subrules are said to be *disjunctively ordered*; they are tested for applicability in the order exemplified by (106), but once a match has been found for one subrule, the subrules yet to be tested are skipped altogether.[40] Disjunctive ordering is opposed to *conjunctive ordering*, which holds for instance for rules abbreviated by the brace notation: under conjunctive ordering the rules are likewise tested one after the other for applicability, but any subrule whose structural description is met is

---

[39] A similar principle applies to the expansion of abbreviations such as C_1^3 'not less than one nor more than three consonants', since these are notational variants of parenthesis statements, e.g. in this case ((C)C)C; they are interpreted exactly like the parenthesis statements to which they are equivalent, e.g. a rule stated as applying before C_1^3 is taken to comprise three subrules applying before CCC, CC, and C in that (disjunctive) order. Cf. Anderson (1974b, 101).

[40] But two disjunctively ordered (sub)rules may apply in the same derivation if the strings to which they apply are disjoint, no input or environment segment for the application of one (sub)rule being an input or environment segment for the application of the other (*SPE* 366). Phelps (1975) brings

applied, even if a previous subrule has applied already: (77) provides an example. The disjunctive application principle ensures that, as soon as (106a) has applied to a form like /terruit/, (106b,c) become inapplicable to that form. In *SPE* it is claimed that the principle holds for *all* rule schemata involving the parenthesis notation.[41]

Sometimes sets of rules are found which seem suitable for abbreviation by the parenthesis notation, and yet this notation cannot be used, because the material whose presence or absence in the affected string is a matter of indifference does not form a continuous substring of that string. A common variety of this phenomenon is when a rule applies to a particular class of segment types in a particular environment, but for one subclass the environmental restrictions are more severe. An example might be a language with a rule that vowels shorten before clusters of two (or more) consonants, but the most open vowel, /aː/, shortens only before three consonants or two word-final consonants. Separately, the two rules would be:

$$\begin{bmatrix} V \\ \geq 2\text{height} \end{bmatrix} \rightarrow [-\text{long}] \ / \ \text{\textemdash\textemdash} CC \qquad\qquad \textbf{107}$$

$$\begin{bmatrix} V \\ 1\text{height} \end{bmatrix} \rightarrow [-\text{long}] \ / \ \text{\textemdash\textemdash} CC \begin{Bmatrix} C \\ \# \end{Bmatrix} \qquad\qquad \textbf{108}$$

But by stating the rules separately we are manifestly missing a generalization. The two rules are not only extremely similar to one another but are quite clearly parts of a single process, it not being surprising that a more open vowel should be more resistant to shortening. How, though, can the rules be collapsed? There is no way of doing so by the parenthesis convention that will give correct results; the reader is invited to try it and see. The numbered brace notation used for (99) offers one possibility:

$$V \rightarrow [-\text{long}] \ / \ \begin{bmatrix} \begin{Bmatrix} \geq 2\text{height} \\ 1\text{height} \end{Bmatrix} \\ 1 \qquad\quad 1 \end{bmatrix} CC \begin{Bmatrix} \begin{Bmatrix} X \\ C \\ \# \end{Bmatrix} \\ 1 \quad 1 \end{Bmatrix} \qquad\qquad \textbf{109}$$

If all we were concerned with was to have a rule that worked, then (109) would be acceptable. But we also wish our rules, so far as possible, to reflect the nature of the phonological processes they profess to describe, and this (109) does not do. Just like (107, 108), it gives two rules, one applying only to non-low vowels, the other only to low vowels; it differs only in that it states their shared features once instead of twice. But the appropriate description of the situation is not this; it is that all vowels shorten but for /aː/ there is a special restriction. There are not two special cases, as (109) implies, but a general and a special case.

---

evidence to suggest that disjunctive rules should be allowed to apply in the same derivation even if the strings in question are only partially distinct, so long as some part of the input to or the environment for the later application was not part of the input to or the environment for the earlier application.
[41] Except for phonetic detail rules, which always apply conjunctively (Anderson 1975, 41). The position taken in the text has been strongly challenged in the last few years, notably by Kiparsky (1973b); the problem will be further discussed in Chapter Seven. It should be noted here that for purposes of rule ordering, a schema consisting of subrules abbreviated by this or any other convention is treated as a single rule; thus subrules can only be abbreviated if they all stand in the same ordering relations to other rules.

Situations of this kind can be captured by the *angled bracket convention*. Basically, this convention is that a schema of the form $X\langle Y\rangle Z\langle W\rangle V$ is interpreted as the disjunctively ordered sequence XYZWV, XZV—i.e. just as if the two angled expressions were a single parenthesized expression. We can now replace (109) by (110):

$$\begin{bmatrix} V \\ \langle 1\text{height}\rangle \end{bmatrix} \to [-\text{long}] / \text{———} CC \left\langle \begin{Bmatrix} C \\ \# \end{Bmatrix} \right\rangle \qquad \textbf{110}$$

This still requires a little care. The first subrule of (110) will correctly shorten /a:/ before three consonants, or two consonants plus word boundary. But if we now omit the angled expressions, the second subrule comes out as:

$$V \to [-\text{long}] / \text{———} CC \qquad \textbf{111}$$

And this will incorrectly shorten *all* vowels before two consonants. The same problem arises whenever particular feature specifications of input segments (as opposed to environment segments) are enclosed within angled brackets, and necessitates an auxiliary interpretative convention:

If P is any expression composed of specified features, then a schema **112** $X\langle Y\rangle Z\begin{bmatrix} W \\ <P> \end{bmatrix} V$, where $\begin{bmatrix} W \\ <P> \end{bmatrix}$ is an input segment and not an environment segment, is interpreted as the disjunctively ordered sequence

$$XYZ\begin{bmatrix} W \\ P \end{bmatrix}V, \ XZ\begin{bmatrix} W \\ \text{not-P} \end{bmatrix}V.^{42}$$

Thus the second subrule of (110) will apply to vowels which are not [1height], i.e. will be precisely (107);[43] only now the restriction of (107) to non-low vowels, instead of having to be stated *ad hoc*, has been presented as an inevitable consequence of the fact that the shortening rule has a special and a general case.

In addition to its use in stating dependencies between parts of an SD, the angled bracket notation can also be used to state dependencies between the SD and the output description. An example may be provided by a nasal assimilation rule found in many modern Greek dialects. Newton (1972, 94) states it thus informally:

A nasal is assimilated completely to a following continuant and in point of **113** articulation to a following occlusive, except that /mn/ remains [mn].

If for the moment we leave that last proviso out of account, the formal statement of the rule is:

$$[+\text{nas}] \to \begin{bmatrix} \alpha\text{lab} \\ \beta\text{cor} \\ \gamma\text{back} \\ \langle +\text{cont} \\ \delta\text{features}\rangle \end{bmatrix} / \text{———} \begin{bmatrix} +\text{cons} \\ \alpha\text{lab} \\ \beta\text{cor} \\ \gamma\text{back} \\ \langle +\text{cont} \\ \delta\text{features}\rangle \end{bmatrix}^{44} \qquad \textbf{114}$$

[42] This convention differs from that of *SPE* 125 n.78 in covering complex expressions formed of specified features as well as single specified features, and in being restricted to input segments. In practice Chomsky and Halle do not apply the convention to segments or boundaries forming part of an environment: see for instance the list of expansions at *SPE* 105.

[43] On the simplifying assumption that the language contains no complex segments.

[44] Note the use of 'features' to mean 'all features not specifically mentioned in this column' and thus,

The first subrule assimilates a nasal completely to a following continuant; the second assimilates the point-of-articulation features of the nasal to those of any following consonant—recall that convention (112) does not apply to output or environment descriptions, so for the second subrule the specifications within angled brackets are simply ignored. We can incorporate the proviso that /mn/ is not affected by using angled brackets a second time, indexing the brackets to show which expression matches which:

$$
\begin{bmatrix} +\text{nas} \\ \langle +\text{lab} \rangle_1 \end{bmatrix} \rightarrow
\begin{bmatrix} \alpha\text{lab} \\ \beta\text{cor} \\ \gamma\text{back} \\ \langle +\text{cont} \\ \delta\text{features} \rangle_2 \end{bmatrix}
\Big/ \text{—}
\begin{bmatrix} +\text{cons} \\ \alpha\text{lab} \\ \beta\text{cor} \\ \gamma\text{back} \\ \langle -\text{nas} \rangle_1 \\ \langle +\text{cont} \\ \delta\text{features} \rangle_2 \end{bmatrix}
\qquad 115
$$

In this particular case (it may not always be so) it makes no empirical difference in which order we expand the abbreviations. If we choose first to expand the abbreviation labelled 1, we find the subrules are as follows:

$$
\begin{bmatrix} +\text{nas} \\ +\text{lab} \end{bmatrix} \rangle
\begin{bmatrix} \alpha\text{lab} \\ \beta\text{cor} \\ \gamma\text{back} \\ \langle +\text{cont} \\ \delta\text{features} \rangle \end{bmatrix}
\Big/ \text{—}
\begin{bmatrix} +\text{cons} \\ \alpha\text{lab} \\ \beta\text{cor} \\ \gamma\text{back} \\ -\text{nas} \\ \langle +\text{cont} \\ \delta\text{features} \rangle \end{bmatrix}
\qquad 116
$$

$$
\begin{bmatrix} +\text{nas} \\ -\text{lab} \end{bmatrix} \rightarrow
\begin{bmatrix} \alpha\text{lab} \\ \beta\text{cor} \\ \gamma\text{back} \\ \langle +\text{cont} \\ \delta\text{features} \rangle \end{bmatrix}
\Big/ \text{—}
\begin{bmatrix} +\text{cons} \\ \alpha\text{lab} \\ \beta\text{cor} \\ \gamma\text{back} \\ \langle +\text{cont} \\ \delta\text{features} \rangle \end{bmatrix}
\qquad 117
$$

Both these subrules are essentially similar to (114). But the first, affecting /m/, does not apply before nasals; this does not make any difference to /mm/, which (114) would not have affected anyway, but it does ensure that /mn/ is unaffected. The second subrule applies to /n/, the only other underlying nasal in the language, and treats it just as (114) did.

An important convention not used in *SPE*, but almost universally adopted since, is the so-called *mirror-image* convention. It frequently happens that a rule which applies *following* some conditioning segment type also applies *preceding* the same segment type: e.g. in Spanish /j/ is deleted either before or after a high

---

by appearing with the same coefficient in both the environment description and the output description, to direct complete assimilation of voice, height, laterality, and all other features not explicitly mentioned in the rule.

vowel. (J. W. Harris, cited by Norman 1973.) Less often, but still with significant frequency, a rule is found to apply in the environment X——Y and also in the environment Y'——X', where Y' is Y with the segment sequence reversed, and X' is X with the segment sequence reversed (if Y or X respectively had more than one segment). Anderson (1974b, 113ff) gives an example from Faroese:

A glide is inserted: 118
(a)   morpheme-initially before a vowel where the previous morpheme ends in a high vowel or glide;
(b)   morpheme-finally after a vowel where the following morpheme begins with a high vowel or glide;
the inserted glide agreeing in backness with the conditioning high vowel or glide, whether the latter precedes or follows it.

Now existing notational devices are quite adequate to enable us to state rules of this sort. Their general form is merely:

$$A \rightarrow B \, / \left\{ \begin{array}{l} X \text{——} Y \\ Y' \text{——} X' \end{array} \right\}$$ 119

But as with rules like (109), so those like (119) do not indicate what is really going on. To accept (119) is to say that it is just an accident that so many rules have this form, and that the relationship between the alternative environments is without significance. Langacker (1969) therefore proposed a convention whereby, instead of stating alternative environments in such cases, a single environment statement was made which could be read either forwards or backwards. The sign of a mirror-image rule is the replacement of the usual oblique stroke (/), read as 'in the environment', by a different symbol (those most used are // and %) which should be read as 'in the mirror-image environment'. (120) has the same effect as (119):

$$A \rightarrow B \, / / \, X \text{——} Y [45]$$. 120

A considerable number of other notational conventions have been used by generative phonologists at various times, but they are not of great importance and usage is not always consistent. There remain many relationships between rules which it is desirable should be formally captured, but for whose capture no notational device has been proposed. In some cases this is because the relationship is 'functional' (Kisseberth 1970a) rather than structural, various rules contributing towards the same 'objective' (e.g. the elimination of complex clusters, contrastive stress patterning for different parts of speech, etc.) by different means. (More on this in Chapter Eight.) But in some cases there are quite marked formal relationships involved: for some proposals about one of these (the situation where underlying A may optionally surface as B and underlying B as A) see Malone (1970) and Brasington (1973).[46] It is legitimate to

[45] A precursor of the mirror-image convention was the *neighbourhood convention* of Bach (1968), whereby an environment given without the usual horizontal bar, in the form / X instead of / —— X, was taken to mean 'either before or after X'. The neighbourhood convention is still used, but it lacks the generality of the mirror-image convention. (For a suggestion that the latter is itself insufficiently general, see D. G. Miller 1976.)
[46] Roca (1975) criticizes Brasington's analysis of the Catalan data on which he bases his proposal, but

doubt the value of devising ever more ingenious notations for capturing formal relationships between phonological rules when formal simplicity is no longer regarded as central to the evaluation of competing grammars. A section heading in Schane (1973a) is 'Notational conventions express linguistic generalizations'; yes, but subject and object are both conspicuously unquantified. Not all formally valid uses of notational conventions express linguistic generalizations, and not all genuine relationships between rules are, or perhaps can be, expressed by notational conventions. A little has already been said, and more will be said hereafter, about the second point; for the first, it will be enough to end this section where we began it, with Schane's own requirement that rules be collapsed only if they involve the same process: for whether two rules involve the same process is not a question that can be answered directly, automatically and simply in terms only of formal relationships between them.

6.5 Boundaries

A phonological representation is not and could not be simply a string of segments represented as feature complexes. Many phonological processes apply only when certain conditions are satisfied which have no reference to the feature make-up of the relevant segments. Among the most important of such conditions are those relating to the position of segments within certain larger phonological units. Very frequent and familiar, for example, are elisions and other phenomena occurring only at the beginning or the end of a phonological word, but there are also units of special significance above and below this size-level.

The units are demarcated by the placement in phonological representations, between the final segment of one unit and the initial segment of the next, of *boundaries*. These are regarded in *SPE* as phonological elements on a par with segments, but differing from them in being marked minus for the feature 'segment' (for which all consonants and vowels are marked plus) and being unspecified for all the phonological features characteristic of segments.[47] Different kinds of boundary are distinguished by a feature or features not used for segments: in *SPE* these features, like all others, are treated as binary[48] and at least two of them are posited, but this implies that the organization of the boundary system is cross-classifying when it appears rather to be hierarchical, and it may well be preferable to distinguish the various types of boundary, either by contrasting specifications

---

Malone had previously shown that a good many other similar pieces of data exist. And see now Brasington (1976).

[47] Lass (1971) and Lightner (1972), noting that a wide variety of phonological processes which occur in the vicinity of consonants occur likewise in the vicinity of boundaries, with to specify the latter (at least word boundary) as obstruent and voiceless, and perhaps for other features; but it must then be arbitrarily stipulated (Lightner 1972, 334f) that such 'segmental' features on boundaries cannot be affected by any phonological rule, and it may be preferable to capture the relationship that undoubtedly exists not by formal means but simply by pointing (as these authors do) to the similarities, both acoustic and in the attitude of the speech tract, between voiceless obstruents and pause.

[48] Segmental features and prosodic features are of course in some cases phonetically multinary though phonologically binary. This distinction is not relevant for boundary features, as boundaries have no phonetic realization (except indirectly, via their effect on segments in their vicinity).

on a single multi-valued feature, or, equivalently, by varying numbers of successive occurrences of a single basic boundary unit.

Four types of boundary appear to be universal. One of these, *syllable boundary*, does not belong to the hierarchy, for the units it demarcates have no relation at all to grammar; it is not referred to at all in *SPE*, and discussion of it will be postponed to Chapter Eight.

The second universal boundary type is *morpheme boundary*, usually symbolized by $+$.[49] This appears between each morpheme and that which follows it, unless some stronger boundary comes at the same place. Its universality follows from the universality of the definition of 'morpheme'.

Many phonological rules apply only when a morpheme boundary is present at a given place in the environment. An interesting example is given in *SPE* 196. Consider alternations in the 'Latin' section of the English vocabulary such as *table:tabulate, angle:angular, circle:circulate*. The alternation is between $[Cl]$ and $[CjUl]$[50], the former appearing word-finally or before inflectional affixes, the latter before most derivational affixes. Since the occurrence of a palatal onglide before $[U]$ (or $[u:]$) is predictable in the 'Latin' vocabulary,[51] we can treat the alternation as one between /Cl/ and /CUl/. But the alternation only occurs where the lateral is the final segment of a morpheme and an affix follows. In other positions we find either non-alternating /Cl/, as in *public*,[52] or non-alternating /CUl/ as in the set *module, modulus, modulate*, etc.[53]

On the face of it there are two possible solutions: to assume underlying /Cl/ and a vowel insertion rule, or underlying /CUl/ and a vowel deletion rule. It proves much easier to state the rule on the former assumption. For the long forms are found in one specific environment: morpheme-final before derivational affixes of the form /VC/ such as *-ate, -al, -ous*. The short forms, on the other hand, are found in several different environments: word-finally; before inflectional affixes; in words not of the 'Latin' vocabulary; and before affixes not of the form /VC/, such as *-i-fy* (cf. *amplify*). Thus a vowel deletion rule would have to have a complex and unrevealing disjunctive environment; a vowel insertion rule, on the other hand, can be stated with quite a simply defined environment—provided we are allowed to mention morpheme boundaries in it.

$$\theta \to U \, / \begin{bmatrix} -\text{cont} \\ +\text{Latin} \end{bmatrix}\!\!-\!\!-\!\!-1 + VC\,[-\text{seg}] \qquad\qquad \textbf{121}$$

Note the requirement that the affix of the form /VC/ must be followed by a boundary (non-segment); if we left out this requirement the rule would apply not

---

[49] Or &, in some earlier work (e.g. Halle 1959).

[50] For the alternation to appear, the C must be a stop.

[51] The onglide does not occur after 'palato-alveolars' or after /r/; after /l/ it is now more or less confined to unstressed medial syllables, and after /s/ it does not occur in stressed initial syllables (*assume* [-sjú:-] but *suture* [sú:-]); after other consonants, in my dialect, the onglide is always present.

[52] Here *-ic* is not an affix; note that no derivative is without *-ic* (*publish* is not an exception, cf. *publication*).

[53] *Model* does not belong to this set; observe that though *model* and *modulate* both have a variety of senses, no sense of the one can reasonably be matched to any sense of the other in the way that, say, *tabulate* matches *table* in its sense 'presentation of data in row and column form'.

only before affixes of the form /VC/ but also before those of the form /VCV/, /VCC/, /VCVC/, etc.

Although there are many rules that apply only when a morpheme boundary is present, there are very few rules which are prevented from applying by the presence of a morpheme boundary. Consequently, in the *SPE* model it is assumed that the presence in a phonological representation of a morpheme boundary is ignored in deciding whether the matrix meets the structural description of a phonological rule; the nasal assimilation rule (115), for example, applies regardless of whether the nasal and the consonant to which it assimilates are separated by a + boundary. The *absence*, on the other hand, of a morpheme boundary specifically required by the SD of a rule can never be ignored.

(The reader may ask how then it is possible to state the 'very few' rules which do apply only if morpheme boundary is *not* present at a particular point. For such rules cf. Wurzel (1970, 183) (German: $e \rightarrow i$ if a palatal consonant follows immediately in the same morpheme); Dell (1973b, 200ff.) (French: $\vartheta \rightarrow \varepsilon$ /——$C_1^n \vartheta [-\text{seg}]$, provided the conditioning consonant(s) belong to the same morpheme as the affected vowel); M. Ohala (1974) (Hindi: schwa deletes subject to certain conditions, one of which is that the schwa must not be the first vowel of a morpheme). Chomsky and Halle (*SPE* 364) recognize the existence of such rules, but do not say how they would state them except that 'the grammar must be complicated in some way'; and later work has not carried the question further, it generally being tacitly assumed that the convention mentioned in the previous paragraph holds except where otherwise stated, and no formal device being employed for the statement of exceptions in this respect.)

The third universal boundary is *word boundary*, customarily symbolized by #. *SPE* seeks to show that the incidence of this is among the phonological phenomena that are determined by syntactic factors: a word boundary is said (*SPE* 366) to be inserted in surface syntactic structure before and after every 'major category' constituent, i.e. every noun, verb, adjective, or phrase including a noun, verb or adjective.[54] Some of these boundaries may be deleted again by language-specific rules; these will relate to such verbs, pronouns, etc., as may, in the language in question, be phonologically non-independent (clitic), and to certain affixes.

The units delimited by # boundaries are not such that they can appropriately be labelled 'phonological words'. Consider for instance the word *departmentalize*. Both grammatically and semantically it is a transparent derivative of the adjective *departmental*, itself a transparent derivative of the noun *department*; so that the word boundary insertion rule would have the following output:[55]

$$[_V \# [_A \# [_N \# \text{department} \# _N]\text{al} \# _A]\text{ize} \# _V] \qquad 122$$

And in no sense could *-al-* or *-ize* be called a 'phonological word'.

The definition of phonological word cannot therefore be based directly on the

---

[54] Neither this formulation nor that of *SPE* of which it is a paraphrase is quite watertight. For example, all noun phrases are major category constituents, even though they may not include a noun—cf. 'he'. It is, however, probably possible in any case to give a universal, exhaustive and not too lengthy list of major categories.

[55] Actually the word boundary after *department-* would probably be deleted by one of the language-

occurrence of word boundaries. Instead, this notion is defined indirectly by way of the notion *word terminus*. A word terminus is either (i) the beginning or end of a sentence or (ii) a word boundary, or sequence of word boundaries, at which a syntactic constituent ends and another begins; and a phonological word is a stretch bounded by word termini which contains no internal word termini.[56] It turns out that normally each phonological word contains one constituent which is a noun, verb or adjective; many also contain various clitics, which may be prepositions, pronouns, particles or other non-lexical forms; a phonological word may or may not contain internal # boundaries. It should be noted that there is no need for a phonological word to coincide with a syntactic constituent.[57]

Consider the sentence

He wanted to departmentalize the libraries fast.   **123**

A plausible surface syntactic structure for (123) would be:

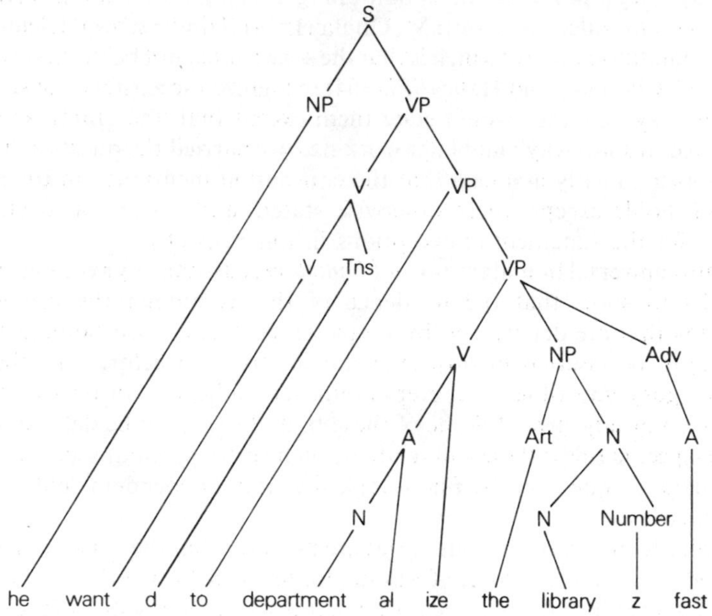

Figure 25

specific rules mentioned above; but that after *-al-* would remain, since *-ize*, like the inflectional affixes, is 'neutral', i.e. has no effect on stress. In (122) syntactic constituent boundaries are indicated in the usual way by labelled bracketing.
[56] Chomsky and Halle's formulation (*SPE* 367) is more rigorous than this informal statement; in particular, it requires that a sentence-internal word terminus be of the form #]X[#, where X may contain further boundaries and brackets but not any segments.
[57] Since the domains for the phonological cycle (see pp. 163–5) are syntactic constituents, and it is essential for the *SPE* theory of rule application that every phonological word be a cyclic domain, this possible failure to coincide could be an embarrassment. Chomsky and Halle therefore (*SPE* 368) devise an algorithm to alter constituent boundaries, after the determination of phonological words, in such a way that every word will be a constituent.
[58] S = sentence, VP = verb phrase, NP = noun phrase; these and N, A, V, Adv are major categories.

If to this (ignoring all but major category labels) we apply the word boundary insertion rule, the result is (125):

$$[_S\# \ [_{NP}\# \ he \ \#_{NP}] \ [_{VP}\# \ [_V\# \ [_V\# \ want\#_V]d\#_V] \ [_{VP}\# \ to \ [_{VP}\# \quad \textbf{125}$$
$$[_V\# \ [_A\# \ [_N\# \ department \ /\!\!/_N]al\#_A]ize\#_V] \ [_{NP}\# \ the \ [_N\# \ library$$
$$\#_N]z\#_N] \#_{NP}] \ [_{Adv} \#[_A\#fast \ \#_A] \# \ _{Adv}]\#_{VP}]\#_{VP}]\#_{VP}]\#_S]$$

Boundary deletion rules specific to English will then remove the $\#$ boundaries after *department-* (cf. note 55) and also after the unemphatic pronoun *he*; the latter change will have the result that *he* will no longer be followed by a word terminus (cf. note 56, a word terminus must include a right-hand (closing) bracket preceded by a $\#$ boundary). In fact, denoting word terminus by (T), the division of the sentence into phonological words will be as follows:

he wanted (T) to departmentalize (T) the libraries (T) fast   **126**

Four phonological words, one of them containing no internal $\#$ boundaries, another (*to departmentalize*) perhaps as many as five; the last two of them syntactic constituents, the first two not (not, at any rate, until the adjustment mentioned in note 57).

Word termini, and the notion of 'phonological word', do not figure in the structural descriptions of rules, though they play an important role in the *SPE* theory of rule application. It is, however, extremely frequent for phonological rules to be conditioned by word boundary in one way or another. Thus *truncation* rules are very common, deleting word-final vowels or consonants or both, with or without further conditions. Or compare the Japanese rule described by McCawley (1968, 124), whereby underlying /p/ becomes a fricative /ϕ/ (whence, in most environments, [h]) in word-initial and intervocalic position:[59]

$$\begin{bmatrix} -\text{voice} \\ -\text{sonorant} \\ +\text{labial} \\ -\text{onomatopoeic} \\ -\text{foreign} \end{bmatrix} \rightarrow [+\text{continuant}] \ / \ \begin{Bmatrix} \# \\ V \end{Bmatrix} \ \underline{\quad\quad} \ V \qquad \textbf{127}$$

Stress rules, again, very typically use either the beginning or the end of the word as a point of reference (cf. (105)).

The last of the universal boundary types is *phonological phrase boundary* or *major pause*. This defines units which form 'the maximal domain of phonological processes'; generally these may be equated with maximal stretches covered by a single intonation contour. No rule can ever apply across a phonological phrase

---

[59]Note how (127) is restricted so as to apply only in two of the four main divisions of the Japanese vocabulary, viz. (non-onomatopoeic) native forms and Chinese loans. This rule, incidentally, answers the doubts of Lightner (1972, 403) about the existence of rules involving the disjunctive environment 'vowel or word boundary', and makes one even more dubious about the proposal to specify word boundary as a voiceless obstruent; in fact one of the few environments in which prevocalic [p] can occur phonetically in Japanese is precisely following a voiceless obstruent, e.g, in *buppin* 'goods'.

boundary. The rules which include these boundaries in their environment descriptions have not been well studied; most of them relate to prosodic features, such as the rule in at least some dialects of Ancient Greek which made the last syllable before a major pause high-pitched:

$$V \rightarrow [+\text{high pitch}] / \text{------} C_0 \text{ [phonological phrase boundary]} \qquad 128$$

An example of a rule conditioned by PPB affecting segmental features may be taken from Classical Sanskrit:

$$\begin{bmatrix} -\text{son} \\ -\text{cont} \end{bmatrix} \rightarrow \begin{bmatrix} -\text{voice} \\ -\text{aspirated} \end{bmatrix} / \text{------} [\text{PPB}] \qquad 129$$

In both cases the treatment before PPB contrasts with the treatment before word boundary: in Ancient Greek the last mora before a word boundary was (according to the most probable interpretation of the evidence) never high-pitched, and in Sanskrit a word-final stop assimilated in voice and nasality[60] to the initial segment (consonant or vowel) of the next word.

In addition to these universal types of boundary, many languages are best analysed as having other boundaries of varying strengths. Chomsky and Halle recognize one such additional boundary for English, which they symbolize by = ; it occurs principally between the elements of words derived from Latin propositional compounds (or formed on the same pattern in modern times) such as *retain, conclude, deform*, etc. This boundary is relevant for several rules of English; for example, there is a rule voicing underlying /s/ which applies, among other environments, in the context V = ------V (so in *resist*, contrast *consist*). In the absence of a = boundary the voicing rule normally applies only where the preceding vowel is tense; thus it does not occur in *asylum* where the sibilant is preceded by no boundary, nor in *solve* where it is preceded by a word boundary (contrast *resolve*), nor in *parasite* where it is preceded by the ordinary morpheme boundary +.[61] Some other languages, as we shall see presently, have considerably larger arrays of boundaries.

How do boundary symbols get into phonological representations, and how (since they are unpronounceable) do they get out again? The universal boundaries are inserted by universal conventions: we have already noted the conventions for inserting + and #; and phonological phrase boundary is inserted at the beginning and end of sentences, and optionally (to some extent according to speech tempo) after certain clauses and noun phrases.[62] The insertion of language-particular boundaries is treated rather vaguely in *SPE*, but Stanley (1973) provides a plausible scheme: in part these boundaries result from rules (doubtless part of the readjustment component—see note 3) which weaken # boundaries, inserted by the universal convention, to boundaries of lower rank, and in part they are directly marked in the lexical entries for the forms in which

---

[60] This applies to all stops; dental stops further undergo complete assimilation if followed by a retroflex, a palatal, or a lateral at the start of the next word.

[61] For a criticism of the use in phonology of boundaries (like =) which lack grammatical motivation, see Ohlander (1976, 141–53).

[62] I follow Bierwisch (1966), whose work remains unsurpassed as a GP treatment of intonation.

they occur, and so appear in surface syntactic structure by the same title as the segments of these lexical items.

When all phonological rules, including the phonetic detail rules, have applied, it is usually assumed that a universal convention erases all boundaries, except that # and stronger boundaries may optionally be, and phonological phrase boundaries obligatorily are, retained and realized as pauses.

The question naturally arises whether there are also other phonological processes which affect boundaries—whether ordinary phonological rules can change one kind of boundary into another, or insert or delete a boundary. *SPE* seems to take the view that the answer is no. I know of no well-motivated rule of boundary deletion, apart from the universal convention mentioned in the last paragraph; though deletion or contraction rules affecting segments adjacent to boundaries may—sometimes must—delete the boundaries as well as the segments. Nor does there seem to be any need to posit phonological rules which insert boundaries:[63] the constraint laid down by Chomsky, Halle and Lukoff (1956) that all boundaries should be syntactically justifiable can be maintained, so long as syntax is taken to include morphology.[64] And rules changing boundaries into other boundaries can perhaps always be assigned to the re-adjustment component,[65] except, again, that the deletion of a segment adjacent to a boundary may sometimes be accompanied by weakening of that boundary. Thus boundaries condition phonological rules but do not undergo them, just like those other unpronounceable elements in phonology—the syntactic and diacritic features.[66]

Distinct from the question of what, if anything, phonological rules can do to boundaries is the question how it is determined whether strings containing boundaries meet the structural descriptions of phonological rules. The position of *SPE* is clear. A morpheme boundary between any two segments in a string is, as already noted, ignored in determining whether that string meets the SD of a rule;[67] otherwise boundaries are treated for this purpose exactly like segments, and a string containing the sequence XBY, where B is a boundary, meets the SD of a phonological rule only if that rule mentions, in the corresponding place, a boundary with no features contradicting those of B.

Almost certainly, *SPE* here is too permissive; by judicious choice of features in rule statement it would be possible to have a rule that applied, say, across

---

[63] The rule of Boundary Insertion once proposed by me for Ancient Greek (Sommerstein 1973, 63) needed to be a phonological rule only because it had to follow the rule of Augmentation; and my arguments for making the latter a phonological rule were not conclusive.

[64] Despite Ross (1972, 278n), the constraint is not falsified by the existence of dialects in which *cranberry* is pronounced with the heterorganic sequence [-nb-] and an unreduced vowel in the second syllable, both indicating the presence of a morpheme boundary after *cran-*. It is true that the putative morpheme *cran-* occurs in no other context; but *berry* does, with precisely the meaning it bears here, and this is sufficient justification for regarding the word as dimorphemic. Chomsky *et al.* cannot have intended to deny the existence of unique-context morphemes such as *cran-*, several of which had become notorious in the literature.

[65] This is true of the Boundary Weakening rule of Sommerstein (1973, 60), which, again, I made a phonological rule on insufficient evidence.

[66] But phonological rules apparently *can* change the position of a boundary in the sequence of segments: cf. R. E. Johnson (1975).

[67] But see p. 145.

morpheme boundary and across word boundary but not across boundaries of intermediate strength, and it is at least highly dubious whether such a rule could occur in a natural language; to that extent the *SPE* theory fails in explanatory adequacy (p. 13). As has been mentioned, the organization of boundaries seems always to be *hierarchical*; the boundaries used in any given language can be arranged in a linear order, from the weakest to the strongest, such that the following constraint can be placed on the conditioning of rules by boundaries:

No phonological rule R may be such that, for some phonological substrings   **130**
X, Y:
(i)   XCY meets R's structural description, where C is a boundary; and
(ii) XBY meets R's structural description, where B is either zero or a boundary weaker than C; and
(iii) XDY does not meet R's structural description, where D is a boundary weaker than C but (if B is not zero) stronger than B.

We now see the advantage of a single, multinary boundary feature or some equivalent. If boundaries are specified by means of a set of binary features, in the *SPE* manner, there is no simple way of ensuring that (130) holds. As soon as we turn to the alternative analysis the problem vanishes. We can posit a single feature [boundary], with a number of possible specifications that varies from language to language, but with [1boundary] always standing for the universal morpheme boundary and [0boundary] for the absence of any boundary; and we can require that all references to boundaries in the structural descriptions of phonological rules be of the form

$$[i \leq . \leq j]\text{boundary} \qquad\qquad \textbf{131}$$

where i may be any non-negative integer and j any such integer greater than or equal to i. This is, in fact, the same convention that we have tacitly been using for other multinary features such as height; we would not expect to find a rule that applied to high and low vowels but not to mid ones, but a rule that applied to mid vowels only, i.e., in a four-height system, contained the specification $[2 \leq . \leq 3$ height], would not surprise us.

The hypothesis we have just been describing was put forward by McCawley (1968), but with an important additional restriction: the value of j in (131) was fixed for each rule. This value was termed the *rank* of the rule. The presence, between two segments of a string otherwise meeting the SD of the rule,[68] of a boundary equal to or stronger than the rank of the rule automatically blocked the rule from applying; but a boundary weaker than the rank of the rule could never be 'too strong', though it might be 'too weak', to allow the rule to apply. This more restrictive hypothesis has proved to be untenable; consider the French rule mentioned on p. 145, for which a morpheme boundary is 'too strong' in some positions but not in others. The SD of the rule is əC₁ₐ[−seg]; this is met by the underlined substring of /rə + də + vən + e/ '(you pl.) become again', but the rule

---

[68] This formulation allows for the possibility that a boundary stronger than the rank of the rule might be required as an *extreme* left- or right-hand environment—what Stanley (1973) calls 'delineation' of rules by boundaries; but I know of no actual case where a rule delineated by a boundary B *must* be assigned a rank weaker than B, and Stanley appears to think no such cases exist.

does not apply: the morpheme boundary after the first schwa is 'too strong' for it. On McCawley's hypothesis this would be possible only if it were the case that the rule could *never* apply to a string with an internal morpheme boundary; yet it constantly does—cf. /ap ə l+ ə + r + a/ → [apɛ ləra] '(he, she, it) will call'. It seems therefore that we cannot impose any restriction severer than (130).

6.6 Syntactic and diacritic features in phonology

We said at the beginning of this chapter that the input to the phonological component includes among other things 'a specification . . . of the hierarchical organization of [the] string into grammatical units' and 'a specification of the syntactic . . . peculiarities of each morpheme'. We must now show what use the phonological component makes of this information.

The available syntactic information may be divided into information about constituent structure and information about the syntactic categorization and features of individual constituents.

6.6.1 Syntactic constituent structure

Constituent structure is primarily relevant to intonation and sentence stress. As we have seen, it determines the insertion of phonological phrase boundary, i.e. the division of a sentence into intonation groups; it also determines such smaller-scale stress-and-intonation contrasts as that between (132) and (133):

M L   M L   132[69]
óld mèn and wómen are exempt from conscription (only young men are liable)
H   L   L M   133
óld mèn and wòmen are exempt from conscription (young people of both sexes are liable)

In (132), 'old men' and 'women' are conjuncts; in (133), 'old' is a modifier of 'men and women'. I am not acquainted with any formal GP account of phenomena of this kind.

But it is not only the prosodic rules that can be conditioned by constituent structure. In Japanese (McCawley 1968, 117) there is a rule deleting high vowels in the following environment (where /:/ is the boundary between the elements of compounds, and I have reformulated the environment in terms of the feature system used in the present work):

$$/ \begin{bmatrix} +\text{cons} \\ +\text{Chinese} \\ \alpha\text{back} \end{bmatrix} \underline{\quad\quad} : \begin{bmatrix} -\text{voice} \\ \beta\text{back} \end{bmatrix} \qquad \textbf{134}$$
where, if $\alpha = +$, then $\beta = +$.

Certain forms, however, unexpectedly fail to undergo the rule though they meet its structural description. The majority of such exceptions are of a single type:

[69] The pitch markings (H = high, M = mid, L = low) are intended only to give an idea of the sort of intonation (sub-) contours that would be associated with the contrasting structures.

F

compounds of three (or more) elements where the vowel which fails to delete directly precedes the major constituent break. Thus /zi+rjoku+kei/ 'magnetometer' retains the vowel at the end of its second element; its constituent structure is

135

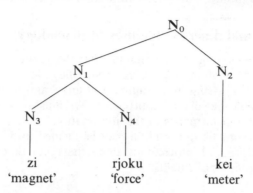

zi	rjoku	kei
'magnet'	'force'	'meter'

The appropriate formulation of the condition appears to be that the deletion rule applies only if the two morphemes which meet at the point where the SD of the rule is met are *sister* constituents.[70]

6.6.2 Syntactic categories

More common with rules of word and lower ranks is the determination of rule applicability by the category (noun, verb, adjective, etc.) to which a word or other piece belongs. This is found both with rules affecting prosodic features and with those affecting segmental features.

The complex rules governing the deletion of word-final consonants and vowels in French are subject to many conditions of this kind (Schane 1967). Most word-final consonants are deleted at the end of a phrase; within the phrase there are restrictions—one of which is that, though deletion applies obligatorily to singular nouns and optionally to plural nouns, it does not apply at all to adjectives, so that surface contrasts may arise between e.g. [œ̃savɑ̃ɑ̃glɛ] 'an English scientist', where *savant* is a noun, and [œ̃savɑ̃tɑ̃glɛ] 'a learned Englishman', where it is an adjective.

Syntactic conditioning of this kind may even affect low-level phonetic rules. Jones (1960, 235) noted that in the South of England there was a tendency to pronounce the vowel [æ] fully long before a voiced consonant; this tendency was most marked in adjectives ending in /-æd/, was also discernible in some nouns, but 'curiously enough' was rare in nouns ending in /-æd/. Evidently the degree of

[70] Two constituents are sisters if the smallest higher constituent containing either of them contains both. Thus in (135) /zi/ and /rjoku/ are sisters. N being the constituent in question (N₃ and N₄ are not higher constituents, being simply the category labels for /zi/ and /rjoku/ themselves); but /rjoku/ and /kei/ are not sisters, since N₁ contains the former but not the latter.—It should be noted that McCawley captures the phenomena here described, not by making the deletion rule directly sensitive to constituent structure, but by having it 'ranked' (p. 150) by a boundary which is for other reasons typical of those compounds where deletion fails to apply. He does not give sufficient data to distinguish between these two possibilities; and whichever version of the rule we choose, it will wrongly predict in certain cases that there will be no deletion.

lengthening is determined by a number of interacting factors, of which syntactic categorization is one.

6.6.3 Syntactic features

In addition to the basic categorization of lexical items as nouns, verbs, etc., the syntactic component of the grammar also imposes many other classifications on them. Nouns may be categorized in the lexicon as countable or uncountable, animate or inanimate, etc., since these classifications frequently affect their syntactic behaviour; they may also be categorized for declensional classes or the like, which may determine the underlying phonological form of certain grammatical morphemes; and in many languages the syntax will assign a case to each occurrence of a noun. Verbs, adjectives and so on likewise have their own subcategorizations. Any[71] of these *syntactic features* may affect the operation of phonological rules.

Sometimes it happens that a rule can only apply if a particular morpheme is present; and sometimes that morpheme can be pinpointed, by a combination of syntactic and phonological specifications, without having to be actually mentioned in the rule. This raises the problem: in such cases, should we formulate the rule so as to refer to a particular morpheme, or to a combination of syntactic and phonological features? There is no mechanical way to the answer. It depends, rather, on the fact that the two modes of formulation say two different things. If a rule applies just to a particular morpheme, then it is really a lexical quirk of that morpheme, on a par with its having an irregular plural or figuring in an idiomatic phrase. But if we say that it applies in the presence of a particular combination of syntactic and phonological features, then we seem to be implying (a) that the rule is at least partly motivated by the desirability of maintaining overt surface marking of the syntactic distinction in question, or possibly of marking it in a consistent manner, and (b) that there is also something about the phonological features mentioned that makes the rule plausible. We will begin with a case where questions of this kind arise.

In Ancient Greek the comparative of adjectives was formed with one of two suffixes, each adjective stem normally taking one suffix to the exclusion of the other. For the vast majority of adjectives the comparative suffix was /tero/; but about eighteen comparatives were formed with a different suffix. The underlying form of this suffix appears to have been /ion/; but, in Attic Greek at least, it never showed up on the surface in this form. Where it was directly preceded by a vowel, this vowel and the initial /i/ of the suffix contracted into a diphthong, as was normal for /Vi/ sequences in Attic; hence [ra͡iɔːn] 'easier', [lɔ͡iɔːn] 'better'.[72]

---

[71] Except for features whose sole *raison d'être* is to account for exceptions to a particular syntactic rule (Zwicky 1970a). Zwicky also asserts that *semantic* features cannot condition phonological rules, except indirectly by way of syntax; this would follow inevitably from the 'standard theory' of generative grammar (p. 4), but that theory in its original form is now known to be unsatisfactory, and it would be unwise to exclude direct semantics-phonology links *a priori*, particularly in the field of intonation. Such links seen in fact to be implicit in Jackendoff's (1972) theory of semantic interpretation.

[72] The forms given are masculine nominative singular: the lengthening and lowering of /o/ is regular in these endingless masculine (and feminine) nominatives.

The other two treatments are less predictable. If the root syllable of the adjective was heavy, i.e. contained a long vowel or was closed by a consonant, the comparative suffix changed to /i:on/:[73] so [hɛ:di:ɔ:n] 'more pleasant', [kalli:ɔ:n] 'fairer', and three or four others. Otherwise—wherever neither of the above two treatments was followed—the suffix was reduced to a monosyllable, its initial vowel becoming a glide, and this glide /j/ then fused with the final consonant of the root by one of a variety of processes which also applied to /Cj/ sequences elsewhere in the language; and—a final twist—the last or only vowel of the root, if short, invariably lengthened. Thus we have derivations like the following:

/thakh+ion/	[tha:tton][74]	'faster'	**136**
/meg+ion/	[me:zdɔ:n]	'bigger'	
/mal+ion/	[ma:llon][74]	'more'	

There are therefore three rules, it would seem, triggered by this comparative suffix and by nothing else: two lengthening rules and a vowel→glide rule; though in fact the first lengthening rule and the vowel→glide rule can, and probably should, be collapsed. Are these rules peculiarities of the morpheme /ion/ as such? If so, then we should assign that morpheme an arbitrary feature—say [+C]—and express the rules as follows:

$$\begin{bmatrix} i \\ +C \end{bmatrix} \rightarrow \begin{cases} [+\text{long}] & / \begin{Bmatrix} V: \\ VC \end{Bmatrix} \ C+ \underline{\quad} \\ [-\text{syll}] & \text{elsewhere} \end{cases} \qquad \textbf{137}^{75}$$

$$V \rightarrow [+\text{long}] \ / \ \underline{\quad} [+\text{cons}] + \begin{bmatrix} -\text{syll} \\ +C \end{bmatrix} \qquad \textbf{138}$$

But is it really accidental that it is a grammatically significant morpheme—the comparative—that is involved in these processes? We may note that /on/ and /ɔ:n/ are rather common as inflexional endings in Greek: they are found in various functions in nouns, adjectives, verbs and participles; in addition many noun and adjective roots end in /on/ and ɔ:n/, so that this comparative suffix is involved in massive homonymy. We may note also that as a result of (137), (138), and the /Vi/ contraction rule, all comparatives formed with this suffix have a long vowel or diphthong in the penultimate[76] syllable; thus the rules between them create an additional marker which, though not uniquely characteristic of comparatives, at least makes it possible to infer that any form ending in [-ɔ:n] or [-on] with a *short* vowel in the preceding syllable is *not* a comparative (unless, of course, it is either (i) a genitive plural of an /ion/ comparative, ending in [on ɔ:n], or (ii) a case-form of a /tero/ comparative; in these forms the danger of homonymy is relatively remote compared with the nominative singular).

[73] All roots taking /i:on/ are heavy, but not all heavy roots take /i:on/; i.e. the rule lengthening /i/ in this context will have some exceptions.
[74] These are neuter or adverbial forms, the adjectival forms being rare or non-existent.
[75] The subrules of (137) must apply disjunctively, but no applicable *SPE* notational convention predicts disjunctive ordering; the example supports Kiparsky's 'elsewhere condition', discussed in Chapter Seven.
[76] In certain case-forms, antepenultimate.

But if the rules are indeed motivated by the desirability of greater distinctiveness for a grammatically significant morpheme, then mention should be made in the rule, if possible, of the grammatical significance of that morpheme; in other words, it should be stated that the rule applies only to comparatives. The two rules which apply only to the morpheme /ion/ should thus preferably be stated in the following manner:

$$\begin{bmatrix} \text{i} \\ +\text{comparative} \end{bmatrix} \rightarrow \left\{ \begin{matrix} [+\text{long}]/ \left\{ \begin{matrix} \text{V:} \\ \text{VC} \end{matrix} \right\} \text{C} \\ [-\text{syll}] \end{matrix} \right\} + \underline{\quad\quad} \text{ on } [-\text{seg}] \qquad \textbf{139}$$

$$\text{V} \rightarrow [+\text{long}] / \underline{\quad\quad} [+\text{cons}] + \begin{bmatrix} \text{j} \\ +\text{comparative} \end{bmatrix} \text{ on } [-\text{seg}] \qquad \textbf{140}$$

(139) and (140) lay proper emphasis on the two crucial features that motivate the rules: that the morpheme is a marker of the comparative, and that its form, /ion/, makes it liable to homonymy.[77]

Another example of a phonological rule partly conditioned by syntactic features would be fronting of back vowels (umlaut) in German. This is confined to particular grammatical categories, and restricted within these. In nouns, for instance, one ending of the nominative plural is identical with one ending of the dative singular, /e/; but the former conditions umlaut (subject to some further restrictions), the latter does not. Among those further restrictions is that plurality does not condition umlaut in neuter nouns—except those of the small declensional class that has /er/ as its plural suffix. Thus, in its application to noun inflexion alone, the umlaut rule must be conditioned by gender, number and declensional-class features.

6.6.4 Diacritic features

So far we have considered only independently motivated syntactic features. But these, in conjunction with phonological features, still cannot account fully for the facts of pronunciation. Some forms unaccountably fail to undergo an otherwise general phonological rule. Some sets of forms behave irregularly with respect to whole sets of rules. To account for these facts two further types of feature are required, often subsumed under the general label of *diacritic features*.

First, we have the straightforward exception.[78] In general, in English, long

[77] The similarity between the structural descriptions of the rules will be noticed; but there does not seem to be any way of collapsing them further into a single rule. As we have already emphasized, not every genuine relationship between rules can be captured by a notational convention.

[78] Much about exceptions is in fact far from straightforward. Where a rule consists of two or more subrules, a form may be an exception to some of the subrules and yet undergo others. Again, it is necessary to distinguish between the kind of exceptional form which fails to *undergo* a rule and the kind of exceptional form which fails to *condition* a rule: a form may be exceptional in one sense and not in the other (Kisseberth 1970b). One and the same morpheme may contain segments that are regular and segments that are exceptional with respect to the same rule: thus in the Russian adjective *deféktnyj* 'defective' the /f/ normally undergoes palatalization, as most Russian consonants do before /e/, but the /d/ normally does not, though /defekt/ is a single morpheme (Holden 1974); for similar examples see Lightner (1972, 360 and 401) and Anderson (1974b, 213). They show that rule-exception features must be assigned to individual segments, not to morphemes as wholes.

syllabic peaks are replaced by their short counterparts of table (86) before the Latin- or French-derived suffixes *-ic, -id, -ish*: note *cone:conic, revive:vivid, final:finish*. Many words ending in *-ic*[79] nevertheless retain a long peak in the preceding syllable, e.g. *strategic, basic, gnomic*. No syntactic or phonological peculiarity of these words can account for their exceptionallity, for they do not have anything in common that is not also shared by words which undergo the shortening rule (also called Laxing). In theory we could invent a phonological peculiarity which would do the job. We might, for example, claim that the vowels in question had, in underlying representation, the feature [+retracted tongue root] and that the Laxing rule applied only to [− retracted tongue root] vowels; we would then require a later rule making all vowels [− retracted tongue root]. Such 'diacritic use of phonological features', as Kiparsky (1968b) termed it, may not be objectionable in all circumstances, but it certainly is objectionable in this case. For it is purely *ad hoc*: there is no other evidence for the supposed retracted-tongue-root vowels (unless, of course, we were to concoct a bit more in the same way) and no particular reason why we should suppose them to be retracted-tongue-root rather than to have any other feature that happens not to be distinctive otherwise in English. Rather we have here a clear case for a *rule feature*.

Any phonological rule (it is normally assumed) can have exceptions.[80] This being so, we can set up a universal set of rule features by positing for each rule R of the phonological component of each language a feature [±R] such that a segment which is [− R] can never undergo rule R even though the string of which it is part satisfies the structural description of the rule. Put otherwise, it is understood that each rule R applies only to segments which are [+R]—this is not being explicitly stated as part of the rule.

It is not, of course, necessary on this ground to mark every segment in the lexicon as regular with respect to every rule in the phonology. Just as we understand [+R] to be part of the SD of every rule, so we can understand that in the lexicon every segment has the value plus for each rule feature for which it is not marked minus. Thus it is never necessary to state in the lexicon that an item is not an exception to a rule—save in two sets of circumstances. The first is if the item happens to belong to a class whose members are normally exceptional. If there is a class of which this is true, it would be missing a generalization to predicate exceptionality separately of every member of the class: we will state by a *redundancy rule* that each segment of each morpheme of the class in question is an exception to such a phonological rule, and then individual members of the class not marked for that rule-feature in the lexicon will be assumed to have the value minus for it. Schane (1967, 47f) gives an interesting example from French. Among the many rules of that language which affect segments that are in some sense final are the following three:[81]

---

[79] Some other apparent exceptions, including those in *-id*, can be accounted for by other independently motivated rules: see *SPE* 180f.

[80] If, however, it is possible to make a principled distinction between phonological and phonetic rules, it may be that the latter are exceptionless.

[81] I have altered the statement of the rules, partly to conform to the feature system used in this book and partly for reasons explained by Chomsky and Halle (*SPE* 353–355); note that Chomsky and Halle are wrong to omit the feature of sonorance from the SD of (141) (their (69)). Doubtless (143) should be generalized to apply to /f/ as well as /s/ (note that it does not apply to /š/).

$$\begin{bmatrix} \alpha\text{cons} \\ -\alpha\text{syll} \\ -\alpha\text{son} \end{bmatrix} \rightarrow \emptyset \ / \ \underline{\qquad} + \ [\alpha\text{cons}] \qquad\qquad 141$$

$$[-\text{son}] \quad \rightarrow \ \emptyset \ / \ \underline{\qquad} \ [\text{PPB}] \qquad\qquad 142$$

$$s \ \rightarrow \ z \ / \ \underline{\qquad} \ \# \ V \qquad\qquad 143$$

These three rules are related in a remarkable way: any form that is an exception to the first of them is also an exception to the other two (but not conversely: /sis/ 'six', for example, is an exception to (142) but not to (141) or for that matter to (143)). The lexicon of French will thus have attached to it the following redundancy rule:

$$[-(141)] \rightarrow \begin{bmatrix} -(142) \\ -(143) \end{bmatrix} \qquad\qquad 144$$

What if the regularity expressed by a redundancy rule of this kind is not perfect? In Desano, for example (Kaye 1971), there is a rule assimilating the value of the feature [nasal] on all segments of a morpheme to its value in the segments of an adjacent morpheme. While, however, all morphemes can condition this rule, not all morphemes can undergo it; in particular noun and verb morphemes are inherently nasal or non-nasal and do not undergo assimilation. Desano thus has a redundancy rule

$$\begin{bmatrix} \left\{ \begin{matrix} +\text{N} \\ +\text{V} \end{matrix} \right\} \end{bmatrix} \rightarrow [-\text{nasality assimilation}] \qquad\qquad 145$$

One verb, /bɨ/ 'old', nevertheless undergoes nasality assimilation, e.g. [bɨ + gɨ] 'old man' but [mɨ̃ + nã] 'old men'. Consequently, this verb must be marked either [+nasality assimilation]—which will be understood to exempt it automatically from any redundancy rules specifying this feature as minus—or directly as an exception to the redundancy rule (145).[82]

One feature of the Desano nasality assimilation rule, as described by Kaye, is that the vast majority of all the morphemes of the language are exceptions to it. Only one lexical morpheme, /bɨ/, undergoes the rule; of grammatical morphemes, three classes (evidentials, classifiers and mood markers) and two unclassifiable morphemes (the question marker and the non-present marker) undergo the rule; four classes (personal endings, directionals, noun finals and verb finals) never undergo it; and case endings, participal endings and probably plural suffixes are divided, some individual morphemes undergoing the rule, some not (Kaye 1971, 51f). It is in fact easier to mark as exceptions those forms and classes which *do* undergo the rule than to mark those which do not.

A rule, in order to undergo which a form has to be an exception, may seem paradoxical. But it corresponds to a reality. Not all linguistic generalizations are

[82] Kaye (1971, 54) is not quite right when he equates these two kinds of marking with one another. Suppose there were a morpheme of French which was an exception to (141) and (142) but not to (143); then to mark it [−(144)] would falsely imply that it underwent rule (142). The marking that *would* be appropriate, [+(143)], thus could not properly be called 'an exception feature to a redundancy rule', which is how Kaye characterizes features of the form [+rule R].

massive affairs covering nearly the whole of the language. Some may affect only four or five forms, and yet be regular for it to be wasteful and also misleading to state it separately for each form to which it applies. There are only seven verbs in English that form a past tense ending in [− ɔːt]; but if we state this simply as an individual lexical quirk of each one of them we arc implicitly claiming that it is an accident that there are no verbs forming past tenses in [-aːt], [-iːt], etc.

A rule of this kind is termed a *minor* rule. Like all other rules, it applies only to segments which are marked plus for its application; but for minor rules the presumption is that, unless otherwise provided by lexical marking or by redundancy rule, every segment is [− R] for every minor rule R.[83]

Often a set of forms behaves exceptionally with respect not just to a single rule, but to a whole set of rules. Such sets of forms often constitute the major vocabulary divisions of a language, such as the 'Germanic', 'Latin' and 'Greek' divisions we have seen to be necessary for English. Such divisions are not necessarily etymologically based. Many languages, such as Japanese (McCawley 1968) and Mohawk (Postal 1968), have classes of words of peculiar formation (like those traditionally called 'onomatopoeic' in Japanese and 'ideophones' in some African languages) which are exceptions to some phonological rules and exceptionally undergo others which ordinary words of similar form would not undergo. In Japanese, the 'onomatopoeic' section of the vocabulary does not undergo the rule spirantizing underlying /p/, is not subject to the phonotactic constraint that a palatalized consonant cannot precede a rounded vowel, does undergo a reduplication rule not otherwise used in the language, etc. The class has a certain degree of syntactic and semantic motivation, in that all its members are manner adverbs; but by no means all manner adverbs are 'onomatopoeic'.

The distinction between 'learnèd' and 'non-learnèd' forms, often referred to in discussion particularly of Romance languages, is really a variety of the vocabulary distinctions based on origin. The 'non-learned' vocabulary of, say, French is that which is 'native' in the sense of having been in the language continuously since before most of the language's present phonological rules entered its grammar, together with later arrivals whose phonological behaviour is similar; the 'learned' vocabulary consists primarily of medieval and modern loans from Latin. Things get more complicated in Romance languages because the 'non-learned' vocabulary itself is for the most part ultimately of Latin origin, so that there is an obvious formal and semantic resemblance between many 'non-learned' forms and corresponding 'learned' forms, e.g. (in French)

[vulwar]	'to wish'	**146**
[vɔlɔ̃te]	'will'	
[naže]	'to swim'	
[natasjɔ̃]	'swimming'	
[ɛspri]	'mind'	
[spirityɛl]	'spiritual'	

[83] Minor rules are not used in *SPE*; their first use in GP (they had already been used in syntax) is apparently by Lightner (1968). — If the Desano nasality assimilation rule were said to be minor, it would obviate the problem of how to state the fact that /bɨ/ undergoes the rule: for there would no

and one is very tempted to derive each pair from a common underlying form. But if we do this, we seem to be saying that one and the same morpheme is learned in some of its occurrences and non-learned in others. If we reject the identification, though, we will be left with numerous homophonous or nearly homophonous pairs of distinct morphemes, which, oddly enough, usually have the same meaning and are in complementary distribution; and, at least as important, we will be implicitly denying that French speakers in any way identify the roots of *vouloir* and *volonté*, of *nager* and *natation*, of *esprit* and *spirituel*—which seems a very dubious claim. The key to a solution in the Romance situation (not necessarily in all such situations in all languages) seems to be that in general it is not morphemes that are or are not 'learned', but words. Surface structures are made up of words; and each word, either in its lexical entry or in the 'word formation rule'[84] by which it is formed, will be specified as learned or non-learned, and the appropriate feature specification will be assigned to each segment of the word.

6.7 Rule ordering

6.7.1 Linear ordering

It has long been recognized that certain phonological processes are more simply and revealingly statable if they are regarded as operating in a particular order, such that the 'later' process can be applied to the output of the 'earlier' but not conversely. We have already seen several examples in passing; let us now consider one more carefully.

Among the phonological rules of present-day Greek are the following three, which are characteristic of the majority of dialects.[85] *Height Dissimilation* raises a mid vowel to high adjacent to a low vowel, and also raises /e/ when adjacent to /o/:

$$\begin{bmatrix} V \\ 2\text{height} \end{bmatrix} \rightarrow [3\text{height}] \ / \ / \ \underline{\hspace{1cm}} \begin{bmatrix} V \\ \leq 2\text{height} \\ +\text{back} \end{bmatrix} \qquad \mathbf{147}^{86}$$

Thus to [kariðéa] 'walnut tree' of the so-called 'Old Athenian' dialects (where height dissimilation does not apply to stressed vowels) corresponds [kariðía] on the Ionian island of Zakinthos (where glide formation, to be mentioned presently, is restricted to unstressed vowels but height dissimilation is not).

---

longer be any need for a redundancy rule about nouns and verbs, and /bi/ could simply be marked as an exception, i.e. as undergoing the rule. The solution, however, is not available for all similar problems. Thus in Lithuanian (Kenstowicz 1970) there is circumflex accentuation in the third person future tense of verbs; if the accented vowel is long and high, the rule does not apply, generally speaking—but in five verbs with accented long high vowels it does.

[84] For word formation rules see Halle (1973).

[85] The discussion which follows is based on Newton (1972). I have formulated the rules, which Newton presents as prose statements, and occasionally have extrapolated slightly from the data he gives.

[86] In Greek vowel height is phonologically only ternary; I have accordingly used [2height] for mid vowels, [3height] for high vowels and glides. Note that /a/ is the only underlying low vowel, so it is a

Glide formation reduces a high vowel to a glide adjacent to any vowel, any stress being transferred to the conditioning vowel:

$$
\begin{bmatrix} V \\ 3\text{height} \\ \langle +\text{stress} \rangle \end{bmatrix} \qquad V
$$
$$
\downarrow \qquad\qquad \downarrow \qquad\qquad\text{(Mirror-image)}
$$
$$
[-\text{syll}] \qquad [\langle +\text{stress} \rangle]
$$

148

Thus in many dialects the sequence of /to/ 'it' and /íða/ 'I saw' is pronounced [tójða] 'I saw it'.

Consonantality effectively neutralizes the distinction between the palatal fricative /ɣ′/ and the glide /j/ from underlying /i/ or /e/: either surfaces as a glide, a nasal or a voiced or voiceless fricative, depending on the preceding segment; if the affected segment is initial, it surfaces as a glide. This appears to be the limit of the effect of the rule in most dialects; in a few, though—those with which we shall be particularly concerned—it applies also to /w/, which it makes consonantal before as well as after a consonant:

$$
\begin{bmatrix} -\text{syll} \\ +\text{cont} \\ +\text{voice} \\ 3\text{high} \\ -\text{lab} \\ -\text{cor} \\ \alpha\text{back} \\ \alpha\text{round} \end{bmatrix} \rightarrow \left\{ \begin{matrix} \begin{bmatrix} +\text{cons} \\ \beta\text{nas} \\ \gamma\text{voice} \\ \langle +\text{lab} \rangle \end{bmatrix} & // & \begin{bmatrix} +\text{cons} \\ \beta\text{nas} \\ \gamma\text{voice} \end{bmatrix} & \begin{bmatrix} \underline{\quad\quad} \\ \langle +\text{round} \rangle \end{bmatrix} \\ \\ [-\text{cons}] & & \text{elsewhere} \end{matrix} \right\}
$$

149

In the mainstream dialects—where the specification [−back] appears instead of [αback, αround], and the first subrule is not mirror-image—this rule has the effect that the word for 'walnut tree' is pronounced [kariðɣ́á]; and it gives rise to a variety of alternations, e.g. [máti] 'eye' ~ [mátχa] 'eyes', [líji] 'it ceases' ~ [élikse] 'it ceased' (where [ks]←[χs] by the regular rule of Manner Dissimilation).

Now in the 'south-eastern' group of dialects (Chios, the Dodecanese, Cyprus), intervocalic voiced fricatives are deleted:

$$
\begin{bmatrix} -\text{son} \\ +\text{cont} \\ +\text{voice} \end{bmatrix} \rightarrow \theta \;/\; V \underline{\quad\quad} V
$$

150

so that alternations arise such as

$$
\begin{aligned}
/\text{as ðóki}/ &\rightarrow [\text{azðóki}] \quad \text{'let him give'} \\
/\text{na ðóki}/ &\rightarrow [\text{naóki}] \quad \text{'let him give'}
\end{aligned}
$$

151

It is evident that the outputs of (150) will contain many vowel sequences meeting the structural descriptions of height dissimilation and glide formation. Let us first

---

true statement that only back vowels can condition height dissimilation; also that both height dissimilation and glide formation are mirror-image rules.

make the simplest possible assumption, viz. that each rule applies whenever its SD is met; and let us consider their effect on an underlying representation such as /aloγás/ 'horse-dealer'.

As it stands this form meets the SD of Voiced Fricative Deletion: so we delete the /γ/, giving the output /aloás/. To this we can apply Height Dissimilation, giving /aluás/; now the SD of Glide Formation is satisfied, and the result of applying this is /alwás/. We now have a glide adjacent to a consonant, and this will be converted by Consonantality (first subrule) into a labial fricative, giving the surface form [alvás].

But this form is found only in south-western Rhodes; in all the other dialects which have rule (150) the surface form is one or other of those given above as intermediate stages: in 'a typical Rhodian dialect', for instance (Newton 1972, 65), it is [aloás]. Now it is not that Height Dissimilation, Glide Formation and Consonantality do not apply in this dialect; pronunciations such as [kariðγ'á] are as normal there as in the south-west of the island. Perhaps then the application of Height Dissimilation is restricted so that such representations as [aloás] are not affected? It turns out that there is no way in which this can be done, short of specifying that Height Dissimilation applies to just those vowel sequences which meet its SD *and* are not derived through the operation of Voiced Fricative Deletion; for there is nothing in the forms themselves to distinguish those which undergo Height Dissimilation from those which do not—unless we give up all hope of capturing any generalization at all by simply listing the formatives which do and those which do not undergo the rule. The same impasse arises with Glide Formation; 'sewer' is [súða] in most dialects outside the south-eastern group, [súa] in most dialects within this group, [sfá] in parts of south-western Rhodes: Glide Formation, like Height Dissimilation, fails to apply just where a vowel sequence apparently susceptible to it has been created by Voiced Fricative Deletion.

There is one way, and one only, to describe the situation without placing any special restriction on the generality of any of the rules in either type of dialect. This is to say that in the dialects having [aloás] and [súa], Voiced Fricative Deletion is *ordered after* the other rules mentioned: that it becomes applicable only when they have already had their chance to apply, so that they cannot apply to its output. More carefully, we may define the statement 'rule R is ordered after rule Q' to mean:

Let the successive stages of a phonological derivation be $P_1, P_2, \ldots, P_{n-1}$, **152** P_n, where P_1 is the underlying representation and P_n the surface representation. Then in every derivation in which P_i differs from P_{i-1} in that rule Q has applied, and P_j differs from P_{j-1} in that rule R has applied, $j > i$.

The principle of cyclic rule application (p. 163) will require some modification of (152), but it does not alter the essential meaning of rule ordering.

What of the south-west Rhodian dialects in which all four rules apply successively—Voiced Fricative Deletion, Height Dissimilation, Glide Formation, Consonantality—to give forms like [alvás] and [sfá]? Two ways of accounting for the facts are open to us. One is to say that in these dialects the four rules are unordered with respect to each other, i.e. apply whenever their structural descriptions are met (leaving aside any ordering relations that may obtain between these and other rules we have not discussed). The other is to say that they are ordered, but that their ordering is not the same as in neighbouring dialects but rather is the order in which they were mentioned earlier in this paragraph.

Empirically the two solutions are exactly equivalent, both giving correct outputs; but they differ in their theoretical implications. For there are three possibilities concerning the role of rule ordering in phonology.

No two rules, in any natural language, are ordered with respect to one   **153a** another.
In at least some languages, some pairs of rules are ordered with respect to   **b** one another; and in at least some languages, some pairs of rules are not.
In every natural language, an ordering relation exists between every rule   **c** and every other rule.

And our second interpretation of the south-west Rhodian data is consistent with either (153b) or (153c), while our first interpretation is consistent only with (153b).

Now if it is possible to uphold (153c), this should be preferred to (153b), because it makes a stronger, more restrictive claim about what is a possible human language. And at the time when *SPE* was written it did appear that (153c) could be upheld; not only that, but also the following further requirement:

Transitivity Condition: if rule Q is ordered before rule R, and rule R before   **154** rule S, then rule Q is ordered before rule S.[87]

Between them, (153c) and (154) constitute the *linear ordering hypothesis*. Leaving aside for the time being the effects of the cyclic principle, the hypothesis entails that all the phonological rules in the language form a sequence, and are applied in the following manner. The first rule in the sequence is tested for applicability and applied or not according to whether its SD is met; in either case the second rule is then tested similarly, and so on to the last. Thus only one rule is tested at each stage, and no rule is tested more than once.

From 1970 onwards, as we shall see in Chapter Seven, attention has been drawn in the phonological literature to numerous sets of data that appear to violate the linear ordering hypothesis; and it now seems probable that the hypothesis cannot be sustained. It remains useful, nevertheless, as a working assumption; and in the presentation of the phonological rules of a language it may be preferable to give them in a linear order, even though it may have to be stated that in certain circumstances (which should be precisely defined) this order is violated, rather than to use some theoretically more correct mode of presentation—because linear ordering makes it easiest for the user to determine the surface form corresponding to a given underlying form.

It is as well to be clear what assertion we are making when we say that (e.g.) in south-west Rhodian Greek, Voiced Fricative Deletion is ordered before Height

[87] Note that (154) is in no way a logically necessary consequence of (152) and (153c): it would be perfectly possible for Q to be ordered before R, R before S, and S before Q, provided only that no one derivation existed in which either (i) all three SDs were met simultaneously, or (ii) the SD of one of the rules was met at a stage when the other two had already applied.

Dissimilation. We are not saying that Voiced Fricative Deletion is historically earlier; the descriptive order of two rules may or may not reflect the historical order.[88] We are not saying that a speaker of the language, every time he uses a form in whose derivation these two rules are involved, actually computes its surface form from the underlying representation, applying the rules in the order stated; GP is not part of (though it does not deny the importance of) a theory of speech production. We are saying only that on the criteria of Chapter One, the best way to describe the mapping between the motivated underlying representations and the actual surface forms is to suppose that where this mapping is mediated (among other processes) both by Voiced Fricative Deletion and by Height Dissimilation, the part of the mapping that involves Voiced Fricative Deletion is closer to the underlying representation than the part involving Height Dissimilation. Everything else is metaphor.

6.7.2 The transformational cycle

In *SPE* there is superimposed on the linear ordering hypothesis another ordering principle known as the principle of the *transformational cycle*. This is an extension to phonology of a standard principle of transformational syntax. The principle may be stated as follows:

> If A and B are syntactic constituents within a given phonological phrase (A **155** may but need not be coextensive with the whole phrase) and A properly includes B, then the whole phonological rule sequence must have had a chance to apply to strings wholly within B before any rule can apply to a string within A which is not wholly within some subconstituent of A. Such a testing of the whole rule sequence for applicability wholly within the constituent B is termed *the B cycle*.
>
> Any rule may be applied on the A cycle notwithstanding that it, or a rule ordered after it, has already applied on the B cycle.

In this way, in theory, the whole rule sequence is applied over and over again within successively larger constituents, with the last cycle allowing them to apply over the whole phonological phrase. In fact it is usually found that the majority of rules apply only once in a derivation: *SPE* handles this by so formulating the structural descriptions of such rules that they can apply only within a constituent which is also a word (cf. pp. 145–7), but it is not clear whether all non-cyclic rules are 'word-level' in this sense.[89] The rules that do apply repeatedly are almost exclusively rules assigning prosodic features:[90] in this domain the cyclic principle

---

[88] On how such discrepancies come to exist, see pp. 242–9.

[89] Fischer-Jørgensen (1975, 249) points out that some non-cyclic rules at least (viz. those of external sandhi) cannot possibly be 'word-level'.

[90] A number of cases have been adduced in which rules assigning segmental features are claimed to apply cyclically: cf. Brame (1972b), Kisseberth (1972a)—who, however, pays very little attention to the principle that the domains of successive cycles are syntactic constituents—and Wilkinson (1974). (Further references, in regard to American Indian languages only, are given by Zwicky 1976.) These cases, however, remain remarkable for their rarity, and several of them have recently been refuted (see, e.g., Truitner and Dunnigan 1975 *contra* Kaye and Piggott 1973). At present no clear verdict can be returned on the general question.

amounts to a claim that the stress and pitch contours of a phonological phrase are largely determined by the inherent stress and pitch features of the constituents of that phrase.

Consider the English word *theatricality*. Since this noun has close syntactic and semantic connections with the adjective *theatrical* and the noun *theatre*, its syntactic and underlying phonological structure might be represented by the labelled bracketing

$$[\#[\#[\#\theta e\text{æ}tr\#_N] + ik + \text{æ}1\#_A] + i + ti\#_N]$$ **156**[91]

How now do the stress rules of English apply to this word? We first consider only the most deeply embedded constituent (the one which does not properly include any other constituent), namely the noun /θeætr/, which a regular principle of English stress assignment[92] will stress on the first syllable. If we were considering *theatre* as a word by itself, we would not proceed to any further stress cycles but apply the word-level rules immediately and so derive the surface representation, [θíətə] or whatever the output may be of the rules of the particular dialect we happen to be describing.

Since, however, we are considering *theatricality*, we proceed to a second cycle, where the string under consideration is the adjective /θéætr + ik + æl/, which at this point, as a result of the previous cycle, has stress on its initial syllable. The adjective, like all *-ical* adjectives, is now assigned primary stress on the syllable preceding *-ical*. This would seem to result in the incorrect stressing *théátrical*, but by convention—apparently a universal convention—the 'new' stress is taken to be stronger than the 'old', or more precisely 'when within a cyclic domain[93] a vowel is assigned the value α for stress, all other vowels with the value α for stress in that domain take instead the value α + 1 [i.e. one degree weaker]' (Kiparsky 1966). Thus, with a new primary stress on the second syllable of *theatrical*, the existing primary stress on the first syllable is automatically downgraded to secondary.

On the third cycle the whole noun *theatricality* is taken into consideration. It is assigned a primary stress on the antepenultimate syllable, the existing stresses being automatically weakened to tertiary on the first syllable and secondary on the second. On this cycle also, since *theatricality* is a word, the word-level rules apply; at least one of these that is relevant also affects stress, the Stress Adjustment rule (*SPE* 84), weakening by one degree all non-primary stresses within the word. By the application of this and the word-level segmental rules we finally derive the surface representation

$$\overset{\overset{4\,3}{}}{[\theta\text{ı}\text{æ}\text{tr}\text{ı}\text{kæl}\text{ı}\text{t}\text{ı}]}$$ **157**

The cycles do not end at the level of the word. Phrase and sentence stress is assigned in the same way, by reassigning primary stress to particular words in successive cycles, with the stresses of words not thus singled out being

---

[91] For this, and the whole derivation, cf. *SPE* 88.
[92] It is not necessary here to give details of the stress assignment rules of English, which are both complex and controversial; only to point out that each cyclic domain in succession is assigned primary stress in the same position where it would bear primary stress were it an independent word.
[93] This is evidently the meaning, though Kiparsky actually says 'innerhalb einer *Konstituente*'.

automatically weakened each time round. At the end of the process there will be just one primary stress in each phonological phrase.[94]

Like other questions of rule ordering, the principle of the transformational cycle is still a matter of dispute, even on the 'home ground' of the cycle, namely stress;[95] but at present cyclic rule application, at least for prosodic features, must be regarded as an established part of GP theory, no one having come near to showing that it can be dispensed with in all cases without loss of generality.

6.7.3 Excursus: the intermingling of phonology and syntax

Mention was made in note 94 of the probability that phrase and sentence stress in English are assigned by rules of the syntactic component. Various other cases have been reported in which rules whose effects and/or conditioning factors are essentially phonological have to be ordered before syntactic rules which have no phonological aspect at all (see Zimmer 1969; Langacker 1970; Cook 1971; Anderson 1974a, 6; Awbery 1975; Tegey 1975); and it might seem that the distinction between the two components, and the very notion of surface syntactic and underlying phonological representations, are thereby called into question. The available evidence, however, seems to show that the *SPE* model is, in this respect, not as radically inadequate as might at first sight appear. It is striking that in every case reported where a phonological rule has to apply before a syntactic rule, either

(i)   the phonological rule affects only prosodic features; or   **158**
(ii) the phonological rule is a deletion; or
(iii) the syntactic rule is a deletion

The conclusion seems to be indicated that prosodic rules and deletion rules may figure in either the syntactic or the phonological component, regardless of whether they are 'syntactic' or 'phonological' rules in an intuitive sense. This need not be regarded as surprising. On the one hand, many linguists have always regarded prosodic features as realizing grammatical elements independent of those realized by segmental features; so it is no more unreasonable that a syntactic rule should introduce a particular combination of prosodic features— say, sentence stress—than that it should introduce a particular combination of segmental features—say, an inflectional affix. On the other hand, it is sometimes hard to distinguish syntactic deletions from phonological deletions; indeed, there are many conceivable data sets which could be accounted for equally well by a deletion rule of either kind; so again it is not surprising that on occasion a deletion with nothing phonological about it may be ordered among the phonological rules, or an essentially phonological deletion among the syntactic rules.

[94] Thus *SPE*; but it seems probable (Bresnan 1971; 1972—cf. though Lakoff 1972 and Langendoen 1975, 553 n.28) that phrase and sentence stress are assigned by rules quite distinct from those which assign word stress. These rules belong to the syntactic component of the grammar, and they apply at the end of each transformational cycle of the syntax. On phonological rules in the syntactic component see the Excursus below (6.7.3).
[95] See for example Ross (1972); Schane (1975); Fudge (1975).

6.8 Underlying representations

6.8.1 Lexical redundancy

In every language, a considerable number of features play no role in the phonology of the language and are completely predictable at all stages of derivation. This is so, for instance, with the features 'retracted tongue root' and 'implosive' in English. But in principle, the final output of the phonological component must specify all features. Need they, then, be specified in underlying representations? Again, it frequently occurs that in underlying representations the value of a feature is completely predictable from its context. On the *SPE* analysis of the English vowel system, there are no underlying vowel-glide sequences; that is, all segments directly preceded by a vowel are [αconsonantal, −αsyllabic]. Must we, then, specify all postvocalic segments for both consonantality and syllabicity, when the value of either feature automatically determines that of the other?

In answering this question we must distinguish in principle—we do not as yet know whether we shall find it necessary to distinguish in practice—between *lexical* and *phonological* representation. The lexicon may be regarded as a store from which elements are extracted, and, as stated on p. 114, gives for each morpheme 'such of its peculiarities as are *not predictable by general rule*'; in principle, therefore, features redundant, either in their particular context or in all contexts, should not be given. Phonological representation is designed to serve as input to the phonological rules, and must therefore contain all information not supplied by *those* rules; and phonological rules are primarily there not to account for redundancies but to account for alternations. Thus there is no necessity that the two conditions 'not predictable by general rule' and 'not supplied by the phonological rules' should coincide.

At one time—and this approach is still reflected in McCawley (1968)—the line taken was that as many features as possible should be left unspecified, both in lexical and in phonological representation. Some of the phonological rules, in addition to or instead of changing the values of already specified features, supplied specifications to previously unspecified features. For example: in Japanese only two contrasting consonants can occur preceded by a vowel and followed by a true consonant, the so-called mora nasal and mora obstruent, which agree in point-of-articulation features with the following consonant.[96] McCawley leaves these features unspecified both in lexical and in phonological representation; the only information there provided about the segments in question is that they are nasals or obstruents as the case may be. The redundant features are supplied by an assimilation rule which is ordered after several of the phonological rules.

That is an example of a set of features which is redundant both within morphemes and across morpheme boundaries. Redundancies of that kind were accounted for by phonological rules; only thus could they be treated in a maximally general way. In other cases, however, intermorphemic and

---

[96] The mora nasal can also occur without a following consonant, in which case it surfaces as a nasalized continuation of the preceding vowel.

intramorphemic constraints differ. In English the surface diphthong [æŭ] does not occur before a labial or velar consonant within the same morpheme.[97] But there is no such restriction across morpheme boundaries, compounds such as *ploughboy* and derivatives such as *endowment* being formed with perfect freedom, so that no motivated *phonological* rule of English can account for the intramorphemic regularity. But that, it was argued, is no reason for including redundant information in a lexical entry; and accordingly, *SPE*, which derives [æŭ] from underlying /ū/, posits the following rule, to be applied in the process of converting lexical into phonological representations, and to hold within morphemes only:[98]

$$C \rightarrow [+\text{coronal}] / \bar{u}—— \qquad \qquad \textbf{159}$$

Such rules were known as *lexical redundancy rules* or *morpheme structure rules*. They could not change feature specifications; they could only apply where the feature(s) mentioned in their output description were unsepecified in the input representation.

Further investigation, however, suggested that this approach was unsatisfactory, and in particular that it was undesirable to leave features unspecified in phonological representations. For, as Stanley (1967) pointed out, by appropriate selection of underlying representations and rules it was possible to devise a language in which non-distinct underlying forms,[99] none of them an exception to any rule, were realized as distinct forms on the surface, contrary to the basic principle that distinct surface forms either realize distinct underlying forms or are in free variation. This might be avoided by requiring that every lexical entry must be phonologically distinct from every other lexical entry,[100] but Stanley showed that this too had undesirable consequences, and concluded that it was necessary to require that no features be left unspecified in phonological representations.

This meant that the 'feature-changing' and 'blank-filling' functions of the phonological component now had to be carried out by completely different sets of rules. Incompletely specified lexical matrices were related to completely specified phonological matrices by lexical redundancy rules, or rather lexical redundancy *conditions*. For Stanley showed that not all lexical redundancies could be satisfactorily expressed in the standard format for phonological rules, which is in effect 'If something has the set of properties X it must also have the set of properties Y.' Two other forms of redundancy conditions are needed:

'All morphemes must have the set of properties Y'; e.g. a language might **160** have a rule that all morphemes must consist of a sequence of syllables of the form CV(C), or that the vowels of a morpheme must agree (harmonize) in tongue root advancement/retraction, etc.

---

[97] Except in some proper names, e.g. *Lowkes, Bowker.*

[98] In *SPE* 196 this rule is said to hold only where a boundary immediately follows; there does not, however, appear to be any empirical objection to the more general form (159) for the rule.

[99] Two phonological representations are non-distinct if and only if: (i) they contain the same number of segments, and (ii) there is no feature which is specified differently in the *i*th segment of one representation and in the *i*th segment of the other. Thus if in corresponding segments a certain feature

'No morpheme may have the set of properties Y'; e.g. a language might have **161** a rule that no morpheme may contain two consonants of the same point of articulation, or two unlike vowels in sequence, etc.

Any condition of the form (160) or (161) is translatable into the standard 'if-then' format; thus the condition that all morphemes consist of a sequence of syllables of the form CV(C) could be expressed in, for example, the form (162):

$$[+\text{seg}] \rightarrow \begin{Bmatrix} [-\text{syll}] \ / \begin{Bmatrix} \# \\ V \end{Bmatrix} \underline{\quad\quad} \\ [+\text{syll}] \ / \ CC \underline{\quad\quad} \end{Bmatrix} \quad\quad\quad 162$$

But as there is no non-arbitrary way of choosing between (162) and various alternative formulations (e.g. one that made use, in the second subrule, of right-hand instead of left-hand environment), the formulation as a 'positive condition' is preferable:

Positive morpheme structure condition: **163**

$CV(C)_1^n$

The completely specified phonological matrices were mapped into phonetic matrices by a set of phonological rules entirely disjoint from the morpheme structure conditions. If, as very frequently happened, a lexical redundancy condition was identical with or very similar to a phonological rule, this could not be given any systematic significance; thus essentially the same facts had often to be stated twice in the grammar.

This unsatisfactory treatment of lexical redundancy has still not been remedied. It is not impossible that the whole notion of lexical redundancy rules at the underlying level is misguided. They play no role in the derivation of surface forms; their sole functions are to make lexical entries more 'economical' and to explicate the distinction that speakers intuitively make between forms that are phonologically admissible in their language (even though they may not actually occur in the lexicon) and those which are inadmissible by reason of containing segment sequences and/or feature combinations excluded by the redundancy rules. The second of these functions, as I have argued elsewhere,[101] can be better carried out by a surface phonotactics (cf. Chapter Eight); the first begs the question whether there is any need to make lexical entries 'maximally non-redundant', and, indeed, how determinate or indeterminate lexical (and even phonological) representations are as regards features that play no role in alternations. Redundancy conditions may themselves be redundant.

6.8.2 Chomsky and Halle's theory of markedness

The final chapter of *SPE*, which stands rather apart from the rest of the book, takes a radically different approach to the problem of lexical redundancy. It

---

is specified (it does not matter how) in one representation and unspecified in the other, that in itself will not make the two representations distinct.

[100] Presumably homophones would for this purpose be regarded as sharing the same lexical entry.

[101] Sommerstein (1974, 73).

proposes the reintroduction of the Praguian notions 'marked' and 'unmarked': for every feature in every possible environment (with perhaps some exceptions such as backness in vowels) one value will be defined as normal or unmarked, the contrary value, of course, being marked. These definitions will be universal. Lexical entries will specify features as marked (*m*) or unmarked (*u*), not as + or −. These specifications will be converted into the usual + and − specifications by a set of universal conventions, and all phonological representations will thus be fully specified. Language-particular lexical redundancy conditions will not be needed, except for some matters of detail. The theory also permits the universal conventions to be used to simplify phonological rule statement in cases where one process (e.g. unrounding) has another (e.g. fronting) as a semi-automatic concomitant.

Markedness theory, as it is called, is not a satisfactory solution to our problem. To know that voiceless obstruents are more normal than voiced obstruents in language generally does not help us if we want to know whether voiced obstruents are or are not admissible in the language we are interested in. If this question is to be answered, a full set of redundancy conditions of the Stanleyan type must be reintroduced, and we are back where we started.

7 Generative Phonology II: Problems in Rule Application

7.1 Simultaneous or iterative application?

How does one apply a rule whose structural description is met at several points? What happens when the output of a rule is of such a form that it could undergo the rule again? These problems are constantly arising; can an answer be given which will hold for all relevant rules in all languages, thus strengthening linguistic theory and limiting the number of possible grammars compatible with any given set of data? Or must we specify the answer separately for each rule?

We can see some of the possibilities by a consideration of the Russian obstruent voicing rule discussed at length in the previous chapter (pp. 116–121). This rule, it will be recalled, assimilates all members of an obstruent sequence to the voicing or voicelessness of the last obstruent in the sequence. In Chapter Six we formulated the rule thus:

$$[-\text{son}] \rightarrow [\alpha\text{voice}] / \underline{\qquad} [-\text{son}]_0 \begin{bmatrix} -\text{son} \\ \alpha\text{voice} \end{bmatrix} \begin{Bmatrix} [+\text{son}] \\ \# \end{Bmatrix} \quad \textbf{164} \ (=(53))$$

This formulation was predicated on two assumptions:

When a form meets the structural description of a rule at two or more **165a** points, the rule is applied simultaneously at all these points.

If the application of a rule creates a structure that satisfies the rule's SD, the **b** rule does not reapply to that structure, except by virtue of the transformational cycle (pp. 163–5) if the rule happens to be one that applies cyclically.

But neither of these assumptions has yet been justified; and it might well be argued that their combination forces the rule to be formulated in a decidedly unnatural way. Presumably, voicing assimilation in obstruent clusters is a matter of anticipation of a glottal state that is going to be required later in the cluster. The basic pattern of such anticipatory assimilation must evidently be to spread from one segment to the immediately preceding segment; in fact, the most natural obstruent voicing assimilation rule would be simply this:

$$[-\text{son}] \rightarrow [\alpha\text{voice}] / \underline{\qquad} \begin{bmatrix} -\text{son} \\ \alpha\text{voice} \end{bmatrix} \quad \textbf{166}$$

But under the assumptions of (165), (166) will not work in Russian. Consider its application to the underlying cluster /tvs^j/ occurring in such a phrase as *ot vs^{j}ej duší* 'with all one's heart'. In that cluster, the SD of (166) is met at two points:

both /t/ and /v/ directly precede an obstruent. So according to (166), each should assimilate to the following obstruent; that is, the former should become voiced and the latter voiceless, giving the incorrect output *[dfsʲ]. The output actually required is [tfsʲ], the phrase being pronounced [atfsʲejduši]. (164), on the other hand, gives the correct outputs, for it directs that every obstruent in the cluster should assimilate to the last obstruent in the cluster, skipping over any number of intervening obstruents.

But what naturalness is there in the first element of a cluster like /tvsʲ/ assimilating (or rather remaining assimilated) to the voicelessness of the last element, when there is a voiced obstruent in between whose glottal state it might have been expected to anticipate? And why should the application of an assimilation rule for obstruents be made to depend on the presence of a non-obstruent or boundary (see the right-hand end of the environment of (164))? May not these infelicities be mere artefacts of the assumptions (165), which between them define what I shall call the *simultaneous once-only* mode of rule application?

Let us leave (165a) standing for the moment and see the consequences of rejecting (165b) and allowing rules to reapply to their own output. If we do this, then rule (166) will affect the cluster /tvsʲ/ as follows:

underlying form	/tvsʲ/	**167**
(166) applied to /t/ and /v/	dfsʲ	
(166) applied to /d/	[tfsʲ]	

Thus it is now possible to state the assimilation rule in its most natural form without getting incorrect outputs. The mode of rule application resulting from the acceptance of (165a) and the rejection of (165b) will be termed *simultaneous iterative* application: under this, rules can reapply to their outputs, but at each iteration they apply simultaneously wherever they are (non-vacuously) applicable.

There is, however, another way of securing correct outputs from (166). At first glance it may seem somewhat *ad hoc*:

If the SD of the rule is met at more than one point, apply it only at the **168** rightmost of such points; then, if after this application the SD of the rule is met at one or more points to leftward of the point at which it was first applied, apply the rule at the rightmost of such points; continue leftward in this way until the rule can no longer be applied non-vacuously anywhere to the left of its last point of application, whereupon it ceases to be further reapplicable.

The derivation of /tvsʲ/ would then go thus:[1]

underlying form	/tvsʲ/	**169**
(166) applied to /v/	[tfsʲ]	

at which point there is no further scope for non-vacuous application of the rule.

This form of rule application will be termed *right-to-left iterative* application.

---

[1] In derivations of this kind I have underlined the rightmost (or, in the case of left-to-right iteration, the leftmost) segment that meets the structural description of the rule; it is to this segment that the rule will apply next.

In the present case it might be claimed that it has some advantage over simultaneous-iterative application, in that it is not necessary, as it was in derivation (167), for underlying /t/ to be first voiced and then devoiced again; but while such 'false steps' may be *prima facie* undesirable, some well-motivated analyses seem to require them (Zwicky 1974). It is more relevant that right-to-left iterative application is appropriate for many other phonological rules and rule types, for some of which simultaneous-iterative application either would not work at all or would work only with much complication of the rules.

I take an example from Mandaic (Malone 1972). This Semitic language had a vowel syncope rule whose effect can be stated as follows:

Delete a short vowel in	**170**
a medial open syllable, or	**a**
an initial open syllable of a disyllabic word.	**b**

Now consider the effect of this rule on a form such as /hawwiy + aθ + iʔ/[2] 'she showed to him'. Both medial vowels meet the SD of syncope, and under either simultaneous once-only or simultaneous-iterative application both would delete, yielding a form /hawwy + θ + iʔ/, which other rules of the language would eventually convert to the surface form *[háwθii]. The attested surface form is [hawwíyθii], from which it is evident that syncope has applied only to one of the two medial vowels. Right-to-left iterative application yields the correct output:

underlying form	/hawwiy + a̱θ + iʔ/	**171**
syncope applied to /a/	hawwiy + θ + iʔ	
SD of syncope no longer met		
assimilation of glottals and		
stress assignment	[hawwíyθii]	

In view of the elaborate interaction of syncope with rules of cluster simplification and epenthesis, documented by Malone, it seems extremely unlikely that the syncope rule could be made to apply correctly under simultaneous once-only or simultaneous-iterative application unless its statement were immensely complicated, and very probably not even then.

It would clearly be possible to define a notion of *left-to-right iterative* application, by interchanging the terms 'left' and 'right' and their derivatives wherever they occur in (168). Such a mode of application would not be helpful in the Russian or Mandaic instances we have considered; it would, in fact, in each case give the same incorrect output as simultaneous once-only application, if the respective rules were to be stated in their simplest form; and, so far as my ingenuity goes, there is *no* way, however complex, of formulating, either in Russian or in Mandaic, a single rule that will yield, under left-to-right iterative application, the outputs yielded by the voicing assimilation and syncope rules, respectively, under right-to-left iterative application.

There are, however, rules for which left-to-right iterative application is necessary. Among these are rules of the type, found in several languages, that assign stress to alternate syllables of a word reckoning from the beginning. Thus

---

[2] This is not quite the underlying form; one rule has applied to it before syncope, spirantizing underlying /t/ postvocalically (Malone 1972, 475).

in Southern Paiute every *even-numbered* vowel in a word is stressed,[3] that is the second, fourth, sixth, etc., vowel in a word. Under simultaneous once-only, simultaneous-iterative, or right-to-left iterative application, a rule to bring this about would have to be formulated thus:

$$V \to [+\text{stress}] \; / \; \# \; C_0V(C_0VC_0V)_0\text{———} \qquad 172^4$$

Left-to-right iterative application makes possible, as Howard (1972) shows, a much simpler rule statement:

$$V \to [+\text{stress}] \; / \; \begin{bmatrix} V \\ -\text{stress} \end{bmatrix} C_0\text{—} \qquad 173$$

The structural description of (173) finds its leftmost match on the second vowel of a word, the first vowel serving as the unstressed vowel required in the environment. Once the second vowel is stressed, it cannot itself serve as environment for the next application of the rule, and so the third vowel of the word cannot undergo the rule, which accordingly applies to the fourth, with the unstressed third vowel as determining environment; and so on through the word. Rule (173) directly expresses the generalization that a Southern Paiute word cannot contain two consecutive stressed syllables, and derives the basic stress pattern of the language directly from this principle and not from syllable-counting.

We have now four modes of rule application at our disposal; and the solution to our original problems might now seem to be merely a matter of brute effort. Check each rule of the types where the mode of application makes a difference, in each language, and see if the same mode can be used with all of them, or if the mode of application is predictable from the type of rule; if the answer is yes, you have made a great discovery.

It is not, of course, quite as simple as that. Often it is open to doubt whether a putative rule is motivated at all. Often it is unclear what is the appropriate choice of underlying form. Often, as we have seen, the data can be accounted for equally well under more than one mode of rule application; thus the simplest version of the Russian voicing assimilation rule (166) gives correct outputs under both simultaneous-iterative and right-to-left iterative application. But clear cases there are, and we have also seen some of them. The Russian voicing assimilation rule has to be made complex and unnatural if it is to work under simultaneous once-only application. The Southern Paiute stress rule can be stated in its simplest form only if it applies iteratively from left to right. The Mandaic syncope rule

---

[3] This is the basic stress pattern; but on the surface the last vowel of a word is never stressed, and a word with only two vowels has stress on the first. I assume that a rule later than the main stress rule transfers any stress on the last vowel of a word to the penultimate vowel if the word has no other stress, and otherwise simply removes stress from the last vowel. Note that Howard's left-to-right rule, which I present below, is criticized by Hastings (1974a) on the ground that a language that stressed *odd*-numbered vowels (such as Finnish) would require a more complex description than a language like Southern Paiute; but the additional complication is very slight (slighter than Hastings, who fails to collapse related rules, makes out).

[4] This is a modified and simplified version of the rule proposed by Chomsky and Halle (*SPE* 347); *their* rule accounts for the peculiar behaviour of word-final syllables and disyllabic words as well as for the basic stress pattern.

perhaps cannot be stated at all except under right-to-left iterative application. These examples provide some of the sort of evidence we need to approach an answer to the questions posed in the first paragraph of this chapter; and even from them we see already that no single mode of application is likely to be universally valid.

In *SPE* simultaneous once-only application is assumed. Since then a variety of proposals have been made, most of which favour some form of directional iteration and seek to predict for each rule, by reference to some aspect of its form or effect, whether it will iterate from left to right or from right to left: see, for example, Howard (1972), Johnson (1972), and Jensen and Jensen (1973). None of these proposals is entirely free of counter-examples, to the extent that they are carefully enough formulated so that it is clear what a counter-example is; and if there is a principle whereby the mode of application of a given rule can be predicted, it still remains to be discovered. At present we can only say that some rules apply once only, others iterate right-to-left, others iterate left-to-right, and content ourselves with marking each rule for one or other of these modes of application.

A fresh proposal for a universal principle of rule application has recently been made by Anderson (1974b). It is that rule application is basically *either* simultaneous-once-only *or* simultaneous-iterative, each rule being marked for one mode of application or the other, but is subject to two important restrictions. *First*, no segment which undergoes a rule can *simultaneously* serve as part of the environment for another application of it. As a result of this constraint a rule (like Russian voicing assimilation or Mandaic syncope) whose structural description is met at more than one point may find itself actually applying at only one, or only some, of these points. In such circumstances, the choice of where to apply the rule and where not to apply it is said to be determined by one of three principles: (i) maximize simultaneous application; (ii) maximize feeding and minimize bleeding; (iii) maximize transparency.[5] The *second* restriction is that when a rule iterates, the same segment cannot undergo it twice. So far no compelling evidence has been produced for or against this new theory of rule application.[6]

7.2 Rule ordering, precedence, and disjunctivity

7.2.1 Counter-evidence to linear ordering

On p. 162 we noted that the *SPE* theory of rule ordering was based on two assertions which then seemed consistent with the available evidence: that every pair of rules in every language exhibited an invariable ordering relation, and that the relation 'is ordered before' was transitive. The first assertion would be falsified if two rules A and B could be found, such that in some derivations A had to apply before B,

[5] For explanation of the notions of 'feeding', 'bleeding', and 'transparency', see 10.1.3.
[6] Only one set of data is cited by Anderson as demonstrating the superiority of his theory to the various theories of 'directional iteration' in that the former but not the latter can handle the data; this concerns a pitch rule in Acoma (Anderson 1974b, 230–4). On the evidence Anderson presents, however, an alternative solution is possible, involving an accent-loss rule iterating from left to right followed by a rule reassigning high pitch to syllables flanked on either side by low-pitched syllables and bearing the independently necessary diacritic feature [+accent ablaut].

and in other derivations B had to apply before A. The second would be falsified if three rules R, S and T could be found, such that there were derivations in which R had to apply before S, derivations in which S had to apply before T, and derivations in which T had to apply before R. Sets of data which seemed to falsify one or the other assertion were familiarly known as *ordering paradoxes,* and in the years following the appearance of *SPE* a sufficient number of these were uncovered to make it extremely dubious whether the hypothesis of universal linear ordering could be maintained. The most important discussion of ordering paradoxes was by Anderson (1969); the example I select from his collection involves a violation of both the assertions which constitute the linear ordering hypothesis.

, The problem concerns four rules of Menomini,[7] which may be informally stated thus:

Reduce any short, non-low vowel to the corresponding high glide in the **174a** following environments: (i) V——V, (ii) V——+, (iii) ——V, (iv) ——+ (the subrules to apply in this order).

Delete any short vowel adjacent to a vowel; if two adjacent vowels are short, **b** delete only the second.

Reduce /a:a:/ to [a:]. **c**

Insert /e/ between a consonant and a following obstruent; insert /j/ between **d** any adjacent vowels that remain after the application of the above three rules.

What are the ordering relations between these rules? At first sight they seem straightforward. The data require (174a) to be ordered before (174b): thus underlying /oe:keoam/ is realized as [we:kewam], not as *[e:kem] or the like as would be the case were (174b) to apply before (174a). There is no crucial ordering between (174b) and (174c), as they are stated above; but if (174c) is ordered after (174b), it becomes unnecessary to require the vowels in the affected sequence to be long; and this is a gain, not only (many might prefer to say, not at all) because it saves two features in the statement of the rule, but also because it is unnatural for a vowel deletion rule to be restricted so as to apply only to long vowels. Rule (174d) consists of a vowel epenthesis and a glide epenthesis: the vowel epenthesis is not crucially ordered with respect to the other rules given, but, as was implied by the way it was stated above, the glide epenthesis *is* crucially ordered after all the other rules affecting the vowel sequences.

Up to this point we seem to have a straightforward case of linear ordering. But now consider how the epenthesis processes (174d) can be formally collapsed into a single rule. This rule will take the form (175):

$$\theta \rightarrow \begin{bmatrix} +\text{son} \\ -\alpha\text{syll} \\ -\text{back} \\ -\text{low} \end{bmatrix} \quad / \ [\alpha\text{syll}] \ \text{———} \ \begin{bmatrix} \alpha\text{syll} \\ \alpha\text{son} \end{bmatrix} \qquad \textbf{175}$$

---

[7] The rules were originally enunciated by Bever in an unpublished MIT doctoral dissertation of 1967, when he reanalysed in GP terms the Menomini data which had been analysed many years before by Bloomfield (1939; 1962).

Despite its collapsed form, this rule remains an instruction to introduce /e/ in one environment and /j/ in another; and such an instruction is more detailed than it needs to be. The information that the inserted segment is syllabic between consonants and non-syllabic between vowels does not need to be specially given here; if nothing at all were said about the matter in (175), these values of syllabicity could be deduced from (174a). By giving (175) in the above form we are implying, what is most implausible, that the choice between /e/ and /j/ as epenthetic segment has nothing whatever to do with the fact that in Menomini intervocalic /e/ becomes a glide anyway.

The logic of this argument demands, in view of the fact that (174a) turns vowels into glides and not *vice versa*, that (175) should be modified so as to introduce a vowel in all cases (which involves only altering the output specification [− αsyll] to [+ syll]) and that (174a) should then be allowed to apply to its output. This is, on two counts, absolutely incompatible with the linear ordering hypothesis. First, we have already seen that the epenthesis rule is crucially ordered after (174a); and so, if we make the proposed modification of (175), we will have the two rules applying in opposite orders in different derivations, contrary to the 'first assertion' of the linear ordering hypothesis. Indeed, it will be worse than that: (174a) will have to apply both before and after the epenthesis rule in one and the same derivation, as witness (176) (adapted from Anderson 1969, 112):

	/aseæ: + æ:n + æmæo/	176
by (174a)	asjæ: + æ:n + æmæw	
by epenthesis	asjæ: + e æ:n + æmæw	
by (174a)	asjæ: + j æ:n + æmæw	
by a later		
assimilation rule	[asi:j æ:næmæw]	

And since epenthesis is also crucially ordered after (174c), which is crucially ordered after (174b), which is crucially ordered after (174a), the application of (174a) to the output of epenthesis will also violate the 'second assertion', the transitivity condition (154). Yet the alternative is in effect to state the restrictions on the distribution of vowels and glides twice over, once in (174a) and a second time as part of the epenthesis rule.

This is only one of a large number of examples which show that the claim that 'it is always possible to order the rules in a sequence and to adhere strictly to this ordering in constructing derivations without any loss of generality as compared to an unordered set of rules or a set ordered on a different principle' (*SPE* 18) cannot be upheld. But what then are we left with? It is evident, both from what we saw in the last chapter and even from the Menomini example we have just been considering, that there must be *some* restrictions on the order in which rules can apply relative to each other; what form can these restrictions take? If it is not appropriate to order the rules of (174) linearly, how *can* we order them?

7.2.2 Alternative hypotheses

7.2.2.1 *Partial ordering*
At this point it may be well to go back to first principles and ask what the

statement 'Rule A is ordered before rule B', as interpreted under the linear ordering hypothesis, actually means. We find immediately that it is equivalent to a conjunction of two statements which are logically quite independent of one another.[8]

Where the same form meets the structural description of both rule A and   **177** rule B, only rule A is applied, though this does not in itself preclude rule B from applying at a later stage of derivation.
No form may undergo rule A, even though it meets that rule's structural   **178** description, if it has already undergone rule B.

We shall call a constraint of type (177) a *precedence* constraint ('A takes (applicational) precedence over B') and one of type (178) a *blockage* constraint ('B blocks subsequent application of A'). Both may be regarded as restrictions on a rule's freedom of application; the natural situation for a rule, as Koutsoudas *et al.* (1974)[9] were the first clearly to point out, is to apply wherever its structural description is met.

Let us, then, remove all the paraphernalia of assumptions (many of them never made explicit) that the linear ordering hypothesis has encouraged, and start with a clean slate. Rules, we will assume, apply freely wherever their SD is met, except as their application may be restricted by precedence or blockage constraints. If the SD of two or more rules is met by the same representation, and it is not the case that constraints render all but one of them inapplicable, let us suppose, with Koutsoudas *et al.*, that they apply simultaneously, if only in order to see where this leads us. What can we then make of the Menomini situation? There are, be it remembered, four rules involved: glide formation, vowel elision, contraction, and epenthesis. It may be most convenient to consider the relationship of each pair of rules separately.

(a) *Glide formation and vowel elision.* The same forms, as we have seen, often meet the SD of both, and, as we have also seen, in such circumstances it is glide formation (174a) that must apply first. A blockage constraint is unnecessary, for no immediate output of vowel elision can meet the SD of glide formation. We limit the constraint, then, to the statement that *glide formation has precedence over vowel elision.*

(b) *Glide formation and contraction.* We recall that contraction, as we previously decided to state it, applied not just to /a:a:/ sequences but also to /aa:/, /a:a/, and /aa/—only the latter three types of sequence never occurred at the stage of derivation where contraction was applicable. We must take care to frame our precedence and blockage constraints in such a way that this arrangement is not upset. For the present we note that although glide formation and contraction may be applicable to the same *form*, they can never apply to the same *vowel*

---

[8] Surprisingly, I know of nobody who drew the distinction I am now going to make in published or even semi-published work before Anderson's recent book (1974b, 196); and even he, having made the distinction, promptly throws it away again and makes no further use of it. The notions that the two types of constraint subsumed under 'ordering' are always Siamese twins, and that for rules to be unordered means that they must apply simultaneously or not at all, have both died hard.
[9] Though not formally published until 1974, this paper had been widely available and influential since 1971.

sequence, so that taking only these two rules into account, no harm could arise if they were to apply simultaneously. Nor is there any reason to prevent either rule from applying to outputs of the other; neither creates, and neither destroys, structures to which the other could apply. So between these two rules we do not need to state any constraint at all.

(c)   *Glide formation and epenthesis.* A representation like /oe:keoam/ meets the SD of both glide formation and epenthesis, and it is evident that for a correct output it must undergo only the former. So *glide formation has precedence over epenthesis*—and the result happens to be that at the points where glide formation has applied the SD of epenthesis is no longer met. By virtue of the distinction between precedence and blockage constraints it nevertheless remains possible, in the absence of a blockage constraint, for glide formation to apply to the output of epenthesis, as we want it to in derivations like (176).

(d)   *Vowel deletion and contraction.* The vowel sequences /aa/, /aa:/ and /a:a/ meet the structural description of both vowel deletion and contraction (in its generalized form)—but it does not in the least matter which of these rules they undergo. Provided that the contraction rule is expressed as a deletion rather than a fusion process, the output will be the same in either case. So no precedence relation needs to be established between the two rules; the relevant vowel sequences may be regarded as undergoing both simultaneously, with, of course, exactly the same effect as if they had undergone either one by itself. Neither rule need be regarded as blocking subsequent application of the other.

(e)   *Vowel deletion and epenthesis.* Vowel deletion, like glide formation, removes vowel sequences which would otherwise condition epenthesis, and hence *vowel deletion has precedence over epenthesis*. Since after the application of epenthesis there are, temporarily, some /VeV/ sequences, it might be thought necessary to block the application of vowel deletion once epenthesis has applied; but these sequences meet not only the SD of vowel deletion but also that of glide formation, and the latter, as we have already seen, will take precedence over the former and automatically prevent its application by abolishing the /VeV/ sequences in question. Once again, therefore, no blockage constraint is required.

(f)   *Contraction and epenthesis.* All representations which meet the structural description of contraction also meet that of epenthesis, but it is contraction that they undergo; so *contraction has precedence over epenthesis*. After epenthesis has applied, there are no more vowel sequences except those discussed in the previous paragraph, so no blockage constraint is needed.

Thus the Menomini data exemplify one only of the two kinds of constraint commonly confused under the name of ordering; and precedence constraints are required only for four of the six rule pairs which we have investigated. All of the rules affecting vowel sequences take precedence over epenthesis; and among these rules, glide formation takes precedence over vowel elision—and that is all. The paradox has evaporated.

It should not be thought that blockage constraints are always as superfluous as they have been shown to be in the present case. In some of the Greek dialects discussed in the previous chapter (pp. 159–163), it is of the utmost importance to correct description that height dissimilation and glide formation should not be able to apply to the output of voiced fricative deletion. Among those rules it is precedence constraints that are superfluous, for no two of them are ever applicable to the same input.

The system of precedence and blockage constraints may be termed (rather inaccurately) the *partial ordering hypothesis*. Like the linear ordering hypothesis, it makes empirical claims about language, which may or may not be borne out (we shall see presently that there is some evidence suggesting that they are not). Like the linear ordering hypothesis, for example, it asserts that the relationships it defines hold constant for each pair of rules throughout the language: thus if rule B has to be regarded as blocking the subsequent application of rule A in one derivation, it has to be regarded as blocking the subsequent application of rule A in every derivation — so that any derivation in which rules B and A applied in that order would be a counter-example to the hypothesis.[10]

How, under the partial ordering hypothesis, is a derivation constructed? Under linear ordering the manner of constructing a derivation is about the simplest imaginable: initially setting $i = 1$, determine whether the SD of the ith rule is met, apply it or not as the case may be, increase i by one and repeat the process until there turns out not to be an ith rule, when the derivation terminates; that (ignoring the cycle) is all. Under partial ordering the procedure is somewhat more complex; it may be stated as (179), where 'prec' means 'has precedence over' and 'bl' means 'blocks subsequent application of'.

a Are there any rules not marked BLOCKED whose SD is met? **179**
   If yes, mark each such rule CANDIDATE and proceed to (b).
   If no, derivation is terminated.
b Are there any pairs of rules (A_i, B_i), both marked CANDIDATE, such that A_i prec B_i?
   If no, proceed to (c).
   If yes, mark the B_i of each such pair RECESSIVE and proceed to (c).
c Apply simultaneously all rules which are marked CANDIDATE and are not marked RECESSIVE; mark each such rule APPLIED, and proceed to (d).
d Are there any pairs of rules (C_i, D_i) such that C_i is marked APPLIED and C_i bl D_i?
   If yes, mark the D_i of each such pair BLOCKED and proceed to (e).
e Erase all CANDIDATE and RECESSIVE markings, and proceed to (a).

Basically, in other words, every rule is tested for applicability at every stage of derivation, unless barred by a blockage constraint; the computation is considerably simplified, therefore, if we make it a practice to posit blockage constraints, not merely where they are necessary, but wherever they are possible. For the Menomini data, for instance, this would mean the addition to the four precedence constraints posited above of two blockage constraints, 'Epenthesis bl Vowel Deletion' and 'Epenthesis bl Contraction'.

We can now see how a derivation such as (176) could arise. The underlying form /aseæ:+æ:n+æmæo/ meets the structural descriptions of three of our four

---

[10] The partial ordering hypothesis in this form was, I believe, my own proposal, dating from about 1972. It still seems to me more satisfactory than the alternative proposals that are in the field, but, like them, it still appears to leave many paradoxes unsolved. It has not till now appeared in print.

rules, glide formation, vowel deletion and epenthesis; but since their order of precedence is as just stated, only glide formation is applied, giving /asjæ:+æ:n +æmæw/. This meets only one structural description, that of epenthesis, which applies giving /asj æ:+eæ:n+æmæw/; and by the application of epenthesis, vowel deletion (whose SD might otherwise have been met at the next stage of the derivation) and contraction are both blocked from being considered for applicability for the rest of the derivation. Only glide formation and epenthesis remain; and the output of the last application of epenthesis meets both of their structural descriptions. But as glide formation takes precedence, it alone applies, giving an output /asjæ:+eæ:n+æmæw/ which subsequent rules (themselves probably related by precedence and/or blockage constraints to some or all of the four with which we have been mainly concerned) convert to the surface form [asi:jæ:næmæw].

For an instance of simultaneous application of distinct rules[11] consider the underlying form /naka:+a:peæ+nasoæ+æo/. This form meets the structural descriptions of *all* our four rules. Epenthesis is recessive with respect to each of the other three, and vowel deletion is recessive with respect to glide formation; but contraction is not recessive with respect to anything, and it can apply at once, that is, simultaneously with glide formation. Thus we both reduce the sequence /a:a:/ and convert three vowels to glides, the output being /naka:+pjæ+naswæ+æw/, which meets the structural descriptions of vowel deletion and epenthesis. The former applies, as having precedence, and the resulting form /naka:+pjæ +naswæ+w/ is no longer amenable to any of the four rules, though later rules convert it to [naka:pi:nasow].

The partial ordering hypothesis retains two of the main features of the linear ordering hypothesis: that in at least some cases, explicit statements have to be made about specific rule pairs, restricting the applicability of one by conditions relating to the application of the other; and that all such statements are valid 'across the board', unambiguously imposing one order to the exclusion of the other. Only the separation of the precedence from the blockage function of 'ordering', and the possibility of leaving rules unordered, distinguish the two hypotheses.

Two other major hypotheses about rule ordering have been put forward since *SPE*. One of these, though it abandons a different plank of the *SPE* platform, is not very dissimilar in its effect from the partial ordering hypothesis; the other is much more radical.

7.2.2.2 *Local ordering*

S. R. Anderson in various works[12] has elaborated a hypothesis known as that of *local ordering*, which abandons, or at least drastically reinterprets, the claim that all ordering statements are valid across the board. In local ordering there are three kinds of ordering constraint, and for every rule pair there must be a constraint of one of these three kinds—unless the rules are so related that the order in which they apply can never make any difference to the output. The first

---

[11] To be distinguished from the simultaneous application of the same rule to different segments, which came under discussion in the first section of the present chapter.
[12] Anderson (1969; 1970; 1972a; 1972c; 1974b).

kind is the straightforward across-the-board ordering constraint 'rule A precedes rule B'; it appears that this is to be interpreted as a conjunction of a precedence and a blockage constraint, no distinction being drawn between these two functions of 'ordering'.[13]

The second and third types of constraint, which are peculiar to the local ordering hypothesis, are based upon the notion of *marked and unmarked orders of application*. This notion is due to Kiparsky (1968a); the fundamental principle is that that order of two rules is *unmarked* which allows them to apply more freely than would the opposite order. For example: if rule A converts forms not meeting the SD of rule B into forms meeting that SD, then A-B is the unmarked ordering of these two rules, other things being equal; for if rule B were to apply first, certain forms would be unable to undergo it for no other reason than that rule A had not yet applied. If, on the other hand, rule A converts forms which do meet the SD of rule B into forms which do not, then—again, other things being equal—the unmarked ordering is B-A: otherwise rule A would drain off ('bleed') forms which might have undergone rule B.

The second possible type of ordering constraint, then, is 'rule A and rule B apply in the unmarked order, whatever that is'. It might be thought that this was merely equivalent to 'A precedes B' or 'B precedes A' as the case may be. It is not, because, as Anderson points out (1969, 116), 'the question of whether a given order of rules is marked or unmarked is not always decidable from an examination of the rules alone ... [but] only with respect to a specific form to which the rules are to apply,' so that one and the same order may be marked in one derivation and unmarked in another.

Thus Icelandic (Anderson 1969, 20–7; 1974b, 141–7) has a rule of umlaut and a rule of syncope. The umlaut rule rounds /a/ to [ǫ] where /u/ follows in the next syllable (or, under certain conditions which do not arise in the forms we shall be considering, in any later syllable in the word). The syncope rule deletes certain vowels in stem-final syllables before endings beginning with a vowel. Very roughly, but adequately for our present purposes, the two rules could be formulated thus:

UMLAUT   180

$$a \rightarrow \phi \ / \underline{\hspace{2cm}} C_0 u$$

SYNCOPE   181

$$\begin{bmatrix} V \\ -\text{stress} \end{bmatrix} \rightarrow \emptyset \ / \ C \underline{\hspace{2cm}} \begin{bmatrix} C \\ +\text{son} \end{bmatrix} + V$$

Consider now how these rules might apply to such underlying forms as /katil +um/ 'kettles (dative)' and /bagg+ul+i/ 'package (dative)'.

---

[13] Note that local ordering assumes that only one rule is applied at each stage of a derivation; in this it follows *SPE*.

Order: umlaut-syncope **182**

	/katil + um/	/bagg + ul + i/
umlaut	(not applicable)	bøgg + ul + i
syncope	[katlum]	[bøggli]

Order: syncope-umlaut **183**

	/katil + um/	/bagg + ul + i/
syncope	katl + um	bagg + l + i
umlaut	køtlum	(not applicable)
	[køtlum]	[baggli]

Thus for /katil + um/, it is the order syncope-umlaut that permits the two rules to apply most freely and thus is unmarked, whereas for /bagg + ul + i/ the unmarked order is syncope-umlaut. And so while an across-the-board constraint would produce the outputs of (182) or of (183) depending on which of the two orderings it imposed, a constraint that umlaut and syncope 'apply in the unmarked order whatever that is' would result in both underlying forms undergoing both rules, giving the outputs [køtlum] and [bøggli]. These are in fact the attested surface forms, so that the 'across-the-board' property of the linear ordering hypothesis is disconfirmed; but it should also be noted that, significantly and typically, the correct outputs will also be given by the partial ordering hypothesis if the umlaut and syncope rules are left *unordered* with respect to each other.

There are certain rule pairs between whose members—sometimes for all derivations, sometimes for a particular class of derivations only—no unmarked order can be defined. Anderson (1969, 113–17; 1974b, 152–60) gives an interesting example from the West African language Kasem. This language apparently has a metathesis rule interchanging the first two vowels of any three-vowel sequence:

$$
\begin{array}{ccc}
V & V & V \\
1 & 2 & 3 \\
\downarrow & \downarrow & \\
2 & 1 &
\end{array}
$$

184

and a truncation rule reducing a sequence of two identical vowels to one. Consider the application of these rules to /pia + a/ and /pia + i/, which are (or may be) the underlying forms of the singular and plural of the Kasem noun meaning 'sheep'.

Order: metathesis-truncation **185**

	/pia + a/	/pia + i/
metathesis	pai + a	pai + i
truncation	(not applic.)	pai

Order: truncation-metathesis **186**

	/pia + a/	/pia + i/
truncation	pia	(not applic.)
metathesis	(not applic.)	pai + i

Thus, while for /pai + i/ the order metathesis-truncation is unmarked, for/pia + a/

neither order allows the rules to apply more freely than would the other. Hence while an across-the-board ordering constraint might be stated for these two rules, if the data warranted one, a constraint requiring unmarked ordering simply could not be stated.

It so happens that no across-the-board ordering constraint will work. The actual surface forms are singular [pia], plural [pæ]. The former can only be derived if truncation is ordered before metathesis.[14] The latter is derived, by a rule of vowel contraction, from /pai/, so that its derivation implies the (unmarked) ordering metathesis-truncation. Anderson's solution to this and a number of similar problems is to introduce a third class of ordering constraint, of which (187) is typical:

Metathesis and truncation apply in the unmarked order, if there is one; if **187** there is no unmarked order, truncation precedes metathesis.

Such a constraint is termed a *contingent* ordering constraint.

It may be asked how the partial ordering hypothesis would handle the Kasem data. The answer is that it would regard metathesis and truncation as unordered. From /pia + i/ would be derived /pai + i/ by metathesis, and thence by truncation /pai/ (→[pæ] by contraction). To /pia + a/ metathesis and truncation, whose SDs are both met, would apply simultaneously: that is, the third segment of the form would simultaneously be (*a*) replaced by zero and (*b*) moved to precede the second segment, resulting in /pθia/, i.e. [pia]. I know of no real set of data that can be handled using a contingent ordering constraint and cannot be handled under the partial ordering hypothesis.

In fact, I know of no real set of data at all that can be accounted for under local ordering but not under partial ordering. And there do seem to be cases which partial ordering can handle and local ordering cannot. One of these is none other than the Menomini paradox considered above, and in particular the derivation (176), involving the rules of glide formation and epenthesis. What is the unmarked order of these rules? There are three points in the underlying form /aseæ: + æ:n + æmæo/ at which one rule or both might be applicable. Let us study the effect of the two possible orderings at each of them.

Order: glide formation-epenthesis   **188**

	/eæ:/	/æ:æ:/	/æo/
glide formation	jæ:	(N.A.)	æw
epenthesis	(N.A.)	æ:eæ:	(N.A.)

Order: epenthesis-glide formation   **189**

	/eæ:/	/æ:æ:/	/æo/
epenthesis	eeæ:	æ:eæ:	æeo
glide formation	ejæ:	æ:jæ:	æjo

The answer is unequivocal: the unmarked order (that which permits the rules to apply more freely) is epenthesis-glide formation. But it is evident that if we apply the rules in this unmarked order, we shall get a completely wrong output, with two

[14] Unless, with Chomsky and Halle (*SPE* 361), we modify the metathesis rule in a manner equivalent to building into its SD part of the SD of truncation.

G

syllables too many; and the only alternative provided by the theory, an across-the-board constraint, will either have the same effect or else make it impossible to apply glide formation to the output of epenthesis at all, despite (176).

This is not the only occasion[15] on which local ordering proves unsatisfactory even in accounting for data which its proposer has specifically discussed in connection with it; and as it has no clear advantage over partial ordering, I do not think it likely to win general acceptance.

7.2.2.3 *No extrinsic ordering*
The other main development in the study of rule ordering began with the startling claim by Koutsoudas *et al.* (1974—cf. note 10) that there is no such thing—more precisely, that the claim 'that in at least some cases, explicit statements have to be made about specific rule pairs, restricting the applicability of one rule by conditions relating to the application of the other' (p. 180) is false. The authors' contentions may be summarized as follows:

The application of phonological rules[16] relative to one another is restricted,   **190a** so far as it is restricted at all, by universal principles making no reference to particular rules or particular languages.

Such apparent cases of rule ordering as are not accounted for by these   **b** principles are spurious: in some cases correct results are given if all rules are allowed to apply freely wherever their structural descriptions are met; where this is not so it will be found that the rules have been incorrectly formulated.

The proposal of Koutsoudas *et al.* must be clearly distinguished, on the one hand from *simultaneous* rule application, on the other from *random sequential* rule application. Under simultaneous application, there are no intermediate stages of derivation: all applicable rules apply simultaneously to the underlying representation, and the resulting representation cannot have any further rules apply to it. Under random sequential application, no more than one rule may apply at each stage of derivation, but this may be any rule whose structural description is then met, and there are no restrictions on rules reapplying. Koutsoudas *et al.*'s proposal is in one way intermediate between these: as in simultaneous application, all rules whose SD is met are to apply, not just one; but as in random sequential application, the resulting representation is again tested to determine whether any rules are applicable, and the derivation continues until no rule has its SD met. This basic mode of rule application (termed *unordered semisimultaneous* by Pullum 1975) is modified only by such universal principles as Proper Inclusion Precedence (below, p. 186).

This no-extrinsic-ordering hypothesis[17] has since been developed, principally by the proposing of further universal principles of rule application, in a long series

---

[15] See the criticisms by Phelps and Brame (1973) of Anderson's (1970) analysis of an apparent ordering paradox in Sanskrit.

[16] Koutsoudas and his associates have also attempted to show that rule ordering is unnecessary in syntax; but an evaluation of their success in that respect falls outside the scope of this book.

[17] *Extrinsic ordering* is the term used for ordering governed by specific statements about specific rules in specific languages, as opposed to sequential application that is not so governed but follows from the conformation of the rules themselves and/or some universal principle.

of papers: see especially Norman (1972), Iverson (1973a; 1973b), Ringen (1972; 1973; 1974), Hastings (1974a; 1974b), Pullum (1976).

To a great extent the hypothesis is justified. The amount of crucial ordering in the phonology of a language is always, on the most generous estimate, far less than would be suggested by a typical *SPE*-type description, particularly if we allow simultaneous application of rules whose application conditions are simultaneously met; and a good deal of what crucial ordering there is can be accounted for by one very well-motivated universal principle which the school of Koutsoudas have put forward, and, less certainly, by other such principles. But there remains a substantial residue for which the only resource of the no-extrinsic-ordering hypothesis is reformulation of rules. The most obvious of such cases, but by no means the only ones, are those in which dialects differ purely in the order of application of two or more rules, such as the modern Greek dialect data discussed on pp. 159–163. In favourable cases the reformulation will merely consist in the addition of a feature or two to one of the affected rules; but more often it will mean building most of the structural description of one rule, and perhaps of several, into the structural description of another—i.e. saying twice or more what, with extrinsic ordering available, would only need to be said once. And sometimes even this is insufficient, as in the Greek case. Recall that in one group of dialects there are three rules:

HEIGHT DISSIMILATION $\qquad$ **191 = 147**

$$\begin{bmatrix} V \\ 2\text{height} \end{bmatrix} \rightarrow [3\text{height}] \; / / \; \text{------} \begin{bmatrix} V \\ \leq 2\text{height} \\ +\text{back} \end{bmatrix}$$

GLIDE FORMATION (mirror-image) $\qquad$ **192 = 148**

$$\begin{bmatrix} V \\ 3\text{height} \\ \langle +\text{stress} \rangle \end{bmatrix} \qquad V$$
$$\downarrow \qquad\qquad \downarrow$$
$$[-\text{syll}] \qquad [\langle +\text{stress} \rangle]$$

VOICED FRICATIVE DELETION $\qquad$ **193 = 150**

$$\begin{bmatrix} -\text{son} \\ +\text{cont} \\ +\text{voice} \end{bmatrix} \rightarrow \emptyset \; / \; V \text{------} V$$

so related that Height Dissimilation and Glide Formation apply only to vowel sequences which do *not* result from Voiced Fricative Deletion; while in another group of dialects Height Dissimilation and Glide Formation are not thus restricted.

In the second group of dialects, we can of course leave the rules unordered. But what of the first? No universal principle can account for the ordering of Height Dissimilation and Glide Formation before Voiced Fricative Deletion, because on the other side of the next hill, so to speak, the ordering is the reverse. Nor can we point to any structural feature by which the forms that do undergo (191) and (192) differ from those which do not. The best we can do is to invent one. Let us say that Voiced Fricative Deletion, in addition to deleting a consonant, makes one of the neighbouring vowels—it does not matter which—[+F]—it does not matter whether F is a diacritic feature or a phonological feature not distinctive in the language—and then restrict Height Dissimilation and Glide Formation so that they apply only to [−F] vowels.

But this is an obvious subterfuge,[18] which no one would think of adopting if extrinsic ordering was available. Nor is it isolated; several similar interdialectal ordering contrasts are known,[19] and there are probably many more lying unrecognized in the dialectological literature. In face of such evidence the no-extrinsic-ordering hypothesis simply cannot be upheld.

It has, however, drawn attention to at least one almost certainly valid principle of rule application, of which a great many orderings formerly thought to be crucial can now be seen to be automatic consequences. This principle has been stated in various forms and under various names over the last few years. The proponents of the no-extrinsic-ordering hypothesis have regarded it primarily as a principle obviating the need for certain ordering constraints; orthodox GP phonologists have regarded it primarily as a more satisfactory statement than had hitherto been available of the conditions for disjunctive application (cf. pp. 138–9). We will turn to the latter aspect lower down (p. 188); for the moment we concentrate on the former.

PROPER INCLUSION PRECEDENCE[20]   **194**

If every (logically possible) form meeting the structural description of rule A also meets the structural description of rule B, and the converse is not the case, then rule A has precedence over rule B.

The value of this principle may be strikingly demonstrated from the Menomini data which we have already found useful more than once. In (195) are shown the structural descriptions of the four rules with which we have been chiefly concerned.

[18] It would not be so if it were part of a general theory which allowed phonological rules to be conditioned by the previous 'history' of the derivation. As we shall see in the concluding section of this chapter, there is perhaps something to be said for such a theory; but to the extent that the object of eliminating extrinsic ordering is to constrain the class of possible grammars, the inclusion of derivational history would leave our last state worse than our first, for derivational history without extrinsic ordering allows a far wider range of grammars than does extrinsic ordering without derivational history. If the use of derivational history is to be justified, it must be (and normally is) done on the basis of data for which extrinsic ordering alone cannot account.

[19] See, for example, *SPE* 342 and Campbell (1973). For a critique of the no-extrinsic-ordering hypothesis from a rather different point of view, see King (1973a) (who is in error if, as it would appear he does, he regards my partial ordering hypothesis as a version of it); and cf. now Vago (1977).

[20] This formulation is eclectic: the antecedent of the conditional is elaborated from Anderson (1972a, 267), the consequent comes from Koutsoudas *et al.* (1974) and other papers in the same tradition. The principle is customarily formulated in terms of the SD of one rule properly including that of the other, but this becomes very hard to interpret when SDs include parentheses, braces, alphas and other notational paraphernalia.

It should be noted that, as Gerald Sanders (in his contribution to Koutsoudas 1975) and Bernard Comrie (*ap.* Pullum 1976, 249) have observed, a principle like Proper Inclusion Precedence is virtually an inevitable corollary of the presence in grammars of pairs of rules in a proper inclusion relation; for were it not for such a principle, the more specific rule of the pair would never get a chance to apply and so would not appear in the grammar.

Glide Formation: (V) $\begin{bmatrix} V \\ -\text{long} \\ -\text{low} \end{bmatrix} \left\{\begin{matrix} V \\ + \end{matrix}\right\}$ **195a**

Vowel Elision: V $\begin{bmatrix} V \\ -\text{long} \end{bmatrix}$ (mirror-image)   **b**

Contraction: $\begin{bmatrix} V \\ +\text{low} \end{bmatrix}\begin{bmatrix} V \\ +\text{low} \end{bmatrix}$ **c**

Epenthesis: $[\alpha\text{syll}]\begin{bmatrix} \alpha\text{syll} \\ \alpha\text{son} \end{bmatrix}$ **d**

It is evident that anything that meets the structural description of either Vowel Elision or Contraction must meet that of Epenthesis, whereas there are structures (e.g. obstruent sequences) that meet the SD of Epenthesis but not those of the other two rules. Hence Vowel Elision and Contraction *automatically* take precedence over Epenthesis, and no extrinsic precedence constraints are required for these two rule pairs. On the other hand, Proper Inclusion Precedence makes no prediction about Glide Formation and Vowel Elision, or about Glide Formation and Epenthesis, and for these rule pairs it might seem that extrinsic constraints must be stated.

Suppose, however, that we divide Glide Formation into subrules with SDs as follows:

(i)   V $\begin{bmatrix} V \\ -\text{long} \\ -\text{low} \end{bmatrix} \left\{\begin{matrix} V \\ + \end{matrix}\right\}$ **196**

(ii) $\begin{bmatrix} V \\ -\text{long} \\ -\text{low} \end{bmatrix}$ V

(iii) $\begin{bmatrix} V \\ -\text{long} \\ -\text{low} \end{bmatrix}$ +

Then Proper Inclusion Precedence would yield the following relationships: (i) has precedence over Vowel Elision and Epenthesis; (ii) has precedence over the same two rules; and the two sub-subrules of which (i) consists have precedence over (ii) and (iii) respectively. The only extrinsic constraint that would then need to be stated would be that (ii) has precedence over (iii); for there is never any need to regulate the relationship between (iii) and Vowel Elision or Epenthesis. It is well to recall that abbreviatory conventions are just that, abbreviatory conventions, and the (sub-)rules they abbreviate do not lose their identity just because they are very like one another.

7.2.2.4 *Unresolved paradoxes*
There remains, whatever hypothesis one adopts about rule ordering, a residue of refractory cases. From time to time we find that this or that pair of rules, in this or that language, is crucially ordered one way for one set of lexical items, and crucially ordered the other way (or unordered) for another set. Thus for many

speakers of French (Dell 1973a, referring to earlier work by C.-J. N. Bailey) the following situation holds:

There is a rule of Vowel Nasalization, making any vowel [+nasal] before a **197a** nasal followed by a consonant or by word boundary.

There is a rule of Liaison, which in close-knit phrases converts the sequence **b** C # V to # CV; it has effects on syllabification, and may protect a word-final consonant from truncation.

In general these rules are unordered, so that a sequence /VN # V/ in a **c** phrase subject to liaison surfaces as [Ṽ.NV]²¹: e.g. *un ami* [œ̃nami] 'a friend', *bien habillé* [bjɛ̃nabije] 'well dressed'.

But in adjective-noun sequences Liaison is ordered before (has precedence **d** over) Nasalization, so that similar segment sequences surface as [V.NV]: e.g. *bon ami* [bɔnami] 'good friend', *en plein hiver* [ɑ̃plɛnivɛːr] 'well into winter' (lit. in full winter).

Neither local ordering nor partial ordering can handle this set of data. Under local ordering, rules can apply in different orders to forms of similar structure only if the applicability of one or both of them is affected by a third rule, which is not the case here. Under partial ordering, as so far conceived, we can only say that Liaison has precedence over Nasalization, or that it does not, across the board; we cannot account simultaneously for (197c) and for (197d). Several similar examples have been reported.²² The only general way out seems to be to allow ordering constraints, like rules, to be conditioned by syntactic factors or even to admit lexical exceptions—and the drawback to that is that, by making it possible to account for just about any restriction on rule applicability, it abandons all hope of setting limits to the power of grammars in this field. Possibly some new principle may be discovered which predicts these apparent exceptions.

7.2.3 On disjunctive application

I mentioned a moment ago that the Proper Inclusion Precedence principle has also been used in recent years to predict when rules apply disjunctively. In *SPE* this depended on a very specific formal relationship between rules: rules were disjunctively ordered if they were capable of abbreviation by the parenthesis or angled-bracket convention. But it came to be found that many rule pairs not so abbreviable had to apply disjunctively; and eventually Kiparsky (1973b) formulated a statement of the conditions under which application was disjunctive, superseding the conditions of *SPE*. This statement, known as the *Elsewhere Condition*, has virtually the same requirements as Proper Inclusion Precedence:

---

²¹ The dot on the line represents syllable boundary: cf. p. 201 below.
²² E.g. by Harris (1973b) and Wilkinson (1974). In these cases (unlike that reported by Dell) one can see the 'reason' for the exceptional ordering: if the rules applied in the same order to all forms alike, it would result in large-scale homonymy or paradigm irregularity. But this, though significant, neither explains the exceptions nor makes them consistent with any existing theory; it is not universally the case that rules always apply in that order which does not lead to homonymy or paradigm irregularity.

ELSEWHERE CONDITION[23]   **198**

Two adjacent rules of the form

(i)   A → B / P——Q

(ii) C → D / R——S

are disjunctively ordered if and only if (a) the set of strings that fit PAQ is a
subset of the set of strings that fit RCS, and (b) the structural changes of the
two rules are either identical or incompatible.

The Elsewhere Condition not only predicts disjunctive ordering in some cases
where the *SPE* conditions exclude it; it also excludes disjunctive ordering in some
cases where the *SPE* conditions predict it. Thus there is a palatalization rule in
Karok which converts /s/ to [š] after a front vowel, with or without an intervening
consonant:

$$s \rightarrow š \; / \begin{bmatrix} -\text{cons} \\ -\text{back} \end{bmatrix} (C) \text{——}$$ **199**

The *SPE* conditions would predict that the two subrules, being abbreviated by
parentheses, would apply disjunctively; thus a sequence /-iss-/ would undergo the
first subrule (with parenthesized material included) and become [-išš-] which
would then undergo the second subrule owing to the disjunctivity principle. But
this is incorrect; the actual surface forms have [-išš-], showing that both subrules
have applied. And the Elsewhere Condition indeed predicts that both will apply;

for the set of strings of the form $X \begin{bmatrix} -\text{cons} \\ -\text{back} \end{bmatrix} CsY$ is not a subset of the set of

strings of the form $X \begin{bmatrix} -\text{cons} \\ -\text{back} \end{bmatrix} sY$.

   We might leave the discussion at this point; but it is clearly undesirable to have
in our linguistic theory two separate and unconnected principles so similar as
Proper Inclusion Precedence and the Elsewhere Condition. Hastings (1974b) has
shown that they can be unified in a single principle which he calls Stifling, and
which, altering his statement somewhat so as to be fully compatible with the
Elsewhere Condition as given above and modified in note 23, we may formulate as
follows:

STIFLING[24]   **200**

   Given two rules of the form

(i)   A → B / P——Q

(ii) C → D / R——S

such that the set of strings that fit P[+segment]Q is a proper subset of the
set of strings that fit R[+segment]S, and the structural changes of the two
rules are either identical or incompatible, and (ii) is not a phonetic rule; then

[23] This is Kiparsky's original statement of the principle; it should probably be amended in two
particulars (Harris 1974). The requirement that the rules be adjacent should be dropped, and
condition (a) should be altered to 'the set of strings that fit P[+segment]Q is a subset of the set of
strings that fit R[+segment]S'. Note also that phonetic rules, as distinct from morphophonemic
rules, always apply conjunctively regardless of the Elsewhere or any other condition (Anderson 1975,
41). For a criticism (not fatal, in my view) of the Elsewhere Condition see A. Howard (1975).
[24] Hastings also seeks to show that two other proposed universals of rule application are mere
consequences of (his version of) Stifling.

a representation that meets the structural descriptions of both (i) and (ii) may not undergo (ii), neither immediately nor at any later stage in the derivation.

7.3 Global constraints and derivational history

In standard GP it is assumed that to determine whether a rule is applicable to a given form, it is necessary to check on three things: whether the form meets the structural description of the rule; whether ordering constraints are satisfied; and whether such universal principles as disjunctivity are satisfied. The thrust of a good deal of recent work, notably by Kisseberth and Kenstowicz,[25] is that this assumption is too restrictive: in particular, that it is sometimes necessary to 'look back' to representations earlier in the derivation than the immediate input to a rule in order to determine whether the rule is applicable. Such rules are said to require reference to *derivational history* or (borrowing a term from syntax) to be subject to *global constraints*.

In no case is reference to derivational history to be assumed lightly. It represents a very great addition to the power of grammars—equivalently, a very great weakening of the content of what we can say about human language. And though some instances seem to me incontrovertible,[26] I know of no compelling evidence[27] against the following restrictions on reference to derivational history (a slightly watered-down version of proposals by Kiparsky 1973a):

Only a *neutralization* rule can 'look back' at derivational history. A rule **201a** A→B/P——Q is a neutralization just in case, at the stage(s) of derivation at which it becomes applicable, there are strings of the form PBQ *not* created by its application.

The only representation to which a rule can 'look back' is the underlying   **b** representation; for example, a condition 'Rule K may apply only if rule J has previously applied' is inadmissible, but a condition 'Rule K applies only to vowels derived from underlying glides' is admissible.

Kisseberth (1973b) gives an example from Klamath, a language of S.W. Oregon.[28] Klamath has a well-motivated rule which converts semivowels to vowels in the environment $C\text{——}\begin{Bmatrix} C \\ \# \end{Bmatrix}$.

[25] See, e.g., Kenstowicz and Kisseberth (1970); Kisseberth (1972a; 1972b; 1973b); Kenstowicz (1973); Kiparsky (1973a); D. G. Miller (1975).
[26] The most striking is that discussed by Kenstowicz (1973) in Tübatulabal, which comes within the restrictions of (201) but not within Kiparsky's original requirements.
[27]. D. G. Miller (1975) claims to have found a non-neutralizing rule which has to look back; but he now (personal communication) believes (as does the present author) that the rule in question ('accent reduction' in Ancient Greek) was in fact a neutralization.
[28] I do not reproduce Kisseberth's argumentation in detail. Reference to derivational history is not *absolutely* required unless Kisseberth's contention is accepted that 'all of the major morphophonemic rules' of Klamath apply cyclically; the evidence for such a cycle is powerful (Kisseberth 1972a), but the proposal remains suspect for more reasons than one (cf. Chapter Six, note 90). In the examples I use Kisseberth's transcription, in which the diacritic ' over a consonant denotes glottalization, and the palatal semivowel is represented by /y/ rather than /j/.

molẘ+a	'is ready'	**202**
molo:+wapk	'will be ready'	
qbatẙ+a	'wraps the legs around'	
qbati:+wapk	'will wrap the legs around'	
sdoly+o:l+a	'finishes advising'	
sdoli:	'advises'	
sʔedw+i:y+a	'counts for someone'	
sʔedo:	'counts'	

In these examples the vowels resulting from the application of this Vocalization rule are long. In certain environments, however, they are normally short, viz:

in $V:C_0$——, e.g.	gi+wk	'because of being/doing'	**203a**
	gmoč+o:k	'because of being tired'	
but:	sʔawi:g+ok	'because of being angry'	
in C_2——$C_0\#$, e.g.	tawy+i:y+a	'curses for someone'	**b**
	tawi:	'curses'	
but:	ta+twi	'curse' (distributive)	
in C_2——C_2, e.g.	nqen+kw+a	'shouts across'	**c**
	nqen+ko+pg+a	'is shouting across'	

But this length alternation applies only to vowels derived by Vocalization from underlying glides; underlying vowels neither shorten in the environments of (203) nor lengthen in the complementary environment. We cannot, though, in standard GP, say 'Shorten vowels in such and such environments *just in case they are derived from underlying glides*'; that is not information that is present in the immediate input to the shortening rule[29]—it constitutes reference to derivational history. The only thing standard GP allows us to do in such circumstances is try to combine Vocalization and length determination into one rule, which would convert glides directly to long or short vowels according to their environment. It can, however, plausibly be argued that such a rule would confuse two separate processes: Vocalization is what Schane (e.g. 1973a) would call a syllable-structure process, whereas length determination is more like the allophonic specification of a feature which for vocalized glides is non-distinctive (even though it is distinctive for underlying vowels). Further, if Kisseberth is right that the major morphophonemic rules of Klamath apply cyclically, there is no way such a composite rule could work. It is therefore most satisfactory to state the two processes as separate rules thus:

VOCALIZATION **204**

$$\begin{bmatrix} -\text{cons} \\ -\text{syll} \end{bmatrix} \rightarrow \begin{bmatrix} +\text{syll} \\ +\text{long} \end{bmatrix} / C \text{——} \begin{Bmatrix} C \\ \# \end{Bmatrix}$$

---

[29] The information could, of course, be put there artificially, by having Vocalization add to the segments affected a rule feature making them subject to the (minor) rule of length determination, or indeed a phonological feature distinguishing them from all other vowels, which feature would then be added to the SD of length determination. Both these expedients are wholly *ad hoc* and no more than notational variants of a global rule.

VOCALIZED GLIDE SHORTENING   205

$$V \rightarrow [-\text{long}] / \left\{ \begin{array}{l} V:C_0 \underline{\hspace{1cm}} \\ C_2 \underline{\hspace{1cm}} \left\{ \begin{array}{l} C_2 \\ C_0 \# \end{array} \right\} \end{array} \right\}$$

condition: the input V was $[-\text{syll}]$ in the underlying representation.

It is noteworthy that the effect of global constraints such as that of (205) is not dissimilar to the effect of what in the previous section we called blockage constraints. Blockage constraints prevent a rule from applying in case a particular other rule has applied, i.e., in effect, they limit the extent to which the input to a rule may differ from the underlying representation. A constraint like that on (205), on the other hand, *requires* the input to the rule to differ from the underlying representation in a particular respect. In view of this it is not surprising that the suggestion has been made (cf. especially Kisseberth 1972b) that blockage constraints be regarded as a special type of global constraint, though it is not clear whether *all* well-motivated blockage constraints can be formulated as global constraints within the restrictions of (201). Precedence constraints are not global, since they relate to immediate inputs which satisfy more than one structural description. This is yet another indication that the blanket term 'rule ordering' covers relationships of two very different kinds.[30]

[30] In addition to the global, or derivational, constraints discussed in this section, it has been suggested that some phonological rules may be subject to *transderivational* constraints. A constraint is transderivational if it makes the application of a rule in one derivation dependent upon properties of another derivation or other derivations; a possible example may come from Terena, where a rule neutralizing the distinction between two types of stress apparently applies only where its application does not result in homonymy, i.e. in there being two derivations which give the same output (Wilkinson 1976). With this cf. note 22 above and Chapter Ten, pp. 247–8. Another form of trans-derivationally constrained rule would be one that applied only where it promoted paradigm regularity; such a rule has been proposed for modern standard Greek by Warburton (1976, 271–4). Cf. Chapter Ten, pp. 246–7.

⑧ Generative Phonology III: Phonological Templates

In the standard GP view, an underlying phonological representation is a sequence of segments and boundaries, the boundaries grammatically motivated, the segments consisting each of a set of phonological, syntactic, and diacritic features. The set of possible underlying representations in a language was determined by the morpheme structure rules, which defined the notion 'phonologically possible morpheme', and by the syntax, which determined which sequences of morphemes were permissible. The set of possible surface representations was not separately defined; it was simply the result of properly applying the rules of the phonological component to the possible underlying representations.

This view had no place for two notions which had long played an important role in phonological thinking. One was the notion of a set of principles directly determining the class of possible surface representations (phonetic or classical-phonemic, according to one's theoretical position)—the *phonotactics* of p. 41. The other was the notion of the syllable: in the hierarchy of grammatically motivated boundaries syllable boundary came nowhere, and expressions like 'syllable-finally' and 'in a closed syllable', long familiar in morphophonemic and allophonic description, were used only informally, to be replaced in formal rule statement by sequences, disjunctions, etc., of segment types.[1] The present chapter is about the rehabilitation of these two neglected notions. Its title makes the point that segments are not, as it were, anarchic individualists; they appear in fixed syntagmatic patterns, almost in slotted frames, and the effects of some phonological rules are not fully comprehensible without consideration of the principles on which these frames or templates are structured.

8.1 Phonotactics

Phonological rules in GP are single isolated entities. Rules which exhibit certain types of structural similarity and have identical ordering restrictions are 'collapsed' into schemata; other rules cannot be. The theory thus makes the implicit claim that where two (or more) rules can properly be regarded as aspects of a single process, they will always be structurally similar in one of the requisite ways and always have identical ordering restrictions. Further, by its rejection of any surface phonotactics, the theory claims that the facts about permissible and

[1] It is typical that although the word 'syllable' and its derivatives are of frequent occurrence in *SPE*, 'syllable' does not figure either in the chapter entitled 'The phonetic framework' or in the subject index.

impermissible segment sequences at the output level are non-significant, the fortuitous product of the restrictions on underlying representations plus the phonological rules.

Both these claims are untenable; but their denial involves far-reaching modifications of established GP theory.

To take the first claim first: there are many cases in various languages where rules whose immediate effects may be radically different and even directly opposite, and which are quite incapable of being collapsed, nevertheless seem in an important sense to serve a common function; in the terminology now generally used, they form a *conspiracy*.

The classic article in this field is Kisseberth's on Yawelmani (Kisseberth 1970a). Yawelmani has, in standard GP terms, a morpheme structure condition barring clusters of more than two consonants. Further, at the phonetic level there are likewise no such clusters; and in word-initial and word-final position not even two consonants may cluster.

Among the phonological rules of Yawelmani are the following:

CONSONANT REDUCTION I   206

$$C \rightarrow \emptyset / CC + \text{——}$$

in certain grammatically defined contexts

CONSONANT REDUCTION II   207

$$C \rightarrow \emptyset / C + \text{——} C$$

VOWEL DELETION I   208

$$\begin{bmatrix} V \\ -\text{long} \end{bmatrix} \rightarrow \emptyset / VC \text{——} CV$$

VOWEL EPENTHESIS   209

$$\emptyset \rightarrow V / C \text{——} C \begin{Bmatrix} C \\ \# \end{Bmatrix}$$

where V = [i] or (irregularly) [a].

VOWEL DELETION II   210

$$V \rightarrow \emptyset / \text{——} V$$

VOWEL DELETION III   211

$$V \rightarrow \emptyset / V +_{\cap} C \text{——} \# \text{ in verbs}$$

Now of course some of these rules can be collapsed. (206) and (207) can, and so can (208), (210) and (211). But the collapsing cannot reveal the *function* of these rules. Every one of them either removes violations of the cluster constraints previously mentioned, or is so formulated as not to be able to introduce any.

It is obvious that Vowel Epenthesis performs in this respect precisely the same function as the two Consonant Reduction rules, and equally obvious that there is in standard GP no formal way to show this. The relevance of the constraints to Vowel Deletion I and III is less obvious; but consider that (208) might have been thus expressed in words:

A short medial vowel is deleted wherever this would not create a cluster of **212** more than two consonants.

and likewise (211) thus:

In monosyllabic verbal suffixes, a final vowel is deleted wherever this would **213** not create a consonant cluster in final position.

The relationship of (210) to the constraints is less obvious still. All noun stems are followed, except in the subjective case, by what may be called a thematic vowel, either /a/ or /i/, in underlying representations. This is of course subject to (208) in appropriate environments. But some nominal suffixes begin with vowels, and before these the thematic vowel does not appear on the surface: it is deleted by (210)—and this apparently is the only motivation for having (210) in the grammar at all. Where then does the thematic vowel not delete? It does not delete word-finally; and it does not delete where its deletion would create an unpermitted cluster. The relationship of (210) to the cluster constraints is thus just this—that the sole motivation for its presence in the grammar is to make possible the following generalization about thematic vowels:

A medial thematic vowel is deleted wherever this would not create a three- **214** consonant cluster.

But all the explanations we have given of the functions of rules (206–211) are prose explanations; our theory gives us no way to express them formally, no way to bring out the fact that the form of all of these rules is affected—and the very existence of four of them determined—by the principle that certain clusters cannot occur in phonetic representations. Thus a generalization is inevitably missed.

This—and examples could be multiplied by investigating the phonology of virtually any language—is powerful evidence for the reality of what I shall henceforward call surface phonotactic constraints. How then was standard GP implicitly, and Postal (1968) explicitly, able to come to the conclusion that such constraints are always and everywhere redundant?

What Postal actually proves (1968, 208ff.) is something less than has usually been assumed: it is that *if* a generative grammar already contains a set of morpheme structure rules or their equivalent and a set of rules defining the possible combinations of morphemes in words, then the possible combinations of segments in words at the phonetic and all intermediate levels are automatically determined. But the all-important antecedent is simply taken for granted: that a grammar must contain morpheme structure conditions constraining underlying representations. Before we can decide whether this antecedent is true, we must ask what the function is of tactic rules in a grammar—whether they be phonotactic or 'morphophonotactic'.

I have argued elsewhere (p. 168) that it is very doubtful whether morpheme structure conditions should be retained in grammars for the sole purpose of enabling predictable information to be omitted from lexical entries; and there have in fact been versions of GP (such as markedness theory: pp. 168–9) in which no features in lexical entries have been left unspecified. So if tactic rules are needed in phonology, it must be for some other reason.

Postal rightly says (1968, 314) that one of the tasks of phonological theory is to provide a means whereby grammars may characterize the notion *possible morpheme* (to which he elsewhere adds tentatively *possible word*). It is for this purpose that tactic rules are needed. An English speaker hearing the sequence of segments [gǽblət] assumes that this is, or at any rate may be, an English word unknown to him. (It is, in fact, an English word that was unknown to the writer until two days before the present passage was originally written.) But if he hears [žablət], he can only suppose that it is some kind of foreign word: for no native or naturalized English word begins with [ž]. Knowledge of this kind is clearly part of what Chomsky would call the 'linguistic competence' of the native speaker of English: it is by virtue of being a speaker of English that one is aware of the difference between the two forms, and so if we believe that a grammar of a given language must include everything that distinguishes that language from other actual or possible human languages, rules expressing the relevant generalizations must be included in a grammar of English. They will not in general have any motivated place among the phonological rules, since not all of them govern alternations; they must therefore be stated as tactic rules.

But having established this, we have by no means established at *what level* these rules should be stated. Can we determine this? Consider under what circumstances the rules are called into use: when our speaker hears a form that does not already belong to his vocabulary. Now either the morphemic composition of the word in question is already known to him, or it is not. If it is known, or at least deducible, the well-formedness of the word will be judged on morphological, not phonological, criteria, since *ex hypothesi* it will already be known whether the constituent morphemes are phonologically well-formed. If, on the other hand, the word is morphologically opaque, will the required principles of phonological well-formedness relate to underlying or to surface representations? Clearly the latter; the other assumption would only be tenable if we could suppose that at first acquaintance with a word whose internal structure, if any, is unknown, an underlying representation could in every case be deduced; and that condition is satisfied only if underlying representations meet a biuniqueness requirement, which in GP they emphatically do not. It follows that the tactic rules that need to be stated apply to *surface* (phonetic or near-phonetic) representations. It is, in fact, the 'morphophonotactic' rules that are redundant.[2]

One irrelevant argument that may have had some weight in the general rejection of surface phonotactics is that the phonotactic rules were normally stated over a classical phonemic representation, and GP claims that there is not in general a level of representation meeting the conditions of classical phonemics. There is, however, no reason why phonotactic constraints could not be stated at the phonetic level (cf. Krivnova and Kodzasov 1972), or at what I have elsewhere called the 'categorial-phonetic' level.[3]

---

[2] Miller (forthcoming), however, presents evidence for the reality of morpheme-structure constraints. It should here be noted that voices had been heard much earlier insisting that a surface phonotactics was essential, e.g. Christensen (1967), K. C. Hill (1969), Johns (1969).

[3] Sommerstein (1974, 72): 'a level of representation . . . having the properties that the only rules still to apply are detail rules and that the last rule to have applied was not a detail rule.' Cf. Shibatani (1973, 88): 'a representation that contains all the necessary articulatory instructions (still in binary terms for

How then can we bring into phonological theory the relatedness of rules that may be structurally quite dissimilar to each other and to phonotactic constraints? Various rather tentative suggestions have been made, none of which anything like covers all the possibilities that can arise: particularly noteworthy are the proposals of Kisseberth (1970a), who uses a form of global derivational constraint rather different from those discussed in the preceding chapter, and Shibatani (1973) and Hooper (1974a), both of whom allow certain phonotactic constraints to function also as phonological rules. In the remainder of this section I will outline my own rather different (but equally tentative and inadequate!) suggestion.[4]

It deals with two types of rule-constraint relatedness, both of which can be observed in the Yawelmani data. Sometimes a rule applies quite generally, except that its application is blocked in those cases where it would create (or perhaps make worse) a violation of a phonotactic constraint. The Yawelmani rules (208) and (211) are of this kind, as their prose paraphrases (212) and (213) indicate. Sometimes, on the other hand, a rule applies *only* where it can remove (or perhaps alleviate) an existing phonotactic violation; the Yawelmani consonant deletion rules (206) and (207), and the epenthesis rule (209), are examples of this.

I have called rules of these two types *phonotactically motivated rules*, the former being *negatively motivated* and the latter *positively motivated*. The most important feature of the proposed theory of phonotactic motivation is that where a rule is phonotactically motivated, such elements of its structural description as are accounted for by the motivating phonotactic constraint(s) are not stated as part of the rule. For the phonotactic constraint(s) is (are) needed in the grammar in any case; there is no point in saying the same thing twice, once in a phonotactic constraint and once in a phonological rule (or perhaps in several phonological rules). Further, we now have a new kind of principle for grouping rules into schemata. Instead of only being able to group rules whose SDs or SCs are similar in certain ways, we can now group rules that remove[5] violations of the same phonotactic constraint. In this way we can convert Kisseberth's 'functional unity' into an authentic structural unity, at least in many cases.

In Yawelmani, as we have seen, there are at the phonetic level no three-consonant clusters, and at word boundary no two-consonant clusters. This may be expressed as a phonotactic constraint in a form analogous to the 'negative' morpheme structure conditions of Stanley (1967):[6]

Negative phonotactic constraint: **215**

$$* \ CC \begin{Bmatrix} C \\ \# \end{Bmatrix} \text{(mirror-image)}$$

---

most parameters) for the characteristics of careful speech.' In practice these two definitions (made quite independently) will come to much the same thing. Shibatani's perhaps being slightly closer to the surface.

[4] Sommerstein (1974). And see Linell (1976) for a good discussion of the role of phonotactic constraints in phonology.

[5] Or, as the case may be, avoid creating.

[6] Cf. pp. 167–8.

As we have seen, the vowel deletion rules (208) and (211) are negatively motivated by this constraint. We can thus ascribe to the constraint, not to the rules, the requirement that these vowel deletions fail to apply when a vowel is preceded or followed by a consonant cluster. Vowel Deletion I will be formulated so as to delete any short vowel between two consonants, and Vowel Deletion III so as to delete any word-final vowel in a verbal suffix of the form CV; the two rules will be combined in a schema marked as 'negatively motivated by (215)', and the restrictions on their application will be imported by means of the universal convention (216):

A rule R negatively motivated by a phonotactic constraint C does not apply   **216**
if its application would create or aggravate[7] a violation of C.

In the case of the vowel deletion rules, the concept of phonotactic motivation made it possible to simplify the actual statement of the rules. This can also sometimes happen in cases of positive motivation. In a language in which all words ended phonetically in vowels, a rule to insert a vowel (say schwa) between any consonant and word boundary would not require any environment statement at all, if stated to be positively motivated by the phonotactic constraint *C# ; for a positively motivated rule never applies unless its application will remove or alleviate[7] a violation of the motivating constraint(s).

However, the object of the theory of phonotactic motivation is not to simplify the statement of phonological rules; and sometimes it will not do so (there is no way to use positive phonotactic motivation to simplify the statement of (206, 207, 209)). Rather the object is to explicate the relationship between phonotactic constraints and phonological rules, and to provide a basis for unifying rules related to the same constraint.

To conclude this section it may be as well to point to some of the inadequacies of the theory just sketched.

(1)   Some phonological rules, though positively motivated in the sense that all their applications remove some phonotactic violation, yet do not seem to be motivated by any single phonotactic constraint; I have suggested (Sommerstein 1974, 92–3) that such rules should be regarded as motivated 'by the phonotactics as a whole', and allowed to apply just where their application would make a string 'fit' the phonotactics better in any way at all. It appears that rules can also be *negatively* motivated by the phonotactics as a whole: from Ohala (1974) it would seem that schwa deletion in Hindi is such a rule.

(2)   By no means all cases of 'functional unity' can be brought within the theory. I have not even suggested how the Yawelmani rule (210) could be related to it; and it cannot, as it stands, be applied to complex cases such as those discussed by Kiparsky (1973a), where, for instance, an early phonological rule, though not itself creating or removing any phonotactic violations, yet creates or removes opportunities for the application of other rules which do have phonotactic effects.

---

[7] The notions of aggravation and alleviation of a phonotactic violation of course need defining; a tentative suggestion in Sommerstein (1974, 76).

(3) Nor is the theory able to recognize the existence of a conspiracy unless that conspiracy is totally successful. If three-consonant clusters, instead of being unknown in Yawelmani, were merely very rare, the language might still have most (though not all) of the rules (206–211), and they would still be functionally related; but it could no longer be said that they were phonotactically motivated. Such cases exist. Attic Greek had a great variety of rules to eliminate vowel sequences within and between words, including vowel contraction, consonant epenthesis, diphthong formation, elision, etc., many of these processes themselves subsuming diverse rules applying in diverse contexts. These rules certainly had a functional unity. Yet the dialect had no phonotactic constraint barring vowel sequences; and so the theory of phonotactic motivation is unable to bring out the relatedness of the rules.

These problems and inadequacies, though, do not call into question the importance of phonotactics in phonological description, nor Kisseberth's insight that rules may be related not just because they apply to similar structures or make similar changes, but because they aim to hit (or to miss) similar 'targets'. How this kind of rule relatedness may be expressed remains in some respects an open question: that it must be expressed somewhere in an adequate theory is beyond dispute.

8.2 The syllable

Perhaps the main reason for the reluctance of GP to operate with the syllable concept has been the apparent difficulty of pinning down that concept itself. Few, however, who have discussed the subject rather than evaded it, have failed to come to the conclusion that the syllable is not an analytic figment, but a reality that needs to be explicated.[8] As Hála (1961) points out, 'persons without linguistic knowledge are capable of dividing words into syllables; persons suffering from subcortical motor aphasia make as many expiratory movements as there are syllables; no matter how slowly one speaks, syllables maintain their existence and ... speech is never decomposed into separate segments.'[9] An adequate linguistic theory must account for this and other related facts (such as the central role of the syllable in many writing systems and many forms of poetry: cf. Meier 1964).[10]

We are still without a satisfactory definition of the syllable. Traditionally, attempts to explicate the syllable concept have proceeded either from the phonetic direction, in terms of muscular movements associated with the respiratory

---

[8] Kohler (1966a; 1966b) was one of these few, arguing that syllable division is either determinable from the segment sequence, in which case it is redundant, or not, in which case it is impossible. The dilemma is a fallacious one. (Try an analogous dilemma in another science: 'the taxonomic classification of an organism is either mechanically determinable from measurements of its parts, in which case it is unnecessary, or not, in which case it is impossible': no one would be persuaded for a moment.)

[9] This last statement does not hold good when speakers are asked specifically to divide an utterance into more and more parts: see Bell (1975, 15).

[10] But note that when Meier speaks of 'ideographische Schriften' he means logosyllabic writing systems; a truly ideographic (or indeed logographic) system would have no relation to phonological units at all.

apparatus or of peaks and troughs of stress or aperture or 'prominence'(whatever that is), or from the phonological direction, as that type of phoneme sequence in terms of which the phonotactics of a given language can be described with the greatest generality.[11] Theories of the syllable up to the early 1960s are usefully surveyed by Kloster Jensen (1963) see also Ladefoged (1975, 219–22).

In recent years there has been a tendency to see the syllable, not as a unit to be extracted from records of muscular or articulatory activity, from phonetic descriptions or phonemic analyses, but as a unit of neural programming. Thus Fry (1964) claims that 'the brain mechanism . . . arranges the time scheme for a complete syllable as a unit', noting various bits of circumstantial evidence, such as that in error correction the syllable is normally treated as the minimal unit, and that delayed auditory feedback is most disturbing to the subject if the delay is approximately equal to the average duration of a syllable. Lehiste (1971) similarly observes that

> if an error is made in the duration of one phoneme, the error is largely compensated for in the following phoneme, which finishes at the originally planned time, despite the fact that it started late. This . . . suggests that articulatory events are programmed . . . not in terms of single phonemes, but in terms of higher-level articulatory units.[12]

If this approach to the problems of the syllable is anywhere near correct, it is both futile to attempt to define the syllable on a phonetic and/or phonological basis and wrong to conclude that, because this cannot be done, the syllable is not a useful concept in phonology. For phonology, the syllable is something given in advance; whether it and its boundaries have phonological effects is an empirical question. The evidence is that they do, and the problem then becomes how to modify GP (or for that matter any other phonological theory) to take account of this.

Very many phonological processes can be expressed with greater generality if the syllable and its boundaries are allowed to be mentioned in their statement. Hooper (1972) gives many examples; perhaps the most striking is that the use of syllable boundary enables us virtually to eliminate from structural descriptions that ubiquitous disjunction $\left\{ \begin{matrix} C \\ \# \end{matrix} \right\}$. Almost always, rules in whose right-hand environment that disjunction figures are better regarded as applying in syllable-final position. We may add two further examples. The subrule (106a) of the Latin stress rule (105)[13] assigns stress to a vowel in the environment

217

$$/ \underline{\hspace{1cm}} C_0 \begin{bmatrix} V \\ -\text{tense} \end{bmatrix} \left\{ \begin{matrix} C_0^1 \\ [-\text{son}] \begin{bmatrix} +\text{cons} \\ +\text{son} \\ -\text{nas} \end{bmatrix} \end{matrix} \right\} VC_0 \#$$

[11] So, in varying terms, O'Connor and Trim (1953), Arnold (1956), Haugen (1956), Fudge (1969), and many others.
[12] The experimental evidence cited by Lehiste does not in fact point to the syllable as such a unit, but rather to (a) the word and (b) the 'rhyme' (the word minus its initial consonantism); this, though, may well be due to the restricted nature of the data investigated.
[13] There is a comparable situation in English, in one respect worse, for in at least four separate rules it

The disjunction is inelegant and not obviously explicable—until we consider that all the evidence suggests that syllable boundaries in Latin were placed according to the following principles:

A single intervocalic consonant goes with the following vowel. **218a**
An intervocalic cluster is generally divided between the end of one syllable and the start of the next; but **b**
An obstruent-liquid cluster goes wholly with the following vowel. **c**

Given these principles, the non-tense vowels whose occurrence in the penultimate syllable of a word permits the antepenultimate vowel to be stressed are all and only those that are syllable-final; and, using a full stop (.) for syllable boundary,[14] the environment statement (217) can be thus revised:

$$ / \text{——} C_0 \left[\begin{array}{c} V \\ -\text{tense} \end{array} \right] \cdot C_0 V C_0 \# \qquad \textbf{219} $$

or better, since the vowels and consonants of the last syllable of the word are absolutely irrelevant to the stress rule (all that matters is that there should be a syllable of some kind between the conditioning non-tense vowel and the word boundary), thus (220), where S denotes an arbitrary syllable:

$$ / \text{——} C_0 \left[\begin{array}{c} V \\ -\text{tense} \end{array} \right] \cdot S \# \qquad \textbf{220} $$

In Attic Greek, the perfect tenses of verbs whose roots began with a consonant normally had a reduplicative prefix consisting of a copy of the initial consonant plus the vowel [e]: e.g.

poiê:tai	'it is (being) done'	**221**
pepoíε:tai	'it has been done'	
klépte:	'he steals'	
kéklophe	'he has stolen'	

There is a fringe of lexical irregularities; but there is also a major subregularity. For certain initial consantisms the reduplicative prefix is not /Ce/ but simply /e/. These were:

/r/: e.g.	ráptetai	'it is stitched'	**222a**
	érraptai	'it has been stitched'	

A cluster ending with an obstruent:[15] e.g. **b**

	spéndetai	'he makes peace'
	éspe:stai	'he has made peace'
	pterû:sthai	'to be given wings'
	epteró:sthai	'to have wings'

---

has to be specially provided that an intervocalic consonant may optionally be followed by a liquid or a glide without rendering the rule inapplicable. See the comments of Chomsky and Halle (*SPE* 241 n.3), and, for the solution, Fudge (1975, 290).

[14] This symbol, used by Anderson (1974b), is preferable to the fashionable but cumbersome $, whose only merit is mnemonic.

[15] Three exceptional verbs with root-initial consantisms of the form (b) or (c) take the /Ce/ prefix.

A voiced consonant followed by a nasal,[15] e.g.   c
      gi + gnɔ́:ske: 'he realizes'
      égnɔ:ke   'he knows'
      mnɛ:monéue: 'he remembers'
      emnɛ:móneuke 'he has remembered'

The high degree of phonological regularity displayed by the alternation suggests that it should be regarded as governed by a phonological rule. But any standard formulation of such a rule would involve an unsatisfactory disjunction:

$$
\text{C} \rightarrow \emptyset /\# \left[\overline{+\text{perfect}} \right] e + \left\{ \begin{matrix} \text{C} \begin{bmatrix} \text{r} \\ -\text{son} \end{bmatrix} \\ \begin{bmatrix} \text{C} \\ +\text{voice} \end{bmatrix} [+\text{nas}] \end{matrix} \right\} \qquad \textbf{223}
$$

What has /r/ got in common with clusters? and why does *any* consonant trigger deletion of the reduplicative consonant if an obstruent follows, but only a *voiced* consonant if a nasal follows (cf. *pepni:gménos* 'stewed' ~ *pní:ge:n* 'to stew')? Some light begins to be shed when we examine Attic syllabification, as revealed by the rules of versification.[16] It turns out that root-initial /r/ is always pronounced long after any prefix (and closes the preceding syllable), and that the clusters figuring in the environment of (223) are almost precisely[17] those whose first member closes the preceding syllable. Thus the proper formulation of Reduplicative Consonant Deletion is

$$
\text{C} \rightarrow \emptyset /\# \left[\overline{+\text{perfect}} \right] e + \text{C.X} \qquad \textbf{224}
$$

It will be noted that the effect of (224) is to avoid a syllable beginning and ending with the same consonant: the rule is in fact dissimilatory. No such motivation for the rule was apparent when it had the form (223).

If we wish to make use of syllable boundaries in GP, we must ask, as we did for other types of boundaries in Chapter Six, how they get into phonological representations, and what effect phonological rules can have on them.

On the first point, various attempts have been made to formulate rules for inserting syllable boundaries into phonological representations, either for particular languages (e.g. Hoard 1971a for English) or universally (e.g. Hooper 1972). I see no reason to believe in the possibility of a universal syllable boundary assignment schema, though certain principles are very definitely 'unmarked' as against others—for example, word boundaries tend also to be syllable boundaries, and the syllabification V.CV is much more common than VC.V. The

---

[16] In Attic verse, a syllable which ends with a short vowel is short (or light) for scansional purposes; any other syllable is long (or heavy).

[17] Only *almost* precisely; for versification indicates that /bl gl/ also are normally syllabified /b.l g.l/. However, the syllabification /.bl .gl/ is also found, though it is rare except word-initially; and contrariwise the reduplicative prefix /Ce/, though regular with these initial consonantisms, is not invariable, certain verbs being sometimes found with /e/. No matter how exactly this undoubted discrepancy should be handled, the general correspondence between syllabification and applicability of (223) is undeniable.

business of working out the detailed rules for syllable boundary assignment in particular languages is important but not very interesting.

As to the effect of phonological rules on syllable boundaries, there are some indications that, in some languages at least, the boundary assignment rules reapply after each phonological rule, but that this process ends at a certain point in the derivation (perhaps to be equated with the transition from phonological to phonetic rules? cf. pp. 205–8), after which fresh rules may apply to delete, and presumably to insert or to shift, certain syllable boundaries.[18] But it is too soon to draw any firm conclusions.

With one exception, it does not at present appear necessary to give explicit recognition in phonological theory to any kind of phonological 'constituent structure' below the level of the syllable. The exception is the *mora*. In many languages syllables fall into two classes, called short and long (or light and heavy), in some into three (called, e.g., short, long, and overlong). It often proves convenient for the statement of phonological rules, especially but not exclusively rules governing prosodic features, to recognize the mora as a unit such that a short syllable consists of one mora and a long syllable of two (and an overlong syllable normally of three). An example may be provided by the Latin stress rule already discussed in this section. The formulation of the first subrule given as (220) is still unsatisfactory in one respect: why should the tenseness of a vowel determine whether the preceding vowel should be stressed? A study of Latin versification (and a variety of other evidence), however, shows us that Latin makes a clear distinction between light and heavy syllables, the light (i.e. one-mora) syllables being just those that end in a non-tense vowel. We may thus reformulate the stress rule in the following manner:

$$S \rightarrow [+\text{stress}] / \underline{\qquad} ((.M).S)\# \qquad\qquad \textbf{225}$$

(where M = mora): the rule is thus seen to be simply a restriction on the number of syllables and moras that may intervene between the stressed syllable and the end of the word.[19]

The syllable and the mora are essential to phonological description, and it may be expected that future work in the field will make much greater use of them than has been the case in the past decade or so.

---

[18] In addition to the treatment in Hooper (1972), these problems have been discussed in as yet unpublished work by A. S. Crompton, with particular reference to the intricate principles governing the occurrence and non-occurrence of schwa in French.

[19] The mora concept, which goes back to antiquity, was made familiar in modern times by Jakobson (1931; 1937), to whom rule (225) in its original form is due; see the discussion in Trubetzkoy (1939), and more recently in McCawley (1968, 58–61; 131–4) and Anderson (1974b).

⑨ Generative Phonology IV: On Constraining the Phonological Rule

In standard GP, phonological rules can do almost anything. Underlying representations may contain segment types never found on the surface; phonological rules may introduce such 'abstract' segment types into intermediate representation, with later rules clearing them away again; the kinds of rules that may be posited, and the kinds of changes they may effect, though in practice constrained by some considerations of phonetic plausibility, are in theory constrained by nothing except the overall simplicity and generality of the grammar. Furthermore, with some relatively minor exceptions,[1] all phonological rules are of similar status, no distinction of theoretical importance being drawn between, for example, rules that rely essentially on grammatical information and rules that do not.

Ever since the appearance of *SPE*, which perhaps represented the apogee of this view of the power of phonological rules, the assumptions of the previous paragraph have come under questioning, in three main directions.

(1) There have been attempts to show that classical phonemics in distinguishing between 'morphophonemic' and 'allophonic' rules, had got hold of a genuine distinction between types of rules with different functions, though it may have drawn the line in the wrong place; and further, that 'higher up' in the derivational process, another distinction is to be drawn between rules of genuinely phonological function and those which exist primarily to provide an exponent for a grammatical category, or to preserve a morphological distinction, or the like.

(2) There have been attempts to limit the power of phonological rules to avoid the possibility of there being underlying representations which, while justifiable by the simplicity-generality criterion, are so 'abstract', so remote from the surface representations, that it seems far-fetched to claim psychological reality for them (as standard GP does); this approach has often been backed by various forms of empirical evidence purporting to show what kinds of underlying/surface discrepancy can be psychologically real and what kinds cannot.

(3) There have been attempts to establish what kinds of phonological processes are 'natural' in human language, and also why they are natural; these processes are then taken to have a special status both in the acquisition of phonology by children and in the structure of the phonological component.

[1] Cf. Chapter Six, note 3 (readjustment rules); there are also 'phonetic detail rules' which convert such feature specifications as are still in binary terms at the categorial-phonetic level (cf. p. 196 with note 3) into specifications for multi-valued phonetic features.

This chapter will deal in succession with these three fields of re-examination, but it should be observed that they are not mutually exclusive: thus the establishment of a typology of natural processes may call into question the reality of such putative rules as cannot be fitted into the typology, or the making of a clear distinction between phonological and morphological rules may remove from the phonological component some of the rules that made necessary excessively abstract underlying representations.

9.1 Morphology, phonology and phonetics

Throughout the history of generative phonology there have been some tentative suggestions that in denying the existence of a classical phonemic level GP has discarded the baby with the bath water. Intuitively there has seemed to be a distinction between rules such as Vowel Shift, which would formerly have been regarded as 'morphophonemic' rules governing alternations between distinct phonological elements, and rules such as those governing the release or non-release, the aspiration or non-aspiration, of English /p t k/, once regarded as 'allophonic' rules governing the realization of the same element in different contexts. It has been recognized, of course, that rules cannot be rigidly divided into two blocks, one morphophonemic, the other allophonic, *if these terms are defined as they were defined by classical phonemicists*; if they could be so divided, the arguments against the possibility of a classical-phonemic level of representation could never have been constructed. Accordingly Schane (1971), who was concerned to argue that a distinction essentially the same as that drawn by classical phonemicists was of importance in accounting for apparent anomalies in the historical development of phonological rules, sought to distinguish, not between morphophonemic and allophonic rules, but between morphophonemic and allophonic *functions*, which might sometimes be performed by the same rule in different contexts: e.g. the Russian obstruent voicing rule discussed on pp. 116–121 would be said to have a morphophonemic function in most contexts, but an allophonic function in its application to /c č x/.

There has been little follow-up to Schane's work; but there has been considerable interest in a distinction, not this time between rule functions but between actual rules, which has become evident in the consideration of various constraints on rule application. With respect to several of these, what may for the time being be vaguely called 'low-level phonetic' rules have been found to behave differently from the general run of phonological rules. For example, the principles governing disjunctive rule application simply do not affect low-level phonetic rules, which always apply conjunctively (cf. Chapter Seven, note 23); and any constraints that may be imposed on phonological rules to avoid excessive 'abstractness' (see 9.2 below) similarly must not apply to phonetic rules (Anderson 1975, 42). These various indications all seem to be connected with the same distinction between rule-types—thus the rules that must not be subject to disjunctive application are much the same as the rules that must be exempt from constraints on absolute neutralization; but where is the line to be drawn, and does it imply that all non-'phonetic' rules must apply before all 'phonetic' rules?

On the first question, the nearest approach to an answer presently available appears to be the following (paraphrased from Anderson 1975):

A rule is phonetic if and only if   **226**
(i) its structural description contains no reference to any non-phonological feature and no reference to any boundary weaker than word boundary; and
(ii) it does not alter from + to − or from − to + the specification of any feature which 'is distinctively specified in underlying forms of the language'.

This definition is clearly related to the criteria for classical phonemic representations, but as clearly distinct from them. The first requirement is simply a rephrasing of a condition on allophonic statements which would have been acceptable to most of those classical phonemicists who regarded the word as the proper domain at least of segmental phonology (e.g. Chao and Jones). In the second requirement the difference from classical phonemics becomes evident: classical allophonic rules may not alter the categorial specification of features which are distinctively specified *for the phoneme(s) in question at the classical phonemic level.*

The qualification 'for the phoneme(s) in question' highlights a possible ambiguity in the part of (226) that I have enclosed in quotation marks. Does 'distinctively specified in underlying forms' mean distinctively specified in all the segments affected by the rule under consideration, or in at least some of those segments, or merely in at least some segments in the language? It can hardly mean the last. Vowel nasalization in English bears all the marks of a phonetic rule. It fully meets condition (226 i); it is thoroughly natural, on general phonetic grounds, in the only environment in which it applies (viz. adjacent to a nasal consonant); it does not apply in an all-or-none fashion, but to different extents depending e.g. on stress, on whether the conditioning nasal consonant precedes or follows or both, on whether a word boundary intervenes, and above all on style of speech. Yet it affects a feature which is distinctive in underlying forms in English (sc. for consonants); and it affects the + / − specification of that feature, for it makes non-nasal vowels nasal. But to take 'distinctively specified' to mean 'distinctively specified in all segments affected by the rule' seems to err equally far in the other direction: it would, for example, make the Russian obstruent voicing assimilation rule a phonetic one, although it reverses the value of one of the most important features in the Russian obstruent system, merely because for three of the twenty or so segment types to which the rule applies voicing is non-distinctive.

Presumably, then, Anderson intends to say that for a rule to be phonetic, it must not reverse the categorial value of any feature unless that feature is always non-distinctive at the underlying level in all segments affected by the rule. If we accept this definition or something like it, we at once see that we cannot say that every non-phonetic rule must apply before every phonetic rule. The rule (70a) governing the distribution of clear and dark allophones of Latin /l/ is phonetic, for this feature never needs to be distinctively specified for /l/ in underlying representations. But the rule that backs vowels before the dark allophone [ł], though it must apply to the output of (70a), is non-phonetic, since backness, whose value it reverses, is distinctive in vowels. Again, in the Le Bourg Blanc dialect of Breton (Jackson 1967; Anderson 1975, 55) we find the following two rules:

$$\text{Mid vowels become mid-low } / \text{------} rC \qquad \textbf{227a}$$

$$\emptyset \rightarrow a \ / \ r \text{------} x\# \qquad \textbf{b}$$

Rule (227a) is phonetic: the allophones of mid vowels in this environment, though lower than in most others, remain distinct from those of the low vowel /a/. Rule (227b) is non-phonetic: it inserts an entire new segment, apparently indistinguishable from the reflex of underlying /a/ And yet (227a) must apply before (227b); for a phonemically mid vowel is phonetically mid-low not only before, e.g., [rx] but also before [rax] if, but only if, the [a] is epenthetic, e.g. [ɛ:rax] 'snow' (from underlying /erx/).

We cannot evade these paradoxes by fixing the definition of 'phonetic rule' so as to make, say, (227a) non-phonetic and/or (227b) phonetic. Certain dichotomies in the structure and application of rules seemed all to relate to the same two great classes of rule, and it was on the basis of these dichotomies that the definition (226) was framed; the sort of alteration in the definition that would be necessary to sustain the claim that all non-phonetic rules apply before all phonetic rules would make the phonetic/non-phonetic distinction incapable of accounting for the evidence on which it was originally set up. Rather, we must accept that phonological and phonetic rules are not to be thought of as forming separate subcomponents of the grammar.

It remains true, however, that with overwhelming frequency phonological rules do apply before phonetic rules; and one naturally asks whether it is possible to state under what circumstances the opposite ordering can obtain. Anderson (1975, 59) notes that in each of the examples he cites of a phonetic rule applying before a non-phonetic rule, the non-phonetic rule is one that is potentially capable of merging the phonetic representations of phonologically distinct forms, and the prior application of the phonetic rule prevents such a merger. Thus in the Breton case, if rule (227a) were not in the grammar, or applied after (227b), the surface reflexes of underlying /erx/ and of a hypothetical */erax/ would be identical; as it is, they are distinguished on the surface, not, as in the underlying forms, by the number of syllables, but by the quality of the mid front vowel, which is lowered (and lengthened) in the underlyingly monosyllabic form, but would be raised (and likewise lengthened) in the other, which would be pronounced *[e̦:rax].

This motivation for the abnormal ordering is in accordance with a very general principle governing particularly the historical development of grammars: that *forms underlyingly distinct should preferably be distinct on the surface, and forms underlyingly identical should preferably be identical on the surface.*

Our Latin example shows that there can also be other motivations for the abnormal ordering of phonetic before non-phonetic rules. There the ordering (which is, by the way, of the kind that does not need to be stated extrinsically at all) is motivated simply by the fact that but for the prior application of the phonetic rule, the non-phonetic rule would have nothing to apply to. The most we can say in general is probably that wherever a phonetic rule does apply before a non-phonetic rule, there must be some special motivation in the form of the rules or in their effect on derivations.

Within the class of rules which we have been calling non-phonetic there remain rules of widely different types. For example, in Attic Greek of the fifth century B.C. my GP description (Sommerstein 1973) included the following two 'phonological' rules:[2]

$$[3\text{height}] \rightarrow [-\text{syll}] / V \text{——} \qquad\qquad 228$$

$$V \rightarrow [+\text{high pitch}] / \# \; C_0 V C_0 + \begin{bmatrix} -\text{participial} \\ 3\text{declension} \\ \begin{cases} +\text{ genitive} \\ +\text{dative} \end{cases} \end{bmatrix} \quad (V)C_0\# \quad 229$$

These rules (which incidentally are crucially ordered, (228) applying before (229)) are in the grammar, so to speak, for totally different reasons. Diphthong Formation (228) is in the grammar because certain types of vowel sequence are impermissible in Attic (which in fact tends to avoid vowel sequences generally: cf. p. 199). Desinential Accent (229) is in the grammar to provide an additional 'marker' or 'exponent' of genitive and dative case in certain nouns and adjectives. Such strictly redundant accentual markers of these secondary cases[3] are also found elsewhere in the language.[4]

The distinction is not solely a question of motivation. It is also evident that it makes no sense to impose any phonetic plausibility constraints on rules like (229); they can make any arbitrary feature change, add or delete whole strings of segments, interchange feature values in the manner of the *SPE* Vowel Shift rule (see Chapter Six, pp. 132–3); whereas rules of the type of (228) do normally (and perhaps should always be required to) 'make phonetic sense'. Thus it has been suggested[5] that rules with phonological motivation are subject to a restriction on the distance that can intervene between the affected segment ('focus') and the determining element in the environment (the details depending on the type of process involved); and again, that rules with phonological motivation cannot be sensitive to the number of syllables a form contains. It would be pointless to impose any constraint of that kind on rules with morphological motivation.

Like the morphophonemic-phonetic distinction, the distinction here being drawn is one that had an analogue in structuralist phonology: it is related, in fact to the four-way distinction among alternation types discussed on pp. 42–3. Most present-day phonologists, however, would recognize only a two-way distinction (those, that is, who recognize any distinction at all): broadly, this distinction would be between those rules whose conditioning can profitably be stated in purely phonological terms and those for which this is not so. The former are

[2] I have modified the formulation of these rules, partly for easier intelligibility, partly to take account of the feature system used in the present work.

[3] I call them so in contradistinction to the primary cases (nominative and accusative) which figure in the 'core' construction subject-verb-object.

[4] Thus in first- and second-declension nouns and adjectives the endings of these cases, if accented, are always accented circumflex (i.e. bear a falling tone), whereas the endings of other cases, if accented, are accented acute (i.e. bear a high tone if the vowel is short, a rising tone if it is long or diphthongal).

[5] Cf. Anderson (1975, 42).

termed *morphophonemic* rules, or *phonological* rules in a narrower than the usual sense; the latter are called *morphological* rules, or, using a term of Bloomfield's (1939) (cf. Matthews 1972),[6] *morpholexical* rules.

Various attempts have been made to provide a definition of morpholexical as opposed to morphophonemic rules. A suggestion of mine (Sommerstein 1975) was this:

A rule which is not phonetic is morphophonemic if and only if   **230**
(a) the alternants which it relates are phonologically similar (i.e. it governs a genuine alternation and a not a suppletion); and
(b) either (i) the conditioning of the rule is purely phonological;
or (ii) the rule is phonetically plausible, and either has some non-simultaneous environment which is phonologically definable or is a natural neutralization.

As well as being complex, this is a fairly broad definition of the notion 'morphophonemic rule': thus it makes it a morphophonemic and not a morpholexical fact that the preterite of *fly* is [flu:] and not *[fləu] (cf., on the one hand, *flown*, on the other, *drove*, *wrote*, etc.) and that *draw*, *know*, *grow*, *throw*, *blow* behave similarly, these being the only English strong verbs to have the vowel [u:] in the preterite. This is because a rule can be formulated for the process that satisfies (230a) and (230b ii):

$$\begin{bmatrix} \text{ə} \\ +\text{ablaut} \\ +\text{preterite} \end{bmatrix} \rightarrow \text{i} \; / \; \underline{\hspace{1.5em}} \text{w} \; \# \qquad\qquad \textbf{231}$$

with this /iw/ subsequently becoming [ju:] or ⌊u:⌋, according to environment, by general rules.

It may well be, however, that the definition (230) would admit as morphophonemic some rules which would violate constraints otherwise valid for morphophonemic rules; and in the phrases 'phonologically similar' and 'phonetically plausible' there is much vagueness and much scope for arbitrary interpretation. A narrower definition of 'morphophonemic rule' may well therefore be preferable. (232) is once again a paraphrase of Anderson.[7]

A rule which is not phonetic is phonological (= morphophonemic) if and   **232** only if its structural description contains no elements other than:

phonological features;   **a**
boundaries recognized by phonological theory;   **b**
labels for major lexical categories such as 'noun' and 'verb';   **c**
diacritic features relating to major vocabulary divisions such as 'native',   **d**
'Chinese', 'learnèd' (cf. Chapter Six, p. 158).
Rules not meeting this requirement are morpholexical.

[6] And for valuable further discussion of the 'grey area' between morphology and phonology, see Matthews (1973; 1974), in particular ch. 11 of the latter work.
[7] Item (d) is added by me. A rule will not, except by accident, serve to provide an exponent for a morphological element or category merely because it applies to forms in some major vocabulary divisions to the exclusion of other such divisions.

By this definition, (231) is classed as a morpholexical rule, since it refers to the morphosyntactic feature 'preterite' and to the purely morphological feature 'ablaut'.

Just as not all morphophonemic rules apply before all phonetic rules, so not all morpholexical rules apply before all morphophonemic rules. We have already seen an example: (228) must precede (229): high vowels and glides need not be regarded as underlyingly distinct ın Ättic, but (229) could not be stated in its present relatively simple form, which requires the stem of an affected noun to be monosyllabic[8] (thereby, incidentally, again demonstrating its morpholexical character, if Anderson's suggested constraint on 'syllable-counting' rules is correct—above, p. 208), unless it applies at a stage of derivation when high vowels and glides *are* featurally distinct; for nouns with monosyllabic stems containing diphthongs are subject to (229)—cf. [paidós] 'of a boy', [klɛːidós] 'of a key', where -*os* is the genitive case ending. Again, in the N.W. Caucasian language Abkhaz (Anderson 1974c, 450; 1975, 50–52) a purely phonological rule of epenthesis, which breaks up clusters of three consonants, must precede the rules of stress assignment, which are morphologically based to a considerable extent; for epenthetic vowels are capable of being assigned stress by these rules. The epenthesis rule must also precede another rule (manifestly non-phonological) which deletes the verbal prefix /j/ 'third person irrational or plural' just in case the noun phrase, agreement with which would be marked by the prefix, directly precedes the verb in question; for when a form like /jə́rtot'] 'they give it to him', where the [ə] is epenthetic and the [j] represents the prefix just mentioned, is immediately preceded by the direct object noun phrase,[9] so that the prefix is deleted, the resulting surface form [ə́rtot'] still has the epenthetic vowel (and still has it stressed), showing that epenthesis must have applied at a stage of derivation when the underlying three-consonant cluster /jrt/ was still intact.

It seems unlikely that all such morphophonemic-before-morpholexical orderings are specifically motivated; Anderson tries to account for the Abkhaz example, and others that he cites, in terms of the transparency principle (below, Chapter Ten), but can only show[10] that, whereas in the *normal* case the transparency principle favours the ordering morpholexical-before-morphophonemic, in *these* particular instances it is neutral as between the two possible orderings: which leaves an explanation still to seek of why this neutrality should be resolved in favour of applying the morphophonemic rule first.

Investigation into the trichotomy of rules sketched in this section is still in its early stages, It may be expected that in the immediate future work in this field will be largely directed to attempts to confirm or refute the conjectures to which I have referred, that phonetic, morphophonemic and morpholexical rules are subject to different constraints on the form they can take, the operations they can perform,

---

[8] It could, of course, have been even simpler if, in the spirit of the last chapter, we had assigned high pitch to the appropriate *syllable* (or mora) rather than to a vowel; if we reformulated (229) accordingly, it would not affect the present argument.

[9] The prefix /j/ is one of a class of verbal prefixes that agree in person, number and gender with the direct object if the verb is transitive, with the subject if it is intransitive: the treatment of intransitive subjects and transitive objects as standing in the same relation to the verb is typical of languages such as Abkhaz with an 'ergative' case system.

[10] Anderson (1975, 57–8).

their mode of application, and other characteristics. For in order for the distinction to be worth making, it must be shown that (say) all morpholexical rules have something in common beyond the defining characteristics that make them count as morpholexical rules. Otherwise the class of morpholexical rules is not much more interesting than the class of rules first postulated on Tuesdays.

9.2 How abstract is phonology?

This was the title of a famous paper by Kiparsky (1968b) which, though it remained unpublished for several years, had an enormous influence on subsequent work in phonology. Its appearance immediately followed that of *SPE*, in which a fairly consistent following of the simplicity-generality criterion had led to the positing of many underlying representations which were remarkably 'abstract' (remote from their surface realizations) with the differences being related only very indirectly to surface alternations—indeed the underlying form of one morpheme was often justified only by alternations observed in a quite different morpheme. For example:

Underlying	Surface		233[11]	
rixt	rājt	'right'		a
rīt	rājt	'rite'		b
lād	lɔ̄əd	'laud'		c
mūdlin	mɔ̄ədlɪn	'maudlin'		d
mūntVn	mawntən	'mountain'		e
long	lɔ̄əŋ	'long'		f
kɔ̄ēn[12]	kɔ̄jn	'coin'		g

Underlying-surface pairings like these exhibited one or more of a number of characteristics which to Kiparsky, and to many since, appeared objectionable.

9.2.1 Problematic features of *SPE*-type analyses

9.2.1.1 The diacritic use of phonological features
Right and *rite* are pronounced alike on the surface; but their derivational morphology differs. There is a fairly general rule of English that 'shortens' vowels (i.e. converts them to their short counterparts in accordance with the pairings given in (86)) where the syllable following the affected vowel is unstressed and is not the last syllable of the word. This rule has applied to *ritual*, a derivative of *rite*; but not to *righteous*, a derivative of *right*, though that too must be regarded as underlyingly trisyllabic. Indeed, if *right* had the same underlying representation as *rite*, and were subject to the same rules, the expected pronunciation of

---

[11] The surface representations given relate to the dialect described in *SPE*, a variety of General American. The transcriptions given by Chomsky and Halle have been modified to fit the conventions of the present work, though the macron, used by them to denote 'tenseness' in vowels, has been retained. The underlying representations in the left hand column are in the precise form given or implied in *SPE*, save that the second vowel of *mountain* is left unspecified where *SPE* (208; 218), contrary to its usual practice, specifies it as schwa.
[12] The vowel symbol in this underlying form is intended to denote a low front rounded vowel.

righteous would be *[rɪšəs], so that another rule, which converts /č/ to [š] before certain suffixes except where a fricative precedes (cf. *requisition* [-šən] but *question* [-čən], *infectious* [-šəs] but *rumbustious* [-čəs]), has also failed to apply. It might be thought reasonable simply to mark *right* as an exception to the two rules which its derivative fails to undergo; one of these rules at least has plenty of exceptions in any case (cf. *SPE* 181). But for two reasons the simplicity-generality criterion suggests another solution. One reason is that one or two words of similar form have similarly exceptional derivatives.[13] The other is that *both* the apparent anomalies can be accounted for at one blow if we take the underlying representation of *right* to be /riCt/, where /C/ is a fricative consonant, which is deleted (with compensatory lengthening of the vowel) at a state in the derivation when the shortening rule and the č→š rule are no longer applicable.[14] The fricative in question must be voiceless, for obstruent clusters within English morphemes are homogeneous in respect of voice; it must contrast with /f θ s š/ and yet, preferably, not make use of any features not already distinctive in the language; it is thus natural to take it to be a velar /x/, the fricative counterpart to /k/.

The simplicity-generality criterion thus leads us to the analysis (233a,b), which (it might well be argued by one not exclusively committed to this criterion) is highly implausible. If we forget about generality, what this analysis is trying to do is account for the double exceptionality of *righteous* by hypothesizing:

two new phonological rules;[15]
an underlying segment that never appears anywhere in surface representations;
a markedly 'abstract' underlying form for a morpheme exhibiting no surface alternations whatever;
an underlying phonological contrast between two identically pronounced morphemes, i.e. 'absolute neutralization'.

Is this justified by the avoidance of two rule-exception features? Can the supposed underlying representations be regarded as in any sense psychologically real? Are there any circumstances under which non-surfacing segments, absolute neutralization, and abstract representations for non-alternating forms, should be

---

[13] At least *nightingale*, if that is indeed to be treated as a derivative of *night* (though even if it is not to be so treated, the [aj] in the first syllable remains an anomaly under the shortening rule, which would be accounted for by an underlying representation /nixt-/). *SPE* 234 also instances *mightily*; but this adverb does not meet the structural description of the shortening rule, for it contains two internal # boundaries (cf. *SPE* 85 on the suffixes -*y* and -*ly*), and there is thus no anomaly in its not undergoing the rule.

[14] Actually, rule-ordering considerations make it necessary, in the *SPE* analysis, for 'compensatory' lengthening to precede the deletion.

[15] One of these is the rule lengthening (tensing) vowels before /x/; the other is the rule deleting /x/. *SPE* claims that both of these 'fall together with other already motivated rules', but in the first case this merely means that there are other rules tensing vowels (and the pre-/x/ tensing rule is not even collapsible with them), and in the second case the 'already motivated rule' is a rule converting /x/ to [h] which is motivated by nothing at all except 'lexical simplicity' (*SPE* 224), that is, in effect, the symmetry of the underlying phonological system. Still a third new rule is necessary if a similar analysis is to be extended to the few forms which show alternations between [g] and zero before nasals—*paradigm(atic)*, *resign(ation)*, etc.

permissible; and if so, what criteria are to replace those of simplicity and generality?

9.2.1.2 *The phonological use of diacritic features*

Diacritic features have the function of triggering or preventing the application of phonological rules in cases where it is not appropriate to assign this function to phonological features. Sometimes two forms which contrast on the surface may have underlying forms which are identical as regards phonological features, differing only in that they belong to different vocabulary divisions or that one is an exception to some rule; and this is unobjectionable, particularly if the exceptional form violates some fairly (but not completely) general phonotactic principle of the language. But is it legitimate to ascribe *all* instances of a particular surface contrast (in general, or in a large class of phonological environments) to an underlying diacritic feature? If one contrast can be so ascribed, why not all contrasts—in which case there would be no need for phonological features, and the Naturalness Condition (p. 108) would lose its meaning?

Chomsky and Halle, having decided to treat the long (tense) syllabic peaks of English as derived by a Vowel Shift rule from underlying vowels differing in one or more features from their surface realizations—[aj] from /ī/, [i:] from /ē/, and so on—were faced with a problem about the source of the surface vowel corresponding to what we have represented as [o:] (in their dialect a tense, low, back, rounded vowel with a centring offglide, transcribed [ɔ̄ʌ]).[16] In monosyllables it so happens that one of the posited underlying tense vowels, /ā/, does not occur; and this is pressed into service as a source for [ɔ̄ʌ], the derivation (ā→āw→āu→āo→ɔ̄ʌ) involving rules most of which, given the general pattern of underlying forms assumed, have at least some independent motivation

But this will not work in polysyllables; for there underlying /ā/ is needed to account for the surface peak pronounced, in this dialect, [āʌ] in words like *father* and *Chicago*. It is not difficult so to formulate the rules that /ā/ surfaces differently in monosyllables and in polysyllables; but it remains necessary to find a source for [ɔ̄ʌ] in polysyllables.

Chomsky and Halle claim that in polysyllables [ɔ̄ʌ] is in complementary distribution with the diphthong which is pronounced [æw] in some dialects, [āw] in others. If this claim were true, it would be possible, by a phonologically watertight (if bizarre) environment statement for one of the rules in the derivation, to derive both diphthongs from /ū/. This is not, in fact, the line that Chomsky and Halle take; and in any case the claim is false.[17] There are thus three alternatives,

---

[16] The offglide, unlike all other postvocalic offglides, is treated by the phonological rules as a vowel, i.e. [+vocalic] in the *SPE* feature system. This is correct in terms of the definition of vocalicity given at *SPE* 302; but it is not clear how the featural distinction between this and other offglides—crucial to the proper working of such derivations as that of *maudlin*—could survive the replacement of this feature by that of syllabicity. The treatment given to the centring offglide also does away with the important generalization that an English word has as many syllables as vowels. It is not *only* the phonological use of diacritic features that casts doubt on the analysis being considered.

[17] The claim is that in polysyllables the diphthong with unrounded first element occurs only before nasal + consonant or before a vowel, while the diphthong with rounded first element never occurs in either of those environments. Chomsky and Halle dispose of such counter-examples as *saunter, launder, trousers* by assuming, without independent motivation, that they are underlyingly

short of a general revision of the whole analysis of the vowel system. One is to derive [ɔʌ] in polysyllables from some other member of the underlying tense vowel system; this probably could not be done without damage to the simplicity and generality of the rules. Another would be to posit an additional underlying tense vowel as the source of this diphthong; this would be *ad hoc*, and one supposed underlying vowel would be inexplicably absent from monosyllables. The third alternative is to derive [ɔʌ] in polysyllables from /ū/, and account for the two disparate realizations of /ū/ via an exception feature on some rule.

The rule chosen is that of 'Glide Vocalization', which converts the diphthongs /ūw āw/ (derived from underlying /ū ā/) to /ūu āu/. This rule, which we have already seen at work in the derivation of [ɔʌ] in monosyllables, has the effect of allowing Vowel Shift to apply to both elements of the diphthong instead of only to the first element; and Vowel Shift and a rule of Rounding Adjustment convert the output /ūu/ of Glide Vocalization to [ɔʌ].

So far the result if Glide Vocalization applies. If, on the other hand, it is prevented from applying, Vowel Shift and Rounding Adjustment will apply only to the first element of the diphthong /ūw/, the surface output then being [āw] or [æw] according to dialect.

This solution works. But it works only by accounting for a surface contrast, on the face of it no different from any other surface contrast, by the presence *v.* absence of a rule-exception feature—a device which, as we have noted, may well be regarded as objectionable, yet in this case appears to be not merely permitted but required by the simplicity-generality criterion.

9.2.1.3 *Abstract representations not justified by alternations*

According to the Naturalness Condition (p. 108), segments are categorized phonetically in the same way in which they are categorized phonologically, unless the facts of the language require otherwise. In all varieties of GP, the main kind of 'fact' that can 'require otherwise' consists in alternation, in situations where one and the same morpheme has diverse phonetic realizations which can plausibly be derived from a single underlying representation.

That single underlying representation cannot be identical with all the phonetic realizations; it is not even desirable to require that it be identical to one of them. For example, in every surface alternant of English *telegraph* at least one of the vowels is reduced:

telegraph	[télɪgra:f]	**234**
telegraphy	[təlégrəf-]	
telegraphic	[telɪgræf-]	

The vowel reduction is environmentally predictable in each case; and the underlying form will have no reduced vowels, being /telegræf/ or the like.

It may not even (this is disputed) be possible to require that each segment of an underlying form shall appear unaltered in some surface alternant. The underlying form /telegræf/ would satisfy that requirement; representations like /rīt/ for *rite*

---

monosyllabic; but no such device will avail in the case of *Maundy (Thursday)* or *gauntlet*, or of *rowdy, frowsy, cowrie, bowdlerize, about, renown,* all of which violate the alleged complementary distribution. Personal and place names violating it are even more numerous.

would not. But even the latter kind of representation would meet a looser requirement expressed, true to the spirit of GP, in terms of features and not of segments: true, no alternant of *rite* has [iː] as its root vowel, but every feature specification of the underlying /ĭ/ is reflected somewhere on the surface—its tenseness in the [āj] of *rite*, its height and frontness in the [ɪ] of *ritual*.

But *SPE* phonology goes beyond this, at the beckoning of the simplicity-generality criterion. English has an alternation in certain lexical items between [æw] and a vowel which Chomsky and Halle transcribe as [ʌ]—a lax mid back unrounded vowel: e.g. *profound:profundity*, *pronounce:pronunciation*, *foundation:fundamental*. The vowel underlying this alternation is said in *SPE* to be /ū/; such an assumption enables the Vowel Shift rule, in particular, to work in the most general manner. But note the feature specifications of the relevant segments:

	æ	w	ʌ	ū	235[18]
high	−	+	−	+
low	+	−	−	−
back	−	+	+	+
round	−	+	−	+
tense	−	−	−	+

Of the five significant features of the underlying vowel, one is not preserved in either of its surface realizations, and two others (highness and rounding) only in the offglide of one of them (an offglide not present in underlying representation). Indeed, the two alternating vowels are more like each other than either is like their supposed common source. It is at points like this that one begins to ask whether the hypotheses implicit in such analyses as these—and hypotheses they are—are empirically testable.

If a main object of positing underlying representations which differ from their surface realizations is to account for alternations, what underlying forms should be set up for morphemes which do not alternate? I do not now speak of morphemes whose failure to alternate is unpredictable: these are simply exceptions. But many languages have numerous morphemes which never appear in environments where they could manifest alternations: in English *ice*, *fiend*, *gate*, *fawn*, *coin*, *groan*, *spoon*, *pound* are among very many instances. It might be thought that such non-alternating forms could simply be given underlying representations identical to their surface representations (low-level rules aside). But the simplicity-generality criterion forbids this. If these morphemes had such 'concrete' underlying representations, it would be necessary to make them exceptions to Vowel Shift and related rules, thus burdening the lexicon with numerous extra rule features: whereas it is possible, at no cost to the grammar, to allow them to undergo the Vowel Shift group of rules in the same way as do alternating forms—so long as we can suppose the underlying representations to be e.g. /īs fēnd gæt fān grōn spōn pūnd/.

I omitted, from that list, the underlying form of *coin*. This word contains a diphthong which *nowhere* in the language takes part in any systematic[19]

---

[18] We here use *SPE* features, and in keeping with *SPE* practice make no use of complex segments.
[19] The qualification 'systematic' is meant to exclude such synchronically genuine but isolated

H

alternations. To make possible the generalization that English contains no underlying vowel-glide sequences, *SPE* 192 derives this diphthong from a low front rounded vowel /ɔ̈/.[20] No matter that phonetically neither this vowel nor any other front rounded vowel occurs in English. No matter that in the languages of the world, low front rounded vowels are extremely rare, and that systems containing low front rounded vowels to the exclusion of high ones are unknown. Symmetry demands that [ɔj] (as the diphthong of *coin* is pronounced in the dialect that *SPE* describes) be derived from a tense monophthong; rules required anyway for other vowels, without addition or modification, will convert /ɔ̈/ to [ɔj]; therefore this analysis *must* be adopted. Some might take it as the *reductio ad absurdum* of the simplicity-generality criterion. But (it may be asked) are the supposed underlying forms for *ice*, *fiend*, etc., any less absurd? They account neither for an alternation nor for a failure to alternate; they are posited for no reason related to the morphemes for which they are posited, but because of alternations in other morphemes; and if they are to be regarded as anything but the sheerest 'hocus-pocus' (p. 49), they imply that English speakers store the lexical item *ice* in the form /ĭs/, though it is never pronounced with a high vowel, and though if someone were (by some fault, presumably, of neural programming) to say

There was a lot of [iːs] on the road this morning   236

it is improbable that anyone would understand. Again the question arises: are there any empirical controls?

9.2.2 Towards a solution

9.2.2.1 *Possible evidence for abstract analyses*
It is clear enough that some restrictions are required on the omnipotence of the simplicity-generality criterion. But what are these restrictions to be? And, logically prior to that question, what is admissible as evidence for determining the nature of the restrictions?

The importance of the latter question will become evident from a consideration of the attempt by Hyman (1970) to use loanword phonology as evidence in favour of a relatively abstract analysis (involving the diacritic use of phonological features). The form of the argument may be thus stated, apart from the particular linguistic data by which Hyman exemplifies it:

Problem: whether, in a given language, to derive some or all instances of   237
surface [Y] from underlying /X/.
Evidence: in nativization of loanwords from other languages, speakers of

---

alternations as *choose:choice*, *voice:vocal*, *conjoin:conjunction*. Any 'rules' to account for these alternations would have to be wholly *ad hoc* (cf. *SPE* 232, fn. 61, on *choice*).
[20] It is not the least of the advantages of doing away with underlying morpheme-structure conditions (cf. Chapter Six, p. 168) that, as Clayton (1976) notes, it automatically rules out arguments such as this of Chomsky and Halle's; for if nothing is directly said in the grammar about what are possible underlying representations, then greater symmetry in the underlying segment or sequence inventory cannot simplify the grammar.

the language under investigation regularly replace [X] of the source language by their own ⌈Y⌉.

Inference: these speakers have a rule X→Y (or a sequence of rules with the same effect) as part of their linguistic competence.

Conclusion: the abstract analysis is justified.

Unfortunately, as D. G. Miller (1973b, 379) points out, (237) is invalid because it can prove too much. Let the investigated language be English, the source languages the Indo-Aryan group, let [Y] be the ordinary voiced stops [b d g] and /X/ the aspirated voiced stops /bh dh gh/; then, if valid, the argument goes through—with the consequence that English voiced stops can be regarded as underlyingly aspirated—which incidentally makes possible the generalization that *all* English stops are underlyingly aspirated.

Clearly the invalid feature of the argument must be the inference from 'speaker replaces [X] by [Y] in loanwords' to 'speaker has a phonological rule X→Y'. It must be the case that the principles governing loan nativization are not necessarily also phonological rules, i.e. principles governing the pronunciation of sentences. One might well suppose that this is because phonological rules determine *surface* representations, whereas loan nativization principles determine the *lexical* representation of borrowed lexical items.

9.2.2.1.1 *Linguistic change* The only kind of evidence for underlying representations that is all but universally regarded as admissible is evidence from linguistic change.

Suppose that, for reasons of the conventional simplicity-generality kind, we wish to posit for some stage of a language (in the past) an underlying segment /θ/, affected by the following phonological rules:

$$[-son] \rightarrow [-cont] \: / \: C \text{———} \qquad\qquad 238$$

$$\theta \rightarrow f \: / \left\{ \begin{matrix} \# \\ V \end{matrix} \right\} \text{———} \qquad\qquad 239$$

Thus there will be no surface [θ], but instead an alternation between [t] and [f], perhaps initially in suffixes after roots some of which end in consonants and others in vowels. Evidence from linguistic change, i.e. from later stages of the language, may confirm this hypothesis in two ways:

(1) As we shall see in Chapter Ten, one form of linguistic change is the loss of a rule or a restriction on its applicability. If rule (238) were lost, or came to apply only (say) after fricatives, then subsequent to that change there would again be surface instances of [θ]. If this happened it would strongly confirm the·validity of the abstract analysis of the earlier *état de langue*.

(2) Suppose, alternatively, that the language had a rule, applying after (238),

$$[-cont] \rightarrow \begin{bmatrix} +son \\ +nas \end{bmatrix} / \: [+nas] \text{———} \qquad\qquad 240$$

This would give rise to such derivations as

Underlying form	/kanθi/	/sintu/	**241**
by (238)	kanti	——	
by (240)	[kanni]	[sinnu]	

Suppose then that at a later stage rules (238) and (240) were reordered. The derivations of (241) would then be changed to:

Underlying form	/kanθi/	/sintu/	**242**
by (240)	——	[sinnu]	
by (238)	[kanti]	——	

This too would confirm the abstract analysis; for instances of [t] which this analysis claimed to be derived from underlying /θ/ would have come to behave differently from underlying /t/. Generally any rule addition, modification or reordering which distinguished in this way between the 'abstractly' derived segments and others would be confirmatory evidence.

This sort of evidence from linguistic change is, of course, not directly available in the case of present-day languages (except to the extent to which change can be observed in progress). It is necessary, from the evidence of past linguistic changes, to determine what sorts of abstract analyses find confirmation of this kind, and thus to formulate restrictions which can then be applied even where linguistic-change evidence is not available.

It should be noted that there is no way in which evidence from linguistic change can *refute* an abstract analysis, except to the following very limited extent: a rule loss or restriction which confirms an abstract analysis may, by its failure to affect certain (usually non-alternating) forms, indicate that speakers had already reanalysed these forms with more 'concrete' underlying representations.[21] Owing to this asymmetry, if a given type of abstract analysis never finds confirmation in linguistic change, this must be regarded as disconfirming its validity.

9.2.2.1.2 *Poetics*   Another form of evidence that has been regarded as capable of confirming the validity of abstract analyses is the evidence of poetic practice. An example of this type of argument may be drawn from Anderson (1969). He had posited for Icelandic an umlaut rule of essentially the following form:

$$a \rightarrow \ddot{o} \ /\!\!-\!\!- \ (C_0 \begin{bmatrix} V \\ +\text{low} \\ -\text{stress} \end{bmatrix})_0 C_0 \begin{bmatrix} V \\ +\text{high} \\ +\text{back} \end{bmatrix} \qquad \textbf{243}$$

This rule gives rise to various alternations between [a] and [ö], chiefly in inflected forms (cf. Chapter Seven, pp. 181–2). There are also, however, some forms, mostly derived nouns, which show [ö] in an environment where (243) might have applied, but without any alternant with [a], at least within the inflectional paradigm: e.g.

---

[21] So the loss of the German final devoicing rule in some Swiss dialects did not affect forms which never preceded an inflectional ending (Kiparsky 1968a, 177); the loss of the English rule deleting postconsonantal /w/ under weak stress, in Early Modern English, did not affect unimorphemic words such as *answer* and *gunwale* (D. G. Miller 1973b, 374–5). (The analyses 'confirmed' by these rule losses were not abstract as the term is normally used, but the examples show what typically happens.)

djöfull 'devil', *jötunn* 'giant'. Can these be regarded as having /a/ in underlying representation? If they can, then /ö/ will not figure at all in the lexical representations of Icelandic morphemes.[22]

This simplification of the underlying vowel system is the principal motivation for treating non-alternating [ö] as derived from /a/; thought there is a weaker motivation in that many of the nouns in question would appear to be morphologically and semantically related to other words in which [a], or some vowel independently known to be derivable therefrom, appears on the surface. But note that if *djöfull, jötunn*, etc., were taken as having underlying /ö/, it would not require the alteration of any phonological (interlevel) rule or the positing of any rule-exception features. It would be a very moot point whether there was sufficient internal justification for the proposed abstract analysis.

We turn therefore to external evidence, and in particular to the so-called Skaldic verse composed in Old Norse from the ninth century onwards. One variety of Skaldic verse has among its rules (which on the whole are observed with a high degree of regularity) a rule of *internal rhyme*. In each line the penultimate syllable holds a dominating position: it is obligatorily long, and it controls internal rhyme according to the following principle:

Each line must contain a stressed syllable ending in the same consonant(s) **244** as the penultimate syllable of the line. In even-numbered lines, this rhyming syllable must also contain the same vowel as the penultimate syllable; in odd-numbered lines, it must contain a different vowel.

Not all actual lines satisfy (244). But of those that do not, the overwhelming majority violate it in exactly the same way: they treat the vowels [a] and [ö] as identical with one another, so that rhymes such as the following are legitimate in even-numbered lines:

all*vald*r	: *sköld*um	**245**
skj*öld*um	: *ald*ri	
kn*örr*	: *varr*ar	

The only principled way of accounting for this is to suppose that vowels could be regarded as equivalent for the purposes of the internal rhyme rule if they were identically represented before the application of umlaut, even if their surface representations were distinct: such conditioning of rules of poetic composition by non-surface phonological representations is found in other poetic traditions.[23]

What is particularly significant for our purpose is that even those instances of [ö] which never alternate with [a] are still treated by the internal rhyme rule as equivalent to [a]; the vowel of *knörr* in (245) is one such. The inference is natural that at the time when poems exhibiting internal rhymes such as those of (245) were being composed, all surface [ö]'s, alternating or not, were derived from underlying /a/'s.

The evidence, however, relates to a period which ended in the early thirteenth century; can it be regarded as having probative value for modern Icelandic? Anderson's argument (1969, 28) is that it can:

[22] 'At least in productive word classes' (Anderson 1969, 37).
[23] Kiparsky (1968c; 1972b) discusses two examples in detail.

It can easily be shown that the older form of the language contained a u-umlaut rule identical in all relevant respects with the modern one . . . . Thus, if it can be shown that . . . umlaut . . . applied in Old Norse [non-alternating forms] as well as [alternating ones], this will constitute strong evidence for the same analysis of modern Icelandic forms.

Perhaps 'strong evidence' is putting it too high. What can be said is that if the evidence of poetic practice indicates that, despite the abstractness of the resulting analysis, we must banish /ö/ from the underlying representations of Old Norse, then, there being no material difference in the general shape of the data or in the rules involved, abstractness cannot be considered in itself an objection to a corresponding analysis in modern Icelandic.

But does the evidence of poetic practice so indicate for Old Norse? Is poetic practice generally a safe guide to phonological analysis? The following considerations must raise very serious doubts.

We supposed too readily above that 'the only principled way' of accounting for the equivalences of (245) was to suppose that rule (244) could apply to non-surface representations. (Call this the *Morphophonemic Hypothesis*.) For there is another possibility, not involving the synchronic grammar at all. It could be that when verse-forms with internal rhyme began to be used, umlaut had not yet come into the language; that when it did come in, syllables which had rhymed before the change continued to be regarded as rhyming after the change though their vowels were no longer phonetically identical; and that out of this situation there became established a general principle of Skaldic verse that [ö] could always be regarded as equivalent to [a]. Poets composing without the aid of writing—and the earliest stages of the Skaldic tradition were surely oral—would have retained these rhymes because otherwise they would have had to give up formulas, phrases, lines that had served them well and their predecessors in the art before them; later generations would have gone on using them because to them, knowing as they did nothing of the earlier pronunciation, [ö] = [a] was simply a permitted licence—theirs not to reason why, theirs merely to make good use of a welcome freedom in a highly constrained form of verse! (Call this the *Conservatism Hypothesis*.)

The Morphophonemic and Conservatism Hypotheses are not mutually exclusive: it may be that one is the best explanation for one set of data in one language, the other for another set in another language. What matters is that there cannot be an immediate inference from poetic rules to phonological rules. The child creating a phonological grammar has no access to long-past states of the language. The poet learning his craft does, in a very qualified sense, have such access: he is learning to continue a consciously elaborated professional tradition which may go back far into the past, and may, like any other professional tradition, contain curious quirks whose rationale is no longer understood.

9.2.2.2 *Some proposed constraints*
Linguistic change, then, is our one trustworthy guide to the question what kinds of 'abstract' analyses should be permissible and what kinds should not be. At present the question is still in a state of flux. It has more than once been proposed[24] that every segment in the underlying representation of a morpheme

[24] By Kiparsky (1968b); more recently by Hooper (1975) in the framework of Vennemann's theory of

should be one that appears on the surface in one or another of its alternants. (We may define an *abstract segment* as a proposed underlying segment that does not meet this condition.) It would, however, seem that there are analyses, shown to be valid by the evidence of linguistic change, which do require the positing of abstract segments.

D. G. Miller (1973b) suggests that all such valid analyses will be found to meet two conditions, originally put forward by Kisseberth (1969). The first of these conditions is that 'the characteristic features of ... underlying non-surfacing segments ... [must be] independently attested on the surface.' The terms 'characteristic' and 'independently' are not explained; the condition appears to amount to this:

> If a given feature in a given segment has the same value in all surface **246** realizations of a morpheme, that must be its underlying value.

It is of interest that this condition would make it impossible for non-alternating [ö] to be taken as derived from underlying /a/ either in Old Norse or in modern Icelandic, despite the apparent poetic evidence to the contrary; it would, in fact, ensure that for all non-alternating segments (and therefore all non-alternating morphemes) underlying and surface forms are identical.[25] The sort of abstract segments which, as far as this condition goes, are permissible include: /uː/ underlying an alternation [oː] ~ [u]; /ž/ underlying an alternation [z] ~ [š]; a little less obviously, /gʷ/ underlying an alternation [k] ~ [w] (velarity and occlusion attested by one alternant, voicing and rounding by the other).

Kisseberth's second condition may be regarded as a sharpening of the generality-simplicity criterion. It may be thus paraphrased:

> Where an abstract segment is posited, there must be some non-arbitrary **247** grounds in the data for positing just that segment rather than a non-abstract segment or another abstract segment.

For example, the fact that an alternation [k] ~ [w] could, so far as condition (246) goes, be underlain by /gʷ/ would not in itself make such an analysis legitimate; for there would remain the possibility, not only of a non-abstract analysis with /k/ or /w/, but also of a variety of other abstract analyses using e.g. /g/, /γ/, /γʷ/, /w̥/. For /gʷ/ to be chosen it must be shown that there are grounds which make it uniquely preferable.

Classical Latin had, in fact, a rather rare alternation between [k] and [w]:

nik + s	'snow' (nom. sg.)	**248**
niw + is	'snow' (gen. sg.)	
wiːk + s + it	'(he) lived'	
wiːw + it	'(he) lives'	
flu(w) + it	'(it) flows'	
fluːk + s + it	'(it) flowed'	

'natural generative phonology'. In earlier versions of this theory the requirement had been the much stronger one that the underlying representation of every morpheme be identical with one of its surface allomorphs.

[25] Except, we may suppose, as regards the application of phonetic rules (see 9.1).

Hockett (1958, 282f), working in the framework of classical morphophonemics, proposed a base form /nig^w/[26] for the root meaning 'snow'; it is not clear whether he would have extended the same analysis to other roots showing the same alternation. P. H. Matthews (1973) discusses the alternation in the manner he so often employs—suggesting many valuable ideas, drawing no firm conclusion. Can we say that the evidence points uniquely to /g^w/? I think we can.

(a) The voiced rounded velar stop [g^w] did occur in Latin on the surface, but only after [ŋ], e.g. [liŋg^{w}a] 'tongue', [aŋg^{w}is] 'snake'. In that position it contrasted with [k g k^w]. The analysis proposed would mean that underlyingly it occurred also after vowels. No other analysis would in this way fill a gap in the distribution of a segment type already existing in the language.

(b) The rules needed to derive the alternant [k] from /g^w/—a rule of delabialization and one of voicing assimilation—have strong independent motivation; the rule needed to derive the alternant [w] is phonetically plausible; in neither case is a diacritic feature needed. No other analysis has all three of these advantages.

(c) The root for 'snow' has a further alternant [niŋg^w]: cf. [niŋg^{w}it] 'it is snowing', and the poetic variant of the noun, [niŋg^{w}eːs] 'snows'. Whatever the explanation of the apparently infixed nasal, this is independent evidence for /g^w/, and /g^w/ only, in this root at least; and it might well seem perverse, when the same alternation is found under the same conditions in 'snow' and in 'flow', to attribute it to underlying /g^w/ in the former and to (say) a diacritic feature in the latter.

All abstractness constraints are constraints on morphophonemic rules only; it is, in fact, only in morphophonemic rules (or rather in what the analyst thinks are morphophonemic rules) that the problem of overuse of the generality-simplicity criterion to posit abstract segments can arise at all. Phonetic rules are in any case too tightly constrained, being unable to alter distinctive feature values; morpholexical rules are not, primarily, in the business of making phonological generalizations, genuine or otherwise.

9.2.2.3 *Another look at English vowels*

Conditions such as (246) and (247) would automatically exclude most of the *SPE* analyses of (233). *Right, laud, maudlin, mountain,* and *coin* are all non-alternating, and the conditions therefore require them to have underlying representations identical to their surface representations. For *long* the only alternant form is [leŋ] (in *length*), and it was indeed to account for this alternation that the underlying representation /long/ was proposed (*SPE* 210). The underlying vowel /o/ certainly meets the spirit of condition (246), being a lax mid monophthong like [e] on the one hand, back like [ɔə] on the other; whether, as condition (247) further requires, the evidence uniquely forces us to accept this underlying

---

[26] Actually /nigw/, but a single consonant seems preferable to a cluster, since /k^w/ in Latin behaved prosodically as a single consonant, e.g. if it occurred intervocalically the preceding syllable remained open.

representation could not be determined without a thorough re-examination of all the rules of English segmental phonology affecting vowels.

The most interesting case is that of *rite*. Conditions (246) and (247) debar anything like the *SPE* Vowel Shift rule from applying to non-alternating forms. What though of the alternations—very widespread ones—to account for which Vowel Shift was set up (cf. pp. 130–1)?

We cannot consider one of these alternations in isolation. In (249) they are listed; the surface representations of the alternants are as in *SPE* (transcriptional modifications here are without substantive import) and the feature system used is also that of *SPE* except that, for convenience only, diphthongs are indicated by such specifications as [back offglide] or [front onglide].

(a) [i] [+high, −low, −back, −tense, −round] **249**
[aj] [−high, +low, +back, +tense, −round, front offglide]
SPE underlying representation:
/ī/ [+high, −low, −back, +tense, −round]

(b) [e] [−high, −low, −back, −round, −tense]
[ij] [+high, −low, −back, −round, +tense, front offglide]
SPE underlying representation:
/ē/ [−high, −low, −back, +tense, −round]

(c) [æ] [−high, +low, −back, −round, −tense]
[ēj] [−high, −low, −back, −round, +tense, front offglide]
SPE underlying representation:
/ǣ/ [−high, +low, −back, +tense, −round]

(d) [ā] [−high, +low, +back, −round, +tense]
[ōw] [−high, −low, +back, +round, +tense, back offglide]
SPE underlying representation:
/ɔ̄/ [−high, +low, +back, +round, +tense]

(e) [ʌ] [−high, −low, +back, −round, −tense]
[æw] [−high, +low, −back, −round, −tense, back offglide]
SPE underlying representation:
/ū/ [+high, −low, +back, +round, +tense]

(f) [ʌ] [−high, −low, +back, −round, −tense]
[jūw] [+high, −low, +back, +round, +tense, front onglide, back offglide]
SPE underlying representation:
/u/ [+high, −low, +back, +round, −tense]

All but one of these underlying representations meet condition (246); but the exception, /ū/, violates it very grossly, having three feature specifications contrary to those of both its supposed realizations: a tense, high, rounded vowel is supposed to be always realized as lax, mid or low, and unrounded.

This could, in isolation, be remedied; an obvious choice to underlie the alternation (249e) would be /a/, which is only one feature removed from [ʌ] and only one from [æ], and which finds no other employment in the *SPE* analysis of English. But even with this alteration, is there any reason to suppose that the analysis would satisfy the unique preferability condition (247)? Several other analyses are conceivable which would meet condition (246) and do not *prima facie* seem likely to require more implausible rules, more diacritic features, etc., than the *SPE* analysis. We might, for example, say that underlying each of the alternations except (249e) is a tense vowel with the same colour as the vocalic element of the diphthongal alternant, i.e. that the vowels underlying (249a–f) were respectively, say /ā ī ē ō ʌ ū/. This might result in such underlying representations as /rāt/ (*rite*), /ob + sīn/ (*obscene*), /tēbl/ (*table*), etc. The 'laxing' and 'tensing' rules would apply more or less as in *SPE* (thus there would be laxing in *ritual*, whose root would then be /rat/; similarly in *obscenity, tabulate*, etc.); then would come a Vowel Shift rule applying mainly to lax rather than tense vowels (in contrast to the *SPE* rule), and operating in approximately the reverse of its *SPE* direction. It could perhaps be expressed (using *SPE* features) in the following way, with four ordered rules:

$$\begin{bmatrix} V \\ -\text{tense} \\ +\text{low} \end{bmatrix} \rightarrow \begin{bmatrix} +\text{high} \\ -\text{low} \end{bmatrix} \qquad\qquad 250$$

That is, /a/ → /ɨ/, The output is /ɨ/ rather than /i/ so as to avoid feeding the main Vowel Shift rule, (251).

$$\begin{bmatrix} V \\ -\text{low} \\ -\text{tense} \end{bmatrix} \rightarrow \begin{bmatrix} -\text{high} \\ \alpha\text{low} \\ -\text{round} \end{bmatrix} \Big/ \begin{bmatrix} -\alpha\text{high} \\ \beta\text{back} \\ \beta\text{round} \end{bmatrix} \qquad 251$$

That is, /i/ → [e], /e/ → [æ], /o/ → [a], and /u/ → [ʌ].

$$a \rightarrow [+\text{tense}] \qquad\qquad 252$$

$$ɨ \rightarrow [-\text{back}] \qquad\qquad 253$$

These are 'adjustment' rules, giving the correct outputs [ā] and [i]; no doubt there are other similar processes with which they could be collapsed, after the manner of the rounding and backness adjustment rules of *SPE*.

Rules (252) and (253) can be allowed to apply without restriction, for the dialect described in *SPE* does not have any instances of [a] or [ɨ] on the surface. The two earlier rules must somehow be restricted so as to apply only to non-alternating forms; this will be necessary in any analysis which accepts condition (246) but retains some form of the Vowel Shift rule.

The object of this *jeu d'esprit* is not to suggest an alternative analysis of the English vowel system; about large parts of that system nothing has been said (which is not to say that with the aid of all the devices *SPE* uses, a consistent and convincing analysis of the whole system could not be worked out). The object has been to suggest that even if the *SPE* analysis could be made to meet the feature attestation condition (246), there is no particular reason to suppose that it would meet the unique preferability condition (247). And if it would not, then we must give up either the two conditions (at least the latter one) or the *SPE* analysis as unjustifiably abstract. This will not affect the fact that [ɪ] and [aj], [æ] and [ej], etc., are morphophonemically related in English. It will affect the manner in which that relatedness is expressed: it will be expressed directly, not indirectly via the claim that in underlying representation the members of each pair are phonologically nearly identical.

Much more importantly, if conditions (246) and (247), or anything like them are correct, much of GP theory will need to be, not necessarily revised, but certainly re-examined; a mechanism here may have been motivated, or a constraint there rejected, solely on the basis of supposed rules which these conditions render indefensible. Such theoretical, re-examination, which far transcends the revision of this or that analysis of a particular language, is well beyond the scope of this book; but it is vitally necessary if what we are aiming at in our linguistic theory is what in Chapter One, p. 13, we called truth.[27] To another aspect of this same search for truth (psychological reality) we now turn.

9.3 Natural phonology

9.3.1 The problem

It is fitting to begin this section with a quotation from *SPE* (400):

> The entire discussion of phonology in this book [*SPE*] suffers from a fundamental theoretical inadequacy. . . . The problem is that our approach to features, to rules, and to evaluation has been overly formal. Suppose, for example, that we are systematically to interchange features or to replace $[\alpha F]$ by $[-\alpha F]$ (where $\alpha - +$ or $-$, and F is a feature) throughout our description of English structure. There is nothing in our account of linguistic theory to indicate that the result would be the description of a system that violates certain principles governing human languages. To the extent that this is true, we have failed to formulate the principles of linguistic theory, of universal grammar, in a satisfactory manner.

Chomsky and Halle's solution to this problem was the theory of markedness, already mentioned, in connection with lexical redundancy, in 6.8.2. This is confessedly not a complete solution but only a contribution to one; and it has failed to satisfy, because it proceeds by asserting *ex cathedra* that certain feature configurations are normal (unmarked) and others abnormal (marked) without offering any insights into why this should be so.[28] In the course of their discussion, however, they take a programmatic look at another possibility (*SPE* 427):

---

[27] I have not attempted to cover all aspects of the 'abstractness controversy' or all points of view put forward. Basic is Kiparsky (1968b); Kiparsky (1973a; 1974a) revises somewhat the position there taken. D. G. Miller (1973b) reviews the controversy up to that date. Hyman (1970), Brame (1972a), Hoard (1972), Jensen (1972) and Schane (1974) argue on various grounds for a less restrictive attitude to abstract analyses. Related to the controversy are the arguments of Skousen (1972) to the effect that many rules generally thought to be phonological are, in their psychologically real form, morphological. The literature of 'natural phonology' and 'natural generative phonology' also contains a fair amount of discussion of the abstractness question; cf. 9.3.

[28] For a detailed and devastating critique of markedness theory see the appendix to Lass and Anderson (1975).

If it should prove possible to define a reasonably short list of . . . 'plausible' phonological processes and show that all—or the majority . of—the phonological processes encountered in different languages belong to this set, this would constitute a very strong empirical hypothesis about language.

Much work since has been devoted to that end, but with an important addition. Chomsky and Halle here say no word about, and do not seem to be interested in, the question which may be crudely phrased as 'What makes plausible rules plausible?' It is generally agreed, for example, that though (254) requires more features in its statement than (255), nevertheless (254) is in an important sense the 'simpler', more 'plausible' rule.

$$[+\text{nasal}] \rightarrow \begin{bmatrix} \alpha\text{labial} \\ \beta\text{coronal} \end{bmatrix} / \underline{\quad} \begin{bmatrix} -\text{syllabic} \\ \alpha\text{labial} \\ \beta\text{coronal} \end{bmatrix} \qquad 254$$

$$[+\text{nasal}] \rightarrow [\alpha\text{coronal}] / \underline{\quad} [\alpha\text{syllabic}] \qquad 255$$

Rule (254) assimilates a nasal in place of articulation to a following consonant; (255) makes all nasals coronal before vowels and non-coronal before consonants. Clearly the word 'assimilation' will figure prominently in any account of the superior plausibility of (254); and clearly assimilation will have to be minutely sub-categorized (*SPE* 428)—for (256), though an assimilation rule, is anything but plausible:

$$[+\text{nasal}] \rightarrow [\alpha\text{syllabic}] / \underline{\quad} [\alpha\text{syllabic}] \qquad 256$$

Rule (256) would make a nasal syllabic before a vowel and non-syllabic before a consonant; it is easy to see that a rule affecting nasals in this environment is far more likely to dissimilate syllabicity than to assimilate it. Chomsky and Halle give another example:

Thus, nasals seem to be quite prone to assimilate the point of articulation of a succeeding consonant, while continuants are apparently all but immune to such assimilation. (*SPE* 428).

All these statements of plausibility, which are clearly going to be quite complex, could of course simply be built into the theory of language as they stand, and this is apparently Chomsky and Halle's intention:

If assimilation were a special process which was available for use whenever necessary, it could be restricted so as to affect only the same features in different segments, or it could be further constrained to affect particular features or sets of features in particular environments. (*Ibid.*)

But any such restriction would be of no real interest unless one of two conditions was met. One condition would be if the restriction were a genuine constraint on the power of phonological rules, such that no rule violating it could be a possible rule of any human language; then, indeed, we would have 'a very strong empirical hypothesis about language'. This possibility is expressly excluded by Chomsky and Halle:

It does not seem likely that an elaboration of the theory along the lines just reviewed will allow us to dispense with phonological processes that change features fairly freely. (*Ibid.*)

Alternatively, something interesting would have been said if it could be shown that the numerous and complex principles of phonological rule plausibility were deducible from simpler, fewer, and more general principles, perhaps having independent motivation outside linguistic theory in the narrow sense. If neither of these conditions is satisfied, all we really have is an attempt to patch up a faulty evaluation measure (simplicity metric) for grammars, which can only conceal the important issues (see Chapter One, p. 12).

9.3.2 Schane's theory of natural processes

S. A. Schane (1972; 1973a; 1973b; 1973c) has taken important steps towards carrying out the programme adumbrated in *SPE* for a typology of plausible phonological processes. In addition to assimilation, the main types of process are considered to be:

(a) *Syllable structure optimization.* It is known that the one universal syllable structure is CV;[29] and the first systematic (not babbling) utterances of children are regularly of this form. One natural motivation for a phonological process can thus be that it serves to bring the structure of some syllables closer than they would otherwise be to the 'ideal' CV shape. Processes of this type would include epenthesis of vowels between adjacent consonants, or of non-vowels (glides, glottal stop, etc.) between vowels in hiatus; vowel contraction, elision, and similar processes; consonant cluster simplification; and the treatment of certain final consonants in French, which are deleted when the next word begins with a consonant, but when it begins with a vowel are retained with a shifting of the syllable boundary, so that an underlying sequence C.#V surfaces as .CV, with syllabification disregarding word boundaries.

(b) *Neutralization*, whereby an underlyingly distinctive feature becomes non-distinctive on the surface in particular environments. Assimilation rules are also in a sense neutralizations; but whereas in assimilation the affected feature takes its surface value from a neighbouring segment, in other forms of neutralization this surface value can be predicted, if at all, only from other considerations. Thus consider the neutralization of a contrast between nasal and oral vowels. If the environment in which such a neutralization occurs is 'before nasal consonants', we would expect the rule to make all vowels nasal in that environment, by assimilation to the nasality of the consonants. If, on the other hand, oral and nasal vowels contrasted only before nasal consonants and the distinction was neutralized elsewhere, this might be regarded as a process of denasalization by assimilation to non-nasal environments. But if the domain of neutralization could not in any way be described as either 'in nasal environments' or 'in non-nasal environments', what then? We would then certainly expect the surface vowels in positions of neutralization to be oral, as they regularly are when there is no nasality contrast at all in a given language; but the process is not an

---

[29] This claim was challenged by Sommer (1970); but see Dixon (1970) and Darden (1971b).

assimilatory one. We may classify it as a neutralization *sensu stricto*, and say that in such neutralization the feature affected normally assumes *the value it would bear if the relevant contrast were entirely absent from the language*—in short, its *unmarked* value: vowels become non-nasal, laterals sonorant, palatalized consonants lose their palatalization, etc. Compare the Prague School treatment of non-assimilatory neutralization (pp. 52–3); but note that in GP it is normally assumed that markedness/unmarkedness is not language-particular and determined by the direction of neutralization, but is universal and determines the direction of neutralization. The unmarkedness of some feature values as against others then has itself to be explained: it appears to be due sometimes to articulatory simplicity, but most often to perceptual considerations, that feature value being unmarked which maximizes the perceptual distance either between one segment and those with which it cooccurs (syntagmatic distinctiveness), or between one segment and those with which it contrasts (paradigmatic distinctiveness).

(c)   *Strengthening and Weakening*. These terms, especially the latter, have long been familiar in the discussion particularly of phonological change, but their definitions have tended to remain intuitive rather than explicit, largely because of the very considerable difficulty of formulating an explicit definition that allows neither too little nor too much. Processes which tend to be regarded as strengthening are, among consonants, the conversion of sonorants to obstruents, voicing to voicelessness, unaspiration to aspiration, shortness to length, voiceless plosives to voiceless affricates, etc.; among vowels, lengthening and diphthongization. Weakening processes for consonants are mostly strengthening processes in reverse; for vowels, they include shortening and reduction to schwa; for both consonants and vowels, deletion is the extreme case of weakening. Frequently, especially among consonants, weakening and strengthening processes resist simple description in terms of the usual phonetic features. The diachronic strengthening process of pre-Germanic known as Grimm's Law is an example: voiceless stops became fricatives (perhaps via an affricate stage), voiced stops became voiceless, and what are conventionally considered to have been voiced aspirate stops (their actual phonetic nature remains obscure) became plain voiced stops. An even more complex strengthening process is reported from Tswana:

> In position after nasals voiced stops become ejectives, nonobstruent continuants become voiceless aspirated plosives, and obstruent continuants become voiceless aspirated affricates (*SPE* 401, referring to Cole 1955).

Normally, strengthening and weakening processes are environmentally controlled, and it seems to be possible to single out some environments as conducive to weakening and others as conducive to strengthening. For consonants, final position tends to be a weakening environment, as does intervocalic position, particularly if the preceding vowel is unstressed; syllable-initial position following a consonant or word boundary, on the other hand, is usually a strengthening environment. For vowels, stressed syllables and open syllables are strengthening environments; unstressed syllables are weakening environments, particularly that which directly follows a stressed syllable, where vowel loss (syncope) is not uncommon. Various attempts have been made to formulate strength hierarchies which, it is hoped, will make it easier to state strengthening and weakening processes in a revealing manner; it is probable that in the end the still unexplicated notion of strength itself will be found to reflect a physiological variable or complex of variables.[30]

Not all plausible rule types can be fitted into this typology, though some of those as yet unmentioned are probably related to it. Stress rules, for instance, have something in common with syllable structure optimization rules; just as the latter tend to create an alternating rhythm of closure (C) and aperture (V) in the speech tract, so stress rules tend to create an alternating rhythm of strong and weak stress; indeed it has even been suggested that the mode of application of iterative stress rules can be determined on this basis.[31] Dissimilation, which Schane (1973a, 61) mentions as without a place in the main typology, may be relatable to neutralization (as above defined) in some cases and to weakening in others; at any rate, though dissimilation has a special kind of triggering factor (an identical or nearly identical articulation in the immediate neighbourhood but not directly adjacent) its effects are sometimes not dissimilar to those of neutralization or weakening processes.[32]

We have had occasion to mention that some plausible process types are articulatorily motivated, some perceptually motivated, and that this distinction sometimes seems to cut across Schane's classification (as in the case of neutralization rules). The logical next step is to base classification on these two motivation types; such a classification has the advantage that there is little reason to suppose it will not be exhaustive. This step has been taken by Reimold (1974), who further argues that for their insightful description the two types of rule need distinct feature systems. The article deals in detail only with the first class, 'articulation-simplifying processes'; these are classified as lenitions (weakenings), assimilations, and 'sloppy timing rules' (really a special class of assimilation, for both alike have to do with changes in the timing of articulatory gestures), and the feature system used is supposed to be so designed that all plausible assimilations are of the form

$$[\alpha F] \rightarrow [\beta F] / \ldots [\gamma F] \ldots \qquad 257$$

where the Greek letters represent numerical feature values, and $\gamma - \beta$ differs less from zero than does $\gamma - \alpha$; that all plausible lenitions are of the form

$$[\delta F] \rightarrow [\varepsilon F] / \ldots \qquad 258$$

[30] There is a useful discussion of strengthening and weakening in Lass and Anderson (1975, ch. 5). An explicit definition of weakening has been put forward by Vennemann (see Hyman 1975, 165): 'a segment X is said to be weaker than a segment Y if Y goes through an X stage on its way to zero', sc. in a natural chain of phonological processes: this is at least not counter-intuitive, and it takes the first step towards explicating weakening, in that we now know what we are talking about.

[31] Jensen and Jensen (1973) claim that stress rules iterate left-to-right or right-to-left, whichever will produce an alternating pattern; so likewise rules which 'affect the number of syllables'.

[32] It may be instructive to examine in this light some of the generalizations about dissimilation in the Romance languages reached by Posner (1961); e.g. that when consonants dissimilate in place of articulation, a less frequent consonant is normally replaced by a more frequent one (i.e. usually a more unmarked one), or that a nasal undergoing dissimilation normally does not become a stop but instead loses its occlusion, becoming a fricative, liquid or glide (weakening)

where ε differs less from zero than does δ; and all features are defined strictly in terms of positions of parts of the vocal tract, with the value being zero where the position is 'neutral', and positive or negative according to the direction of departure from the neutral position. Strengthening is not mentioned presumably because, along with syllable-structure optimization and (most) neutralization processes, it is regarded as a perceptually motivated or 'differentiation' process, and of these processes and their associated feature system no detailed account is given in Reimold's article.

One proposal by Schane (1972; 1973b; 1973c) goes beyond typology. He suggests that there is a fixed universal set of natural rules.[33] Particular languages select rules from this set and may impose *constraints* on their applicability. This suggestion is not, as it might seem, empirically vacuous; Schane shows how it can be used to explain some facts about the behaviour of exceptions in phonology which have always been taken for granted, but which in standard GP find no explanation.

French may be analysed as having a consonant deletion rule, or rules, with the following effect:

nasals delete before any consonant or major boundary;   **259**
liquids and glides delete before major boundary, or before morpheme boundary when a consonant follows; provided that (1) a liquid or glide can delete only if preceded by /e/ or /i/, and (2) /r/ in monosyllables cannot delete at all;
obstruents delete before major boundary, or before morpheme boundary when a consonant follows; provided that (1) velars delete only if a nasal precedes, and (2) /b f v z/ do not delete at all.[34]

Clearly we are dealing here with a single process; but it is very doubtful whether in standard GP it can be formulated as a single rule, and if it can such a rule would certainly be very complex. More important is the consideration of exceptions. Some forms, such as *abdomen*, which meet the structural description of the rule do not undergo it; this is the ordinary kind of exception and creates no special problems. But other forms which do *not* meet the SD of the rule *do* seem to undergo it, e.g. *cul* [ky] 'arse', *escroc* [εskro] 'swindler', whose underlying final consonants are guaranteed by derivatives such as *culot* [kylo] 'bottom', *culasse* [kylas] 'breech (of rifle)' *escroquer* [εskrɔke] 'swindle'. In standard GP there are two possibilities for the description of this situation. One would be to extract the restrictions on the applicability of the deletion rule, which *cul, escroc*, etc., violate, and state them as redundancy rules in the readjustment component (cf. Chapter Six, p. 115 and note 3), e.g.

[33] For a rather similar approach cf. Chen (1974a): again, particular languages are made to fill in details of the structural descriptions of rules which are essentially universal (Chen calls the universal schemata 'metarules').
[34] This last proviso will only hold if the plural ending, which surfaces as [z] in positions of liaison and zero elsewhere, is analysed as /s/, in violation of the Kisseberth conditions on abstractness; the analysis which (259) presupposes may possibly also violate these conditions in other respects. I leave the analysis standing, for I do not think that such doubts as may exist about the validity of parts of it affect the points discussed in the text.

$$\begin{bmatrix} +\text{son} \\ -\text{nas} \end{bmatrix} \rightarrow [-\text{Cons. Deletion}] \; / \quad \begin{bmatrix} V \\ \begin{Bmatrix} +\text{low} \\ +\text{back} \\ +\text{round} \end{Bmatrix} \end{bmatrix} \underline{\quad\quad} \qquad\qquad \textbf{260}$$

$$\begin{bmatrix} -\text{son} \\ +\text{back} \end{bmatrix} \rightarrow [-\text{Cons. Deletion}] \; / \; [-\text{nas}] \underline{\quad\quad} \qquad\qquad \textbf{261}$$

The forms which exceptionally undergo consonant deletion would then be lexically marked as exceptions to (260), (261), and similar rules. This device has its drawbacks. The most important of them is this: what principled reason is there in GP theory for extracting the restrictions in this way, other than the handling of the exceptions? Could they not be stated in the ordinary way as part of the SD of the deletion rule or rules? It is unlikely that the analysis using (260) and (261) is any simpler than the alternative, and (260) involves a suspect disjunctive environment.

The other possible solution is not to use rules like (260) and (261), but to mark *cul, escroc,* etc., as *positive exceptions* to the deletion rule, meaning that they undergo the rule even though they do not meet its structural description. This device must be used with some care: in particular, it is necessary, rather than clumsily, to state just what part of the structural description can be disregarded—otherwise we might, e.g., have the final consonant of *escroc* deleting before a morpheme boundary followed by a *vowel,* so that the derivative verb will be assigned, impossibly, some such pronunciation as *[ɛskroe].

Neither of these devices can explain why the forms which can be 'positive exceptions' are so curiously restricted. To be specific: only consonants can undergo the rule when its structural description is not met, and they can only undergo it when followed by a consonant or a major boundary. Why so? It would be perfectly possible to make words ending in a vowel 'positive exceptions'; perfectly possible to rig exception features in such a way as to delete any (or indeed every) segment of a word like *escroc*; perfectly possible to extract as a redundancy rule the restriction that deletion applies only to consonants, or the restriction that it does not apply when a vowel follows, and allow forms to be exceptions to such a redundancy rule. Why does none of these things occur, and, more important, why are we morally certain that none of them *could* occur?

Schane hypothesizes that the French consonant-deletion rule and all similar rules in other languages are restricted versions of a single, universal rule, which he states as follows:

$$C \rightarrow \emptyset \; / \; \underline{\quad\quad} ([-\text{segment}]) \begin{Bmatrix} C \\ \text{pause} \end{Bmatrix} \qquad\qquad \textbf{262}$$

where 'pause' is presumably to be understood as 'potential pause', i.e. the end of a phonological word (cf. pp. 145-7). The process is a natural one, either as weakening or (more solidly) as syllable-structure optimization.[35]

---

[35] In which case it might perhaps be more simply and insightfully formulated as applying before C_0. (where . = syllable boundary).

No doubt there are languages in which (262) applies without restriction. No doubt there are other languages in which it does not apply at all. In French and other languages intermediate between these extremes, the rule applies subject to constraints, which may be expressed in the form of redundancy rules. Formally these do not appear to differ from rules like (260) and (261). In reality there is all the difference in the world. (260) and (261) were expressed as redundancy rules purely in order to avoid marking lexical items as positive exceptions. The constraints on (262) are expressed as redundancy rules because *the theory precludes their being expressed in any other way*; *all* non-universal conditions on the application of phonological rules[36] must be expressed as redundancy rules marking certain classes of lexical items as exceptions to the phonological rule, or subclasses within such exceptional classes as not being exceptions,[37] while the phonological rules themselves are left in their simple, general, universal form.

The constraints necessary to ensure that the effect of (262) in French will be as stated in (259) are detailed below; my presentation of them differs from Schane's in various non-essential respects. The constraints are to be applied in the order in which they are given.

$$[-\text{nasal}] \rightarrow [-(262)] \qquad\qquad\qquad \textbf{263}$$

$$\begin{bmatrix} C \\ \langle +\text{sonorant} \rangle \end{bmatrix} \rightarrow [+(262)] \; / \quad \left\langle \begin{bmatrix} V \\ -\text{low} \\ -\text{round} \\ -\text{back} \end{bmatrix} \right\rangle \underline{\qquad} [-\text{segment}] \qquad \textbf{264}$$

$$r \rightarrow [-(262)] \; / \; \# \; C_0 V \underline{\qquad} C_0 \; \# \qquad\qquad \textbf{265}$$

$$\{b, f, v, z\} \rightarrow [-(262)] \qquad\qquad \textbf{266}$$

$$\begin{bmatrix} -\text{sonorant} \\ +\text{back} \end{bmatrix} \rightarrow [-(262)] \; / \; [-\text{nas}] \underline{\qquad} \qquad \textbf{267}$$

Consider now how the applicability of (262) to the final consonant of a word like *mer* 'sea' can be determined. As a non-nasal, it is first marked minus for the rule by (263); then plus by (264), being a word-final sonorant preceded by a non-low front unrounded vowel; and finally minus again by (265), being /r/ in a monosyllable. Thus, although this final consonant meets the structural description of (262), it fails to undergo the rule, and remains undeleted on the surface.[38]

And what of *cul* and *escroc*? Their final consonants[38] will be marked in the lexicon as exceptions to redundancy rules (263) and (267) respectively; the effect

[36] At least of such phonological rules as embody natural processes; truly 'crazy' rules (cf. Bach and Harms 1972), which are not relatable to any natural process, will (if they exist, and are genuinely phonological rather than morpholexical) have to be differently treated.

[37] Note that a redundancy rule like (264), which assigns a plus-rule feature, does not create positive exceptions; the feature [+(262)] means, as plus-rule features usually do, that the rule in question applies *if its structural description is met*. The theory precludes the possibility of (262), or any other natural process, applying to a form which does not meet its universal structural description; there is no way to formulate a redundancy rule to make this possible.

[38] Rule features assigned by these redundancy rules, like other rule features, will be features of individual segments and not of morphemes as wholes: cf. Chapter Six, note 78.

of this will be that no rule will mark them as not undergoing (262), and they will therefore undergo it, yielding the correct surface forms. And this does not leave open the undesirable possibilities made available by a redundancy rule solution in standard GP (cf. pp. 230–1); by virtue of the formulation of the universal rule and the ordinary interpretation of minus and plus rule features, it is impossible for *any* segment *ever* to be deleted by (262) except a consonant followed by a pause or (with or without an intervening boundary) by a consonant. (Cf. note 37.) The actual non-occurrence of such deletions is no longer merely a curious, expected and yet unexplained fact; it is an automatic consequence of a linguistic universal.

9.3.3 Stampe's 'natural phonology'

The notion of a universal typology of natural processes has likewise been prominent in the work of David Stampe, which in the last few years has issued in an entirely new model of the phonological component, termed *natural phonology*.

In Stampe's early work (1969; 1973), the emphasis is laid on the innateness of natural processes and on their role in the acquisition of language. There is a fixed universal set of natural processes, and the child about to acquire language 'knows' *all* of these in advance—they are part of his *faculté de langage* on the same footing as other linguistic universals. Moreover, in the first stages of language acquisition he *applies* them all; this accounts for the very restricted phonological repertoire he displays in these early stages. For the only syllable types to appear on the surface will be those which no natural process converts into something else; and since if all natural processes applied freely 'they would reduce all phonological representations to [pa] or some such verbal pabulum' (Stampe 1973, 46), this or something like it will be the child's sole initial output. For we cannot account for this restricted repertoire by supposing the child unable to articulate more complex syllables; he has already articulated them (in babbling) and remains capable of using them in mimicked utterance and other not strictly linguistic performances (much as adult English speakers are perfectly capable of uttering clicks, but not, as a rule, capable of making linguistic use of them).

In the course of language acquisition, this primitive phonological component, comprising all and only the natural processes, is modified in four ways. Some natural processes are *suppressed*; one of the first to go, in English and many other languages, is the process making all consonants occlusive (which would permit only stops and nasals). Some natural processes are *limited* by the addition or tightening of contextual restrictions: thus the natural process of palatalization applies in some languages before all front vowels, in others only before the maximally palatal vowel /i/, in others, such as English, only before the yet more palatal glide /j/ (its effect is seen in such frequent, if sometimes stigmatized, pronunciations as [sčú:dnt] or [čú:zdɪ]); evidently the natural process in its primitive form applies before all front vowels, and various languages place various degrees of limitation on it.[39] Some natural processes become subject to *ordering constraints* which limit their applicability as genuine ordering constraints always

---

[39] Similarly, the primitive process of palatalization presumably applies to all consonants, and in Russian it remains in very much this state; in English it is 'limited' so as not to apply to labials. On some of the forms palatalization can take, see Chen (1974a).

do. Stampe (1973, 48) gives an interesting example of this, which incidentally shows how a natural process can remain alive in a speaker's competence even when in normal speech there is nothing for it to apply to:

> Research on the acquisition of phonology ... suggests that conditions on underlying representation in a language originate as innate processes which, in child speech, often apply near the surface to cause actual substitutions, and then (instead of being suppressed) are ordered so that they are manifest only in restrictions on underlying representations. Furthermore, in relaxed and allegro speech, certain constraints on underlying representation appear in low-level substitution, through unordering.
>
> For example, children's pronunciation of English often exhibits an innate process deleting glottal stops, so that [bʌʔn̩] 'button' becomes [bʌn̩]. When these deleted glottals at last appear in the child's speech we might assume that the child has suppressed the deletion process. In fact it appears that he has merely ordered it to the north of[40] the process which substitutes glottal for [t], and that it is this deletion process (not an unrelated, coincidental condition) which accounts for the inadmissibility and unpronounceability of nonderived glottal stops in English. It is no accident, therefore, that adult relaxed speech commonly exhibits deletion (via unordering) of derived glottal stops. Nor is it an accident that in foreign words ... glottal stops which cannot be analysed in the English system as derived from [t] are deleted.

Note there the appeal to the evidence of 'relaxed and allegro speech'; in these styles, we observe, natural processes may be to some extent (let us say) desuppressed, derestricted and/or deordered.

The fourth kind of modification of the primitive phonological component is the addition of *learnt rules*. Not all the rules of the adult phonological component are natural processes or relics of natural processes, motivated in the last resort by physiological or perceptual factors; some are characteristic of particular languages and have no motivation other than that they account for alternations in these languages. They are acquired by the language learner on the basis of alternations existing in the data to which he is exposed. The paradigm example of such a learnt rule is Velar Softening in English—which, we may note, is never found as an allegro-speech rule, or applying out of its place in the ordering, or applying to newly borrowed morphemes as, say, glottal stop deletion does.

It is natural now to ask whether there are criteria for determining which phonological 'rules' reflect natural processes and which are learnt rules. The criteria proposed in recent formulations of natural phonology[41] are essentially criteria of function. One and the same substitution may be a natural process in one language and a learnt rule in another: thus vowel harmony, an obvious

---

[40] This does not reflect a geographical theory of rule application, but a double metaphor: north of = above = before.

[41] The most useful published sources for natural phonology are Stampe (1969; 1972; 1973) and Bjarkman (1975). See also P. D. Miller (1973) and Lovins (1974); Dressler (1974) for some cautionary remarks on the validation of natural processes, and Rhodes (1973; 1974) for a variant version of the model. Stampe's doctoral dissertation (University of Chicago, 1973) may be described as the unpublished bible of the theory. Natural phonology must be sharply distinguished from *natural generative phonology*, for which see note 47.

candidate for membership in the universal set of natural processes, is in modern Turkish a learnt rule.

(What are the implications of this for language acquisition? The child brings a ready-made natural process of Vowel Harmony to the task of learning Turkish, as he would bring it, along with all other universal natural processes, to the task of learning any language. If the Turkish rule is nevertheless a learnt one, does this mean that the child, in spite of finding massive evidence in the data presented to him that a Vowel Harmony rule of some kind is operating, nevertheless suppresses it completely and acquires a learnt rule which is much the same as the natural process but has restrictions and exceptions of a non-phonetic nature? Rather than accept this, some might well think it preferable to follow, in essence, Rhodes (1973), and set up a third class of substitutions (*natural rules*, as Rhodes calls them), which may be regarded as relics of primitive natural processes, subjected to contextual restrictions (some of them non-phonetic) and to ordering constraints, and applying among the learnt rules, from which only their origin distinguishes them. Some of the criteria listed below (one thinks particularly of 5 and 7) may then relate to the distinction between natural and other rules, rather than to that between processes and rules. If a natural process can become a rule in the historical development of a language (Rhodes 1974; Bjarkman 1975), why should the same thing not happen in the ontogenetic development of a language learner? Below, for simplicity, I follow the dichotomy of Bjarkman; but I am by no means convinced that it is preferable to the trichotomy of Rhodes.)

The criteria distinguishing natural processes from learnt rules may be stated as follows; they are paraphrased from Bjarkman (1975). It may be noted that a theory of phonology incorporating these criteria makes a very strong empirical claim about language: the theory will be falsified by a single example of a substitution which has at least one feature which the theory assigns uniquely to natural processes and at least one which the theory assigns uniquely to learnt rules.

(1) Learnt rules never apply to constrain the shape of lexical representations (i.e. as lexical redundancy rules); some natural processes do so apply, others do not.

(2) Learnt rules are capable of being accidentally violated by slips of the tongue; natural processes are not.

(3) Learnt rules may be optional, but this optionality is not related to speed and style of speech; natural processes are often optional with respect to these factors—it is by the application of a greater number of natural processes that fast, 'slurred' speech differs from slow, 'distinct' speech.[42]

(4) Learnt rules can be suspended by conscious effort; thus, in the case of Velar Softening, a facetious form like *electrl*[*k*]*ity* is not at all hard to pronounce. Natural processes are never individually suspendable in this way; in more

---

[42] Bjarkman (1975, 68) says in so many words that learnt rules are *never* optional; but this statement must be interpreted in the light of the distinction he draws between 'optionality' and 'suspendability', and seems to mean much the same as the statement in another version of the paper (Bjarkman 1974, 15) that 'processes are often optionally acquired, relative to style and speed of articulation. Rules apparently never have this property.'

careful speech fewer natural processes will apply, but this difference will affect all natural processes alike, not just one at a time.

(5) Learnt rules are not restricted in the feature substitutions they can make; natural processes can make only 'minimal' substitutions (apparently meaning one feature at a time—though they are also capable of deleting and, presumably, inserting segments).[43]

(6) Learnt rules always have 'abstract and non-phonetic environments requiring reference to, say, some specific morphemes, lexical items, or non-phonetic boundaries' (Bjarkman 1975, 70)—or, we may add, grammatical categories or features, diacritics, etc.; natural processes never have environments of this kind, being automatic and exceptionless.[44]

(7) Learnt rules may or may not have obvious phonetic motivation; natural processes always do.

(8) Learnt rules are always context-sensitive; natural processes may be context-free.[45]

(9) Learnt rules may be crucially ordered; no natural process is ever crucially ordered before any rule or process, except in the case of those natural processes which apply in the lexicon (cf. 1).[46]

(10) Learnt rules are not sychronically productive. This does not mean that, for instance, no new word in English will show the effect of Velar Softening; any neologism in *-icity, -icist*, etc., will do so when it comes into general use. It does mean that no new *morpheme* will show the effect of Velar Softening or any other learnt rule; in other words, learnt rules do not apply to nativize loanwords. Natural processes always can so apply (though, as in other circumstances, their application may be optional depending on style; the more careful the style, the more closely the pronunciation of a recent loanword is likely to approximate its pronunciation in the source language, and if this is adversely evaluated by hearers it will be as pedantry, not as facetiousness).

It does not come within our scope here to describe the proposals made within the general framework of natural phonology about the organization of the phonological component of a grammar. Three features are prominent in many of them:

(a)   A subset of the natural processes determine the segment inventory in the

---

[43] I take it that when Bjarkman says that 'rules make more radical substitutions' he means that they *may* do so.

[44] Is it really the case, as this criterion claims, that every substitution which violates one of the necessary conditions for natural-process status will be found to have non-phonetic elements in its structural description?

[45] Hence rules which are neither context-sensitive nor members of the universal set of natural processes are barred from phonology altogether.

[46] Natural processes, however, which apply both in the lexicon and late in the phonology (as glottal stop deletion does in 'relaxed' speech in English) are subject to this no-ordering condition as regards their phonological function, though exempt from it in their lexical function. The no-ordering condition may also be expressed by saying that the natural processes of a given language constitute (optionality aside) true generalizations about what is and is not pronounceable in that language; if a surface form violates a natural process, it can only be because the process has optionally not applied, not because it has been obligatorily prevented from applying by an ordering constraint.

lexicon; these are sometimes called 'paradigmatic' or 'dominant' natural processes.

(b) Aside from these, all natural processes apply after all learnt rules.

(c) There is a significant level of representation between the lexical and the phonetic, termed the *natural phonemic* level; it is characterized by being the level 'above' which all substitutions remain within the constraints imposed by the dominant natural processes, and 'below' which this ceases to be the case (so that segment types are introduced which are not permitted in the lexicon). All learnt rules apply above the natural phonemic level; it is not clear whether the natural phonemic level falls after the application of some of the non-dominant ('syntagmatic') natural processes as well.

But the basic distinction between learnt rules and natural processes in no way stands or falls with these proposals, or even with the correctness of every one of the criteria listed on pp. 235–6. Natural phonology must be regarded as one of the most important developments in phonological theory, if not the most important, since GP itself.[47]

[47] 'Natural generative phonology', a theory developed over the last few years mainly by T. Vennemann and J. B. Hooper, is primarily interested in the naturalness, not of rules, but of underlying representations, on which it places very tight constraints; one version even denies the existence of underlying representations, regarding all phonological rules as merely well-formedness conditions on surface representations (and therefore requiring them to be true generalizations about surface representations). For the development of the theory see Vennemann (1972a; 1972b; 1973; 1974a; 1974b) and Hooper (1974a; 1974b; 1975; 1977).

⑩ On Phonological Change

10.1 The description of phonological change

Every child, when he learns his first language, creates its grammar—semantics, syntax and phonology—anew; and sometimes the grammar he creates is not identical with the grammar of those from whom he learns the language. Later in life too his vocabulary, his syntax and morphology, his pronunciation, may all undergo changes—changes which must be represented somehow in his grammar, if we define that as the sum of his internalized knowledge about the language. What are the major types of change that can at either of these stages affect the phonological component of the grammar? We are not at present interested in the process(es) by which these changes take place, or in the causes of these processes; these questions we shall take up in 10.2 and 10.3. For the moment we ask only what their effect is on the grammar.

10.1.1 Restructuring

Phonological change can be subdivided into two great classes: change in *underlying representations* and change in *rules*. It is likely that the complete overhaul and *restructuring* of the phonological component, necessitated by changes in underlying representations, is something that only young children are capable of; only they can start with a clean slate. Restructurings take place when previous changes have removed or attenuated the evidence for positing some rule or rules, so that the original underlying representations have become too 'abstract' for the child to recover. Such a restructuring took place (or will take place, according to your point of view on abstractness!) when Vowel Shift ceased (ceases) to be a phonological rule of English—most forms with underlying /e:/ coming to have underlying /i:/, those with /æ:/ changing to /ej/, etc. Restructuring may take many forms, and there is almost no limit to the number of rules it can affect at once or the manner in which it can affect them; for any appreciable 'concretization' of underlying representations is likely to make several rules wholly or partly redundant.

10.1.2 Rule change

10.1.2.1 *Rule addition*
Rule change, on the other hand, has a relatively slight effect on the grammar, but

may affect the output considerably (whereas a major restructuring may well have no effect on the output at all, but only on how the output is arrived at). Its most common form is no doubt *rule addition*: the phonological component comes to contain a rule that it did not contain before. When English vowels shifted, when French final consonants (some of them) deleted, when Mohawk came to epenthesize vowels in the environment consonant———resonant, all these were represented in the grammars of these languages as rule additions.

The natural place where one would expect a rule to be added is at the end of the phonological component, as a process applied to the output of the old grammar to produce a new output. It is a matter of controversy whether a new rule can be 'inserted' at a point where it is ordered before existing rules. King (1973b) flatly denies the possibility, whereas in earlier discussions of phonological change from the GP point of view (e.g. Postal 1968) it had been accepted. At present there is no clear counter-evidence to King's claim that new rules are added 'at the "break" between the phonological rules proper and the phonetic rules', whence they may afterwards—perhaps very soon afterwards—come, by reordering (see below), to apply earlier in the derivation.[1]

10.1.2.2 *Rule loss*

There are other phonological changes which cannot be accounted for as rule additions, at any rate not in any revealing way. Sometimes, for instance, phonological rules disappear from grammars. Kiparsky (1968a) gives the following interesting example.

Most High German dialects have a rule making all word-final obstruents voiceless:

$$[-\text{son}] \rightarrow [-\text{voice}] / \underline{\quad} \# \qquad \textbf{268}$$

This sets up alternations between voiced and voiceless obstruents, notably in stem-final position: so to the nominative form [bunt] 'league' corresponds a genitive [bundəs]. Beside this morpheme there is a non-alternating adjective meaning 'mottled', predicative-adverbial form [bunt], neuter nominative-accusative prenominal form [buntəs]. The motivated underlying forms for the stems are naturally /bund/ 'league' and /bunt/ 'mottled'.

But certain Swiss dialects do not have these alternations. In these dialects morphemes of the /bund/ type show voiced obstruents in all positions, i.e. [bund] as well as [bundəs], while those of the /bunt/ type show voiceless obstruents everywhere as in other dialects. On the face of it, these dialect differences could be accounted for historically in three ways.

---

[1] King provides references to earlier literature. Of later work, note Pyle (1974, 277f), who provides an excellent example of rule insertion which cannot be explained away—but the inserted rule should probably be classified as morpholexical; Chen (1974b, 55–72), whose argument may be interpreted as showing that rule insertion is possible before relatively new rules which are not yet obligatory over the whole lexicon, if such rule insertion can serve to prevent homonymy; D. Cohen (1975), who suggests, without very cogent evidence, that rule insertion occurs always and only where the added rule is required to precede an existing rule by the principle of Proper Inclusion Precedence (p. 186); and Robinson (1976), who provides some evidence for a more general version of King's principle, claiming that 'items newly subject to a rule, by virtue either of rule addition *or of rule generalization*, add it at the end of their phonological derivations'.

First possibility: rule (268) was never added to the grammars of the dialects that now do not show its effects. This possibility is ruled out by the fact that several non-alternating forms, known to have had final voiced obstruents at one stage, now have final voiceless obstruents in these dialects as much as in others. Two forms instanced by Kiparsky are *ab* 'off' and *weg* 'away', where the orthography correctly represents the pronunciation of an earlier period; in both standard German and the non-devoicing Swiss dialects they are pronounced [a:p ve:k]. It is evident that (268) must have applied in the non-devoicing dialects at some stage.

Second possibility: at some stage after the introduction of rule (268), the non-devoicing dialects added another rule voicing final consonants. This possibility is even less satisfactory than the first: it makes incorrect predictions not only for the problem forms but also for *bunt* 'mottled' and other forms which ended in a voiceless consonant at all material times.

Third possibility: rule (268) was once present in the grammars of these dialects and was then lost; or, equivalently (but pointlessly), we could claim that a rule was added before (268) making every form in the language an exception to it. In either case the underlying voiced obstruents of relevant forms would come to the surface again, *except* where the underlying representation had changed—as for *ab* and *weg* it evidently had.

It should be observed that Kiparsky (1971) claims that rules which constitute true surface generalizations (as the devoicing rule does in those German dialects which have it) cannot be lost. If this is correct, the non-devoicing dialects must somehow have acquired new forms with final voiced obstruents which brought it about that the devoicing rule no longer expressed a true surface generalization. This apparently happened through the addition of a rule of final schwa deletion whereby [bundə], for example, became [bund] (Stampe 1969). This 'opacification' of existing rules through the addition of new ones is one of the most typical features of phonological change; it may in the end make a phonetic rule phonological, or a phonological rule morphological (cf. J. W. Harris 1973a), or cause the 'rule inversion' and restructuring of underlying forms discussed by Vennemann (1972b).

10.1.2.3 *Simplification*

Rule loss, then, is a possible kind of phonological change.[2] Another kind is *simplification*,[3] which, following Kiparsky, we may divide into two subclasses.

In the first type of simplification, a rule previously applying to a restricted class of segments or in a restricted environment loses some or all of the restrictions so that it comes to apply more generally. This corresponds to what in traditional historical linguistics is known as analogical extension.

Quite generally, for example, in English, the underlying clusters /mb ng/[4] in

---

[2] On rule loss see further Darden (1970; 1971a) and D. G. Miller (1973a).

[3] Rule *complication* can also occur, generally as an indirect result of other changes (cf. Bach and Harms 1972); it is not a form of primary phonological change except where, as sometimes happens, a more complex rule is also more natural.

[4] The evidence for positing underlying /mb/ is rather shaky; but even if in English [m] is in fact never underlain by /mb/, (269) would still be the best formulation of the post-nasal deletion rule for

word-final position are pronounced [m ŋ], as in *climb, long* (contrast *clamber, longer*). Most English dialects thus have a rule like (269).

$$\begin{bmatrix} -\text{continuant} \\ +\text{voice} \end{bmatrix} \rightarrow \theta \;/\; \begin{bmatrix} +\text{cons} \\ +\text{son} \\ -\text{coronal} \end{bmatrix} \underline{\qquad} \# \qquad\qquad \textbf{269}$$

In some dialects, however, notably in the southern United States, underlying /nd ld/ are simplified in the same way. The generalization would appear to be that in these dialects the rule applies to voiced stops after any sonorant consonant except /r/: that is, after those sonorant consonants which have a central closure (cf. p. 103):

$$\begin{bmatrix} -\text{continuant} \\ +\text{voice} \end{bmatrix} \rightarrow \theta \;/\; \begin{bmatrix} +\text{sonorant} \\ +\text{central closure} \end{bmatrix} \underline{\qquad} \# \qquad\qquad \textbf{270}$$

Rule (270) is more general than (269); and it is also simpler both in a formal sense and, one intuitively feels, in a real sense.[5]

Now assuming, as must surely be the case, that the dialects which now have rule (270) originally had rule (269), can the change be accounted for as rule addition? In theory it can. We could say that these dialects added (270) as a new rule and that consequently (269) became vacuous and was lost. Provided that rule loss is admitted as possible, any apparent case of rule generalization can be accounted for in this way; but to do so is to claim that the formal resemblance between the new and the old rule is a coincidence—or, to put it otherwise, that the existence in the grammar of (269) had nothing to do with the fact that it was (270) and not some other rule that was added. It is far more satisfactory to view the change as a straight simplification, (269) being directly replaced by its more general form (270).[6]

So far the first variety of simplification, which corresponds to the traditional category of analogical extension. The second variety of simplification affects not, or not only, the domain of the rule, but its application; it consists of, or includes, a change in the output description of the rule. The most typical and interesting cases are those where a rule which previously had different effects in different environments comes to have the same effect in all cases. Kiparsky sees this as corresponding to what is traditionally known as analogical 'levelling'; but the correspondence is not particularly close, since analogical levelling normally involves the disappearance or restriction of one or more of a number of alternating allomorphs, whereas the variety of rule simplification we are considering does not eliminate alternations except in the extreme case where it amounts to rule loss (where the uniform effect of the simplified rule is a null effect).

---

mainstream English, since it would be pointless to complicate the rule to prevent it from applying to /mb/ if /mb/ is in any case never in the right environment for it to apply.

[5] Note that the clusters /lb lm/, to which (270) would apply, are simplified by earlier rules whose effect is to delete the first rather than the second consonant; these rules apply in all dialects.

[6] The formal relationship between the two rules may be even closer if, as I suspect, /r/ in American (and some other) dialects of English is non-consonantal; GP analyses have always treated it as consonantal, yet it has no 'close constriction ... in the upper part of the vocal tract' (pp. 98–9). If /r/ is non-consonantal, the left-hand environment of (270) becomes [+cons, +son]—exactly that of (269) with the omission of the requirement of non-coronality.

Kiparsky's example for this type of simplification comes from umlaut in Germanic, in particular High German. In Old High German, the effect of umlaut was to front all vowels before /i/ in the next syllable; in general, other features of the vowels were not affected, but underlying /a/ had [e], not [æ], as its umlauted counterpart, although the counterpart of /a:/ was [æ]. At this stage, then, the umlaut rule was:

$$
\begin{bmatrix} V \\ \langle -\text{long} \rangle \\ \langle 1\,\text{height} \rangle \end{bmatrix} \rightarrow \begin{bmatrix} -\text{back} \\ \langle 2\text{height} \rangle \end{bmatrix} / \underline{\quad} C_0 i \qquad\qquad 271
$$

In standard German this is still the form of the rule, except that its environment is now morphological instead of phonological. But in many modern dialects the umlauted counterpart of /a/ is [æ]. This is not due to a general lowering of /e/: no such lowering has taken place. Nor does it reflect an older situation than that represented by (271): for even in these dialects, forms historically umlauted but synchronically non-alternating exhibit [e], showing that these dialects once had a rule like (271), which has since been simplified (simplified, that is, so far as its input and output descriptions are concerned) to (272):

$$
V \rightarrow [-\text{back}] / \text{ in certain contexts} \qquad\qquad 272
$$

10.1.2.4 *Reordering*

The last major type of phonological rule change affects not the form of rules but their ordering. We have seen in Chapters Six and Seven that closely related dialects often contain the same rules applying in different orders: generally the contrast is between a dialect in which, under the partial ordering hypothesis (pp. 176–180), no extrinsic ordering constraint needs to be stated, and one which does require such a constraint. The dialectological evidence itself creates a presumption that an alteration in the order in which rules apply—which will usually mean the addition or the loss of an extrinsic ordering constraint—is a possible linguistic change; and of this there is abundant confirmatory evidence.

A case of the loss of an ordering constraint may perhaps be cited as an illustration. As far back as we know, ancient Greek had a rule reducing underlying /s/ to an aspirate:

FRICATIVE WEAKENING   273

$$
\begin{bmatrix} -\text{sonorant} \\ +\text{continuant} \end{bmatrix} \rightarrow h / \begin{Bmatrix} \# \\ V \end{Bmatrix} \underline{\quad} V
$$

A rule of later origin (so much later that several dialects never acquired it) created new instances of intervocalic [s] by the simplification of /ns/ clusters, some underlying, some themselves derived from more complex underlying clusters:

NASAL DELETION[7]   274

$$
\begin{array}{ccc}
V & [+\text{nas}] & \begin{bmatrix} -\text{son} \\ +\text{cont} \end{bmatrix} \\
\downarrow & \downarrow & \\
[+\text{long}] & \emptyset &
\end{array}
$$

[7] This is the form the rule takes in most of the dialects in which it is found; in others /Vns/ surfaced as [Vjs], e.g. [pajsa] 'all'.

In most dialects these rules continued to apply[8] in the order in which they had entered the language, which required a constraint that nasal deletion blocked subsequent application of fricative weakening; thus underlying /pant +ja/ 'all (nominative singular feminine)' had the following derivation:

		275
	/pant+ja	
by glide assimilation	pantsa	
by cluster simplification	pansa	
by nasal deletion	[pa:sa]	

to which fricative weakening could not apply.

But in three well-separated areas[9] we find [pa:ha] and similar forms, indicating clearly that in the dialects of these areas fricative weakening was applying to the output of nasal deletion, i.e. that they had lost the blockage constraint. In the same set of dialects fricative weakening also applies to many other forms which in most dialects do not undergo it; that is, *several* ordering restrictions applying to this rule have been dropped. It is evident that in some circumstances, at least, the loss of an ordering constraint must be an extremely natural form of phonological change, if it can thus occur in much the same way in three dialect groups independently.

10.1.3 Factors determining the direction of rule change

Various attempts have been made to determine under what circumstances rule reordering is a natural change and under what circumstances not. The first proposal, by Kiparsky (1968a), may most simply be expressed in the following form:

It is natural for ordering constraints to be lost; it is not natural for them to   276 be added.

This formulation is essentially due to Anderson (1969); Kiparsky's own formulation, in terms of the linear ordering hypothesis, is necessarily of a functional kind ('Rules tend to shift into that order which allows their fullest utilization in the grammar'). In this connection Kiparsky introduced the now popular terms *feeding* and *bleeding* order. A rule *feeds* another if, like nasal deletion in relation to fricative weakening in the dialects listed in note 9, it creates representations to which the other can apply; an ordering constraint which prevents feeding imposes a *counterfeeding* order on the rules concerned (thus the order fricative weakening—nasal deletion is counterfeeding). A rule *bleeds* another if, like vowel deletion in relation to epenthesis in Menomini (Chapter Seven, p. 178), it removes representations to which the other could have applied; if the precedence constraint which gives rise to bleeding is lost, the resulting relationship between the two rules is *counterbleeding*. For a full typology of rule

---

[8] So long as fricative weakening remained a phonological rule; it is not unlikely that in many of the dialects in which reordering did not take place, a restructuring eventually removed fricative weakening from the grammar, or at least relegated it to the status of a morpholexical rule.
[9] In the (first millennium B.C.) dialects of Laconia and Argolis, on the east side of the Peloponnese peninsula; of Elis, in its north-western corner; and of Cyprus.

relationships along these lines see Newton (1971)—to whom the useful terms 'counterfeeding' and 'counterbleeding' are due—or Koutsoudas *et al.* (1974).

In the form (276) Kiparsky's principle has the apparent advantage of making the permitted kinds of reorderings simplifications in an obvious sense, since they remove statements from the grammar. It may be asked how, given (276), new ordering constraints can ever get into the grammar: will not all extrinsic ordering in the long run disappear? The answer is that new ordering constraints enter the grammar as accidental by-products of changes of quite different kinds. Rule additions, for instance, can give rise to new blockage constraints: added rules typically apply, as we have seen, after all other phonological rules, and even if an added rule creates representations to which an existing phonological rule might apply, the existing rule normally will not apply to these representations. Restructurings too may create new ordering constraints. All (276) claims is that the addition of an ordering constraint is not a natural form of *primary* linguistic change.

However, (276) appears to be inadequate on empirical gounds. One of the earliest counter-examples to be discovered to the principle comes from two varieties of Canadian English (King, 1968; 1972).[10] Both dialects appear to have, among other rules, the following two:

CENTRALIZATION   277

$$a \rightarrow \wedge / \underline{\qquad} \begin{bmatrix} -\text{cons} \\ -\text{syll} \end{bmatrix} [-\text{voice}]$$

T-VOICING   278

$$t \rightarrow [+\text{voice}] / \begin{bmatrix} V \\ +\text{stress} \end{bmatrix} (\begin{bmatrix} -\text{cons} \\ -\text{syll} \end{bmatrix}) \underline{\qquad} V$$

Unconstrained application of (277) and (278) to a form such as /tajprajtr/ 'typewriter' yields (after resonant syllabification) [tʌjprʌjtǝr]. This output is found in one of the two dialects with which we are concerned, and is fairly certainly to be accounted for, in the historical sense, by the supposition that *t*-voicing was added to a grammar which already contained centralization, rather than by the reordering of two rules originally added in the opposite order; the evidence for this comes from the dialectal distribution of the two rules, which strongly suggests that centralization predates, while *t*-voicing postdates (and in Canada very much postdates), the main period of the establishment of substantial English-speaking populations in North America.

If the historical evidence is correctly interpreted, then according to (276) it should not have been possible for any dialect to alter its grammar by imposing the constraint that *t*-voicing has precedence over centralization, a constraint that would result in *typewriter* being pronounced [tʌjprajtǝr]; and the pronunciation [tʌjprajtǝr] should not be found at all except in such dialects as have never had, or have lost, the rule of centralization. Yet this is the pronunciation of *typewriter* in

---

[10] The data are due to Joos (1942); the rules (not exactly in the form given here) to Halle (1962).

the second of our two varieties of Canadian English (and words of analogous form are analogously pronounced); and that though in this dialect the rule of centralization is in full force (e.g. [rʌjt] 'write' as in the first dialect). The inference seems inevitable that in the second dialect a rule reordering has occurred of a type not permitted by (276). In the terminology of p. 243, a counterbleeding relationship has become a bleeding one.[11]

Recent work has identified three major factors influencing the direction of rule reordering (and, in all probability, exercising an important directive influence on phonological change generally). The factors do not seem to form a hierarchy: it does not appear that any one of them universally outweighs any other.

10.1.3.1 *Phonetic transparency*
Very roughly speaking, the easier it is to infer from surface phonetic representations the existence of a phonological rule, the more *transparent* the rule is said to be. A rule can be non-transparent (*opaque*) phonetically in one of three ways (Kiparsky 1971; 1973a):

If the rule does not represent a true surface generalization, i.e. if there are **279a** surface forms which meet its input and environment descriptions but not its output description;

If, in some derivations in which the rule has applied, the environmental **b** conditions which made its application possible are no longer evident on the surface;

If there are surface forms which meet the input, output, and environment **c** descriptions of the rule, and hence 'look as though' they have been derived by the rule, but in whose derivation the rule has in fact played no part.

In those Ancient Greek dialects that had surface forms such as [pa:sa], Fricative Weakening (273), if a phonological rule at all, was opaque in sense (a); the reorderings in Laconian and other dialects either eliminated or substantially reduced this opacity. In the Canadian English dialect in which *typewriter* is pronounced [tʌjprʌjtər], Centralization (277) is opaque in sense (b), for in this dialect centralized vowels can occur before a consonant which on the surface is *voiced*, whereas (277) provides for vowels to be centralized before a *voiceless* consonant; in the [tʌjprajtər] dialect this opacity is eliminated. Opacity of type (c) is characteristic of neutralization rules, in a broad sense of that term: [ná:sɪsɪzəm] *narcissism* 'looks as though' it has undergone Velar Softening (cf. *criticism*, etc.), but has not (cf. *Narcissus*, *narcissoid*).[12]

In each of these senses of opacity, transparent rules, other things being equal, are more natural than opaque rules; and rules tend, other things being equal, to shift into that order which maximizes their joint transparency.[13] The Canadian

---

[11] This particular counter-example has been shown by Hogg (1976) to be suspect, since there *may* have been restructuring of underlying forms in the second dialect; it is, however, not isolated.

[12] Not in the dictionaries; but a psychologist might use it any day as a neologism, perhaps not even realizing it was one (cf. e.g. *schizoid*), and he certainly wouldn't expect its final syllable to be pronounced [-kojd].

[13] Kisseberth (1973a) finds that where, of two rule orderings, one would maximize transparency of type (a) and the other would maximize transparency of type (b) or (c), it is the former ordering that is more natural; blatant surface violations are less easily tolerated than is surface unclarity as to whether a rule has applied or not.

English example shows that the naturalness of increasing transparency can override the unnaturalness of adding a new ordering constraint.

10.1.3.2 *Minimization of Allomorphy*

It has long been recognized that one of the basic factors in linguistic change is a drive towards uniformity of morpheme realization, towards an ideal situation where each morpheme has one and only one surface phonetic form—an ideal never attained, because this factor is never the only one at work: the effect of this drive has usually been known as 'analogical levelling'. It is to be expected that this will be a factor in determining favoured directions for rule reordering, and this indeed proves to be the case. The effect is seen most strongly within inflectional paradigms, and for this reason the principle has sometimes been termed *paradigm regularity*. It was proposed as a principle for rule reordering by Kiparsky (1971).

King (1972) gives an example of a reordering determined by paradigm regularity. Middle High German had at one stage the following two rules:

SYNCOPE   **280**

$$
\begin{bmatrix} e \\ -\text{stress} \end{bmatrix} \rightarrow \emptyset \; / \; \left\{ \begin{array}{cc} h \text{——} & \begin{bmatrix} -\text{voice} \\ +\text{coronal} \end{bmatrix} \\ [+\text{nasal}] \text{——} & t \end{array} \right\}
$$

LENGTH DETERMINATION   **281**

$$
V \rightarrow \begin{cases} [+\text{long}] \; / \text{——} \quad [\text{syllable boundary}] \\ [-\text{long}] \; / \text{——} \; CX \; [\text{syllable boundary}] \end{cases}
$$

This was the order in which the rules entered the language, and it was also, for some time, the order in which they applied. It was a transparent order: length determination created no surface violations of syncope, nor consonant sequences that 'looked as though' derived by syncope, nor did it destroy the consonantal environment that had conditioned syncope. But it gave rise to paradigm irregularity as some verbal roots came to have long or short vowels on the surface according as they had or had not undergone syncope:

	/won + e/	/won + e + t/	**282**
	'I dwell'	'he dwells'	
by syncope	——	won + t	
by length			
determination	[woːne]	[wont]	

And subsequently the two rules were reordered, length determination now being blocked from applying to the output of syncope. This made length determination opaque in the worst sense, sense (279a) (cf. note 13); but it removed the paradigm irregularity:[14]

[14] It is not clear what principle (276) would say about this reordering. If we suppose that the rule of length determination *taken as a whole* is non-iterative—i.e. that the length of a given vowel can only be determined once by the rule—then the change from derivation (282) to (283) represents the loss of an ordering constraint—a change from bleeding to counter-bleeding. If, however, we suppose that, except as prevented by ordering constraints, either subrule of length determination applies whenever

	/won+e/	/won+e+t/	**283**
by length determination	wo:n+e	wo:n+e+t	
by syncope	[wo:ne]	[wo:nt]	

It cannot, however, be concluded from this that paradigm regularity overrides transparency where they conflict. In the Canadian English example discussed above (pp. 244–5), the innovating dialect accepted paradigm irregularity—[rʌjt] 'write' but [rajtɪŋ] 'writing'—for the sake of the transparency of Centralization.[15]

10.1.3.3 *Maintenance of Contrast*

If language 'prefers' that identical grammatical/semantic units should have identical phonetic realizations (minimization of allomorphy), it also 'prefers' that distinct grammatical/semantic units should have distinct phonetic realizations. The notion has been familiar, as 'avoidance of homonymy', since the investigations of Gilliéron early in this century (which were concerned mainly with the field of vocabulary); it is equally applicable to phonology. It can be seen at work most clearly in languages where the incidence of homonymy is in any case high and but for rule reordering would be even higher, such as those of China.

Chen (1974b; cf. Chen 1976, 220–5) gives a spectacular example. Between the years 800 and 1200 approximately (which mostly falls within the period known as that of Late Middle Chinese) Chinese underwent a series of vowel changes which may be collectively termed *i*-umlaut. From documentary evidence and from the general principles governing such movements within vowel space, it can be established with a high degree of confidence that the sequence of these changes was as given below.

$$ɑ \rightarrow a \qquad \qquad \textbf{284}$$

$$a \rightarrow ia \, / \begin{bmatrix} C \\ +\,back \end{bmatrix} \!\!\!-\!\!\!- X \qquad \textbf{285}$$
$$(\text{where } X \neq i)$$

$$ia \rightarrow ie \, / \, \underline{\qquad} (i) \, \# \qquad \textbf{286}$$

$$ie \rightarrow i \, / \, \underline{\qquad\quad} i \qquad \textbf{287}$$

---

its structural description is met, then the change represents the *addition* of an ordering constraint ('syncope blocks subsequent application of length determination') and is analogous to, though it cannot be identified with, a change from feeding to counter-feeding.

[15] Nor is the counter-example isolated: cf. King (1973b), who concludes that 'there may ... be competition between the two principles with factors presently unknown that contribute to deciding the outcome.'

A variant of the principle of minimization of allomorphy is discussed by Comrie (ms.), who shows that an otherwise general alternation may be levelled in forms where the 'phonetic distance' between the alternants is greater than normal for that alternation: thus all the lexical exceptions to soft mutation in Welsh are words beginning with /g/, and /g/ happens to be the only one of the stops subject to soft mutation which the rule, when it does apply, deletes altogether (whereas other voiced stops become voiced fricatives, and voiceless stops become voiced stops).

$$i \rightarrow \left\{ \begin{array}{l} \ddot{\imath} / \begin{bmatrix} +\text{coronal} \\ +\text{strident} \end{bmatrix} \text{-----} \# \\ i / [\,+\text{labial}\,] \text{-----} \# \end{array} \right\}$$ **288**

To apply the rules in the order in which they came into the language is equivalent to applying them freely: the relationship is a feeding one, and no extrinsic constraints are required. This order of application is also a very transparent one—completely transparent in the most important sense, that of (279a). It neither promotes nor hinders paradigm regularity, because Chinese has to all intents and purposes no paradigms. And yet in the dialect ancestral to present-day standard Mandarin the rules were reordered. The new order was almost the reverse of the old: (288 286 287 285 284). Three of the four feeding relationships had become counterfeeding, and there was a high degree of opacity, with (284) creating instances of [a] that did not undergo (285) though in the appropriate environment to do so, and similarly (285) creating instances of [ia] that did not undergo (286) though in the appropriate environment to do so. What could have motivated the reordering?

Chinese, as has been noted, is notoriously a language with a high degree of homonymy: at a rough estimate, and ignoring all lexical items outside the 'core' vocabulary, there were over three times as many distinct lexical items in Late Middle Chinese as there were distinct phonetic shapes for them,[16] and over four times as many in present-day Mandarin. And had the original order of application of (284–288) been maintained, the degree of homonymy (which has, it will be noted, increased in any case over the intervening centuries) would have increased further still. In particular, the seven distinct eighth-century syllable-final sequences /ɑ a ia ɑi ai iai i/ would have been reduced to four if preceded by a dental sibilant, and to three if preceded by a velar or guttural; whereas in actual fact modern Mandarin retains six contrasting sequences in the former environment and five in the latter. The reordering has also made possible the retention of three further pairwise contrasts in other environments, which under the original order would have suffered merger. Avoidance of homonymy, maintenance of contrast, or as one is very tempted to call it *semantic transparency*[17] has overridden both the principle of non-addition of ordering constraints and the principle of phonetic transparency.[18]

In discussing rule reordering we have trespassed somewhat into the province of 10.3 below, largely because it is connection with rule reordering that several of the major determining factors behind phonological change have been most clearly discussed in the GP framework. For the purpose of the present section let us merely note that rule reordering is a possible form of phonological change; that on a partial ordering hypothesis it will appear now as the loss of an ordering constraint, now as the addition of a constraint, now, perhaps, as the replacement of one constraint by another; and that while we can see several factors which make

---

[16] Phonetic shapes distinguished only by tone are, of course, treated as distinct in this calculation.
[17] The term is due to Kisseberth (1973a); it has not yet caught on, but it is very felicitous.
[18] But it does not universally override these principles: note that (286) and (287) have retained their original order in the ancestor of present-day Mandarin, even though reordering would have resulted in less homonymy.

some logically possible reorderings natural and others unnatural, it is at present for the most part impossible to say why, in a particular case, one factor or group of factors has prevailed over another to bring about, or to prevent, a reordering.[19]

10.2 The process of phonological change

In the previous section we discussed and classified types of phonological changes, treating them all the time virtually as if they were instantaneous events. So, indeed, they seem sometimes to have been regarded in early GP writings on the subject. This view is now generally recognized to be untenable. It is, for one thing, based on Chomsky's conscious fiction (1965b) of 'an ideal speaker-listener, in a completely homogeneous speech-community': a notion valuable for certain purposes, but not a useful basis for a study of historical events, which happen to real people, among whom 'no language community is homogeneous' (Hoenigswald 1963, 39). Again, if all phonological changes are instantaneous, it should never be the case that at a given stage in the history of a language a phonological change is *in progress*: it could only be either not yet begun or already completed. Yet it is often possible, in languages whose histories are even fairly well documented, to pick out three *états de langue* in temporal sequence, of which the second shows some phonological change compared with the first, while in the third stage what is clearly the same change has been carried further, or applies in additional contexts, or applies to more lexical items, etc. This has been known for a long time. Thus (to paraphrase Jakobson 1929, 49) in the history of Russian certain extra-short high vowels, known as 'weak jers', have been lost; and it appears that this loss occurred earliest in such words as were particularly frequent in allegro speech. Evidently jer loss began as a fast-speech rule and spread later to other styles; while it was still a fast-speech rule, the only lexical items to show its effects quite generally (not only in speech but even in writing) will have been those that were common in fast speech; and such the documentary evidence indicates to have been the case. Jakobson, in noting the facts, does not suggest he is saying anything new; the history of almost any language could probably furnish examples. It is true that perhaps none of these examples is literally incapable of being accounted for by a theory of instantaneous change; what has traditionally been regarded as a single change taking place over a period can always be viewed instead as a succession of lesser changes taking place instantaneously. In one sense GP *must* so regard it; for a phonological grammar consists of discrete units (features and their specifications, and the other elements

[19] Most of the major papers on rule reordering have already been referred to in text or notes. See also Kisseberth (1972b), on the naturalness of bleeding relationships; Wilkinson (1974), who finds that three Telugu rules apply to nouns in a different order from that in which they apply to verbs, because if they applied in the same order there would be excessive homonymy among nouns; and Laferriere (1975), who argues that reordering tends to create allomorphy where it is 'functional' (i.e. corresponds to 'major grammatical category divisions') and to eliminate it elsewhere, and implies that there is no independent principle of transparency. Halle and Keyser (1971, 131) seem to imply yet another motivation for reordering, viz. to create a situation where similar rules have identical ordering relations so that they can be collapsed into a schema; but King (1973b) has argued that the motivation for reordering in the case in question was regularization of the position of stress (a variant of the principle of minimization of allomorphy).

that go to make up phonological rules), and any change in such a grammar can only be discontinuous (except perhaps in the phonetic detail rules). But we must not let this attitude lead us to deny the reality of the large-scale changes: jer loss in Russian was none the less a single historical process because it did not take place all at once. To the question whether phonological change is sudden or gradual, the only possible answer is 'Both'. As change in discrete grammars, it is necessarily discontinuous and sudden. But there are at least three senses in which it can be meaningfully termed gradual.

10.2.1 The continuity of sound-change

Above, we entered a caveat to the statement that phonological grammar change was necessarily discontinuous 'except perhaps in the phonetic detail rules'. These rules do not restrict themselves to the very limited number of specifications for each feature allowed to morphophonemic rules: they determine (aside from free variation) a precise pronunciation. It has usually been supposed in GP, explicitly or tacitly, that even at the phonetic level there is a universal, finite and not very high limit on the number of specifications for each feature (positions along each phonic axis); but I know of no empirical evidence supporting this position, and it may well be that detail rules, for some features at least, do not select one of a number of discrete regions along an axis, but instruct the articulatory apparatus to aim at a particular target-point on a continuum. If so, a possible form of linguistic change would be a shifting of this target-point, which might be very finely adjustable; and detail-rule change would then correspond in its effects, though not in its mechanism, to the neo-neogrammarian notion of sound-change as interpreted by Hockett (1958; 1965), in which the articulatory loci of allophones for a given speaker wander about according to his auditory experience of realizations of these allophones in his own and others' utterances. What matters for us at present is not how or why articulatory 'fine-tuning' comes to pass, but that it is not inconsistent with GP to suppose that it *can* come to pass.

Recent work has reduced a fair amount of evidence that articulatory fine-tuning is a genuine phenomenon. Thus Labov (see Labov 1972b), investigating vowels in New York English, found that for each individual within a single speech community, the relative heights of two long mid vowels, which he symbolized as /eh/ and /oh/, 'narrowly determined' the position in vowel space of the long low vowel /ah/: vowel space appeared to be being treated as a continuum. with the positions of various contrasting vowels within it being interdependent and finely adjusted. It was entirely reasonable for Weinreich *et al.* (1968) to deduce from evidence of this kind that 'these quantitative relationships imply the *steady movement* [emphasis mine] of a vowel along one dimension in coordination with other vowels moving along other dimensions.' Nothing seems to be gained by talking about discrete coefficients of height or backness, rather than about the actual positions of vowels in articulatory space or of their formants in acoustic space.

What starts as articulatory fine-tuning, affecting only phonetic detail rules, may sooner or later affect phonological rules as well, if a target-point shifts so far that it crosses or approaches the boundary between categorially distinct specifications for some feature—e.g. from [−long] to [+long], or from velar to palatal. The result may be classifiable as a rule addition, a simplification or even (especially if a contrast is obliterated) a restructuring.

While, however, articulatory fine-tuning almost certainly exists, it seems unlikely that *all*-phonological change takes place in this way, even if we disregard the so-called 'minor sound change processes' such as metathesis, haplology, and assimilation/dissimilation of non-adjacent consonants, which it is hard to conceive of as coming about by articulatory fine-tuning. There is considerable evidence for the existence of a very different kind of phonological change, exhibiting a very different kind of gradualness; and to this we must now turn.

10.2.2 Lexical diffusion

Sound-change of the classic type, brought about by articulatory fine-tuning, is 'lexically abrupt but phonetically gradual':[20] it affects all segment types with a given set of feature specifications in a given phonetic environment, regardless of lexical or grammatical factors, but until phonologized it proceeds by insensible stages. One might alternatively conceive of a form of phonological change that was 'lexically gradual but phonetically abrupt': where a feature value changed directly from − to + , from [2height] to [3height], etc., without intermediate stages, but where this change might percolate gradually through the lexicon, now infecting one lexical item, now another, perhaps taking centuries to become complete, perhaps never becoming complete but losing impetus and leaving a scattering of lexical items as unaltered 'residues', perhaps losing impetus at a much earlier stage so that only a few lexical items are affected by the change—in which case the handbooks will call the change 'sporadic'.

The idea is not a new one. Jer loss in Russian non-allegro speech is presented by Jakobson (see p. 249) as having taken place in a fashion which, if it is not explicitly said to be lexically gradual, is certainly lexically staged. Fries and Pike (1949, 41) suggest that

> in the process of change from one phonemic system to a different phonemic system of the same language, there may be a time during which parts of the two systems exist simultaneously and in conflict within the speech of single individuals. The incoming contrasts or sounds may be already present, but not completely extended throughout all the words of the language.

And Malkiel's formidably detailed word-by-word, morpheme-by-morpheme investigations into the history of the Romance languages lead him (Malkiel 1967) to assume that phonological change is lexically gradual without even thinking the matter worthy of discussion, and to ask:

> Does it not stand to reason that [the] preliminary scouting and groping—as speakers unconsciously feel their way towards a possible break-through which, once it is a *fait accompli*, linguists will class as sound-shift,—should be directed towards points of least resistance? These are just such points, in the edifice of

[20] My recollection is that I first heard this phrase and its antithesis, or something like them, in a seminar talk by W. S-Y. Wang.

language, as might cause the existing structure to yield through pressure independently applied by miscellaneous processes, such as metathesis, dissimilation, lexical or affixal analogy, etc.

Malkiel here not only takes lexical gradualness for granted, but also—despite his use of the phrase 'stand to reason'—puts up a highly plausible empirical hypothesis about what kind of lexical items will be the first to be affected by an incipient change. He suggests that a shift [ð] → [r] may be incipient in present-day Spanish; as yet it is detectable only as a 'sporadic' change affecting a scattering of lexical items, in most of which it can be accounted for by the 'miscellaneous' processes mentioned by Malkiel, but the claim is—and only the future can bear it out—that what is going on is not just a few odd cases of dissimilation, analogy, etc., but the beginnings of a sound-shift.[21]

If some phonological changes proceed by lexical diffusion, situations can arise which are impossible with lexically abrupt sound-change. For example, if two incompatible changes are spreading across the lexicon at the same time, we may, after the event, find some lexical items showing the effect of one of these changes, others of the other, quite unsystematically. Thus corresponding to Middle Chinese [-ai], present-day Peking Chinese has [-a] in some lexical items, [-ai] in others, apparently at random. There is no case for explaining the data by analogical effects, and no positive evidence for dialect borrowing; we are witnessing the effects of 'competition' between two sound-shifts that were at one time spreading across the lexicon of Middle Chinese:

$$- ai \rightarrow \ -a \qquad\qquad \textbf{289a}$$

$$- ai \rightarrow \ - aei \qquad\qquad \textbf{b}$$

Or it may be that (289a) ceased to be active before it had affected the whole lexicon, and that (289b), coming later, could only attack those lexical items which had not undergone (289a). A celebrated problem in the history of pre-Ancient Greek may just possibly have a similar explanation: corresponding to proto-Indo-European /j/ we find in some Greek words [h], in others [dz],[22] again apparently at random. It could be that a shift [j] → [ĵ] → [dz] had begun to affect some lexical items at a very early period, but had petered out leaving a majority of relevant lexical items unshifted; the later shift [j] → [ç] → [h] will then have applied to such lexical items as had not undergone the earlier shift. Note that this explanation requires us to assume lexical diffusion only for the earlier shift; the later one may have proceeded in the same way, or may have been due to articulatory fine-tuning.

A slightly more complex situation appears in another Chinese example. One of the changes that have supervened between Middle Chinese and present-day Peking Chinese is the monophthongization of certain diphthongs whose first element was in Middle Chinese distinctively short:

$$ăi \rightarrow ĕ \quad ĕi \rightarrow ĕ \quad ău \rightarrow ŏ \qquad\qquad \textbf{290}$$

---

[21] Many other scholars have held similar points of view on what has since been termed lexical diffusion. See for instance Sapir (1921, 180); Martinet (1955, 187); Posner (1961), who tentatively put forward a suggestion similar to Malkiel's; Sommerfelt (1962, 75); and Hoenigswald (1964, 207).
[22] Whence in some dialects, such as Attic, [zd], and from the 3rd c. B.C. [zz].

Another was a neutralization whereby the distinctive feature of shortness vanished from the language: [ă] merged with [a], [ĕ] with [e], and so forth. It would appear that at one stage both changes were spreading across the lexicon from different starting-points, and accordingly some lexical items underwent (290) before being affected by neutralization, while others underwent neutralization first. The two orderings would result in different Modern Peking reflexes:

291a	-ăi	**b**	-ăi
by monophthongization	-ĕ	by neutralization	[-ai]
by neutralization	-c	(SD of monophthongization	
by a later process	[-ɤ]	no longer met)	

And in fact, in Modern Pekingese, both reflexes are found in different lexical items, and there are also some items in which there is free variation between them.

As yet the study of the lexical diffusion of phonological change is still in its infancy.[23] One of its most important tasks in the future will be to determine whether, among the main forms of phonological change (roughly classifiable as vowel shifts, assimilations, syllable-structure simplifications, stress shifts, etc.), there are some which are never implemented by lexical diffusion and/or some which invariably involve lexical diffusion: perhaps it will ultimately be possible to tell in all cases, merely from the end-effect of a phonological change, whether it was a 'phonetic' change, acting on the output of the grammar through articulatory fine-tuning, or a strictly 'phonological' change acting directly on the grammar itself—the phonological rules and perhapd even the underlying representations—and working by lexical diffusion. This is not very likely; but that such a dichotomy can be meaningfully made, even if it proves to be not always possible to assign any given change to one or other of its wings, that is highly likely.

10.2.3 Social spread

Typically divisions or gradations within a community, whether of class, sex, race, locality, or anything else which is socially important (in many periods and places, religion; in others, political orientation; in contemporary American cities, membership of one or another street gang), are accompanied by linguistic differentiae more or less profound, and more or less within the speakers' awareness. Clearly this fact is potentially relevant to linguistic change—not so much to its initiation as to its spread and establishment. When a speaker first becomes aware of an innovation, it is as something used by other people. Whether and to what extent he adopts the innovation may well be thought likely to depend on his attitude to those other people. Are they members of his own group? Then he may adopt the innovation quickly as a sign of group solidarity, particularly if the group is one which regards itself as downtrodden. Are they members of a

[23] But it possesses a considerable literature, from which the Chinese examples in the text have been culled. See especially Wang (1969); Wang and Cheng (1970); Chen and Hsieh (1971); Chen (1972); and Chen and Wang (1975), according to whom phenomena analogous to lexical diffusion are to be found in infant phonology.

group to which he would like to belong but doesn't? Then he may imitate them or even over-imitate them, falling into hypercorrectness: this can of course happen whether the 'prestige' form is innovative or not (e.g. when a speaker who normally pronounces *heart* as [aːt] hypercorrects by pronouncing *art* as [haːt]) and may thus itself create new innovations. Are the innovators members of a group towards which the speaker's own group is hostile, or which they regard (whether or not they would admit it) as inferior? Then he will do his best to avoid the innovation, and, if he is a prescriptive grammarian, stigmatize it as wrong; though he may well himself use much of the time when he is not being self-conscious, and his children are even more likely to (for the strongest linguistic influence on children is other children, as anyone who lives in a city with a substantial immigrant population can verify for himself).

The more complex the society, the greater the variety of fates that can befall an innovation; and the subject here being briefly touched on is a vast one.[24] But after a long period of neglect, it is now becoming clearer and clearer that social factors are of vital importance in the spread and establishment of linguistic changes of all kinds. It does not lie within the scope of this book to do more than call attention to this development.

10.3 The causes of phonological change

Perhaps that plural, *causes*, is the most important thing in this section. The warning of Grammont (1933, 175) is still not sufficiently appreciated:

> The error of most of those who have concerned themselves with the question [of the causes of phonetic change] has been precisely this: when they recognized a cause . . . , they believed that it was the sole cause and wanted to refer everything to it.

There are a great number of factors which can contribute to precipitating a phonological change, and it is probably rare for a single change to result from a single factor.

10.3.1 Factors already discussed

Several such factors have already emerged from the discussion earlier in this chapter. Restructurings result from an excessively abstract phonological component (p. 238). Rule reorderings tend to increase phonetic and semantic transparency and reduce allomorphy, from which it follows that all of these can be factors motivating change, and not only change by reordering. Lexical diffusion tends to begin from 'points of least resistance' as Malkiel calls them (p. 251);

---

[24] The fundamental work in the field is that of William Labov. His most important contributions are collected in Labov (1972b); see also Labov (1969; 1972a; 1974) and Weinreich *et al.* (1968). Labov's work has stimulated a good deal of research, particularly on American English. The Labovian paradigm also promises to make it possible to describe more satisfactorily what has been called the *polylectal competence* of the language user—his ability to cope easily with a wide range of variation in the speech of those who 'speak the same language' as he does—and is thus of value for synchronic as well as diachronic linguistics; or rather, as many would argue, it shows that the distinction usually drawn between synchronic and diachronic study is an artificial one. On this see Bailey (1973).

therefore the various factors he mentions can likewise motivate change. We have noted that an innovation may start life as a hypercorrection: before Labov had brought this out, Hoenigswald (1960) had suggested that phenomena similar to hypercorrection were at the back of most cases of what had generally been thought of as classic 'phonetically gradual' sound-change. If an innovation can spread for reasons of group solidarity, perhaps it can also be initiated for similar reasons. Among the large number of other causal factors that have been noted, the following are perhaps worth special mention.

10.3.2 Ease of articulation

This is one of the oldest proposals, and there is obviously some truth in it—in the case of assimilation, for example. It is hard at present to prove physiologically that a given sequence of articulations is easier than another; but where a substitution is common both as a phonological change and as a fast-speech rule, it is reasonable enough to suppose that it makes for ease of articulation.

10.3.3 Structural imbalance

The group of factors subsumable under this head was brought into prominence by A. Martinet, though there had been precursors.[25] Languages, it is said, seek on the one hand to exploit their contrasts maximally, and on the other to ensure that contrasting phonemes are perceptually far enough apart to obviate the possibility of confusion. If there is a 'hole in the pattern', a 'case vide', an unused combination of feature values, another phoneme may shift to fill the hole; if, on the other hand, there is an excessive number of phonemes within a given area of phonetic space, one of them may shift out of the area. In either case, such a shift may set up a chain reaction by creating a new imbalance at another point.

A classic case of the first kind is cited by Martinet (1952) from the dialect of Hauteville in Savoy. At one stage of the history of this dialect there were low vowels /ɛ a/ but no /ɔ/; then the following developments took place, all at about the same time:

$$
\begin{array}{ll}
a \rightarrow \mathfrak{o} & \qquad\qquad \textbf{292} \\
\varepsilon \rightarrow a \\
\tilde{\varepsilon} \rightarrow \varepsilon \\
\tilde{e} \rightarrow \tilde{\varepsilon}
\end{array}
$$

This may be explained in the following way: /a/ shifted to fill the hole in the pattern; by so doing it created a new hole. Partly for this reason, and partly because the proximity of /ɛ̃/ was a threat to its distinctiveness, /ɛ/ concomitantly shifted towards, and eventually to, /a/; and so on down the rest of the chain. The chain ended where it did because no structural gain could come from any simple shift of a neighbouring vowel to fill the gap created by the lowering of /ẽ/; for this gap, far from constituting an asymmetry, actually increased symmetry, since /ẽ/

---

[25] See especially Martinet (1952; 1955). The notions of imbalance and of chain reaction go back at least to Sapir (1921, 182), cf. also Haudricourt (1939) and Haudricourt and Juilland (1949/1970). Interesting exemplification is given by Moulton (1960; 1962).

had been the only non-low nasalized vowel. The resulting vowel system contained the same number of phonemes as before, but more evenly distributed over vowel space; there was complete symmetry and less perceptual overcrowding in the mid and low front region (though more crowding in the mid and low back region—here perhaps lie the seeds of future change).

Such a chain, which begins with a shift into a 'case vide' creating a new 'case vide', is sometimes termed a *drag chain*. The converse type of chain, the *push chain*, is motivated primarily by semantic transparency. Suppose that, for whatever reason, a sound shift is in progress which will lead, if unchecked, to the merger of two phonemes. Sometimes, of course, such a merger actually takes place. But sometimes the phoneme whose territory is being encroached upon may itself shift away from the encroaching phoneme, and perhaps in turn encroach upon a third phoneme, which may in turn shift away, etc., etc.

A simple example may be taken from the early history of Germanic. It is conventional to posit for proto-Indo-European three basic sets of plosive consonants: voiceless stops, voiced stops, and a third set, usually taken to be voiced aspirated stops of the kind still found in Indo-Aryan languages. In all I.E. languages outside India the last-named set have proved unstable, and often (as in Balto-Slavonic) they have merged with the plain voiced stops. In Germanic, however, the development was different. The plain voiced stops, when encroached upon, tended to devoice, thus maintaining their distinctness from the former voiced aspirates; this in turn resulted in a more fortis pronunciation of, and a greater delay of voice onset in, the original voiceless stops, which became aspirated and ultimately fricative. This was the end of the chain; for until these developments there had been only one fricative phoneme in the language, and none of the newly created fricative phonemes threatened to merge with it.

Considerations of structural imbalance may inhibit changes as well as promoting them. A phoneme which is fully 'integrated', to use Martinet's term—one which is part of a fairly extensive pattern of fully exploited contrasts, and whose disappearance would leave a 'case vide'—tends to maintain its distinctness even if it occurs relatively rarely and signals important distinctions even more rarely. Thus, as Vachek (1962) notes, English /ŋ ž/ show no tendency to disappear—and he might have added /ð/: the existence of these phonemes exemplifies general patterns of English phonology—every type of plosive is found in the labial, alveolar and velar positions; every obstruent occurs voiceless and voiced—which their disappearance would destroy. In contrast the survival of /h r/ is in jeopardy, though they are far more important to the communicative efficiency of the language.

10.3.4 Language contact

Language contact, as an agent of phonological change, is not to be forgotten. The development in English of a voicing contrast in fricatives is primarily due to the introduction, from Early Middle English onwards, of large numbers of French and Latin loans; in Old English voicing in fricatives had been entirely determined by environment. This massive borrowing has likewise revolutionized the principles of English stress assignment. Again, the Romance languages that developed secondary distinctions of vowel-length (French, Franco-Provençal, north Italian) were precisely those that adjoined Germanic-speaking territory and acquired a considerable population bilingual in a Romance and a Germanic language.[26] More strikingly still, the indigenous languages of Australia, out of contact with other languages for many millennia, and divided into not less than twenty-seven families (all, it would seem, related, but only distantly), still have virtually a common phonemic system except in one region; and that region is the extreme north-west of Australia, where there is known to have been contact with a Papuan language.[27] The extent to which language contact can change phonological systems depends on many factors, notably the extent of borrowing (the effect of Chinese phonology on Japanese has been considerable, on English virtually nil) and the extent of pre-existing similarity between the phonological systems of the borrowing language and the source language (thus Turkish, which has borrowed fairly heavily in vocabulary from Arabic, has tended strongly to adapt the loans to its own phonological system).

All these factors, and no doubt others too, can motivate phonological change. Some of them, such as language contact or the phenomena investigated by Labov, are primarily of a social nature; others are more purely linguistic. Kiparsky (1974b) has sought to reduce the factors of the latter kind to three: ease of production, ease of perception, and ease of acquisition.[28] He argues that available evidence suggests that if a potential change motivated by one of these factors would have bad effects with respect to another, this does not inhibit the change from going ahead: it 'seem[s] to take place anyway, and [is] then followed by further change which corrects the damage done by the first'—itself, perhaps, having further deleterious effects at another point. Equilibrium is never reached.

10.3.5 Drift

But neither this, nor any other hypothesis I know of, has satisfactorily explained certain sets of data to which attention was called as long ago as 1921 by Sapir. Sapir develops the concept of 'phonetic drift', or a secular trend immanent in language, varying in strength and direction from one language to another, but capable of being realized almost identically and, as it seems, independently, in related but distinct languages; for example, he shows (1921, 171ff) how umlaut developed independently in English and German, and concludes:

> There was evidently some general tendency or group of tendencies at work in early Germanic, long before English and German had developed as such, that eventually drove both of these dialects along closely parallel paths.

Sapir neither shows nor professes to show what these 'general tendencies' were or where they were located; and the facts remain to be explained. It is likely enough that there is a straightforward explanation in the particular case of

---

[26] Haudricourt and Juilland (1949/1970, 45).
[27] Wurm (1972).
[28] Ease of production and perception corresponds to the more arbitrary notion of 'derivational markedness' in the very full discussion of the same problem by D. G. Miller (1973a).

English and German umlaut;[29] but the example is not isolated. Thus Sapir invites us to place side by side the following forms of proto-West-Germanic, modern English and modern German:

PWG:	fo:t	fo:ti	mu:s	mu:si	**293**
English:	fʊt	fi:t	mæws	majs	
German:	fu:s	fy:se	maws	mojze	

We may well feel, as he comments,

> that today the English and German forms resemble each other more than does either set the West Germanic prototypes from which each is independently derived. Each . . . illustrates the tendency to reduction of unaccented syllables, the vocalic modification of the radical element under the influence of the following vowel, the rise in tongue position of the long middle vowels . . . , the diphthongizing of the old high vowels . . . . These dialectic parallels cannot be accidental. They are rooted in a common, pre-dialectic drift.

If such secular trends exist (and while Sapir may have overstated his case a little, there is certainly *something* that needs explanation), there must be an assignable cause for them; and it cannot be anything in the nature of a linguistic universal,[30] because this will not explain why languages differ in this respect, nor why related languages tend to show similar drifts.[31] Perhaps the last word on this, and on phonological change generally, can be left to Sapir himself (1921, 183):

> What is the primary cause of the unsettling of a phonetic pattern and what is the cumulative force that selects these or those particular variations of the individual on which to float the pattern readjustments we hardly know. Many linguistic students . . . have tried to dispose of the problem by bandying such catchwords as 'the tendency to increased ease of articulation' or 'the cumulative result of faulty perception' (on the part of children, say, in learning to speak). These easy explanations will not do. 'Ease of articulation' may enter in as a factor, but it is a rather subjective concept at best. Indians find hopelessly difficult sounds and sound combinations that are simple to us; one language encourages a phonetic drift that another does everything to fight. 'Faulty perception' does not explain that impressive drift in speech sounds which I have insisted upon. It is much better to admit that we do not yet understand the primary cause or causes of the slow drift in phonetics, though we can frequently point to contributing factors.

---

[29] Cf. Hockett (1958, 518): it may well be that the fronting of vowels before /i/ in the next syllable was a low-level phonetic fact of West Germanic in general, and that it was only the phonemicization of this phonetic fact that occurred independently in the dialects (consequent mainly on the loss or lowering of the conditioning /i/).

[30] As Foley would apparently have it ('The basis of rule repetition is the existence of a set of universal phonological rules', Foley 1971, 382). But Foley's work (1971; 1972a; 1972b) is important as drawing attention—or trying to draw attention—to this long-neglected subject of secular trends.

[31] Aspects of the problem are discussed by Posner (1975) and one possible explanation adumbrated. Another relevant consideration is that similar and closely related languages will have similar points of structural instability, which may well be amenable to similar changes; these changes will then themselves produce secondary points of instability which are the same in each language, and so on.

Of how many things in phonology besides 'drift' would that last sentence be true! We know a great deal; we understand a great deal less. But, as we have seen from time to time in this book, signs are not wanting to show from what directions understanding is likely to come.

Abbreviated Titles

AL	*Acta Linguistica (Hafniensia)*
ArchL	*Archivum Linguisticum*
BSOAS	*Bulletin of the School of Oriental and African Studies*
BSOS	*Bulletin of the School of Oriental Studies*
CLS	*Papers from the (Fourth, Fifth, ...) Regional Meeting, Chicago Linguistic Society*
FL	*Foundations of Language*
GUMSLL	*Georgetown University Monograph Series on Languages and Linguistics*
IJAL	*International Journal of American Linguistics*
JAOS	*Journal of the American Oriental Society*
JIPA	*Journal of the International Phonetic Association*
JL	*Journal of Linguistics*
JPhon	*Journal of Phonetics*
Lg	*Language*
LInq	*Linguistic Inquiry*
PiL	*Papers in Linguistics*
SiL	*Studies in Linguistics*
StGr	*Studia Grammatica*
StudL	*Studia Linguistica*
SWRJ	*Selected Writings of Roman Jakobson I: Phonological Studies.* The Hague: Mouton. 1962
TCLC	*Travaux du Cercle Linguistique de Copenhague*
TCLP	*Travaux du Cercle Linguistique de Prague*
TPS	*Transactions of the Philological Society*
ZPhon	*Zeitschrift für Phonetik, Sprachwissenschaft und Kommunikationsforschung*

References

ALI, L. H. and R. G. DÀNILOFF 1972: 'A cinefluorographic-phonologic investigation of emphatic sound assimilation in Arabic', in *Proceedings of the 7th International Congress of Phonetic Sciences.*

ALLEN, W. S. 1951: 'Some prosodic aspects of retroflexion and aspiration in Sanskrit', *BSOAS* **13**, 939–46.

1956: 'Aspiration in the Hārautī nominal', in *Studies in Linguistic Analysis*. Oxford: Basil Blackwell.

1973: *Accent and rhythm*. Cambridge: University Press.

ANDERSON, S. R. 1969: *West Scandinavian vowel systems and the ordering of phonological rules*. Bloomington: Indiana University Linguistics Club.

1970: 'On Grassmann's Law in Sanskrit', *LInq* **1**, 387–96.

1971: 'On the description of "apicalized" consonants', *LInq* **2**, 103–107.

1972a: 'On nasalization in Sundanese', *LInq* **3**, 257–68.

1972b: 'Mirror image rules and disjunctive ordering', in *Proceedings of the 7th International Congress of Phonetic Sciences.*

1972c: 'Icelandic u-umlaut and breaking in a generative grammar', in Firchow *et al.* (ed.), *Studies for Einar Haugen*. The Hague: Mouton.

1974a: 'On the typology of phonological rules', in *Papers from the Parasession on Natural Phonology*. Chicago: Chicago Linguistic Society.

1974b: *The organization of phonology*. New York: Seminar Press.

1974c: 'On dis-agreement rules', *LInq* **5**, 445–51.

1975: 'On the interaction of phonological rules of various types', *JL* **11**, 39–62.

1976: 'Nasal consonants and the internal structure of segments', *Lg* **52**, 326–44.

ANDERSON, S. R. and W. BROWNE 1973: 'On keeping exchange rules in Czech', *PiL* **6**, 445–82.

ARNOLD, G. F. 1956: 'A phonological approach to vowel, consonant and syllable in modern French', *Lingua* **5**, 253–87.

AWBERY, G. M. 1975: 'Welsh mutations: syntax or phonology?', *ArchL* n.s. **6**, 14–25.

BACH, E. 1968: 'Two proposals concerning the simplicity metric in phonology', *Glossa* **2**, 128–49.

BACH, E. and R. T. HARMS 1972: 'How do languages get crazy rules?', in Stockwell and Macaulay (1972).

BAILEY, C. J. N. 1973: *Variation and linguistic theory*. Arlington, Va.: Center for Applied Linguistics.

BELL, A. E. 1970: 'Syllabic consonants', *Working Papers in Language Universals* (Stanford) **4**, B1 ff.

1975: 'If speakers can't count syllables, what can they do?' Bloomington: Indiana University Linguistics Club.

BENDOR–SAMUEL, J. T. 1966: 'Some prosodic features in Terena', in Bazell *et al.* (ed.), *In Memory of J. R. Firth*. London: Longmans.

BHATIA, T. K. 1976: 'On the predictive role of the recent theories of aspiration', *Phonetica* **33**, 62–74.

BIERWISCH, M. 1966: 'Regeln für die Intonation deutscher Sätze', *StGr* **7**, 99–201.

1967: 'Skizze der generativen Phonologie', *StGr* **6**, 7–33.

BJARKMAN, P. C. 1974: 'Rule order and Stampe's natural phonology'. Bloomington: Indiana University Linguistics Club.

1975: 'Toward a proper conception of processes in natural phonology', *CLS* **11**, 60–72.

BLOCH, B. 1948: 'A set of postulates for phonemic analysis', *Lg* **24**, 3–48.

1950: 'Studies in colloquial Japanese IV: phonemics', *Lg* **26**, 86–125.

BLOCH, B. and G. L. TRAGER 1942: *Outline of linguistic analysis*. Baltimore: Linguistic Society of America.

BLOOMFIELD, L. 1926: 'A set of postulates for the science of language', *Lg* **2**, 153–64.

1933: *Language*. New York: Holt.

1939: 'Menomini morphophonemics', *TCLP* **8**, 105–115.

1962: *The Menomini language*. New Haven: Yale University Press.

BOTHA, R. P. 1971: *Methodological aspects of transformational generative phonology*. The Hague: Mouton.

BRAME, M. K. 1972a: 'On the abstractness of phonology: Maltese ˢ ', in Brame (ed.), *Contributions to Generative Phonology*. Austin: University of Texas Press.

1972b: 'The segmental cycle', in Brame (ed.), *Contributions to Generative Phonology*.

BRASINGTON, R. W. P. 1973: 'Reciprocal rules in Catalan phonology', *JL* **9**, 25–34.

1976: 'Have we inhibitions related to universal rules?', *JPhon*. **4**, 75–81.

BRESNAN, J. W. 1971: 'Sentence stress and syntactic transformations', *Lg* **47**, 257–81.

1972: 'Stress and syntax: a reply', *Lg* **48**, 304–325.

BÜHLER, K. 1931: 'Phonetik und Phonologie', *TCLP* **4**, 22–52.

BUTLIN, R. T. 1936: 'On the alphabetic notation of certain phonetic features of Malayalam', *BSOS* **8**, 437–47.

CAMPBELL, L. 1973: 'Extrinsic ordering lives.' Bloomington: Indiana University Linguistics Club,

1974: 'Phonological features: problems and proposals', *Lg* **50**, 52–65.

CHAO, Y. R. 1934: 'The non-uniqueness of phonemic solutions of phonetic systems', *Academica Sinica, Bulletin of the Institute of History and Philology* **4**, 363–97. Also in Joos, ed., *Readings in Linguistics I*. (Chicago: Chicago University Press, 4th ed., 1966.)

CHEN, M. Y. 1972: 'The time dimension: contribution towards a theory of sound change', *FL* **8**, 457–98.

1974a: 'Metarules and universal constraints in phonological theory', in *Proceedings of the 11th International Congress of Linguists*.

1974b: 'Natural phonology from the diachronic vantage point', in *Papers from the Parasession on Natural Phonology*. Chicago: Chicago Linguistic Society.

CHEN, M. Y. and H-I. HSIEH 1971: 'The time variable in phonological change'. *JL* **7**, 1–13.

CHEN, M. Y. and W. S-Y. WANG 1975: 'Sound change: actuation and implementation', *Lg* **51**, 255–81.

CHOMSKY, N. 1965a: *Current issues in linguistic theory*. The Hague: Mouton.

1965b: *Aspects of the theory of syntax*. Cambridge, Mass.: MIT Press.

CHOMSKY, N. and M. HALLE 1968: *The sound pattern of English*. New York: Harper & Row. (Cited as *SPE*.)

CHOMSKY, N., M. HALLE and F. LUKOFF 1956: 'On accent and juncture in English', in Halle *et al.* (ed.), *For Roman Jakobson*. The Hague: Mouton.

CHRISTENSEN, B. W. 1967: 'Glossématique, linguistique fonctionnelle, grammaire générative et stratification du langage', *Word* **23**, 57–73.

CHRISTIE, W. M. 1976: 'Another look at classical phonemics', *Language Sciences* **39**, 37–9.

CLAYTON, M. L. 1976: 'The redundance of underlying morpheme-structure conditions', *Lg* **52**, 295–313.

COHEN, A. 1952: *The phonemes of English*. The Hague: Martinus Nijhoff.

COHEN, D. 1975: 'On predictable rule-insertion'. Bloomington: Indiana University Linguistics Club.

COLE, D. T. 1955: *Introduction to Tswana grammar*. London: Longmans.

COLLINDER, B. 1951: 'Three degrees of quantity'. *StudL* **5**, 28–40.

COMRIE, B. S. ms.: 'Morphophonemic exceptions and phonetic distance', unpublished paper, King's College, Cambridge.

CONTRERAS, H. 1969: 'Simplicity, descriptive adequacy, and binary features', *Lg* **45**, 1–8.

CONTRERAS, H. and S. SAPORTA 1960: 'The validation of a phonological grammar', *Lingua* **9**, 1–15.

COOK, E-D. 1971: 'Phonological constraint and syntactic rule', *LInq* **2**, 465–78.

CRYSTAL, D. 1969: *Prosodic systems and intonation in English*. Cambridge: University Press.

1975: *The English tone of voice*. London: Edward Arnold.

DARDEN, B. J. 1970: 'The fronting of vowels after palatals in Slavic', *CLS* **6**, 459–70.

1971a: 'Diachronic evidence for phonemics', *CLS* **7**, 323–31.

1971b: 'A note on Sommer's claim that there exist languages without CV syllables', *IJAL* **37**, 126–28.

DAVIDSEN–NIELSEN, N. 1969: 'English stops after initial /s/', *English Studies* **50**, 321–38.

1975: 'A phonological analysis of English *sp, st, sk* with special reference to speech error evidence', *JIPA* **5**, 3–25.

DELL, F. 1973a: 'Two cases of exceptional rule ordering', in Kiefer and Ruwet (ed.), *Generative Grammar in Europe*. Dordrecht: Reidel.

1973b: *Les règles et les sons: introduction à la phonologie générative*. (Collection Savoir.) Paris: Hermann.

DIXON, R. M. W. 1970: 'Olgolo syllable structure and what they are doing about it', *LInq* **1**, 273–76.

DRESSLER, W. 1974: 'Diachronic puzzles for natural phonology', in *Papers from the Parasession on Natural Phonology*. Chicago: Chicago Linguistic Society.

FANT, C. G. M. 1971: 'Distinctive features and phonetic dimensions', in G. E. Perren and J. L. M. Trim (eds.), *Applications of Linguistics*. Cambridge: University Press. Also in Fant, *Speech Sounds and Features*. (Cambridge, Mass.: MIT Press, 1973.)

FIRTH, J. R. 1935: 'Phonological features of some Indian languages', in *Proceedings of the 2nd International Congress of Phonetic Sciences*; also in Firth, *Collected papers 1934–1951* (London: Oxford University Press, 1957).

    1948: 'Sounds and prosodies', *TPS* 1948, 127–52.

FISCHER-JØRGENSEN, E. 1952: 'On the definition of phoneme categories on a distributional basis', *AL* 7, 8–39.

    1975: *Trends in phonological theory; a historical introduction*. Copenhagen: Akademisk Forlag.

FLIFLET, A. L. 1962: 'Gespannte und ungespannte Vokale', *StudL* 16, 24–8.

FOLEY, J. 1971: 'Phonological change by rule repetition', *CLS* 7, 376–84.

    1972a: rejoinder to V. B. Cohen's 'Foleyology', *CLS* 8, 458–62.

    1972b: 'Rule precursors and phonological change by metarule', in Stockwell and Macaulay (1972).

FRIES, C. C. and K. L. PIKE 1949: 'Coexistent phonemic systems', *Lg* 25, 29–50.

FROMKIN, V. 1970: 'The concept of "naturalness" in a universal phonetic theory', *Glossa* 4, 29–45.

FRY, D. B. 1964: 'The function of the syllable', *ZPhon* 17, 215–21.

FUDGE, E. C. 1969: 'Syllables', *JL* 5, 253–86.

    1975: 'English word stress: an examination of some basic assumptions', in Goyvaerts and Pullum (1975).

GIMSON. A. C. 1970: *An introduction to the pronunciation of English*. 2nd ed. London: Edward Arnold.

GOYVAERTS, D. L. and G. K. PULLUM (ed.) 1975: *Essays on the sound pattern of English*. Ghent: E. Story-Scientia P.V.B.A.

GRACE, E. C. 1975: 'In defence of *vocalic*', *Language Sciences* 36, 1–6.

GRAMMONT, M. 1933: *Traité de phonétique*. Paris: Delagrave.

GREENBERG, J. H. 1962: 'Is the vowel-consonant dichotomy universal?', *Word* 18, 73–81

    1970: 'Some generalizations concerning glottalic consonants, especially implosives', *IJAL* 36, 123–45.

HAAS, W. 1957: 'The identification and description of phonetic elements', *TPS* 1957, 118–59.

HÁLA, B. 1961: 'La syllabe, sa nature, ses origines et ses transformations', *Orbis* 10, 69–143.

HALLE. M. 1959: *The sound pattern of Russian*. The Hague: Mouton.

    1962: 'Phonology in generative grammar', *Word* 18, 54–72.

    1972: 'Theoretical issues in phonology in the 1970s', in *Proceedings of the 7th International Congress of Phonetic Sciences*.

    1973: 'Prolegomena to a theory of word formation', *LInq* 4, 3–16.

    1975: 'Confessio grammatici', *Lg* 51, 525–35.

HALLE, M. and S. J. KEYSER 1971: *English stress: its form, its growth, and its role in verse*. New York: Harper & Row.

HALLIDAY, M. A. K. 1964: 'Intonation in English grammar', *TPS* 1963, 143–69.

HANKAMER, J. and J. AISSEN 1974: 'The sonority hierarchy', in *Papers from the Parasession on Natural Phonology*. Chicago: Chicago Linguistic Society.

HARMS, R. T. 1966: 'The measurement of phonological economy', *Lg* 42, 602–11.

HARRIS, J. W. 1973a: 'Morphologization of phonological rules: an example from Chicano Spanish', in Campbell *et al.* (ed.), *Linguistic Studies in Romance Languages*. Washington: Georgetown University Press.

    1973b: 'On the order of certain phonological rules in Spanish', in Anderson and Kiparsky (ed.), *Festschrift for Morris Halle*. New York: Holt, Rinehart & Winston.

    1974: 'Evidence from Portuguese for the "Elsewhere Condition" in phonology', *LInq* 5, 61–80.

HARRIS, Z. S. 1944: 'Simultaneous components in phonology', *Lg* 20, 181–205.

    1945: 'Navaho phonology and Hoijer's analysis', *IJAL* 11, 239–46.

    1951: *Methods in structural linguistics*. Chicago: Chicago University Press.

HASTINGS, A. J. 1974a: 'Howard's directional theory and the unordered rule hypothesis', in *Papers from the Parasession on Natural Phonology*. Chicago: Chicago Linguistic Society.

    1974b: 'Stifling'. Bloomington: Indiana University Linguistics Club.

HAUDRICOURT, A. G. 1939: 'Quelques principes de la phonologie historique', *TCLP* 8, 270–72.

HAUDRICOURT, A. G. and A. G. JUILLAND 1949/1970: *Essai pour une histoire structurale du phonétisme français*. 2nd ed. The Hague: Mouton.

HAUGEN, E. 1950: *The First Grammatical Treatise.* (*Lg* Monograph No. **25**.) Baltimore: Waverly Press.
  1956: 'The syllable in linguistic description', in Halle *et al.* (ed.), *For Roman Jakobson*. The Hague: Mouton.
HAUGEN, E. and W. F. TWADDELL 1942: 'Facts and phonemics', *Lg* **18**, 228–37.
HENDERSON, E. J. A. 1948: 'Notes on the syllabic structure of Lushai', *BSOAS* **12**, 713–25.
  1949: 'Prosodies in Siamese', *Asia Major* n.s. **1**, 189–215; also in Palmer (ed.), *Prosodic analysis* (London: Longmans, 1970).
  1951: 'The phonology of loanwords in some South-East Asian languages', *TPS* 1951, 131–58.
  1966: 'Towards a prosodic statement of Vietnamese syllable structure', in Bazell *et al.* (ed.), *In Memory of J. R. Firth*. London: Longmans.
HIGGINBOTTOM, E. 1965: 'Glottal reinforcement in English', *TPS* 1964, 129–42.
HILL, A. A. 1958: *Introduction to linguistic structures*. New York: Harcourt Brace.
HILL, K. C. 1969: 'Some implications of Serrano phonology', *CLS* **5**, 357–65.
HILL, T. 1966: 'The technique of prosodic analysis', in Bazell *et al.* (ed.), *In Memory of J. R. Firth*. London: Longmans.
HIRST, D. J. 1976: 'A distinctive feature analysis of English intonation', *Linguistics* **168**, 27–42.
HJELMSLEV, L. 1948: 'Structural analysis of language', *StudL* **1**, 69–78.
  1954: 'La stratification du langage', *Word* **10**, 163–88.
  1961: *Prolegomena to a theory of language*. Trans. F. J. Whitfield. 2nd ed. Madison: University of Wisconsin Press.
HOARD, J. E. 1971a: 'Aspiration, tenseness, and syllabication in English', *Lg* **47**, 133–40.
  1971b: 'The new phonological paradigm', *Glossa* **5**, 222–68; also in Goyvaerts and Pullum (1975).
  1972: 'Naturalness conditions in phonology, with particular reference to English vowels', in M. K. Brame (ed.), *Contributions to Generative Phonology*. Austin: University of Texas Press.
HOCKETT, C. F. 1942: 'A system of descriptive phonology', *Lg* **18**, 3–21.
  1947a: 'Peiping phonology', *JAOS* **67**, 253–67.
  1947b: 'Componential analysis of Sierra Popoluca', *IJAL* **13**, 258–67.
  1954: 'Two models of grammatical description', *Word* **10**, 210–34.
  1955: *Manual of phonology*. Bloomington: Indiana University Press.
  1958: *A course in modern linguistics*. New York: Macmillan.
  1961: 'Linguistic elements and their relations', *Lg* **37**, 29–54.
  1965: 'Sound change', *Lg* **41**, 185–204.
  1968: *The state of the art*. The Hague: Mouton.
HOENIGSWALD, H. M. 1960: *Language change and linguistic reconstruction*. Chicago: Chicago University Press.
  1963: 'Are there universals of linguistic change?', in Greenberg (ed.) *Universals of Language*. Cambridge, Mass.: MIT Press.
  1964: 'Graduality, sporadicity, and the minor sound change processes', *Phonetica* **11**, 202–15.
HOGG, R. M. 1976: 'The status of rule reordering', *JL* **12**, 103–23.
HOLDEN, K. T. 1974: 'Assimilation rates of borrowings and phonological productivity'. Bloomington: Indiana University Linguistics Club.
HOOPER, J. B. 1972: 'The syllable in phonological theory', *Lg* **48**, 525–40.
  1974a: 'Aspects of natural generative phonology'. Bloomington: Indiana University Linguistics Club.
  1974b: 'Rule morphologization in natural generative phonology', in *Papers from the Parasession on Natural Phonology*. Chicago: Chicago Linguistic Society.
  1975: 'The archi-segment in natural generative phonology', *Lg* **51**, 536–60.
  1977: *An introduction to natural generative phonology*. New York: Academic Press.
HOWARD, A. 1975: 'Can the "Elsewhere Condition" get anywhere?', *Lg* **51**, 109–27.
HOWARD, I. 1972: 'A directional theory of rule application in phonology', *University of Hawaii Working Papers in Linguistics* IV 7; also available from Indiana University Linguistics Club.
HSIEH, H.-I. 1976: 'On the unreality of some phonological rules', *Lingua* **38**, 1–19.
HYMAN, L. M. 1970: 'How concrete is phonology?', *Lg* **46**, 58–76.
  1975: *Phonology: theory and analysis*. New York: Holt, Rinehart & Winston.
ISAČENKO, A. V. 1956: 'Hat sich die Phonologie überlebt?', *ZPhon* **9**, 311–30.
IVERSON, G. K. 1973a: 'A guide to sanguine relationships'. Paper presented at the Indiana University Rule Ordering Conference; now in Koutsoudas (1975).
  1973b: 'Speculations on counterfeeding'. Bloomington: Indiana University Linguistics Club.
IVIĆ, P. 1965: 'Roman Jakobson and the growth of phonology', *Linguistics* **18**, 35–78.

JACKENDOFF, R. S. 1972: *Semantic interpretation in generative grammar*. Cambridge, Mass.: MIT Press.

JACKSON, K. H. 1967: *A historical phonology of Breton*. Dublin: Dublin Institute for Advanced Studies.

JAKOBSON, R. 1929: 'Remarques sur l'évolution phonologique du russe', *TCLP* 2.

1931: 'Die Betonung und ihre Rolle in der Wort- und Syntagmaphonologie', *TCLP* 4, 164–82.

1937: 'Über die Beschaffenheit der prosodischen Gegensätze', in *Mélanges . . . J. van Ginneken*. Paris. Also in *SWRJ*.

1942: *Kindersprache, Aphasie und allgemeine Lautgesetze*. Uppsala. Also in *SWRJ*. Trans. A. R. Keiler as *Child language, aphasia and phonological universals* (The Hague: Mouton, 1968).

1949: 'On the identification of phonemic entities', *Recherches structurales* (= *TCLC* 5) 205–13.

1960: 'Kazańska szkoła polskiej lingwistyki i jej miejsce w światowym rozwoju fonologii', *Biuletyn Polskiego Towarzystwa Językoznawczego* 19, 3–34; translated in *Selected Writings of Roman Jakobson II: Word and Language* (The Hague: Mouton, 1971) 394–428.

1962: 'Retrospect', in *SWRJ*.

JAKOBSON, R., C. G. M. FANT, and M. HALLE 1952: *Preliminaries to speech analysis*. Cambridge, Mass.: MIT Press.

JAKOBSON, R. and M. HALLE 1956: *Fundamentals of language*. The Hague: Mouton.

1957/1968: 'Phonology in relation to phonetics', in *Manual of Phonetics* (1st ed. 1957, ed. Kaiser; 2nd ed. 1968, ed. Malmberg). Amsterdam: North-Holland.

JENSEN, J. T. 1972: 'Hungarian evidence for abstract phonology', in *Proceedings of the 7th International Congress of Phonetic Sciences*.

JENSEN, J. T. and M. E. 1973: 'Ordering and directionality of iterative rules'. Paper presented at the Indiana University Rule Ordering Conference. Now in Koutsoudas (1975).

JOHNS, D. A. 1969: 'Phonemics and generative phonology', *CLS* 5, 374–81.

JOHNSON, C. D. 1972: *Formal aspects of phonological description*. The Hague: Mouton.

JOHNSON, R. E. 1975: *The role of phonetic detail in Coeur d'Alène phonology* (Doctoral dissertation, Washington State University). Ann Arbor: Xerox University Microfilms.

JONES, D. 1950. *The phoneme: its nature and use*. Cambridge: Heffer.

1960: *An outline of English phonetics*. 9th ed. Cambridge: Heffer.

JOOS, M. 1942: 'A phonological dilemma in Canadian English', *Lg* 18, 141–44.

1962: 'The definition of juncture and terminals', in *Proceedings of the 2nd Texas Conference on Problems of Linguistic Analysis in English*. Austin: University of Texas Press.

KAYE, J. D. 1971: 'Nasal harmony in Desano', *LInq* 2, 37–56.

KAYE, J. D. and G. L. PIGGOTT 1973: 'On the cyclic nature of Ojibwa T-Palatalization', *LInq* 4, 345–62.

KENSTOWICZ, M. J. 1970: 'The Lithuanian third person future', in *Studies Presented to Robert B. Lees by his Students*. Edmonton: Linguistic Research Inc.

1973: 'On the application of rules in pre-generative phonology'. Paper presented at the Indiana University Rule Ordering Conference. Now in Koutsoudas (1975).

KENSTOWICZ, M. J. and C. W. KISSEBERTH 1970: 'Rule ordering and the asymmetry hypothesis', *CLS* 6, 504–19.

1973: (ed.) *Issues in phonological theory*. The Hague: Mouton.

KIM, C-W. 1970: 'A theory of aspiration', *Phonetica* 21, 107–16.

KING, R. D. 1968: 'Root versus suffix accent in the Germanic present indicative', *JL* 4, 247–65.

1972: 'A note on opacity and paradigm regularity', *LInq* 3, 535–8.

1973a: 'In defense of extrinsic ordering'. Paper presented at the Indiana University Rule Ordering Conference. Now in Koutsoudas (1975).

1973b: 'Rule insertion', *Lg* 49, 551–78.

KINGDON, R. 1958: *The groundwork of English intonation*. London: Longmans.

KIPARSKY, P. 1966: 'Über den deutschen Akzent', *StGr* 7, 69–98.

1968a: 'Linguistic universals and linguistic change', in Bach and Harms (ed.) *Universals in Linguistic Theory*. New York: Holt, Rinehart & Winston.

1968b: 'How abstract is phonology?', now in Fujimura (ed.) *Three Dimensions of Linguistic Theory*. Tokyo: TEC Co. Ltd., 1974.

1968c: 'Metrics and morphophonemics in the Kalevala', in Gribble (ed.), *Studies Presented to Professor Roman Jakobson by his Students*. Cambridge, Mass.

1971: 'Historical linguistics', in Dingwall (ed.) *A Survey of Linguistic Science*. College Park: University of Maryland Linguistics Program.

1972a: 'Explanation in phonology', in Peters (ed.) *Goals of Linguistic Theory*. Englewood Cliffs: Prentice-Hall.

1972b: 'Metrics and morphophonemics in the Rigveda', in Brame (ed.), *Contributions to Generative Phonology*. Austin: University of Texas Press.

1973a: 'Abstractness, opacity and global rules'. Paper presented at the Indiana University Rule Ordering Conference. Now in Fujimura (ed.), *Three Dimensions of Linguistic Theory* (Tokyo: TEC Co. Ltd., 1974).

1973b: ' "Elsewhere" in phonology', in Anderson and Kiparsky (ed.), *Festschrift for Morris Halle*. New York: Holt, Rinehart & Winston.

1974a: 'Phonological representations', in Fujimura (ed.), *Three Dimensions of Linguistic Theory*. Tokyo: TEC Co. Ltd.

1974b: 'On the evaluation measure', in *Papers from the Parasession on Natural Phonology*. Chicago: Chicago Linguistic Society.

KISSEBERTH, C. W. 1969: 'On the abstractness of phonology: the evidence from Yawelmani', *PiL* 1, 248–82.

1970a: 'On the functional unity of phonological rules', *LInq* 1, 291–306.

1970b: 'The treatment of exceptions', *PiL* 2, 44–58.

1972a: 'Cyclical rules in Klamath phonology', *LInq* 3, 3–33.

1972b: 'Is rule ordering necessary in phonology?', in Kachru *et al.* (ed.), *Issues in Linguistics: Papers in Honor of Harry and Renee Kahane*. Champaign-Urbana: University of Illinois Press.

1973a: 'The interaction of phonological rules and the polarity of language'. Paper presented at the Indiana University Rule Ordering Conference. Now in Koutsoudas (1975).

1973b: 'On the alternation of vowel length in Klamath: a global rule', in Kenstowicz and Kisseberth (1973).

KLOSTER JENSEN, M. 1963: 'Die Silbe in der Phonetik und Phonemik', *Phonetica* 9, 17–38.

KOHLER, K. J. 1966a: 'Is the syllable a phonological universal?', *JL* 2, 207–208.

1966b: 'Towards a phonological theory', *Lingua* 16, 337–51.

KOUTSOUDAS, A. (ed.) 1975: *The application and ordering of grammatical rules*. The Hague: Mouton.

KOUTSOUDAS, A., G. SANDERS and C. NOLL 1974: 'On the application of phonological rules', *Lg* 50, 1–28.

KRÁMSKÝ, J. 1974: *The phoneme*. Munich: Wilhelm Funk Verlag.

KRIVNOVA, O. F. and S. V. KODZASOV 1972: Review of Postal (1968), *Linguistics* 94, 111–27.

KURATH, H. 1957: 'The binary interpretation of English vowels: a critique', *Lg* 33, 111–22.

LABOV, W. 1969: 'Contraction, deletion, and inherent variability of the English copula', *Lg* 45, 715–62.

1972a: 'The internal evolution of linguistic rules', in Stockwell and Macaulay (1972).

1972b: *Sociolinguistic patterns*. Philadelphia: University of Pennsylvania Press.

1974: 'On the use of the present to explain the past', in *Proceedings of the 11th International Congress of Linguists*.

LADEFOGED, P. 1965: 'The nature of general phonetic theories', *GUMSLL* 18, 27–42.

1967: *Three areas of experimental phonetics*. London: Oxford University Press.

1971: *Preliminaries to linguistic phonetics*. Chicago: University Press.

1972a: 'Phonetic prerequisites for a distinctive feature theory', in Valdman (ed.), *Papers in Linguistics and Phonetics to the Memory of Pierre Delattre*. The Hague: Mouton.

1972b: 'Phonological features and their phonetic correlates', *JIPA* 2, 2–12.

1973: 'The features of the larynx', *JPhon* 1, 73–83.

1975: *A course in phonetics*. New York: Harcourt Brace Jovanovich.

LAFERRIERE, M. 1975: 'Rule exceptions, functionalism, and language change', *Canadian Journal of Linguistics* 20, 161–82.

LAKOFF, G. 1972: 'The global nature of the Nuclear Stress Rule', *Lg* 48, 285–303.

LAMB, S. M. 1971: 'The crooked path of progress in cognitive linguistics', *GUMSLL* 24, 99–123; also in Makkai and Lockwood (ed.), *Readings in Stratificational Linguistics* (University: University of Alabama Press, 1973).

LANGACKER, R. W. 1969: 'Mirror image rules II: lexicon and phonology', *Lg* 45, 844–62.

1970: 'English question intonation', in *Studies Presented to Robert B. Lees by his Students*. Edmonton: Linguistic Research Inc.

LANGENDOEN, D. T. 1968: *The London school of linguistics*. Cambridge, Mass.: MIT Press.

1975: 'Finite-state parsing of phrase-structure languages and the status of readjustment rules in grammar', *LInq* 6, 533–54.

LASS, R. 1971: 'Boundaries as obstruents: Old English voicing assimilation and universal strength hierarchies', *JL* 7, 15–30.

1976: *English phonology and phonological theory*. Cambridge: University Press.

LASS, R. and J. M. ANDERSON 1975: *Old English phonology*. Cambridge: University Press.

LEHISTE, I. 1970: *Suprasegmentals.* Cambridge, Mass.: MIT Press.
   1971: 'Temporal organization of spoken language', in Hammerich *et al.* (ed.), *Form and Substance: Phonetic and Linguistic Papers Presented to Eli Fischer-Jørgensen.* Copenhagen: Akademisk Forlag.
LIEBERMAN, P. 1970: 'Towards a unified phonetic theory', *LInq* **1**, 307–322.
LIGHTNER, T. M. 1968: 'On the use of minor rules in Russian phonology', *JL* **4**, 69–72.
   1972: *Problems of phonological theory.* Edmonton: Linguistic Research Inc.
LINDAU, M. E. 1975: *Features for vowels* (Doctoral dissertation, University of California at Los Angeles). Ann Arbor: Xerox University Microfilms.
LINELL, P. 1976: 'On the structure of morphological operations', *Linguistische Berichte* **44**, 1–29.
LISKER, L. and A. S. ABRAMSON 1971: 'Distinctive features and language control', *Lg* **47**, 767–85.
LOCKWOOD, D. G. 1969: 'Markedness in stratificational phonology', *Lg* **45**, 300–308.
   1972a: 'Neutralization, bi-uniqueness, and stratificational phonology', in Makkai (ed.), *Phonological Theory: Evolution and Current Practice.* New York: Holt, Rinehart & Winston.
   1972b: *Introduction to stratificational linguistics.* New York: Harcourt Brace Jovanovich.
LOVINS, J. 1974: 'Why loan phonology is natural phonology', in *Papers from the Parasession on Natural Phonology.* Chicago: Chicago Linguistic Society.
MALKIEL, Y. 1967: 'Multiple vs. simple causation in linguistic change', in *To Honor Roman Jakobson: Essays on the Occasion of his Seventieth Birthday.* The Hague: Mouton.
MALONE, J. L. 1970: 'Two hypotheses on the origin of an Aramaic apocope-paragoge process', *Glossa* **4**, 206–211.
   1972: 'The Mandaic syllable-adjustment circuit and its historical origins', *CLS* **8**, 473–81.
MARTIN, S. E. 1956: Review of Hockett (1955), *Lg* **32**, 675–705.
MARTINET, A. 1952: 'Function, structure and sound change', *Word* **8**, 1–32.
   1955: *Économie des changements phonétiques.* Bern: Francke.
MATHESIUS, V. 1929: 'La structure phonologique du lexique du tchèque moderne', *TCLP* **1**, 67–84; also in Vachek (ed.), *A Prague School Reader in Linguistics* (Bloomington: Indiana University Press, 1964).
   1934: 'Zur synchronischen Analyse fremden Sprachguts', *English Studies* **70**, 21–35; also in Vachek (ed.), *A Prague School Reader in Linguistics.*
MATTHEWS, P. H. 1972: *Inflectional morphology.* Cambridge: University Press.
   1973: 'Some reflections on Latin morphophonology', *TPS* 1972, 59–78.
   1974: *Morphology.* Cambridge: University Press.
MCCAWLEY, J. 1967: 'Le rôle d'un système de traits phonologiques dans une théorie du langage', *Langages* **8**, 112–23. Trans. in Makkai (ed.), *Phonological Theory: Evolution and Current Practice* (1972) (New York: Holt, Rinehart & Winston).
   1968: *The phonological component of a grammar of Japanese.* The Hague: Mouton.
   1973: 'On the role of notation in generative phonology', in Gross *et al.* (ed.), *The Formal Analysis of Natural Language.* The Hague: Mouton.
   1974: Review of Chomsky and Halle (1968), *IJAL* **40**, 50–88. Reprinted with corrections in Goyvaerts and Pullum (1975).
MEIER, G. F. 1964: 'Silbenkern und Sonorität', *ZPhon* **17**, 369–78.
MILLER, D. G. 1973a: 'On the motivation of phonological change', in Kachru *et al.* (ed.), *Issues in Linguistics: Papers in Honor of Harry and Renee Kahane.* Champaign-Urbana: University of Illinois Press.
   1973b: 'Some theoretical implications of Greenlandic phonology', *PiL* **6**, 371–427.
   1975: 'On constraining global rules in phonology', *Lg* **51**, 128–32.
   1976: 'On mirror-image rules', *LInq* **7**, 383–8.
   forthcoming: 'Some theoretical and typological implications of an IE root structure constraint'.
MILLER, P. D. 1973: 'Bleaching and coloring', *CLS* **9**, 386–97.
MOULTON, W. G. 1960: 'The short vowel systems of northern Switzerland', *Word* **16**, 155–82.
   1962: 'Dialect geography and the concept of phonological space', *Word* **18**, 23–32.
NEWTON, B. E. 1971: 'Ordering paradoxes in phonology', *JL* **7**, 31–53.
   1972: *The generative interpretation of dialect.* Cambridge: University Press.
   1975: Review of Allen (1973), *Lg* **51**, 472–5.
NORMAN, L. 1972: 'The insufficiency of local ordering', *CLS* **8**, 490–503.
   1973: 'Bi-directional rules and non-extrinsic ordering', Paper presented at the Indiana University Rule Ordering Conference. Now in Koutsoudas (1975).
O'CONNOR, J. D. and O. TOOLEY 1964: 'The perceptibility of certain word boundaries', in Abercrombie *et al.* (ed.), *In Honour of Daniel Jones.* London: Longmans.

o'connor, J. D. and J. L. M. trim 1953: 'Vowel, consonant and syllable—a phonological definition', *Word* **9**, 103–122.

ohala, M. 1974: 'The schwa-deletion rule in Hindi: phonetic and non-phonetic determinants of rule application'. Bloomington: Indiana University Linguistics Club.

ohlander, s. 1976: *Phonology, meaning, morphology: On the role of semantic and morphological criteria in phonological analysis.* Göteborg: Acta Universitatis Gothoburgensis.

palmer, F. R. 1956a: 'Gemination in Tigrinya', in *Studies in Linguistic Analysis*. Oxford: Basil Blackwell.

1956b: ' "Openness" in Tigre', *BSOAS* **18**, 561–77.

phelps, e. 1975: 'Iteration and disjunctive domains in phonology', *Linguistic Analysis* **1**, 137–72.

phelps, e. and M. K. brame 1973: 'On local ordering of rules in Sanskrit', *LInq* **4**, 387–400.

pierce, J. E. 1965: 'The phonemes of English', *Linguistics* **17**, 36–57.

1966: 'Phonemic composition of English morphemes', *Linguistics* **20**, 60–71.

pike, K. L. 1947: 'Grammatical prerequisites to phonemic analysis', *Word* **3**, 155–72.

1952: 'More on grammatical prerequisites', *Word* **8**, 106–121.

pilch, H. 1965: 'Zentrale und periphere Lautsysteme', in *Proceedings of the 5th International Congress of Phonetic Sciences*.

1968: *Phonemtheorie: Erster Teil.* 2nd ed. Basel: Karger.

posner, R. R. 1961: *Consonantal dissimilation in the Romance languages.* Oxford: Basil Blackwell.

1975: 'Ordering of historical phonological rules in Romance', *TPS* 1974, 98–127.

postal, P. M. 1966: Review of Martinet's *Elements of General Linguistics*, *FL* **2**, 151–86.

1968: *Aspects of phonological theory.* New York: Harper & Row.

pullum, G. K. 1975: 'On a nonargument for the cycle in Turkish', *LInq* **6**, 494–501.

1976: 'Sequential and simultaneous rule application in Spanish phonology', *Lingua* **38**, 221–62.

pyle, c. 1974: 'Why a conspiracy?', in *Papers from the Parasession on Natural Phonology*. Chicago: Chicago Linguistic Society.

reighard, J. 1972: 'Labiality and velarity in consonants and vowels', *CLS* **8**, 533–43.

reimold, P. 1974: 'Phonologische Feature-Systeme und die strukturelle Definition natürlicher phonologischer Regeln', *Linguistische Berichte* **33**, 27–46.

rhodes, R. A. 1973: 'Some implications of natural phonology', *CLS* **9**, 530–541.

1974: 'Non-phonetic environments in natural phonology', in *Papers from the Parasession on Natural Phonology*. Chicago: Chicago Linguistic Society.

ringen, c. o. 1972: 'On arguments for rule ordering', *FL* **8**, 266–73.

1973: 'Vacuous application, iterative application, reapplication, and the unordered rule hypothesis.' Paper presented at the Indiana University Rule Ordering Conference; now in Koutsoudas (1975).

1974: 'Obligatory-optional precedence: a reply to Malone', *FL* **11**, 565–70.

robins, R. H. 1957: 'Aspects of prosodic analysis', *Proceedings of the University of Durham Philosophical Society* **B 1**, 1–12; also in Palmer (ed.), *Prosodic Analysis* (London: Longmans, 1970).

1967: *General linguistics: an introductory survey.* 4th impr., with corrections and additions. London: Longmans.

robinson, o. w. 1976: 'A "scattered" rule in Swiss German', *Lg* **52**, 148–62.

roca, i. m. 1975: 'Phonetics is not phonology', *JPhon* **3**, 53–62.

rood, d. s. 1975: 'The implications of Wichita phonology', *Lg* **51**, 315–37.

ross, J. R. 1972: 'A reanalysis of English word stress: Part I', in Brame (ed.), *Contributions to Generative Phonology*. Austin: University of Texas Press.

sampson, G. R. 1974: Review of Lockwood (1972b), *Lingua* **34**, 235–51.

sapir, e. 1921: *Language.* New York: Harcourt Brace.

1925: 'Sound patterns in language', *Lg* **1**, 37–51.

1933: 'La réalité psychologique des phonèmes', *Journal de Psychologie Normale et Pathologique* **30**, 247–265. Translated as 'The psychological reality of phonemes' in Mandelbaum (ed.), *Selected Writings of Edward Sapir* (Berkeley: University of California Press, 1949).

schane, s. a. 1967: 'L'élision et la liaison en français', *Langages* **8**, 37–59.

1971: 'The phoneme revisited', *Lg* **47**, 503–21.

1972: 'Natural rules in phonology', in Stockwell and Macaulay (1972).

1973a: *Generative phonology.* Englewood Cliffs: Prentice-Hall.

1973b: 'The formalization of exceptions in phonology', in Gross *et al.* (ed.), *The Formal Analysis of Natural Language.* The Hague: Mouton.

1973c: 'The treatment of phonological exceptions: the evidence from French', in Kachru *et al.* (ed.),

Issues in Linguistics: Papers in Honor of Henry and Renee Kahane. Champaign-Urbana: University of Illinois Press.

1974: 'How abstract is abstract?', in *Papers from the Parasession on Natural Phonology.* Chicago: Chicago Linguistic Society.

1975: 'Noncyclic English word stress', in Goyvaerts and Pullum (1975).

SHIBATANI, M. 1973: 'The role of surface phonetic constraints in generative phonology', *Lg* **49**, 87–106.

SKOUSEN, R. 1972: 'On capturing regularities', *CLS* **8**, 567–77.

SLEDD, J. H. 1962: 'Notes on English stress', in Hill (ed.), *Proceedings of the 1st Texas Conference on Problems of Linguistic-Analysis in English.* Austin: University of Texas Press.

SOMMER, B. A. 1970: 'An Australian language without CV syllables', *IJAL* **36**, 57–8.

SOMMERFELT, A. 1962: *Diachronic and synchronic aspects of language.* The Hague: Mouton.

SOMMERSTEIN, A. H. 1973: *The sound pattern of Ancient Greek.* Oxford: Basil Blackwell.

1974: 'On phonotactically motivated rules', *JL* **10**, 71–94.

1975: 'The margins of morphophonemics', *JL* **11**, 249–59.

SPRIGG, R. K. 1954: 'Verbal phrases in Lhasa Tibetan', *BSOAS* **16**, 134–56; 320–50; 566–91.

1966: 'Phonological formulae for the verb in Limbu as a contribution to Tibeto-Burman comparison', in Bazell *et al.* (ed.), *In Memory of J. R. Firth.* London: Longmans.

STAMPE, D. 1969: 'The acquisition of phonetic representation', *CLS* **5**, 443–54.

1972: 'On the natural history of diphthongs', *CLS* **8**, 578–90.

1973: 'On chapter nine', in Kenstowicz and Kisseberth (1973).

STANLEY, R. 1967: 'Redundancy rules in phonology', *Lg* **43**, 393–435.

1973: 'Boundaries in phonology', in Anderson and Kiparsky (ed.), *Festschrift for Morris Halle.* New York: Holt, Rinehart & Winston.

STAROSTA, S. 1971: Review of Lyon's *Introduction to Theoretical Linguistics, Lg* **47**, 429–47.

STEVENS, K. N. 1972: 'Segments, features, and analysis by synthesis', in Kavanagh and Mattingly (ed.), *Language by Ear and by Eye.* Cambridge, Mass.: MIT Press.

STEWART, J. M. 1967: 'Tongue root position in Akan vowel harmony', *Phonetica* **16**, 185–204.

STOCKWELL, R. P. 1972: 'The role of intonation: reconsiderations and other considerations', in Bolinger (ed.), *Intonation.* Harmondsworth: Penguin Books.

STOCKWELL, R. P. and R. K. S. MACAULAY (ed.) 1972: *Linguistic change and generative theory.* Bloomington: Indiana University Press.

SWADESH, M. 1934: 'The phonemic principle', *Lg* **10**, 117–29.

1947: 'On the analysis of English syllabics', *Lg* **23**, 137–50.

TEGEY, H. 1975: 'The interaction of phonological and syntactic processes: examples from Pashto', *CLS* **11**, 571–82.

TRAGER, G. L. 1962: 'Some thoughts on juncture', *SiL* **16**, 11–22.

TRAGER, G. L. and H. L. SMITH 1951: *An outline of English structure.* (*SiL* Occasional Papers, **3**.) Norman, Oklahoma: Battenburg Press.

TRUBETZKOY, N. S. 1939: *Grundzüge der Phonologie* = *TCLP* **7**. Translated by J. Cantineau as *Principes de phonologie* (Paris: Klincksieck, 1949). Translated by C. Baltaxe as *Principles of phonology* (Berkeley: University of California Press, 1969).

TRUITNER, K. L. and T. DUNNIGAN 1975: 'Palatalization in Ojibwa', *LInq* **6**, 301–316.

TWADDELL, W. F. 1935: 'On defining the phoneme'. Baltimore: Linguistic Society of America. Also in Joos (ed.), *Readings in Linguistics I* (4th ed., Chicago University Press, 1966).

VACHEK, J. 1962: 'On the interplay of external and internal factors in the development of language', *Lingua* **11**, 433–8.

1966: *The linguistic school of Prague.* Bloomington: Indiana University Press.

VAGO, R. M. 1977: 'In support of extrinsic ordering', *JL* **13**, 25–41.

VANDERSLICE, R. 1972: 'The binary suprasegmental features of English', in *Proceedings of the 7th International Congress of Phonetic Sciences.*

VANDERSLICE, R. and P. LADEFOGED 1972: 'Binary suprasegmental features and transformational rules of English word-accentuation', *Lg* **48**, 819–38.

VENNEMANN, T. 1972a: 'Phonological uniqueness in natural generative grammar', *Glossa* **6**, 105–116.

1972b: 'Rule inversion', *Lingua* **29**, 209–242.

1973: 'Phonological concreteness in natural generative grammar', in Shuy and Bailey (ed.), *Toward Tomorrow's Linguistics.* Washington: Georgetown University Press.

1974a: 'Restructuring', *Lingua* **33**, 137–56.

1974b: 'Words and syllables in natural generative grammar', in *Papers from the Parasession on Natural Phonology.* Chicago: Chicago Linguistic Society.

VOGT, H. 1954: 'Phoneme classes and phoneme classification', *Word* **10**, 28–34.

WANG, W. S-Y. 1967: 'Phonological features of tone', *IJAL* **33**, 93–105.
  1968: 'Vowel features, paired variables, and the English vowel shift', *Lg* **44**, 695–708.
  1969: 'Competing changes as a cause of residue', *Lg* **45**, 9–25.
WANG, W. S-Y. and C-C. CHENG 1970: 'Implementation of phonological change: the Shuāng-fēng Chinese case', *CLS* **6**, 552–9.
WARBURTON, I. P. 1976: 'On the boundaries of morphology and phonology: a case study from Modern Greek', *JL* **12**, 259–78.
WATERSON, N. 1956: 'Some aspects of the phonology of the nominal forms of the Turkish word', *BSOAS* **18**, 578–91.
WEINREICH, U., W. LABOV and M. L. HERZOG 1968: 'Empirical foundations for a theory of language change', in Lehmann and Malkiel (ed.), *Directions for Historical Linguistics*. Austin: University of Texas Press.
WELLS, R. S. 1945: 'The pitch phonemes of English', *Lg* **21**, 27–39.
  1947: Review of Pike's *The Intonation of American English*, *Lg* **23**, 255–73.
  1949: 'Automatic alternation', *Lg* **25**, 99–116.
WELMERS, W. E. and Z. S. HARRIS 1942: 'The phonemes of Fanti', *JAOS* **62**, 318–33.
WILKINSON, R. W. 1974: 'Tense/lax vowel harmony in Telugu: the influence of derived c ontrast on rule application', *LInq* **5**, 251–70.
  1976: 'A homonymy-avoiding transderivational constraint in Terena', *IJAL* **42**, 158–62.
WILLIAMSON, K. 1970: 'The definition of a tone language', in *Proceedings of the 10th International Congress of Linguists*.
WURM, S. 1972: *The languages of Australia and Tasmania*. The Hague: Mouton.
WURZEL, W. U. 1970: *Studien zur deutschen Lautstruktur = StGr* **8**.
ZIMMER, K. E. 1969: 'On specifying the input to the phonological component', *FL* **5**, 342–8.
  1970: 'On the evaluation of alternative phonological descriptions', *JL* **6**, 89–98.
ZWICKY, A. M. 1970a: 'Auxiliary reduction in English', *LInq* **1**, 323–36.
  1970b: 'Class complements in phonology', *LInq* **1**, 262–4.
  1972: 'Note on a phonological hierarchy in English', in Stockwell and Macaulay (1972).
  1974: 'Taking a false step', *Lg* **50**, 215–24.
  1975: 'The strategy of generative phonology', in Dressler and Mareš (ed.), *Phonologica 1972*. Munich: Wilhelm Fink Verlag.
  1976: 'Bibliography on cyclical segmental rules', *IJAL* **42**, 267–8.

Index of names

Index of languages

General index

Note: Notational conventions are not separately indexed, but grouped in a single entry 'Notational conventions'.